# INTERNATIONAL DIFFERENCES IN GROWTH RATES

CENTRAL ISSUES IN CONTEMPORARY ECONOMIC THEORY
AND POLICY

General Editor: **Mario Baldassarri**, *Professor of Economics, University of Rome
'La Sapienza', Italy*

*Published titles*

Mario Baldassarri (*editor*)
INDUSTRIAL POLICY IN ITALY, 1945-90

Mario Baldassarri (*editor*)
KEYNES AND THE ECONOMIC POLICIES OF THE 1980s

Mario Baldassarri (*editor*)
OLIGOPOLY AND DYNAMIC COMPETITION

Mario Baldassarri (*editor*)
THE ITALIAN ECONOMY: HEAVEN OR HELL?

Mario Baldassarri and Paolo Annunziato (*editors*)
IS THE ECONOMIC CYCLE STILL ALIVE?: THEORY, EVIDENCE
AND POLICIES

Mario Baldassarri and Massimo Di Matteo (*editors*)
INTERNATIONAL PROBLEMS OF ECONOMIC INTERDEPENDENCE

Mario Baldassarri, John McCallum and Robert Mundell (*editors*)
DEBT, DEFICIT AND ECONOMIC PERFORMANCE

Mario Baldassarri, John McCallum and Robert Mundell (*editors*)
GLOBAL DISEQUILIBRIUM IN THE WORLD ECONOMY

Mario Baldassarri and Robert Mundell (*editors*)
BUILDING THE NEW EUROPE
Volume 1: The Single Market and Monetary Unification
Volume 2: Eastern Europe's Transition to a Market Economy

Mario Baldassarri, Luigi Paganetto and Edmund S. Phelps (*editors*)
INTERNATIONAL ECONOMIC INTERDEPENDENCE,
PATTERNS OF TRADE BALANCES AND ECONOMIC POLICY
COORDINATION

Mario Baldassarri, Luigi Paganetto and Edmund S. Phelps (*editors*)
PRIVATIZATION PROCESSES IN EASTERN EUROPE: THEORETICAL
FOUNDATIONS AND EMPIRICAL RESULTS

Mario Baldassarri, Luigi Paganetto and Edmund S. Phelps (*editors*)
WORLD SAVING, PROSPERITY AND GROWTH

Mario Baldassarri, Luigi Paganetto and Edmund S. Phelps (*editors*)
INTERNATIONAL DIFFERENCES IN GROWTH RATES: Market
Globalization and Economic Areas

Mario Baldassarri and Paolo Roberti (*editors*)
FISCAL PROBLEMS IN THE SINGLE-MARKET EUROPE

# International Differences in Growth Rates

## Market Globalization and Economic Areas

Edited by

**Mario Baldassarri**
*Professor of Economics*
*University of Rome 'La Sapienza'*
*Italy*

**Luigi Paganetto**
*Professor of Economics and*
*Dean of the Faculty of Economics and Business Administration*
*University of Rome 'Tor Vergata'*

and

**Edmund S. Phelps**
*McVickar Professor of Political Economy*
*Columbia University, New York*

**St. Martin's Press**

in association with
*Rivista di Politica Economica*, SIPI, Rome
and
CEIS, University 'Tor Vergata', Rome

338.9
I6192

First published in Great Britain 1994 by
THE MACMILLAN PRESS LTD
Houndmills, Basingstoke, Hampshire RG21 2XS
and London
Companies and representatives
throughout the world

A catalogue record for this book is available
from the British Library.

ISBN 0–333–61043–1

Printed and bound in Great Britain by
Antony Rowe Ltd
Chippenham, Wiltshire

First published in the United States of America 1994 by
Scholarly and Reference Division,
ST. MARTIN'S PRESS, INC.,
175 Fifth Avenue,
New York, N.Y. 10010

ISBN 0–312–12344–2

Library of Congress Cataloging-in-Publication Data
International differences in growth rates : market globalization and
economic areas / edited by Mario Baldassarri, Luigi Paganetto, and
Edmund S. Phelps.
p.   cm. — (Central issues in contemporary economic theory and
policy)
Includes index.
ISBN 0–312–12344–2
1. Economic development.   2. Regional economic disparities.
I. Baldassarri, Mario, 1946–   .  II. Paganetto, Luigi.
III. Phelps, Edmund S.   IV. Series.
HD75.I585  1994
338.9—dc20                                          94–21619
                                                         CIP

# Contents

# I - HUMAN CAPITAL AND GROWTH

# How Robust
# Is the Growth-Machinery Nexus?

## J. Bradford De Long - Lawrence H. Summers
Harvard University,                    World Bank, Washinghton
Cambridge (Mass.)

## 1. - Introduction

This paper provides evidence showing, for a variety of samples of economics and for a variety of periods, that in the cross-country distribution of growth rates there is a very strong connection between machinery investment and productivity growth. In this paper we continue the research project we began in *Equipment Investment and Economic Growth* (De Long-Summers [18]) (*).

In that paper we used data from Summers and Heston [55], [56], and from detailed benchmark estimates of national economy price and quantity structures from the UN International Comparison Project (Kravis-Lipsey [31]; Kravis-Heston-Summers [29] and [30]). We demonstrated that in that particular data set covering the 1960-1985 period, both a 61-economy sample including both rich and poor nations and a 25-economy sample of rich nations showed a very strong connection between growth and investment in machinery and equipment.

Here we use additional data to show that this strong growth-machinery nexus was not an artifact of the particular cross-section or the particular sample period of De Long and Summers [18]. Here we show that a strong growth-machinery nexus can be found in data-

---

(*) *Advise:* the numbers in square brackets refer to the Bibliography in the appendix.

bases reaching as far back into the past as 1870. Moreover, the patterns found in De Long and Summers [18] for the post -World War II era hold not just for the cross-section sample analyzed there but for other post-World War II economies not in our previous database as well. And the patterns hold for post-World War II years outside our previous 1960-1985 sample.

These findings give our earlier argument enhanced authority. The models we use and regressions we estimate here were specified in 1990, long before we had begun to collect the additional data underlying the results reported in this paper. Yet our specifications, *ex ante* from the standpoint of the data we have collected since 1990 analyzed, fit this paper's data as well as they fit the data analyzed in De Long and Summers [18]. They show an association of machinery investment and output per worker growth much stronger than we would expect under the standard growth-accounting assumption that the return to investors is the marginal social product of investment.

In addition, the data we analyze in this paper supports our belief that the growth-machinery nexus arises from strong *causal* links between machinery investment and growth. We report instrumental variables regression, using as instruments variables that are in large part the results of policy choices made by governments, and that have direct effects on machinery investment rates and only indirect effects on output per worker growth. Such instrumental variables regressions reveal the same association between growth and machinery as our least-squares regression. This strengthens our confidence that the bulk of the growth-machinery investment relationship arises from a causal nexus between machinery and growth, and that policies undertaken to generate more or less machinery investment by altering the incentives of investors and firms in market economies have large effects on economic growth rates.

We organize the argument of this paper in five sectins, including this brief introduction. The second section summarizes our previous work. The third section presents evidence from additional periods outside the 1960-1985 sample analyzed in De Long and Summers [18]. The fourth section presents evidence from additional nations not included in our previous cross-section.

The fifth section discusses interpretations. In it we argue that the association of growth and machinery is much stronger than one would anticipate if the source of the connection were the added production that growth-accounting studies attribute to capital. We also present instrumental variables results that strongly speak for the claim that policies that succeed in altering the incentives of market participants and changing rates of machinery investment have large effects on growth. We also discuss informal and anecdotal evidence suggesting that policy interventions to change the rate of machinery investment that are not market-conforming — of which the most substantial have been the policies of "forced industrialization" undertaken in the centrally-planned economies of the twentieth century — yield much lower benefits.

The sixth section provides a brief recapitulation of our main points.

## 2. - The Growth-Machinery Nexus: Previous Evidence

De Long and Summers [18] regressed the growth rate of GDP per worker over 1960-1985 (in international dollars as estimated by Summers and Heston [55]) on the estimated share of GDP devoted to machinery investment over 1960-1985 (1). Our basic regressions controlled for three of the most obvious growth related factors: labor force growth, other forms of investment, and the productivity gap *vis-à-vis* the world's industrial leaders. Labor force growth determines the degree to which investment equips new workers with capital rather than raising the capital-labor ratio. The productivity gap *vis-à-vis* the richest nations measures the potential gains from the adoption of best-practice technologies and organizations. The share of GDP devoted to non-machinery investment measures the rate of non-machinery capital accumulation.

Graph 1 and table 1 present a summary of our results in De Long and Summers [18], using our sample of the 61 non oil exporting nations for which we had U.N.ICP data to use to construct estimates

---

(1) We estimated the machinery and equipment investment share by multiplying the average share of investment in GDP by ICP benchmark-year measures of the share of investment devoted to machinery and equipment.

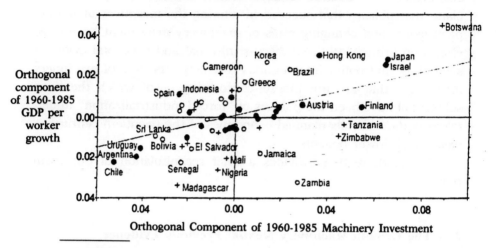

GRAPH 1

PARTIAL SCATTER OF GROWTH
AND MACHINERY INVESTMENT
FROM DE LONG-SUMMERS [18]

Legend:

● High:              ○ Intermediate:          + Low:
> 25% of 1960 US     < 25% and > 10%;         < 10% of 1960 US

of machinery investment over 1960-1968 (2). Graph 1 plots the partial scatter of machinery investment and GDP per worker growth. Its vertical axis measure that component of 1960-1985 GDP per worker growth orthogonal to the three "control" independent variables in the basic regression shown in the first column of table 1. Its horizontal axis measures that component of the 1960-1985 real machinery investment share orthogonal to the same three controls. The graph shows point-by-point the information on the partial correlation of machinery investment and GDP per worker growth contained in the cross-country sample of De Long and Summers [18].

Table 1 reports a sampling of regression equations estimated in De Long and Summers [18]. The first column provides our basic specification, using just machinery investment and our three most basic controls as independent variables. The second sample reports

_____

(2) And using our 1991 vintage of machinery investment estimates.

regressions for a high-productivity sample containing just those nations with 1960 levels of GDP per worker more than twenty-five percent of the US value; such economies had already exhibited substantial economic growth over the previous half-century and possessed the human and physical infrastructure necessary to take advantage of modern machine technologies. The third column reports a regression including among the independent variables five politico-economic variables which Barro [10] stresses as likely to have substantial influence on growth rates: the annual rates of political assassinations and coups over 1960-1985, 1960 primary and second-ary school enrolment rates, and the average 1960-1985 share of government consumption expenditures in GDP. The fourth column reports a regression including continent dummies. And the last two columns report regressions for subperiods of the 1960-1985 period.

In all of the regressions in table 1, machinery investment has a strong and precisely estimated association with economic growth. In the basic regression in column one, the control variables — initial

TABLE 1

BASIC REGRESSION RESULTS
FROM DE LONG-SUMMERS [18]

| Independent variables | 1960-1985 Basic Regression | High-productivity sample | Barro variables included | Continent dummies included | 1960-1975 | 1970-1985 |
|---|---|---|---|---|---|---|
| Machinery investment Share of GDP | 0.265 (0.065) | 0.337 (0.054) | 0.275 (0.070) | 0.288 (0.072) | 0.279 (0.086) | 0.276 (0.062) |
| Non-machinery investment Share of GDP | 0.062 (0.035) | 0.015 (0.033) | 0.029 (0.037) | 0.022 (0.038) | −0.011 (0.043) | 0.040 (0.047) |
| Labor force growth | −0.031 (0.198) | −0.002 (0.146) | −0.001 (0.203) | 0.143 (0.285) | 0.019 (0.233) | −0.217 (0.270) |
| GDP per worker gap vis-à-vis the US | 0.020 (0.009) | 0.030 (0.009) | 0.039 (0.013) | 0.029 (0.012) | 0.039 (0.016) | 0.038 (0.017) |
| $R^2$ | 0.291 | 0.662 | 0.391 | 0.385 | 0.263 | 0.236 |
| SEE | (0.013) | (0.008) | (0.012) | (0.012) | (0.015) | (0.016) |
| n | 61 | 25 | 61 | 61 | 61 | 61 |

GDP per worker levels, labor force growth rates, and non-machinery investment rates — each account for less than 5% of the variability of output per worker growth rates. By contrast, differences in machinery investment account for a quarter of the growth rate variance. An increase of four percentage points in the share of GDP devoted to machinery investment is associated with an increase in the growth of GDP per worker of 1% per year. Over the 25 years of the sample such an increase in growth rates cumulates to a difference of 30% in the final level of GDP per capita: differences in machinery investment are associated with substantially important differences in productivity growth.

To put this association in perspective, this implies that a difference in machinery investment rates of one cross-country standard deviation is associated with a difference in growth rates of nearly half of the cross-country standard deviation. Differences in machinery investment are associated with a sizeable share of differences in output per worker growth rates.

Other writers have stressed still other factors as potential influences on growth. Alesina and Rodrik, 1991, endogenize politics and trace links from high inequality to slow growth. Agarwala [3], Balassa [7], [8], and many others have documented links between openness to international trade and growth. Still other factors that have received emphasis are the allocation of entrepreneurial talent to positive- as opposed to zero-sum activities (Murphy, Shleifer and Vishny [42]), the appropriate mix of human capital (Kremer [32]), financial policy (Levine [35]), and incentives for research and development (Romer [48]). We argue in De Long and Summers [18] that while these other factors have significant and important partial correlations with growth (3), their inclusion in the list of independent variables has little effect on the estimated magnitude of the machinery-growth nexus.

The strong association means that differences in machinery investment account in a statistical sense for essentially all of the extraordinary growth performance of many fast-growing nations —

---

(3) But note that in many cases their coefficients are not robust to changes in the specification. See LEVINE - RENELT [36].

for example, Japan — relative to the sample as a whole. Conditional on the initial GDP per worker gap and the achieved rates of growth of the labor force, Japan has achieved a relative GDP per worker growth rate edge of 2.2% per year over 1960-1985 relative to the average pattern seen in the sample, given the values of the control variables in the basic regression. Conversely, deficient machinery investment can account in a statistical sense for the relatively poor performance of many slow-growing nations. Argentina, for example, has suffered a relative GDP per worker growth rate deficit of 2.1% per year over 1960-1985, relative to the sample average. In both the case of Argentina and the case of Japan, more than four-fifths of this difference is accounted for in the framework of table 1 by their high or low quantities of machinery investment.

The results of De Long and Summers [18] leave open only two potential reasons for doubting that machinery investment is indeed a key factor in the economic growth of market economies. The first reason is that there is a possibility that causality runs the other way - from fast growth to high machinery investment rather than from high machinery investment to rapid growth. We provided a number of pieces of evidence that investment rates were the cause and growth rates the effect. Of these, the most powerful was the negative association of machinery prices with machinery quantities and with growth: if high investment were induced by high demand for capital goods as a result of rapid growth driven by other factors, then machinery prices should be high, not low, in fast-growth high machinery-investment economies. But the issue of causality is a delicate and important one that no collection of evidence can definitively close.

The second reason is that in initial exploratory studies of any topic there is always a dynamic relationship between the specification and the data (4). Specifications are always adjusted at the margin to fit

---

(4) In this case, as we noted in DE LONG-SUMMERS [18] we omitted transport equipment from our key investment aggregate not on theoretical grounds but because of its relatively low correlation from growth. In addition, we had begun our paper believing that it would focus on the relationships between a price structure favorable to investment and economic growth. Our shifting of topic to document the association of machinery investment and growth was a result of the extraordinary strength in our dataset of the relationship between the quantity structure of an economy and its rate of growth.

the peculiarities of the particular data set. And the questions ultimately asked are shaped by the questions the database appears
capable of answering. Given this interplay, standard *t*-statistics
overstate the confidence with which one can draw conclusions. As a
result, tests of empirical hupotheses on newly constructed, independent datasets are very valuable. Hypotheses that pass such tests on
new, independent data are thereby endowed with extraordinary force.
We now turn to the task of providing such tests.

### 3. - The Growth-Machinery Nexus:
### Evidence from Additional Periods

In this section we show that the patterns found in De Long and
Summers [18], for the 1960-1985 subperiod of the post-World War II
era hold not just for that period but for other periods as well — the
decade of the 1950s, the (very short) period since the end of the De
Long and Summers [18] sample, and most important for a dataset
containing evidence on machinery investment in the very long run
since 1870 as well. The next section continues the task of providing
tests of the hypotheses of De Long and Summers [18] on new,
independent data. In it we show that the patterns hold not just in the
cross-section sample analyzed by De Long and Summers [18] but also
for a sample made up of other economies not included in our previous
database.

The regression specifications we estimate here were published,
specified, and fixed as of early 1991, long before we had begun to
collect the additional data underlying our results. Thus the empirical
results in this and the following section greatly enhance the authority
of our earlier findings. In this paper our *ex ante* specifications fit the
data we have collected more recently as well as they fit the data we
originally analyzed in De Long and Summers [18] (5). In all the

---

(5) One dimension along which the specification of DE LONG-SUMMERS [18] was
explicitly *ex post* was its omission of transport equipment from its equipment aggregate.
As JONG-WHA LEE [33] has pointed out to us, Liberia and Panama appear to have
enormous relative amounts of investment in transport equipment because of the large
share of the world's ocean-going fleet registered in those two flag-of-convenience

samples and over all of the time periods that we have examined, there is a strong association between machinery investment and output per worker growth. This association is much stronger than we would expect to see under the standard growth-accounting assumption that the return to investors is the marginal social product of investment. Our results strongly support "new thinking" in the theory of economic growth, largely derived from the work of Paul Romer (6), which stresses the connection between productivity growth and investment broadly defined, and sees large gaps between the private profitability and the social utility of various components of investment.

## 3.1 *Machinery and Growth in the Very Long Run*

De Long [17] argued that machinery investment and growth were closely associated not just in the post-World War II period but in the longer-run as well by regressing growth on machinery investment in a small very long run panel of currently-industrialized nations. The sample was of necessity small. It consisted of six industrial nations for which data are available (Canada, Germany, Italy, Japan, the United Kingdom, and the United States) plus a seventh nation once among the world's leaders in living standards: Argentina (7). On the other hand, the panel covered most of economic growth since the industrial revolution. It extended from 1870 to 1980.

De Long [17] showed a close association between output per capita growth and a "net concept" of machinery investment (the

---

countries. Nevertheless, we continue to exclude transport equipment from the machinery investment aggregate studied in this paper in order to gain the advantage of a specification fixed and known to have been fixed *ex ante*.

(6) See PAUL ROMER [47], [49], [50].

(7) The sample was restricted to such a narrow base because of data availability. Long-run national product estimates of the necessary quality are rare, for economic historians are luxuries usually found only in rich nations. Any quantitative examination of the correlates and determinants of long-run growth is subject to severe sample-selection biases that effectively remove from consieration these issues and factors which ABRAMOVITZ [2] groups under the heading of "social capability". The nations for which long-run data on factor accumulation are available had a pre-twentieth century history of experience with entrepreneurship, market exchange, and early modern technologies. Thus, as DE LONG [13] noted, any conclusions drawn from such a narrow base are somewhat fragile.

change in the gross machinery stock) (8). Here we demonstrate that such a close association holds for this very long-run panel between output per worker growth and gross machinery investment as well. The estimates of machinery (and non-machinery) investment used in De Long [17] are transformed into estimates of gross machinery (and non-machinery) investment as a share of GDP by assuming an eight-year life for machinery and a thirty three-year life for structures (9).

There are three differences between the data used here and those used in De Long [17]. First, here we use output per worker. Second, here we use not a net but a gross investment concept of machinery investment. Third, here we use the relative price structure for GDP, machinery investment, and investment in structures of the US in 1929 rather than the US in 1970 as our benchmark for determining real investment shares of national product.

The first two of these changes from the specification of De Long [17], were adopted to make the regressions in this section directly comparable to other regressions in this paper. The third was adopted in order to make the relative price structure used to calculate real values correspond more closely to the average of relative price structures actually found in the sample.

The very long-run data base we use here covers seven nations, Canada, Germany (the Bundesrepublik after World War II), Italy, Japan, the United Kingdom (including southern Ireland until 1913), and United States, and Argentina, over eight periods, (1870 to 1885, 1885 to 1900, 1900 to 1913, 1913 to 1929, 1929 to 1938, 1938 to 1950, and 1950 to 1965, and 1965 to 1980).

We divide the past century into periods of roughly fifteen-years, with some of the division dates offset to match the course of the business cycle and the outbreak of war or the substantial completion

---

(8) DE LONG [17] gave two reasons for his specification: first, that the change in the gross capital stock is the appropriate measure of the outward shift in a production function made possible by new investment and is thus the theoretically most favored concept of investment; second, that (as MADDISON [37] notes) estimates of pre-World War II capital stocks are for the most part more solidly based than are estimates of investment flows. Estimates of changes in capital stocks can thus be constructed with fewer auxiliary assumptions than are required to construct gross investment estimates.

(9) Results reported below were not sensitive to changes in the assumed rate of retirements.

GRAPH 2

PARTIAL SCATTER OF MACHINERY
AND GROWTH FOR THE VERY LONG RUN PANEL

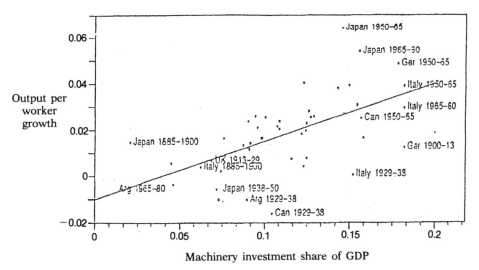

Machinery investment share of GDP

of reconstruction. This frequency of observation was chosen because we wished to focus on long-run shifts in growth rates produced by shifts in the production potential of economies, and not on short run cyclical fluctuations produced by shifts in the relative rate of employment of resources (10).

In choosing among different possible estimates of growth rates and investment shares we stay as close as possible to the estimates compiled by Angus Maddison, whose database has had a substantial influence on conceptions of long-run growth in a comparative perspective. Estimates of output per capita were drawn from Maddison

---

(10) The fifteen-year frequency of observation was chosen to avoid confusing short-run business cycle fluctuations with long-run shifts in rates of economic growth. If the data were examined year-by-year a substantial proportion of identifying variance would come from business cycle fluctuations. In recessions output drops because productive resources have become slack, not because the reduced pace of investment has significantly reduced the output that could be produced if capacity utilization and employment were at their normal levels. Such business cycle fluctuations would generate an association between investment and growth independent of the links between capital accumulation and long-run full-employment productive capacity.

[37]. Estimates of machinery investment were compiled from individual national sources, in most cases once again the same sources used by Maddison.

Graph 2 shows the partial scatter of gross machinery investment and output per worker growth rates for the very long-run panel. Each data point represents the experience of one of the seven nations in the sample for one of the roughly fifteen-year periods into which the century 1870-1980 is divided. The other independent variables in the regression, with their effects held constant in graph 2, are the relative productivity gap vis-à-vis the US at the start of the period, the rate of labor force growth, the rate of gross investment in non-residential construction, and whether a nation was on the losing side in the Second World War (11).

Table 2 reports regressions for the very long-run panel. Like table 1, table 2 shows a very strong association between machinery investment and growth. The coefficient on machinery investment is approximately the same as in De Long and Summers' [18] study of the post-World War II era: each one percentage point rise in the machinery investment share of GDP is associated with a one quarter of one percentage point rise in the annual growth rate of output per worker. This partial association is strong and accounts for a relatively large share of the variation in output per capita growth: a one standard deviation increase in machinery investment is associated with a one-half standard deviation rise in output per worker growth. And the coefficient of the machinery investment variable is precisely estimated, with a *t*-statistic more than twice as large as any other variable (save the World War II loss dummy).

In addition to the basic specification, table 2 also reports the effects of adding to the list of independent variables estimates of primary and seconday school enrolment rates, era dummies, and nation dummies. Inclusion of the educational enrolment variables has no effect on the machinery investment coefficient, and the educational enrolment variables have little partial association with growth (12).

---

(11) A First World War loss dummy was dropped after proving insignificant.

(12) This does not necessarily imply that human capital accumulation is unimportant for growth. It more likely means only that estimates of enrolment rates are bad measures of human capital accumulation.

TABLE 2

GROWTH REGRESSIONS
FOR THE VERY LONG RUN PANEL

| Independent variables | Basic specification | Education variables | Era controls | Nation controls | Both era and nations controls |
|---|---|---|---|---|---|
| Machinery investment .. | 0.249 | 0.241 | 0.195 | 0.329 | 0.288 |
| | (0.055) | (0.066) | (0.058) | (0.061) | (0.083) |
| Non-machinery invest-ment ................. | 0.009 | 0.012 | 0.033 | 0.094 | 0.060 |
| | (0.044) | (0.045) | (0.045) | (0.048) | (0.053) |
| Pdty gap *vis-à-vis* US .... | 0.017 | 0.014 | 0.020 | 0.021 | 0.029 |
| | (0.008) | (0.010) | (0.008) | (0.019) | (0.022) |
| Labor force growth...... | 0.449 | 0.960 | 0.514 | 0.683 | 0.719 |
| | (0.426) | (0.518) | (0.426) | (0.421) | (0.511) |
| Log primary enrolment/ population .............. | | 0.014 | | | |
| | | (0.009) | | | |
| Log secondary enrolment/ population .............. | | 0.004 | | | |
| | | (0.002) | | | |
| World War II loser? .... | 0.038 | −0.041 | −0.050 | −0.035 | −0.049 |
| | (0.009) | (0.009) | (0.010) | (0.008) | (0.010) |
| Nation controls? ........ | no | no | no | si | si |
| Era controls? .......... | no | no | si | no | si |
| $R^2$ ................... | 0.531 | 0.623 | 0.666 | 0.723 | 0.804 |
| *SEE*................... | 0.0142 | 0.0142 | 0.0132 | 0.0124 | 0.0111 |
| *n* .................... | 48 | 41 | 48 | 48 | 48 |

Inclusion of era dummies reduces the machinery investment coefficient by about one-fifth of its magnitude, or one standard error. Inclusion of nation dummies raises it by one and a half standard errors. Only one of the era dummy variables, that for 1929-1938, is significantly different from zero. Only two of the nation dummy variables, Argentina and Japan, are significant, with Argentina low and Japan high. Thus there is no strong evidence that important nation- or era-specific effects have been omitted from the independent variables and are thus biasing the results.

Graph 3 shows the partial scatter of machinery investment and growth controlling for nation and era effects. The variations in machinery investment shown on the horizontal and growth rates shown on the vertical axis are those portions orthogonal not only to labor force growth, non-machinery investment, and relative backwardness, but also to nation- and era-specific average growth rates. For example, post-World War II Argentina is in the lower left hand quarter of graph 3 but not of graph 2. Post-World War II Argentinian growth has been slow and machinery investment low not so much in absolute terms as relative to the (high) post-World War II average rates of growth and investment in the economies in the panel.

Nevertheless, the differences between graphs 2 and 3 are not of overwhelming importance. Controlling for nation- and era-specific factors does not greatly distort the pattern of identifying variance, and the partial scatter in graph 3 appears largely similar to the partial scatter in graph 2. This should not come as a surprise: it is implicit in the relatively small sizes and low significance levels of the nation- and era-specific dummy variables.

GRAPH 3

### PARTIAL SCATTER OF MACHINERY INVESTMENT AND GROWTH FOR THE VERY LONG RUN PANEL CONTROLLING FOR NATION AND ERA EFFECTS

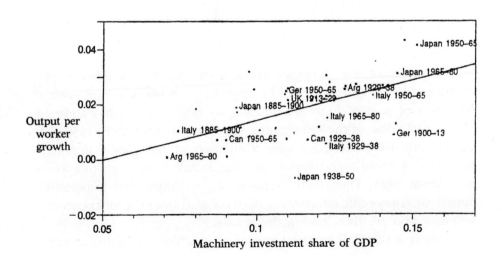

## 3.2  *Backcasts: 1950-1960*

Yet another potential source of information about the growth-machinery nexus is the comparative performance of economies in the 1950s before the beginning of the De Long and Summers [18] sample. We have constructed estimated of machinery investment rates in the 1950s for 54 countries. As always, we omit high-income oil-exporting nations and centrally-planned economies from our sample. For the OECD nations, estimates of machinery investment in the 1950s are derived from the official OECD estimates of the current-price machinery investment share, adjusted to international dollars.

For other nations our estimates of machinery investment in the 1950s were constructed by multiplying Summers and Heston's [55] estimates of investment shares in the 1950s by our own estimates of the machinery investment share of total investment calculated for the previous subsection. The non-OECD data are therefore of relatively low quality: they contain no new information about the division of investment between machinery and structures. The OECD data do contain substantial amounts of information about the division of investment between categories in the 1950s. We report regressions both for the sample of all 54 nations and for the OECD alone.

Graph 4 plots the partial scatter of growth and machinery investment in the 1950s. Table 3 presents regressions covering the 1950s for various modifications of our basic specification and sample. The decade of the 1950s is a period only forty percent as long as that covered by the basic 1960-1985 regressions of De Long and Summers [18]. As a result of the shortness of the sample, we are not surprised that the standard errors of the regression and the coefficients are relatively large. But note the magnitude of the machinery investment coefficient: it is almost exactly the same as for the 1960-1985 sample (although it is not very precisely estimated). Graph 4 and table 3 show that the growth-machinery nexus is as strong in the 1950s as over 1960-1985.

Graph 4 shows that the high growth-high machinery countries in the 1950s were a slightly different set than they were later on. In the 1950s Germany especially is a high growth-high machinery investment country. Brazil, which is a moderate investment-high growth

GRAPH 4

PARTIAL SCATTER OF GROWTH
AND MACHINERY INVESTMENT IN THE 1950s

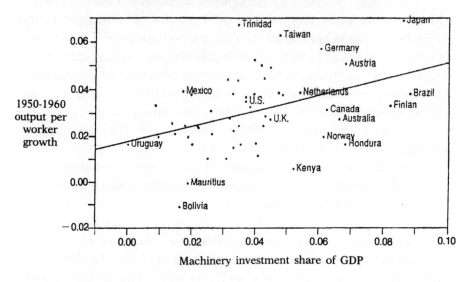

Machinery investment share of GDP

country in many of our regressions covering the 1960-1985 period, is as a high investment-moderate growth country in the 1950s. The 1950s are a somewhat different "natural experiment", possessing a somewhat different pattern of variation in machinery investment than found in subsequent post-World War II yeras.

The first two columns of table 3 report regressions for all 54 nations and for just the OECD nations. The association of machinery and growth is somewhat weaker in the OECD sample. To some degree this may arise because of the endogeneity of OECD membership: Australia, Japan, and New Zealand joined the group in the early 1960s. It seems reasonable to suppose that had rich South American nations like Uruguay and Argentina not stagnated during the 1950s they would have joined as well. If the possession by Uruguay, Argentina, and Chile of low machinery investment shares and low growth rates in the 1950s excluded them from the OECD sample, it is not surprising that the OECD sample does not show as strong a relationship between machinery investment and economic growth.

Some evidence supporting this hypothesis is contained in the

TABLE 3
GROWTH REGRESSIONS FOR THE 1950s

|  | Basic specification | OECD nations only | High-pdty(**) economies only(*) | Basic with (*) schooling variables | Basic with continent dummies |
|---|---|---|---|---|---|
| Machinery investment .... | 0.332 | 0.218 | 0.384 | 0.260 | 0.274 |
|  | (0.109) | (0.130) | (0.122) | (0.126) | (0.111) |
| Non-machinery investment | 0.020 | −0.013 | 0.027 | 0.008 | −0.001 |
|  | (0.047) | (0.066) | (0.075) | (0.049) | (0.047) |
| Pdty gap *vis-à-vis* US .... | 0.035 | 0.061 | 0.065 | 0.048 | 0.043 |
|  | (0.011) | (0.010) | (0.013) | (0.014) | (0.013) |
| Labor force growth ...... | −0.338 | 0.272 | 0.083 | −0.107 | 0.152 |
|  | (0.212) | (0.240) | (0.233) | (0.247) | (0.335) |
| Primary school enrolment |  |  |  | 0.020 |  |
|  |  |  |  | (0.011) |  |
| Secondary school enrolment .................. |  |  |  | 0.012 |  |
|  |  |  |  | (0.019) |  |
| $R^2$ .................... | 0.338 | 0.721 | 0.595 | 0.398 | 0.493 |
| SEE .................... | 0.0154 | 0.0092 | 0.0129 | 0.0150 | 0.0142 |
| n ..................... | 54 | 20 | 28 | 54 | 54 |

(*) Enrolment rates as a fraction of the school-age population in 1960.
(**) Economies with 1985 output per worker levels at least one-quarter that of the United States.

third column of table 3. It shows that the machinery investment coefficient estimated for the 1950s is very large when the sample is selected not by OECD membership but by initial 1950 levels of output per worker.

The fourth and fifth columns show that the inclusion of additional variables (in this case school enrolment rates and continent dummies) does not have a large effect on the estimated machinery investment coefficient. The association between machinery investment and growth does not appear to be result of the omission of human capital formation variables, or of fixed continent-specific factors.

### 3.3 *Forecasts: 1985-1989*

Relatively few years have elapsed since the 1985 end of the sample period used in  De Long and Summers [18]. It would be somewhat surprising if we were able to precisely estimate the relationship between growth and machinery for such a short period. As Easterly [20] *et Al.* have pointed out, there is enormous temporary year-to-year variation in cross-country growth rates that has a variance approximately twelve times as great as the cross-country variance in trend growth rates. Thus the share of growth rate variance that we could ever hope to explain in a cross-country regression over a five year period is much smaller than the share of variance we could hope to explain over a longer sample period like that of  De Long and Summers [18]. Moreover, the high residual variance implies that coefficients will almost surely be imprecisely estimated.

Nevertheless, graph 5 and table 4 report regressions for the very short 1985-1989 period with a sample of seventy-one economies. For

GRAPH 5

## PARTIAL SCATTER OF GROWTH
## AND MACHINERY INVESTMENT 1985-1989

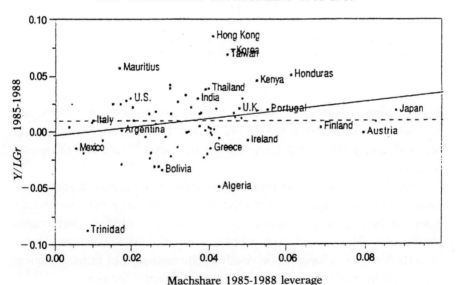

Machshare 1985-1988 leverage

TABLE 4

GROWTH REGRESSION FOR THE 1985-1989 PERIOD

| Independent variables | Basic specification | OECD nations only | High-pdty (*) economies only | Basic with continent dummies |
|---|---|---|---|---|
| Machinery investment | 0.391 | 0.096 | 0.261 | 0.248 |
| | (0.199) | (0.167) | (0.275) | (0.201) |
| Non-machinery investment .............. | 0.113 | 0.061 | 0.075 | 0.081 |
| | (0.072) | (0.140) | (0.119) | (0.073) |
| Pdty gap *vis-à-vis* US | 0.058 | 0.015 | 0.078 | 0.040 |
| | (0.025) | (0.020) | (0.039) | (0.026) |
| Labor force growth .. | −1.512 | −0.107 | −2.087 | −1.941 |
| | (0.432) | (0.670) | (0.584) | (0.508) |
| $R^2$ ................ | 0.286 | 0.075 | 0.317 | 0.426 |
| SEE ................ | 0.0282 | 0.0141 | 0.0319 | 0.0264 |
| n ................. | 71 | 20 | 38 | 71 |

(*) Economies with 1950 output per worker levels at least one-quarter that of the United States.

the OECD nations the estimates of machinery investment shares are derived from official OECD year-to-year estimates of national product adjusted to the 1985 ICP benchmark. For other nations in the De Long and Summers [18] sample the share of machinery in total investment over 1985-1989 was set equal to the ratio in the 1985 ICP benchmark year (13). Thus for non-OECD nations the estimated machinery investment rates over the 1985-1989 period are of low quality.

The results in table 4 show that in trying to estimate the association of machinery and growth over 1985-1989, we have pushed beyond the limits of the questions that the data can effectively answer. In the first column of table 4 the machinery investment coefficient is in its standard range (0.391). But it is very imprecisely estimated. Its 0.95 confidence interval ranges from − 0.007 to 0.789. For the OECD sample the machinery investment coefficient is not of high magnitude.

(13) For nations outside the DE LONG-SUMMERS [18] sample, the share of machinery in total investment over 1985-89 was imputed from proxy variables as described for the sample of «additional nations" in section 4 below.

And for the other regressions in table 4 the standard errors are even higher than in table 1.

Graph 5 shows why the machinery investment coefficient is so imprecisely estimated. The residual variance of 1985-1989 growth rates is enormous, with a standard deviation of 2.8% per year. With such a high residual variance, it is surprising that the data speak as strongly as they do in support of the growth-machinery connection. The regression results in table 4 and the scatter in graph. 5 are welcome confirmation of their opinions to those who already believe that there is a strong growth-machinery nexus. But they would be entirely unconvincing to any who were even slightly skeptical.

## 4. - The Growth-Machinery Nexus: Evidence from Additional Nations

Our original study covered a sample of some sixty-odd economies that had been at some point or other closely studied by the *UN International Comparison Project*. The ICP had constructed estimates of national relative price and quantity structures for specific benchmark years denominated in a common "international dollar" unit. The ICP allowed for cross-national comparisons orders of magnitude more accurate than any made before (Kravis, Heston and Summers [30]). We used estimates of the share of total investment devoted to machinery equipment derived from the benchmark-year data of Kravis, Heston and Summers [30] and of other versions of the ICP to estimate the share of machinery investment in GDP over 1960-1985, and merged our machinery investment estimates with the cross-country comparative national growth accounts of Summers and Heston [55], [56].

As we pointed out in De Long and Summers [18], these estimates we used are not especially good estimates of machinery investment. They depend heavily on the ratio of machinery to total investment in the benchmark years being a good proxy for the average ratio of machinery to total investment. Moreover, these estimates are confined to those economies that served as benchmarks in the ICP.

## 4.1 *Extending the Sample*

Alternative ways of estimating real rates of machinery investment allow us to construct estimates for economies not included in the sample of De Long and Summers [18]. There are many variables that could serve as proxies for the extent of an economy's machinery investment effort. As Warner [57] has demonstrated, the bulk of machinery and equipment are imported from abroad in all except the very richest economies. Trade statistics are thus a fruitful source of data on machinery investment. As De Long and Summers [18] showed, the relative price of machinery and equipment has a high correlation with the rate of machinery investment. For economies for which direct machinery investment data are lacking, data on price structures can help impute machinery investment estimates.

Aitken [1] has constructed estimates of the relative price of machinery in the 1980s. Lee [33] has compiled estimates of real machinery and equipment imports over 1960-1985. Our strategy in this subsection is to use these correlates of machinery investment to construct machinery investment estimates for economies not in the sample of De Long and Summers [18] and to show that the regressions we reported hold true for out-of-sample data.

Table 5 reports regressions of machinery and equipment investment rates over 1960-1985, as estimated in De Long and Summers [18], on proxies for the investment effort devoted to machinery. The sample in the first three columns of table 5 excludes the machinery-exporting economies of the G7. The sample also excludes the African outliers Tanzania, Zambia, and Zimbabwe, which De Long and Summers [18] estimated to have high shares of machinery investment in GDP, yet which have no capital goods producing sectors and import only small quantities of machinery from the industrial core (14). We omit these nations as well as the G7 nations from the sample used in determining the relationship between machinery investment rates and the available proxies for machinery investment effort.

---

(14) We believe that our previous estimates of their rates of machinery investment are overstated, perhaps because of our failure to note that benchmark year we were using was also a peak year in the construction of the Chinese-built Tanzania-Zambia railroad.

TABLE 5

MACHINERY INVESTMENT RATES AS A FUNCTION
OF CAPITAL GOODS IMPORTS,
TARIFF STRUCTURES, AND RELATIVE PRICES

| Sample | Excludes G7 | Excludes G7 | Excludes G7 | Includes G7 |
|---|---|---|---|---|
| Investment share of GDP.. | 0.0979 | 0.0978 | 0.0794 | 0.1994 |
| | (0.0359) | (0.0321) | (0.0470) | (0.0461) |
| Productivity gap *vis-à-vis* US ................... | 0.0242 | 0.0330 | 0.0257 | −0.0251 |
| | (0.0158) | (0.0130) | (0.0191) | (0.0174) |
| Aitken estimates of machinery prices ......... | 0.1473 | | −0.1256 | −0.3157 |
| | (0.0978) | | (0.1079) | (0.1289) |
| Imports of machinery as a share of GDP ........... | 0.8357 | 0.9167 | 0.9804 | 0.1674 |
| | (0.1681) | (0.1351) | (0.2579) | (0.2058) |
| 1980s tariffs on machinery | | | 0.0049 | |
| | | | (0.0094) | |
| $R^2$ .................... | 0.774 | 0.745 | 0.656 | 0.647 |
| SEE ................... | 0.0108 | 0.0105 | 0.0115 | 0.0163 |
| $n$ ..................... | 34 | 39 | 29 | 40 |

At Table 5 shows, nearly three quarters of the variation in machinery investment can be predicted from these proxies for machinery investment effort. Of the proxies the best predictor is the share of machinery imports in GDP. It is a direct "output" proxy, while the other proxy variables are more estimates of machinery investment "effort". In the table 5 regressions, the most significant positive outlier of the economies in the De Long and Summers [18] sample is Brazil, which has a regression residual more than twice as large as any other positive residual. According to Lee [33], Brazil imported only 0.8% percent of GDP in machinery investment on average over 1960-1985. Yet the ICP benchmarks of Brazil's machinery share of investment and Brazil's high general investment share of GDP led us to estimate that Brazil achieved a relatively high average rate of machinery investment: 4.1% of GDP over 1960-1985.

We believe that this large residual is a consequence of the import substitution development strategy that Brazil chose to follow over this particular part of the post-World War II period. Brazil has eschewed imports of machinery and equipment, and has to a large degree attempted to build its own capital goods producing industries from scratch. It has achieved a surprising degree of success. Thus we are not greatly disturbed by the inability of our proxies to account for machinery investment in Brazil.

Using the first regression equation in table 5, we impute estimates of 1960-1985 machinery investment rates for 27 economies not included in the original De Long and Summers [18] sample. Table 6 reports results from our basic specifications over the 1960-1985 period, using as our sample only those economies not included in the De Long and Summers [18] database.

Even though the sample is a small one, the machinery investment coefficient remains reasonably precisely estimated. Moreover, it remains in the high range seen in the other regressions. And once again the estimated machinery investment coefficient is little affected by the inclusion of continent dummies, of rates of schooling, or of Barro's collection of five political and educational variables.

Graph 6 reports the partial scatter of growth and machinery investment in the regression underlying the first column of table 6. Graph 6 shows that the sample of the additional economies contains one extreme observation: Singapore. But the large and significant estimated machinery investment coefficient is not a product of the inclusion of Singapore in the sample. Indeed, the inclusion of Singapore significantly lowers the estimated machinery investment coefficient. The presence of Singapore in the sample does markedly increase the precision of the estimates. If Singapore were excluded from the sample, the standard errors in table 6 would be approximately twice as large.

Angola and Mozambique possess extremely large negative residuals. They are poor countries that have undergone long and bloody civil wars with US and South African-backed guerrilla movements. They have also attempted, like other African countries such as Zimbabwe, to introduce large elements of central planning and socialist production into their economies. These factors seem to us more than enough to account for their disappointing growth rates.

TABLE 6

MACHINERY INVESTMENT AND GROWTH OVER 1960-1985
FOR ECONOMIES NOT IN THE
DE LONG SUMMERS [18] SAMPLE

| Independent variables | Basic specification | Including schooling variables | Including continent dummies | Including Barro variables |
|---|---|---|---|---|
| Machinery investment .. | 0.350 | 0.264 | 0.244 | 0.243 |
| | (0.116) | (0.123) | (0.129) | (0.099) |
| Non-machinery invest-ment ............... | 0.072 | 0.048 | 0.060 | 0.021 |
| | (0.052) | (0.062) | (0.082) | (0.050) |
| Pdty gap *vis-à-vis* US .. | 0.038 | 0.067 | 0.026 | 0.062 |
| | (0.025) | (0.029) | (0.032) | (0.024) |
| Labor force growth .... | −0.217 | −0.089 | −0.190 | −0.162 |
| | (0.444) | (0.506) | (0.593) | (0.397) |
| $R^2$ ................. | 0.450 | 0.526 | 0.569 | 0.761 |
| SEE................. | 0.0144 | 0.0141 | 0.0145 | 0.0108 |
| n .................... | 27 | 27 | 27 | 27 |

GRAPH 6

PARTIAL SCATTER OF GROWTH
AND MACHINERY FOR ECONOMIES
NOT IN DE LONG-SUMMERS [18] SAMPLE

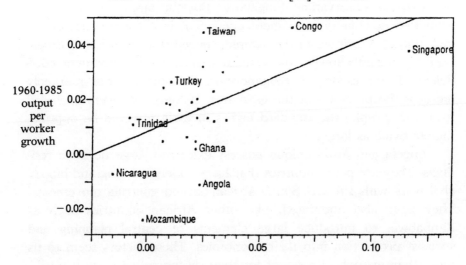

Estimated machinery investment as a share of GDP

Taiwan possesses an extremely large positive residual in graph 6: nearly three percentage points per year of growth faster than predicted from the regression equation in column one of table 6. Machinery investment and the other basic variables in De Long and Summers [18] do not account for more than four-ninths of growth rate variation. Adding Barro's [10] politico-economic and education variables to the list of growth-causing factors accounts for another thirty percent of the growth rate variance, but does not help account for the rapid growth of Taiwan.

Given the large magnitude of the residuals that remain, and the small size of the sample of additional nations, it is striking that the regressions are as consistent with those of De Long and Summers [18], as they are. The sample of economies analyzed in this subsection — a sample relying exclusively on new data, including only economies not analyzed in our original De Long and Summers [18] — shows the same pattern as did our earlier work. Machinery investment is strongly associated with output per worker growth. Machinery investment by itself accounts for a large share of growth rate variation. And machinery investment has a much larger association with growth than other forms of investment.

## 4.2 *Maximum 1960-1985 Cross Section Regression*

To summarize the evidence on the strength of the association of machinery and growth in the 1960-1985 period, it is worth combining all of the sources of data on machinery investment and estimating the regression of output per worker growth on machinery investment for the maximum cross-section sample (15). Table 7 reports such regres-

---

(15) Machinery investment data underlying graph 7 and table 7 come from three sources. For OECD nations, the estimates of machinery investment over 1960-1985 are those underlying graph 10 and equation 4, calculated by taking year-by-year OECD estimates of machinery investment shares of national product and deflating them to 1985 internatinal dollars. For the additinal natins not included in the DE LONG-SUMMERS [18] sample, and for Tanzania, Zambia and Zimbabwe, for which the volumes of machinery imports are grossly inconsistent with previous calculations of machinery investment rates, the estimates of machinery investment over 1960-1985 are those imputed from the proxies for machinery investment effort. For other non-OECD nations included in the DE LONG-SUMMERS [18] sample, the estimates of machinery investment are averages of the values imputed from the proxies and the original De Long and Summers estimates.

sions, and graph 7 reports the partial scatter of growth and machinery investment.

As would be expected, the results estimated in graph 7 and table 7 are somewhat stronger than those estimated by De Long and Summers [18]. The $t$-statistic on the machinery investment variable is 7.09 in the first column of table 7, but only 4.07 in the analogous regression in De Long and Summers [18]. In the maximum cross-section the regression accounts for 45 percent of the variation in output per worker growth rates, as opposed to 29% in our previous sixty-odd nation sample.

Significant variation in output per worker growth rates remains unaccounted for. The maximum share of growth rate variance acounted for in the regressions of table 7 is 60%. Many observations continue to show large residuals, as graph 7 displays. A number of the outliers with negative residuals are a number of sub-Saharan African nations with semi-socialized economies: Angola, Madagascar, Mozambique, Zaire, and Zambia. A number of the economies that show large negative residuals (Angola, Mozambique, and Nicaragua) have suffered through long and destructive civil wars.

TABLE 7

### MACHINERY INVESTMENT AND GROWTH OVER 1960-1985 FOR THE MAXIMUM CROSS SECTION

| Independent variables | Basic specification | Schooling variables | Continent dummies | Barro variables |
|---|---|---|---|---|
| Machinery investment .... | 0.342 | 0.318 | 0.302 | 0.293 |
| | (0.049) | (0.055) | (0.053) | (0.054) |
| Non-machinery investment | 0.048 | 0.020 | 0.014 | 0.020 |
| | (0.028) | (0.029) | (0.032) | (0.028) |
| Pdty gap *vis-à-vis* US .... | 0.032 | 0.043 | 0.033 | 0.050 |
| | (0.008) | (0.010) | (0.010) | (0.010) |
| Labor force growth ...... | 0.018 | 0.015 | 0.091 | 0.013 |
| | (0.161) | (0.178) | (0.227) | (0.171) |
| $R^2$ .................... | 0.464 | 0.486 | 0.497 | 0.553 |
| SEE.................... | 0.0126 | 0.0123 | 0.0124 | 0.0117 |
| $n$ ..................... | 89 | 88 | 88 | 88 |

GRAPH 7

### PARTIAL SCATTER OF 1960-1985 GROWTH
### AND MACHINERY INVESTMENT
### FOR THE MAXIMUM EXTENDED CROSS SECTION

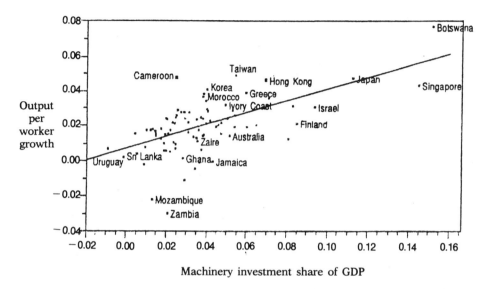

Machinery investment share of GDP

Prominent amoing the positive residuals are some of the most rapidly growing East Asian economies: Hong Kong, Korea, and Taiwan, in addition to countries like Morocco, the Cameroon, the Congo, and most prominently Botswana in Africa. A high rate of machinery investment is not the sole determinant of rapid growth. Indeed, some of the East Asian economies now put forward as models for rapid development do not display extraordinarily high rates of machinery investment, although some — Japan and Singapore, and to a lesser extent Hong Kong — do.

All of the samples and periods considered in this and the previous section carry the same message. In all cases regressions using new data strongly confirm our previous claim that the growth-machinery nexus is strong and robust. The very long run panel data set, the cross-section regression covering the 1950s alone, the weak results for the 1985-1989 period, and the regression using as its sample the 27 additional nations all use databases that have no overlap with that of

De Long and Summers [18]. If our earlier conclusions were due to some specific peculiarity or feature of our previous data, then these tests of our hypotheses should have revealed their fragility. Our own confidence that the correlations set out in De Long and Summers [18] are in fact robust features of industrialization has been greatly strengthened by the extra data we have presented in this and the previous section.


## 5. - Interpretation

### 5.1 *Productivity: Is the Growth-Machinery Correlation the "Normal" Return to Investment?*

The partial association of machinery investment and growth is, of course, much stronger than one would expect under the assumption that the private returns to factors of production are equal to their social marginal products. This shows itself as a strong correlation between machinery investment and total factor productivity growth. Graphs 8 and 9 plot partial scatters of two different estimates of total factor productivity growth and machinery investment. Equations 1 and 2 beneath the graphs report regressions of the estimates of total factor productivity growth on machinery investment and on the productivity gap *vis-à-vis* the US.

In the first case, graph 8, total productivity is calculated assuming that the net returns to capital do not diminish but are a constant 12%, chosen to approximately match both real rates of return earned by investors and the regression coefficients on non-machinery investment that we have estimated above, and in De Long and Summers [18].

Graph 9 allows for diminishing returns to capital by assuming a Cobb-Douglas production function with a capital share of 40% and a labor share of 60%, and uses Summers and Heston's [55] estimates of capital-output ratios to calculate the variation in profit rates across countries. Because of the limited number of nations for which Summers and Heston make capital stock estimates, the sample is relatively small: twenty-nine nations.

GRAPH 8

### PARTIAL SCATTER OF TOTAL FACTOR PRODUCTIVITY GROWTH AND MACHINERY INVESTMENT, 1985-1989

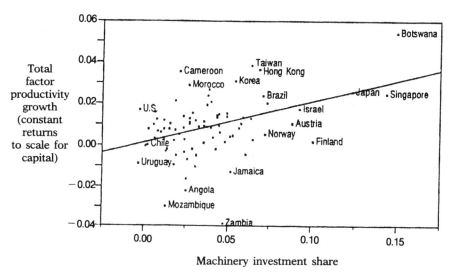

*(1) Gdp/Wkr Gr=*  + 0.039 *(Rel. Gdp Gap)*  + 0.198 (mach inv.)
          (0.008)                    (0.048)
     *n* = 88     *R*2 = 235     *SEE* = 0.130

According to both sets of total factor productivity estimates, a large productivity gap does provide significant opportunities for total factor productivity growth through "catch-up" (16). According to equation *(1)*, a country that in 1960 had an output per worker level one-third that of the U.S. would have closed almost half of the gap by 1985 had it managed to achieve the same rate of machinery investment and residual factors as the US.

But the more important feature of graphs 8 and 9 is that a high rate of machinery investment is associated with very rapid total factor productivity growth. Over a twenty-five year period, a country de-

---

(16) Regressions including education rates, labor force growth rates, and non-machinery investment rates as possible determinants of productivity growth did not produce significant differences.

Graph 9

PARTIAL SCATTER OF TOTAL FACTOR PRODUCTIVITY GROWTH
AND MACHINERY INVESTMENT
1960-1985

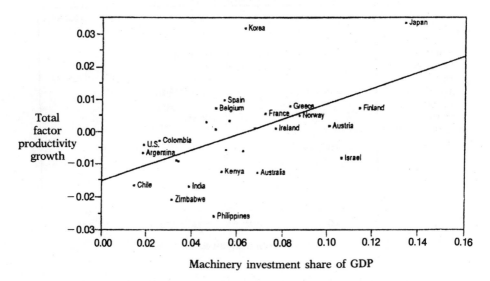

Machinery investment share of GDP

$$(2)\ Gdp/Wkr\ Gr = +\ 0.027\ (Rel.\ Gdp\ Gap)\ +\ 0.240\ (\text{mach inv.})$$
$$(0.011) \qquad\qquad\qquad (0.073)$$
$$n = 29 \qquad R2 = 0.312 \qquad SEE = 0.114$$

voting one additional percentage point of GDP per year to machinery
investment raises relative output per capita at the end not only by the
direct growth-accounting effect of a higher capital stock (a cumulative
matter of 2.4%) but also by the association of machinery investment
with total factor productivity growth (a matter of an additional 5%).
Such total factor productivity gains are *not* realized by economies that
devote resources to non-machinery investment.

Similar conclusions follow from estimates of the level of output
per worker today as a function of the machinery and non-machinery
capital stocks. Table 8 reports regressions for a twenty-nine country
sample, using data from Summers and Heston [55], of output per
worker *levels* on stocks of machinery and equipment capital per
worker, of non-residential structures capital per worker, and on the

TABLE 8

## 1985 OUTPUT PER WORKER LEVELS
## AS A FUNCTION OF MACHINERY CAPITAL STOCKS

| | | | | |
|---|---|---|---|---|
| Machinery capital stock | 0.466 | 0.510 | 0.492 | 0.460 |
| | (0.103) | (0.098) | (0.077) | (0.108) |
| Structures capital stock | 0.031 | 0.067 | | 0.029 |
| | (0.081) | (0.077) | | (0.083) |
| Secondary school enrolment rate ........... | 0.177 | | 0.120 | 0.191 |
| | (0.139) | | (0.128) | (0.150) |
| Primary school enrolment rate ........... | | | | −0.063 |
| | | | | (0.228) |
| $R^2$ ................. | 0.852 | 0.843 | 0.852 | 0.853 |
| SEE ................ | 0.111 | 0.113 | 0.110 | 0.114 |
| $n$ ................... | 29 | 29 | 29 | 29 |

secondary school enrolment rate. All variables are normalized so that the United States in 1985 is equal to one.

In the first colomn the level of output per worker is regressed on all three of the three independent variables, which together account for eighty-five percent of the variation in output per worker (17). Of these three, the stock of machinery investment per worker is by far the most closely associated with the level of output per worker.

An increase in the machinery capital stock per worker of one percentage point of the US level carries with it an increase in output per worker of 0.47% points of the US level. The US machinery stock per worker has been approximately one-third of output per worker, and so a one dollar difference across countries in machinery capital per worker is associated with a $1.50 difference in gross output per worker. This is far greater than growth-accounting calculations would suggest: even with a fifteen percent net rate of return on capital and a ten percent depreciation rate on machinery, a given dollar of machinery capital contributes capital services of only $0.25 to the

---

(17) Residuals are not heteroskedastic: there is no evidence that they are an increasing function of scale.

GRAPH 10

PARTIAL SCATTER OF OUTPUT PER WORKER LEVEL
AND MACHINERY CAPITAL STOCK PER WORKER

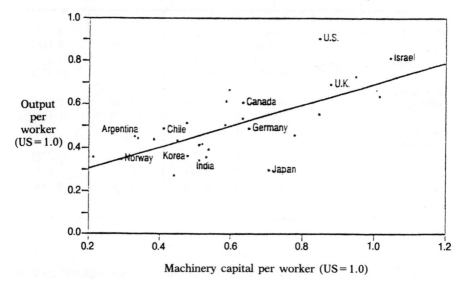

Machinery capital per worker (US=1.0)

economy, only one sixth as much as the regression coefficients in table 8.

The structures capital stock has no significant association with output per worker levels. Education variables are positively related to output per worker variables, but their effects are not precisely estimated, and are an order of magnitude smaller than the association of machinery capital stocks and output per worker levels. The other columns of table 8 show that omitting variables, or including an extra education variable does not markedly affect the partial association of the machinery capital stock and the output per worker level.

The point-by-point information about the partial association is shown in graph 10, which displays the partial scatter of output per worker levels and machinery capital stocks. Interestingly, Japan is not an especially influential observation in this partial scatter. Relative to its levels of school enrolment, it has not a high but a moderate level of output per worker. And relative to its levels of school enrolment, Japan fails to have a high and in fact has a relatively low machinery capital stock per worker. The influential observations in graph 10 are economies like that of the US, Israel, and the UK in the first, and Argentina, India, and Korea in the third quadrant.

The association between machinery stocks and output per worker levels would not convince any skeptics that machinery is a key factor in economic growth. Skeptics will point to the very large size of the estimated correlation: $1.00 extra in machinery capital per worker buys you $1.50 extra in output per worker. There is a more than even chance that this correlation arises because of feedback: rich countries invest more in dollar terms than do poor countries, and have higher capital stocks. It is hard to think of *any* model of economic growth in which there is not a rough one-for-one proportional association of productivity levels with capital stocks. Nevertheless, it is noteworthy that the weight in this roughly proportional association is entirely on the machinery stock, and not at all on the structures capital stock per worker.

## 5.2 *Causality*

Does the strong growth-machinery nexus mean that machinery investment cuses rapid growth, or that rapid growth induces high machinery investment? In De Long and Summers [18], we have argued that machinery investment was the cause and growth the effect. Here we attempt to strengthen the case for interpreting the growth-machinery nexus as a causal link.

The most powerful piece of evidence presented in De Long and Summers [18] for attributing causal significance to the machinery-growth nexus was the strong *negative* association between machinery prices on the one hand and machinery investment and growth on the other. If high rates of investment were a consequence rather than a cause of growth, one would expect the price of machinery to be high in rapidly-growing countries because of strong demand pressing on the limits of available supply.

This argument is simple supply-and-demand. Fast growth could increase machinery investment by raising profits and shifting the derived demand for machinery investment to the right. This would

GRAPH 11

### IDENTIFICATION FROM THE CORRELATION
### OF MACHINERY PRICES AND QUANTITIES

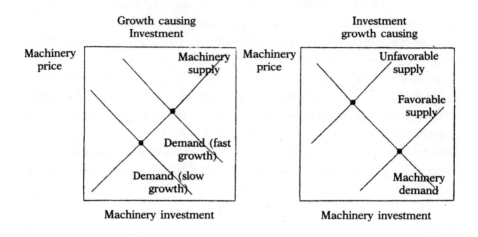

move the economy upward and outward along a machinery supply curve, as shown in the first panel of graph 11. In such a case, we would see rapid growth go together with high machinery investment and relatively high machinery prices.

In fact, rapid growth turned out to be associated with low relative machinery prices. Graph 12 shows relative machinery prices, relative machinery investment rates, and GDP per worker growth rates for the dataset used in De Long and Summers [18]. It shows a strong negative relationship between machinery prices and quantities. It also shows that the high-quantity low-price economies are predominantly the fast-growing economies. This suggests that high machinery investment comes about through a move down and to the right along a machinery supply curve, as is shown in the second panel of graph 11.

Here we report additional evidence, using a number of instruments plausibly more closely related to machinery supply conditions than to economic growth impulses produced by outside factors. We use three sets of instruments. First, we use our measures of national relative price structures from De Long and Summers [18]; the structure of relative prices in an economy is largely a function of its

GRAPH 12

MACHINERY PRICES, MACHINERY INVESTMENT,
AND OUTPUT GROWTH

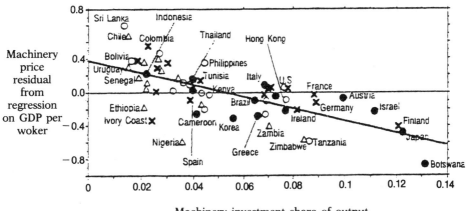

Machinery investment share of output

---

*Legend:*

● Top growth quartile;     ✗ Second growth quartile;     ○ Third growth quartile;
△ Bottom growth quartile

level of development and of the economic policies pursued by the government.

Second, we use openness to trade as measured by World Bank estimates of tariff and non-tariff barriers in the 1980s, and by the average share of imports in GDP over 1960-1985; tariff and non-tariff barriers are the result of explicit policies; the import share is in large part a product of past policy decisions and how they have shaped an economy's openness to the world market. Third, we use Lee's *et Al.* [34], estimates of real machinery imports from the industrial core of the OECD; this provides us with an estimate of the effort devoted to machinery investment independent of errors or biases in the UN ICP benchmarks.

We have substantial confidence in the value of these instruments. We do not find it credible that rapid growth generated by exogenous sources leads to a relative price structure that makes it easy and cheap to invest in machinery, and hence to a high machinery investment share. We do not find it credible to suppose that rapid growth generated by other sources leads economies to quickly dismantle their trade barriers and become more open to machinery imports, and thus to higher machinery investment. We are less confident in the exogeneity of machinery imports, but we do think this instrumental variable provides us with a valuable control for biases and errors in the ICP benchmark-year estimates of quantity structures, on which so much of our data ultimately rest.

Table 9 reports our instrumental variable results using 1960-1985 as our sample period, and using the machinery investment estimates constructed for the maximum cross-section sample. Graph 13 reports the partial scatter of growth and machinery investment in the different second-stage regressions.

The results using the relative price of machinery as an instrument for the machinary investment quantity are similar to results reported in De Long and Summers [18]. The estimated equation is shown in the second column of table 9, and the partial scatter in the first panel of graph 13. Results using the quantity of capital goods imported

TABLE 9

**INSTRUMENTAL VARIABLES REGRESSIONS OF GROWTH
ON MACHINERY INVESTMENT**

|  | All instruments | D&S equip. price | Lee mach. imports | Barriers imports (*) |
|---|---|---|---|---|
| Equip. share .......... | 0.278 (0.215) | 0.320 (0.115) | 0.324 (0.117) | 0.229 (0.126) |
| Non-mach share ...... | 0.019 (0.062) | 0.039 (0.043) | 0.048 (0.041) | 0.056 (0.043) |
| L Gr 1960-1985 ...... | −0.183 (0.315) | −0.013 (0.240) | −0.024 (0.199) | −0.044 (0.220) |
| Y/Y US 1960.......... | 0.030 (0.022) | 0.033 (0.012) | 0.027 (0.013) | 0.019 (0.014) |
| $R^2$ .................. | 0.128 | 0.230 | 0.243 | 0.168 |
| SEE.................. | 0.0146 | 0.0146 | 0.0145 | 0.0146 |
| n .................... | 38 | 57 | 77 | 67 |

(*) World Bank estimates of tariffs and non-tariff barriers on machinery imports in the 1980s, and the average share of imports in GDP over 1960-1985.

according to Lee [34] as an instrument produce the equally strong results shown in the third column of table 9, with the partial scatter shown in the second panel of graph 13. However, the quantity of capital goods imported may well not be exogenous — the relative price structure of an economy as measured by the relative price of machinery has a better claim to being independent of the residual in the growth rate equation — and this regression should be interpreted as primarily a check on the reliability of our ICP benchmark data.

A better claim to exogeneity is possessed by variables that indirectly help determine the quantity of capital goods imported, but that are explicitly the result of economic policy choices. Tariffs and non-tariff barriers on machinery and equipment directly affect investors' and importers' willingness to purchase machinery from abroad, and are clearly variables determined by economic policy. The average share of imports in GDP is also, largely, a variable determined by the sum total of policy stances that affect "openness": a larger share of trade in GDP has an immediate effect increasing machinery imports by increasing the potential pool of foreign exchange that could be used to buy foreign machinery.

Results using these "openness" determining variables as instruments are shown in the fourth column of table 9, and the partial scatter is shown in the third panel of graph 13c. These results are somewhat weaker in support of machinery investment as a key to growth than those portrayed in graphs 13a and 13b, but they still give a very prominent place to machinery investment as a determinant of growth. The final panel of graph 13d presents the partial scatter from the first regression in table 9, using all of the instruments. Unfortunately the sample size is relatively small, and the standard error of the machinery investment coefficient is relatively large. However, the point estimate is the same as in the other instrumental variables regressions.

Different economies are the most influential observations in the different panels of graph 13, for each panel captures a somewhat different dimension of the machinery-growth scatter and uses a somewhat different sample. Nevertheless, they all generate qualitatively similar conclusions.

GRAPH 13

## PARTIAL SCATTERS OF GROWTH AND MACHINERY INVESTMENT
## FROM SECOND-STAGE INSTRUMENTAL VARIABLES REGRESSIONS

### *a) Instrument: Machinery Prices*

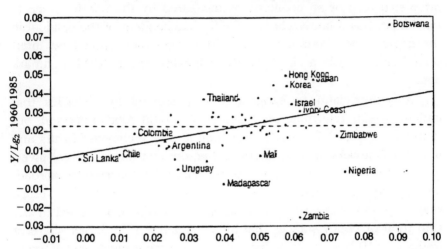

### *b) Instrument: Machinery Capital Imports*

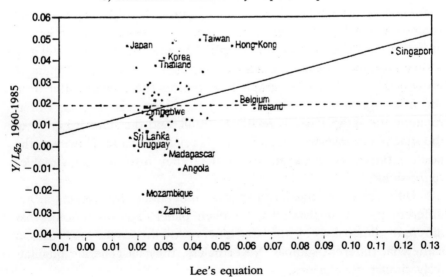

Lee's equation

GRAPH 13 *continued*

### c) *Instrument: Openness variables*

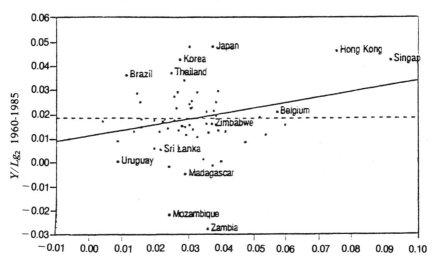

equation *NTB, T* e *X*

### d) *Instruments: All*

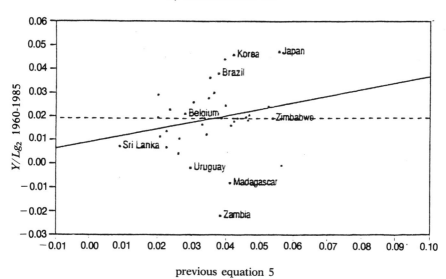

previous equation 5

### 5.3 *Argentina's Stagnation*

Still another powerful line of evidence that the association between machinery investment and economic growth is a causal one, and that a high rate of machinery investment is more than a signal that fundamentals are attractive, comes from analyzing exemplary case studies. Argentina's disappointing post-World War II growth history provides a particularly apposite example. According to Carlos Díaz-Alejandro, the rise of Perónism unintentionally crippled the Argentine economy's ability to invest in machinery. Díaz-Alejandro's tracing the sources of Argentinian post-World War II stagnation to the same factors that our cross-country regressions suggest are important determinants of growth lends very powerful support to our argument.

Up to the late 1950s, Argentina was a country as rich as any in continental Europe. In 1929 Argentina had been perhaps fifth in the world in automobiles per capita (Flick [21]). In 1913 Buenos Aires had been perhaps thirteenth among cities of the world in telephones per capita (Hobsbawm [24]). Yet hy the late 1970s (even before the oil shock induced borrowing sprees of the 1970's and the recession of 1980-1982 led to the Latin American debt crisis, and the subsequent

GRAPH 14

### POST-WORLD WAR II ARGENTINE
### AND EUROPEAN GDP PER CAPITA GROWTH

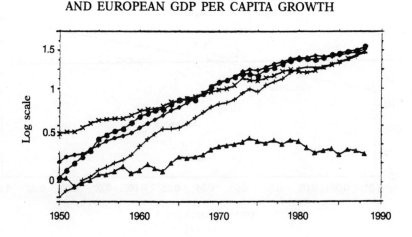

decade of decline in the 1980s) Argentina had become a third rather than a first world country. Graph 14, taken from De Long and Eichengreen [12], shows the relative erosion of Argentine productivity and living standards.

Like all countries outside of the inner industrial core, Argentina imported a large share of its machinery and equipment from abroad, primarily from Britain. This was efficient: first Britain and then the United States had enormous comparative advantages in producing producers' durable capital goods, and international transportation costs are a negligible fraction of the cost of such high value products. This pattern was destroyed by the Great Depression, which left Argentina justifiably suspicious of the free-trade order. America and Britain had, during the Depression, taken aggressive steps to shut Argentina out of their domestic markets and so preserve their own domestic employment at its expense.

In this environment an army officer, Juan Domingo Perón, gained mass political support by advocating a political program of national reassertion and populist redistribution. Perón embarked on a program of populist redistribution. Agricultural marketing boards were established to limit the price of food, and to keep rural monopolies from gouging urban workers. The growth of unions and the organization of workers was supported, in order to allow the urban working classes a fair chance to bargain against their employers. Urban wages were boosted. Perón's policies were popular. As Díaz Alejandro writes: «[f]avoring domestic consumption over exports pleased the urban masses, and strengthening import restrictions pleased urban entrepreneurs. All who would lose, it appeared, were foreigners who had to do without Argentine wheat and beef and could not sell manufactures to Argentina, and oligarchs who had previously profited from the export-import trade and their association with foreign investors».

All of Perón policies twisted terms of trade against rural agricultural and in favor of urban industrial goods. Real wages for urban workers and profits for urban manufacturers rose, while real incomes of rural workers and landlords fell. Imports rose, and exports fell. The resulting foreign exchange shortage provided Perón with only unattractive options, of which the best appeared to be the rationing of whole classes of imported goods. Perón and his advisors chose this alternative, believing that a dash for growth, a maintenance of his redistributive policies, and a reduction in dependence on the world economy was good for Argentina.

Administrative controls were used to allocate newly-scarce foreign exchange. The consequences appeared minor in the short run: the raw materials and intermediate goods needed to maintain current operations had first priority. But machinery and equipment, last in the queue, could not be imported. As a result, the early 1950s saw a huge rise in the relative price of capital goods. Before 1945, Argentina's relative price structure had been about average for a country of its level of wealth and industrialization. By the early 1950s the relative price of producer durable goods in Argentina was two or three times world levels. Thus the net effect of Perónist economic policies was an extraordinary rise in real capital goods relative prices in the 1940s, and a concommitant fall in investment in machinery and equipment. Each percentage point of national product saved produced less than half as much in terms of real investment after the war than would have been the case under other, liberal, outward-oriented economic policies (18).

Perón was overthrown and departed Argentina for Spain in 1953. But successor governments did not reverse his policies: the political forces he had mobilized still had to be appeased. Argentinian governments have remained committed to relative autarky, favoring urban over rural producers, terms of trade that disadvantaged rural producers, overvalued exchange rates, and unstable monetary policies throughout the post-World War II period. The government's hostility to foreign trade and foreign investment, and its desire to redistribute income towards the politically-powerful urban working classes produced an extraordinary rise in the relative real price of machinery and equipment — and a consequent fall in the rate of investment in

---

(18) The macroeconomic distortions that crippled Argentinian real investment were accompanied by microeconomic distortions as well. Diaz Alejandro laments that "the price mechanism became a tool to redistribute income rather than to allocate resources.... Severe bottlenecks had been allowed to develop in transportation, electricity, the supply of machinery and equipment, oil, and rural goods... the government neither allowed the price mechanism to reflect these imbalances in a steady fashion nor took effective measures to remedy them by public investment".

machinery and equipment capital stock. This, Díaz-Alejandro believed, was the principal source of slow Argentinian growth after World War II. Post-World War II Argentina has had a healthy national savings rate, but it has not been able to transform these savings into real investment in machinery and equipment.

It is difficult to interpret Argentina's low rate of machinery investment in the post-World War II world as a response to slow growth and low anticipated profits. Demand for that quantity of machinery that is imported and produced has in fact been relatively high: firms have been willing to purchase the quantities supplied at relative prices far exceeding world levels (Díaz-Alejandro [4]). It is much more natural to see Argentina's low rate of machinery investment as a result of the economic policies it has adopted, in which case the relative stagnation that has in the post-World War II era reduced Argentinian relative living standards relative to those in Western Europe by two-thirds is powerful evidence of a causal link from machinery investment to growth.

## 5.4 *Caveat*

One *caveat* is necessary. There is substantial evidence that the centrally-planned communist-ruled economies of the twentieth century commanded that huge fractions of GDP be devoted to machinery investment, yet they have not realized rapid productivity growth. There is other evidence that boosts in machinery investment that are not the results of market processes do not appear to produce large productivity gains. Machinery investment-boosting policies that are not market-conforming yield much lower benefits than our cross-section regressions suggest. If machinery investment does indeed have massive external benefits, then why didn't Stalin's Russia — apparently investing a greater share of total output in machinery over 1929-1973 than Japan did over 1950-1973 — even begin to overtake the industrial west? (19).

---

(19) The USSR's gross investment share of GDP in peacetime years from 1929 to 1973 appears to have been between thirty and forty percent, of which approximately one-third was machinery. Yet output per worker growth over this period was probably no greater than the OECD average: less than two percent per year.

One interpretation is that we have given an incorrect interpretation to our data. In spite of our attempts to control for outside souces of growth, it may be that the growth-machinery nexus arises not because machinery investment causes rapid growth but because a high rate of machinery investment is a signal that other fundamental factors that make for rapid growth are favorable. In spite of our attempts to control for other factors, it may be that the growth-machinery association arises because a high rate of machinery investment and low relative prices for machinery are signals of general administrative and social competence.

A second interpretazion is that the Soviet Union's high rate of investment in machinery and equipment did give it a much higher growth rate than it would otherwise have attained. Disappointing productivity growth in the Soviet Union would then be attributed not to the failure of investments in machinery to help workers learn skills and organizations learn procedures for efficiently handling modern technologies, but to the extraordinary costs of coordinating economic activity by the dead hand of the communist party. Under this interpretation we should dismiss the experience of the Soviet Union and the other centrally-planned economies (and perhaps of semisocialized economies like those of Tanziania and Mozambique as well) as having been generated by a regime too different from that of mixed and market economies to yield any useful lessons.

We are attracted to yet a third interpretation: one that attempts to resolve the apparent inconsistency between the strong cross-section correlation of machinery and growth in market economies, and the failure of high rates of machinery investment to trigger rapid productivity growth in centrally-planned economies. A given investment in machinery can have large external benefits if learning-by-using helps to create a workforce experienced and competent at handling modern technologies, and helps organizations to develop the rules of thumb and standard operating procedures necessary to produce efficiently that other firms can imitate. If these are the channels through which machinery investment produces external benefits, then it makes sense that few such external benefits would be generated by investments in inappropriate technologies. There is no gain to creating a workforce trained at technologies that subtract value. There is no advantage in the opportunity to copy the operating procedures of a money-losing organization. This leads us to suspect that the largest external benefits from machinery investment will arise from those investments that make the highest profits.

This line of thought suggests that growth is likely to be increased by investment-promoting policies that were market conforming: policies that alter the marginal incentives of producers and investors and induce them to undertake machinery investment projects that had previously just failed to meet hurdle rates. However, growth is *not* likely to be much increased by investment-promotions that are market-replacing. Policies that command pre-chosen large scale investments in machinery whether or not they meet direct cost-benefit tests are not likely to generate investment in kinds of machinery that have high private benefit-cost ratios. Thus we should not be surprised when the commands for more machinery investment issued by Joseph Stalin lead to an economic structure in which workers and organizations have skills and operating procedures that are value-substracting.

For an example closer to home, we should also not be surprised when the commands for more machinery investment issued by GM Chairman Roger Smith in the 1980s did not accelerate productivity growth in GM. General Motors invested more than 63 billion dollars in plant and equipment in the 1980s, more than four times current stockholders' equity, and enough to have purchased Toyota twice over (Keller [28]). But GM's massive 1980s investment program failed *ex ante* market tests. In the 1980s the stock market valued GM as worth only half as large a multiple of earnings or cash flows as its competitors like Honda or Volvo (only the extraordinary entrenchment of US executives allowed Roger Smith to go through with his investment program given the stock market's extraordinary low valuation of its likely outcome).

By contrast, the American steel industry also invested heavily in the 1980s. But the firms that did the investing in the steel industry were small firms, with prospects that the stock market saw as favorable *ex ante*, with few of the bureaucratic problems and inefficiencies of their larger competitors. And productivity in the American steel industry in the 1980's did grow rapidly (Barnett and Crandall [9]).

Thus we are attracted to an interpretation that stresses the importance of machinery investment in a market context. Market signals and allocation processes may well be essential to generating the type of machinery investment that is associated with rapid productivity growth.


## 6. - Conclusion

We have documented here, as we argued before in De Long and Summers [18], a very strong connection between machinery investment and productivity growth. This strong growth-machinery nexus can be found in databases reaching as far back into the past as 1870, and is as strong in the economies and subsections of the post-World War II era not analyzed in our previous work. All of our regressions show an association of machinery investment and output per worker growth much stronger than we would expect under the standard growth-accounting assumption that the return to investors is the marginal social product of investment.

We have also reported instrumental variables regressions that produce the same association between growth and machinery. Our instruments are in large part variables determined by economic policy that have direct effects on machinery investment rates, and only indirect effects on output per worker growth. Thus we conclude that the bulk of the growth-machinery investment relationship arises from a causal nexus between machinery and growth. The most plausible mechanism is that workers' skills and organizations' capacities to handle technologies are largely learned-by-doing. We believe that policies undertaken to generate more or less machinery investment by altering the incentives of investors and firms in market economies have large effects on economic growth rates.

However, we suspect that even though machinery investment is a key to growth, market tests of the value of investment projects are essential to making machinery investment realize its productive promise. We suspect that the kinds of machinery investment promoted by market-conforming policies are the right kinds of machinery investment, and that the kinds of machinery investment produced by command mechanisms are relatively unproductive. Thus we believe that policies to shift incentives toward making machinery investment cheaper and easier are likely to yield enormous benefits. But we also believe in the essential role of market mechanisms: any governments that took the correlations we have documented here as evidence that they should embark on large-scale programs to control and direct machinery investment through command mechanisms would, we believe, be making a very large mistake.

BIBLIOGRAPHY

[1] AITKEN BRIAN: *Measuring Trade Policy Intervention: A Cross-Country Index of Relative Price Dispersion*, Washington (DC), World Bank, 1991.

[2] ABRAMOVITZ MOSES: «Catching Up, Forging Ahead, and Falling Behind», *Journal of Economic History*, n. 46, 1986, pp. 385.

[3] AGARWALA RAMGOPAL: *Price Distorsion and Growth in Developing Countries*, Washington (DC), World Bank, 1983.

[4] ALEJANDRO DIAZ (ed.): *Essays on the Economic History of the Argentine Republic*, in CARLOS F. - ALEJANDRO DIAZ New Haven, Yale University Press, 1970.

[5] ARNDT H.W.: *Economic Development: The History of an Idea*, Chicago (Ill.), University of Chicago Press, 1987.

[6] BALASSA BELA A.: *Comparative Advantage, Trade Policy, and Economic Development*, New York, New York University Press, 1989.

[7] — —: *Development Strategies in Semi-Industrial Economies*, in BELA BALASSA - JULIO BERLINSKI et AL., published for the World Bank, Baltimore, Johns Hopkins University Press, 1982.

[8] — —: *The Structure of Protection in Developing Countries*, in BELA BALASSA, published for the International Bank for Reconstruction and Development and the Inter-American Development Bank, Baltimore, Johns Hopkins Press, 1971.

[9] BARNETT DONALD - CRANDALL ROBERT: *Up from the Ashes: The Rise of the Steel Minimill in the United States*, Washington (DC), Brookings Institution, 1986.

[10] BARRO ROBERT: «Economic Growth in a Cross Section of Countries», *Quarterly Journal of Economics*, vol. 106, n. 2, May 1991, pp. 407-44.

[11] — —: «Government Spending in a Simple Model of Endogenous Growth», *Journal of Political Economy*, vol. 98, n. 5, October 1990, pp. 5103-26.

[12] DE LONG J. BRADFORD - EICHENGREEN BARRY J.: *The Marshall Plan as a Structural Adjustment Program*, London, Centre for Economic Performance, 1991.

[13] BATES ROBERT: *Markets and States in Tropical Africa: The Political Economy of Agricultural Policies*, Berkeley (CA), University of California Press, 1981.

[14] BAUMOL WILLIAM - BEATTY BLACKMUN - SUE ANNE - WOLFF EDWARD: *Productivity and American Leadership: the Historical Record*, Cambridge (MA), MIT Press, 1990.

[15] BERGSON ABRAHAM: *The Real National Income of Soviet Russia since 1928*, Cambridge (Mass.), Harvard University Press, 1961.

[16] DE BEVER LEO - WILLIAMSON JEFFREY: «Saving, Accumulation and Modern Economic Growth: The Contemporary Relevance of Japanese History», *Journal of Japanese Studies*, n. 4, Winter 1978, pp. 125-67.

[17] DE LONG J. BRADFORD: «Productivity and Machinery Investment: A Long Run Look 1870-1980», *Journal of Economic History*, vol. 53, n. 2, June 1992.

[18] DE LONG J. BRADFORD - SUMMERS LAWRENCE H.: «Equipment Investment and Economic Growth», *Quarterly Journal of Economics*, vol. 106, n. 2, May 1991, pp. 445-502.

[19] DOWRICK STEVEN - NGUYEN DUC-THO: «OECD Comparative Economic Growth 1950-1985: Catch-Up and Convergence», *American Economic Review '79*, n. 5-6, December 1989, pp. 1010-30.

[20] EASTERLY WILLIAM: «Economic Policy and Economic Growth», *Finance and Development*, vol. 28, n. 3, September 1991, pp. 10-4.

[21] FLINK JAMES J.: *The Automobile Age*, Cambridge (Mass.), MIT Press, 1988.

[22] GROSSMAN GENE - HELPMAN ELHANAN: *Innovation and Growth in the Global Economy*, Cambridge (Mass.), MIT Press, 1991.

[23] HAWITT EDWARD: *Reforming the Soviet Economy: Equality versus Efficiency*, Washington (DC), Brookings Institution, 1988.

[24] HOBSBAWM E.J.: *The Age of Empire, 1875-1914*, 1st American edition 1917, New York, Pantheon Books, 1987.

[25] HOUNSHELL DAVID: *From the American System to Mass Production: The Development of Manufacturing Technology in the United States*, Baltimore (MD), Johns Hopkins University Press, 1984.

[26] JOHNSON CHALMERS: *MITI and the Japanese Miracle*, Palo Alto (CA), Stanford University Press, 1982.

[27] JONES CHARLES: *Economic Growth and Producer Durables Prices*, Cambridge (MA), MIT, 1991.

[28] KELLER MARYANN: *Rude Awakening: The Rise, Fall, and Struggle for Recovery of General Motors*, New York, Morrow, 1989.

[29] KRAVIS IRVING - HESTON ALAN - SUMMERS ROBERT: *International Comparisons of Real Product and Purchasing Power*, Baltimore, (MD), Johns Hopkins University Press, 1978.

[30] — — . — — . — —: *World Product and Income: International Comparisons of Real Gross Product*, Baltimore, (MD), Johns Hopkins University Press, 1982.

[31] KRAVIS IRVING - LIPSEY ROBERT: «The International Comparison Program: Current Status and Problems», in PETER HOOPER - J. DAVID RICHARDSON (eds.): *International Economic Transactions: Issues in Measurement and Empirical Research*, Chigaco (Ill.), University of Chicago Press, 1991.

[32] KREMER MICHAEL: *The O-Ring Theory of Economic Growth*, Cambridge (Mass.), Harvard University, 1991.

[33] LEE JONG-WHA: *Trade, Distortion, and Growth*, Ph. D. thesis, Cambridge (Mass.), Harvard University, 1992.

[34] LEE JONG-WHA - SWAGEL PHIL - TAN LING HUI: *Measuring Trade Distortions*, Cambridge (Mass.), Harvard University, 1991.

[35] LEVINE ROSS: «Stock Markets, Growth, and Policy», *Journal of Finance*, 1991.

[36] LEVINE ROSS - RENELT DAVID: «A Sensitivity Analysis of Cross-Country Growth Regressions», forthcoming, *American Economic Review*, 1992.

[37] MADDISON ANGUS: *Phases of Capitalist Development*, Oxford (UK), Oxford University Press, 1982.

[38] — —: *Economic Growth in the Twentieth Century*, Paris, Oecd, 1989.

[39] — —: *Dynamic Forces in Capitalist Development: A Long-Run Comparative View*, New York, Oxford University Press, 1991.

[40] MAGAZINER IRA - REICH ROBERT: *Minding America's Business*, New York, Harcourt Brace Jovanovich, 1982.

[41] MANKIW N. GREGORY - ROMER DAVID - WEIL DAVID: «A Contribution to the Empirics of Economic Growth», *Quarterly Journal of Economics*, vol. 107, n. 2, May 1992, pp. 407-38.

[42] MURPHY KEVIN - SHLEIFER ANDREI - VISHNY ROBERT: «The Allocation of Talent: Implications for Growth», *Quarterly Journal of Economics*, vol. 106, n. 2, May 1991, pp. 503,30.

[43] PATRICK HUGH - ROSOVSKY HENRY: *Asia's New Giant: How the Japanese Economy Works*, Washington (DC), The Brookings Institution, 1976.

[44] POLLARD SIDNEY: *Peaceful Conquest: The Industrialization of Europe 1760-1970*, Cambridge (UK), Cambridge University Press, 1982.

[45] PRESTON RICHARD: *American Steal: Hot Metal Men and the Resurrection of the Rustbelt*, New York, Prentice Hall, 1991.

[46] REBELO SERGIO: «Long-Run Policy Analysis and Long-Run Growth», *Journal of Political Economy*, vol. 99, n. 3, June 1991, pp. 500-23.

[47] ROMER PAUL: «Increasing Returns and Long Run Growth», *Journal of Political Economy*, vol. 95, n. 5, October 1986, pp. 1002-37.

[48] ——: *What Determines the Rate of Growth and Technological Change?*, Washington (DC), World Bank, 1989.

[49] ——: «Capital, Labor, and Productivity», *Brookings Papers on Economic Activity*, 1990.

[50] ——: «Endogenous Technological Change», *Journal of Political Economy*, vol. 98, n. 5, October 1990, pp. 971-1109.

[51] ROSENBERG NATHAN: «Capital Goods, Technology, and Economic Growth», *Oxford Economic Papers*, n. 15, 1963.

[52] ——: «Technological Change in the Machine Tool Industry, 1840-1910», *The Journal of Economic History*, December 1963.

[53] ROSOVSKY HENRY: «What Are the "Lessons" of Japanese Economic History», in A. YOUNGSON (ed.): *Economic Development in the Long Run*, New York, St. Martin's Press, 1972.

[54] SUMMERS LAWRENCE: «What is the Social Rate of Return on Capital Investment?», in DIAMOND PETER: *Growth, Productivity, Unemployment: Essays to Celebrate Bob Solow's Birthday*, Cambridge (Mass.), MIT Press, 1990.

[55] SUMMERS ROBERT - HESTON ALAN: «The Penn World Table, Version V», *Quarterly Journal of Economics*, 1991.

[56] —— - ——: «A New Set of International Comparisons of Real Product and Prices: Estimates for 130 Countries», *Review of Income and Wealth G4*, March 1988, pp. 1-25.

[57] WARNER ANDREW: *The Debt Crisis, World Investment Cycles, and American Exports*, Ph. D. thesis, Harvard University, 1991.

[58] YOUNG ALWYN: «A Tale of Two Cities», NBER, *Macroeconomics Annual*, 1992.

# The Role of Human Capital and Political Instability in Economic Development

**Jess Benhabib · Mark M. Spiegel**
New York University

## 1. - Introduction

The recent growth accounting literature (Barro [2]) has concentrated on estimation of aggregate production functions to investigate the determinants of economic growth. Typically, the methodology followed in this literature entails regressing per capita income growth on a set of ancillary variables in an effort to determine the characteristics which are thought to contribute positively or adversely to economic growth. In addition, these studies have attempted to estimate the contribution of factors of production to economic growth once one has properly accounted for differences in country characteristics through introduction of these ancillary variables.

Because of data constraints, the literature has often attempted to proxy the variables relevant to growth accounting by those which are directly observable. For example, although physical capital stocks are necessary to estimate the growth accounting equations, the literature has usually used gross investment rates as a proxy for physical capital accumulation (Barro [2]) (1). In addition, human capital has been

---

(1) An exception is the work of MANKIW - ROMER - WEIL [13]. In their study, they are able to generate a specification in terms of investment rates by assuming that all countries are in their steady state.

*Advise:* the numbers in square brackets refer to the Bibliography in the appendix.

proxied in the literature by enrollment ratios or literacy rates. At best, however, enrollment ratios represent investment levels in human capital. Literacy is a stock variable, but there are important empirical problems associated with the use of literacy as a proxy for human capital (2).

This paper continues work by Benhabib and Spiegel [4] in which estimates of physical and human capital stocks are used in growth accounting equations. We begin with estimation of a standard Cobb-Douglas production function in which labor and human and physical capital enter as factors of production. In the context of this estimation, we also examine the impact of two ancillary variables which indicate the severity of political conflict and distortionary economic policy, as well as the role played by initial levels of per capita income.

One of our main findings concerns the role of human capital in explaining the growth of per capita income. In our first set of results, we find that human capital growth is either insignificant, or has a significant but negative effect in explaining per-capita income growth. This result is robust to a number of alternative specifications, as well as to the possibility of bias which is encountered when regressing per capita income growth on accumulated factors of production (3).

These findings shed some doubt on the traditional role given to human capital in the development process as a separate factor of production. Nevertheless, human capital accumulation has long been stressed as a pre-requisite for economic growth. In the remainder of the paper, we examine alternative specifications that allow human capital to play a role in the development process and in the determination of per capita income growth.

First, it may be that standard growth accounting equations misspecify the role played by human capital. Below, we introduce an alternative model which allows human capital levels to directly affect aggregate factor productivity through two channels: following Romer [17], we postulate that human capital may directly influence productivity by determining the capacity of nations to innovate new tech-

---

(2) These include quality of measurement differences across countries, biases introduced by the skewness of sampling towards urban areas, and the fact that developed countries typically have literacy rates which are close to unity.

(3) See section 2 and appendix.

nologies suited to domestic production. Furthermore, we adapt the Nelson and Phelps [14] model to allow human capital levels to affect the speed of technological catch-up and diffusion. We assume that the ability of a nation to adopt and implement new technology from abroad is a function of its domestic human capital stock. In our model, at every point in time there exists some country which is the world leader in technology. The speed with which nations "catch-up" to this leader country is then a function of their human capital stocks.

The combination of these two forces, domestic innovation and catch-up, produces some noteworthy results: first, under certain conditions, in particular when the innovation parameter dominates, growth rates may differ across countries for a long time due to differences in levels of human capital stocks. Second, a country which lies below the "leader nation" in technology, but possesses a higher human capital stock, will catch up and overtake the leader in a finite time period. Third, the country with the highest stock of human capital will always eventually emerge as the technological leader nation in finite time and maintain its leadership as long as its human capital advantage is sustained.

We test the specification indicated by this alternative model below. In particular, our model assigns a positive role to the levels of human capital in growth accounting. Our results below confirm that per capita income growth indeed depends positively upon average levels of human capital, although not always measurably at a 5% confidence level. In addition, our results also indicate that distortionary economic policy hinders economic growth, although indices of political instability fail to enter directly in the determination of per capita income growth rates.

Second, although the growth of human capital may not be significant in explaining relative growth rates on its own, the levels of aggregate human capital may act as an engine for attracting factors, such as physical capital, which do contribute measurably to per capita income growth. Lucas [11] suggested that physical capital fails to flow to poor countries because of their relatively poor endowments of complementary human capital. Below, we investigate this relationship by examining the determinants of cross sectional gross investment rates as a share of the capital stock. In addition, we find that political instability and exchange rate overvaluation have an influence on investment rates, particularly when one omits the highly collinear human capital variable.

Our results indicate that levels of human capital play an important role in attracting physical capital. In addition the ancillary variables, namely political instability and distortionary price policies, are found to measurably inhibit physical capital accumulation, although not always measurably at the five percent confidence level.

The following section introduces the methodology used in the standard growth accounting regressions and provides an overview of the generation of the physical and human capital stock variables. Section 3 then introduces the alternative theoretical model in which human capital plays a role in determining productivity, rather than entering on its own as a factor of production. Section 4 empirically tests this alternative specification, including the robustness of the results to the inclusion of the ancillary variables. Section 5 then investigates empirically the relationship between human capital stocks and physical capital accumulation rates. Section 6 concludes.

## 2. - Growth Accounting with Human Capital as a Factor of Production

### 2.1 *Methodology and Data*

The standard growth accounting methodology with human capital specifies an aggregate production function in which per capita income, $Y$, is dependent upon three input factors: labor, $L$, physical capital, $K$, human capital, $H$, and a technology factor, $A$. Assuming a Cobb-Douglas technology, $Y = AK^{\alpha}L^{\beta}H^{\gamma}$, and taking logs, this production function can be approximated in growth terms as:

(1) $$\Gamma Y = \Gamma A + \alpha \Gamma K + \beta \Gamma L + \gamma \Gamma H + \varepsilon$$

where $\Gamma X$ represents the growth rate of $X$, $\Gamma X = (X_T - X_0)/X_0$.

A difficulty associated with estimating aggregate production functions such as equation *(1)* concerns the possibility that because physical and human capital are accumulated factors, they will be correlated with the error term ε. This would imply the possibility of biased estimates. In the appendix, we attempt to assess the size of the bias using a bootstrap procedure. The results suggest that a coefficient bias, if one exists, is likely to be positive, so that one would tend to overestimate the dependence of per capita income growth on physical and human capital accumulation.

Estimation of equation *(1)* in the standard growth accounting framework entails assuming that the growth of *A* is identical across countries and regressing per capita income growth on rates of factor accumulation in order to estimate the magnitudes of α, β and γ. In addition, a number of "ancillary variables" are commonly introduced to adjust for productivity differences, such as proxies for political instability and distortionary activity.

In practice, data for physical and human capital stocks are not available for large cross-country samples. However, Benhabib - Spiegel [4] provide physical capital stock estimates using the flow data from the Summers-Heston [18] data set, and estimating initial physical capital stocks by positing that a fixed-point relationship exists in logs between the capital-output ratio of a nation and its capital-labor ratio. The methodology used in the generation of these data sets as well as the generated data used in the regression analysis is reported in the appendix of this text.

In addition, human capital stock estimates have been constructed by Kyriacou [9]. Kyriacou estimates human capital stocks by first estimating the relationship between the educational attainment of the labor force from 1974 through 1977, which is available for 42 countries, and past values of human capital investment, such as enrollment in primary, secondary, and tertiary education. His methodology used in the construction of the data used in this study is also described in greater detail in the appendix.

Per capita income and population growth data are acquired from the Summers-Heston [18] data set. In addition, we add ancillary variables to incorporate cross-country differences in political stability and the severity of distortionary activity.

As in Benhabib-Spiegel [4], we use the Gupta [7] index of political instability. Gupta uses discriminant analysis to measure the influence of ten explanatory variables on incidents of political violence. The variables considered by Gupta include the number of political demonstrations, the number of riots, the number of strikes, the number of deaths from political violence, the number of assassinations, the number of armed attack events, the number of political executions, the occurrences of successful coups d'etat, the occurrence of unsuccessful coups d'etat and the nature of government (4).

To proxy for distortionary activity, we examine the degree of exchange rate overvaluation of a country as measured by Dollar [5]. Dollar measures the degree to which countries have an over-valued real exchange rate in 1975, correcting for the Balassa effect, that is the tendency of non-tradables to command higher prices in the richer and developed nations. He accounts for this effect by first examining the relationship between price levels and incomes across countries, and then measuring the degree of divergence of a country's real exchange rate from that of the United States which is unexplained by the Balassa effect.

In theory it is possible for distortionary prices to increase growth rates by inducing higher levels of savings and investment. On the other hand distortions, in particular exchange rate overvaluation, may signal an inward orientation that can create an inhospitable climate for foreign investment, hindering capital accumulation from abroad. Alternatively, inward orientation may result in wasteful expenditure on the creation of intermediate inputs (Romer [16]).

Note that the effects of inward orientation which hinder factor accumulation will already be accounted for through the introduction of realized rates of factor accumulation in the regressions below. However, if exchange rate overvaluation has a negative impact upon per capita growth rates in specifications which include factor accumulation rates, the evidence will indicate productivity effects of distortionary trade policies, such as those suggested by Romer.

---

(4) See BENHABIB - SPIEGEL [4] for a critical discussion of the appropriateness of the Gupta index for use in the growth accounting equations as a proxy for political instability.

## 2.2 *Results*

The results for regressions run on per capita income growth from 1965 through 1985 is reported in table 1, using the 7% depreciation rate Benhabib-Spiegel [4] capital stock data (5). Regressions were run using ordinary least squares and White's heteroskedasticity-consistent covariance estimation method. One can see that capital stock growth rates, *dK*, enter positively and significantly at the 1% confidence level in all the specifications, as would be predicted by the Cobb-Douglas production function. The capital coefficient is estimated to be approximately 0.25.

However, since the capital stock data are generated regressors, they are likely to be measured with error. Therefore, the regression is likely to have underestimated $\alpha$. The standard response to this problem is the reverse regression method. While the direct estimate of $\alpha$ will be biased towards the origin, the reverse regression estimate of $\alpha$ will be biased away from the origin, so that the true coefficient estimate will lie between these points. For example, the coefficient on $\alpha$ estimated from the reverse regression specification for Model 3 is equal to 0.385. The true coefficient estimate should lie somewhere between these two values.

The coefficient on population growth rates, *dPOP*, also enters with the expected negative coefficient, and is generally significant at the 1% confidence level (6). Note that the magnitude of the coefficient estimate on population growth is very sensitive to the inclusion or exclusion of initial income. For example, Model 2 estimates $\beta$ to be equal to 0,57, while Model 5 only estimates its value to be 0.25. It follows that the data may or may not indicate the presence of diminishing returns depending upon whether initial income is included in the growth accounting specification.

As in Benhabib-Spiegel [4], we find that human capital growth, *dHK*, consistently enters with a negative point estimate, although

---

(5) All regressions reported in this paper were also run with the 10% depreciation rate assumption. The result with this data set were universally similar and in some cases even stronger than those reported here. These results are available upon request.

(6) The exception is Model 2, in which it enters significantly at the 5% confidence level.

TABLE 1

### GROWTH ACCOUNTING REGRESSIONS (1965-1985) (*)
(human capital included as factor of production)

| Dep var | dGDP 1965-1985 | dGDP 1965-1985 | dGDP 1965-1985 | dGDP 1965-1985 | dGDP 1965-1985 | dGDP 1965-1985 |
|---|---|---|---|---|---|---|
| Constant .... | 0.014 (0.003) | 0.016 (0.003) | 0.083 (0.030) | 0.061 (0.031) | 0.119 (0.038) | 0.096 (0.038) |
| dK ........ | 0.253** (0.037) | 0.250** (0.041) | 0.260** (0.035) | 0.250** (0.044) | 0.250** (0.037) | 0.241** (0.046) |
| dPOP ...... | −0.429** (0.172) | −0.454* (0.206) | −0.707** (0.187) | −0.603** (0.208) | −0.748** (0.197) | −0.612** (0.210) |
| dHK........ | −0.024 (0.015) | −0.043* (0.021) | −0.032 (0.020) | −0.021 (0.019) | −0.037 (0.025) | −0.025 (0.024) |
| LGPO ...... | — | — | −0.008* (0.003) | −0.005 (0.004) | −0.011** (0.004) | −0.008 (0.004) |
| OIL ........ | — | 0.005 (0.014) | — | — | — | — |
| PIQ ........ | — | — | — | −0.002 (0.003) | — | −0.002 (0.003) |
| INWARD .... | — | — | — | — | −0.008 (0.005) | −0.009 (0.006) |
| AFRICA .... | — | 0.005 (0.014) | — | — | — | — |
| LAAMER .... | — | −0.007 (0.005) | — | — | — | — |
| Obs ........ | 80 | 80 | 80 | 70 | 78 | 69 |
| F-stat ...... | 49.187 | 25.292 | 41.592 | 25.114 | 32.654 | 20.609 |
| R-squared .. | 0.660 | 0.675 | 0.689 | 0.662 | 0.694 | 0.666 |

(*) 1965-1985. Capital stock estimated by iterative method with 7% assumed depreciation rate.

usually insignificantly at a 5% confidence level. This result is robust to the inclusion of African and Latin American dummies in Model 2. African and Latin American countries experienced large rates of human capital accumulation and disappointing per capita income growth rates during the sample period. However, one can see that including dummies for these countries actually raises the absolute value of the negative point estimate on human capital accumulation. This implies that the experience of these nations cannot totally explain the surprising result reported here. Both region dummies are insignificant, with the *AFRICA dummy* actually entering with a surprising positive sign once one accounts for its poor factor accumulation experience.

The negative point estimate on human capital accumulation is robust to the inclusion of the log of initial wealth, *LGPO*, as shown in Model 3. This implies that this surprising result also cannot be explained by the negative correlation between human capital accumulation and initial per capita income. Initial income itself robustly enters with a negative parameter estimate, usually either significant or close to a 5% confidence level. This provides some support for the convergence hypothesis.

Models 4, 5 and 6 introduce ancillary variables to incorporate other factors which may play a role in determining per capita growth rates. *PIQ* represents average levels of the political instability coefficient obtained from Gupta [7] and *OVER* represents the degree of overvaluation of the real exchange rate as measured by the Dollar [5] index. All of these variables enter with the expected negative sign, although none significantly at a 5% confidence level. The *OVER* variable comes relatively close, entering at 12% and 11% confidence levels respectively in Models 4 and 6. In addition, if a dummy for oil-exporting nations is included, the *OVER* variable enters significantly in Model 6 and enters at a 7% significance level in Model 4.

More importantly, the factor accumulation parameter estimates exhibit stability with respect to the inclusion of various combinations of these ancillary variables. This stability is desirable in the light of studies which show that the results of cross-country growth accounting of this type are likely to be sensitive to the specification chosen (Levine and Renelt [10]).

Table 2 displays the results of the same set of regressions run for the period 1970 through 1985. By and large, the results are quite similar: physical capital growth and population growth both enter significantly with their expected signs. The somewhat higher coefficient on physical capital accumulation is now closer to its traditional factor share. The coefficient on physical capital accumulation now enters in the direct regression as high as 0.29, and its reverse regression coefficient for Model 3 is equal to 0.454. Human capital again enters with its surprising negative point estimate, although

TABLE 2

### GROWTH ACCOUNTING REGRESSIONS (1970-1985) (*)
(human capital included as factor of production)

| Dep var | dGDP 1970-1985 | dGDP 1970-1985 | dGDP 1970-1985 | dGDP 1970-1985 | dGDP 1970-1985 | dGDP 1970-1985 |
|---|---|---|---|---|---|---|
| Constant .... | 0.013 (0.004) | 0.015 (0.004) | 0.094 (0.033) | 0.069 (0.035) | 0.097 (0.036) | 0.071 (0.038) |
| dK ........ | 0.272** (0.039) | 0.266** (0.049) | 0.291** (0.033) | 0.253** (0.033) | 0.299** (0.041) | 0.260** (0.041) |
| dPOP ...... | −0.536** (0.148) | −0.485* (0.231) | −0.902** (0.209) | −0.677** (0.204) | −0.705** (0.228) | −0.494* (0.225) |
| dHK........ | −0.043 (0.031) | −0.062 (0.039) | −0.065* (0.029) | −0.053 (0.029) | −0.035 (0.029) | −0.026 (0.031) |
| LGPO ...... | — | — | −0.009** (0.004) | −0.007 (0.004) | −0.008* (0.004) | −0.006 (0.004) |
| OIL ........ | — | 0.000 (0.016) | — | — | — | — |
| PIQ ........ | — | — | — | −0.001 (0.004) | — | −0.001 (0.004) |
| INWARD .... | — | — | — | — | −0.013* (0.006) | −0.012* (0.005) |
| AFRICA .... | — | 0.001 (0.010) | — | — | — | — |
| LAAMER .... | — | −0.009 (0.006) | — | — | — | — |
| Obs ........ | 89 | 89 | 89 | 77 | 87 | 76 |
| F-stat ...... | 45.444 | 23.236 | 39.745 | 21.907 | 33.778 | 19.894 |
| R-squared .. | 0.616 | 0.630 | 0.654 | 0.607 | 0.676 | 0.634 |

(*) 1965-1985. Capital stock estimated by iterative method with 7% assumed depreciation rate.

generally not significantly. Initial per capita income again enters negatively and usually significantly at the 5% confidence level.

The ancillary variables do not markedly affect the parameter estimates on the factor accumulation variables. The *OVER* variable now enters significantly negative at a 5% level of significance. Again, introduction of a dummy for oil-exporting countries increases the coefficient on this variable, and hence its significance, so that it enters for this period at a 1% level of significance. However the political instability variable remains highly insignificant, and enters with the wrong sign.

## 3. - An Alternative Model for Growth Accounting

Despite the plausible parameter estimates obtained for physical capital and population growth rates in Tables 1 and 2, the small role indicated for human capital in the standard growth accounting equations is somewhat troubling. Human capital accumulation is commonly cited as a pre-requisite for development and most countries have government policies which encourage human capital accumulation.

As early as 1966, Nelson and Phelps [14] pointed out that simply including an index of education or human capital as an additional input would represent a gross misspecification of the productive process. Instead, they argued that education facilitates the adoption and implementation of new technologies, which are continuously invented at an exogenous rate. In particular, they suggested that the growth of technology, or the Solow residual, depends on the gap between its level and the level of "theoretical knowledge", $T(t)$:

$$(2) \qquad \frac{\dot{A}}{A} = c(H)\left[\frac{T(t) - A(t)}{A(t)}\right]$$

One can see through the specification in equation *(2)* that the rate at which the gap is closed will depend on the level of human capital, $H$, through the function, $c(H)$, where $\partial c/\partial H > 0$. The theoretical level of knowledge is taken to grow exponentially, so that $T(t) = T(0)\,e^{\lambda t}$. This model implies that the Solow residual, or the growth of total factor productivity, is influenced by $H$ in the short run. However, in the long run, the Solow residual must settle down to a rate of $\lambda$.

More recent theories have modeled the growth of $A$ directly as a function of the educational level $H$, emphasizing the endogenous nature of growth and technical progress (Lucas [11]). Romer [17] has studied the role of market incentives that determine the allocation of $H$ between the production of goods and inventive activities which enhance the growth of $A$, while treating the total quantity of $H$ as exogenous. For simplicity, we will abstract from these important issues relating to the allocation and production of $H$. We assume that $H$ is exogenously given and that a higher level of $H$ causes a higher level of growth in $A$.

For the purpose of our cross-country comparisons, however, we cannot ignore the diffusion of technology between countries. We adapt the Nelson and Phelps [14] framework to allow for the "catch-up" of technology, not to an exogenously growing theoretical level of knowledge, but to the technology of the leading country. For example, for a country $i$ we specify the growth rate of total factor productivity as follows:

$$(3) \quad \frac{\dot{A}_i(t)}{A_i(t)} = g(H_i) + c(H_i) \left[ \frac{\text{Max } A_j(t) - A_i(t)}{A_i(t)} \right] \quad i = 1 \dots n,$$

where the endogenous growth rate $g(H_i)$ and the catch-up coefficient are non-decreasing functions of $H_i$. Therefore, the level of education not only enhances the ability of a country to develop its own technological innovations, but also its ability to adapt and implement technologies developed elsewhere.

Equation *(3)* then represents a system of differential equations which are easily analyzed. First we note that a lead country with the highest initial $A$, say $A_L(0)$, will be overtaken by some other country that has a higher level of education. This follows because the lead country grows at the rate $g(H_L)$, or $A(t) = A_L(0) e^{g(H_L)t}$, while the growth rate of a country with a higher $H$, say $H_i$, is larger than $g(H_i)$, since it is also affected by the catch-up factor. Thus $A_i(t) > A_i(0) e^{g(H_i)t}$, and since $g(H_i) > g(H_L)$, there exists some $\tau$ such that for $t > \tau$, $A_i(t) > A_L(t)$. Once country $i$ is in the lead however, it can also be overtaken by another country with a lower initial level of technology $A_j(0)$, $[A_j(0) < A_L(0)]$, but which has a higher level of education, such that $g(H_j) < g(H_L)$.

Note that the technology level $A_L$ of a leader country $L$ cannot be overtaken by another country with a lower level of education. If the follower country, say $F$, ever caught up, we would have $A_L - A_F$, and the catch-up component of the growth in $A$'s would be equalized, leaving the country with the higher education level to surge ahead (7).

The observations above imply that irrespective of the distribution

---

(7) For the leading country with the highest $A$, say $A_m$, this would be true even if the functions $c(H)$ differed across countries since $\text{Max}_j A_j - A_m = 0$.

of initial levels of technology, given by the vector $A(0)$, at some time $\hat{t}$ the country with the highest level of education must overtake the technology level of all other countries and maintain that lead into the future, unless of course it loses its educational advantage. The dynamics of technology can then easily be characterized beyond $\hat{t}$, and without loss of generality we take $\hat{t} = 0$. The technology level of the leading country, say $m$, grows at the rate $g(H_m)$, so that $A_m(t) = A_m(0) e^{g(H_m)t}$. In general, the growth rates of $A_i$, for every $i$, are given by:

(4) $$\frac{\dot{A}_i(t)}{A_i(t)} = g(H_i) + c(H_i)\left[\frac{A_m(0) e^{g(H_m)t} - A_i(t)}{A_i(t)}\right]$$

which can be simplified to:

(5) $$\frac{\dot{A}_i(t)}{A_i(t)} = [g(H_i - c(H_i)] + c(H_i)\left[\frac{A_m(t)}{A_i(t)}\right]$$

this equation has a simple solution:

(6) $$A_i(t) = [A_i(0) - \Omega A_m(0) e^{[g(H_i) - c(H_i)]t} + \Omega A_m(0) e^{g(H_m)t}]$$

where:

(7) $$\Omega = \left[\frac{c(H_i)}{c(H_i) - g(H_i) + g(H_m)}\right]$$

In the case studied by Nelson and Phelps [14], $g(H_i) = 0$ and $H_i$ affects the growth of $A_i$ only in transition: the asymptotic growth rate is given by the exogenous growth rate of technology. In the case above, the effects of $g(H_i)$ on the growth of $A_i$ persist if $g(H_i) > c(H_i)$ and the convergence to a common growth rate takes much longer than in the case of Nelson and Phelps [14]. Nevertheless, in the long run, the leader must still set the pace as the growth induced by $g(H_m)$ eventually overwhelms the other growth component $g(H_i)$ in each country. This can immediately be seen from the asymptotic ratio $A_i(t)/A_m(t)$:

$$(8) \quad \lim_{t \to \infty} \frac{A_i(t)}{A_m(t)} = \lim_{t \to \infty} \left[ \frac{A_i(0) - \Omega A_m(0)}{A_m(0)} \right] e^{[g(h_i) - c(H_i) - g(H_m)]t} + \Omega$$

which simplifies to:

$$(9) \qquad\qquad \lim_{t \to \infty} \frac{A_i(t)}{A_m(t)} = \Omega$$

since $[g(H_i) - c(H_i) - g(H_m)] < 0$. It follows that $A_i$ and $A_m$ asymptotically grow at the same rate $g(H_m)$.

Nonetheless, a few simple simulations show that the transition period may be extremely long. Note also that a country with a very low level of $A$ can have a much higher growth rate than the leader because of the catch-up effect, while others that are closer to the leader, both in their technology level and their educational attainment, may in fact have lower growth rates than the leader because the catch-up effect may be insignificant relative to the educational gap. It follows that it may be difficult to observe the positive effect of education on the growth of total factor productivity. Therefore, to the extent that low educational attainment leads to or is associated with low levels of technology and income, it may be necessary to control for the catch-up effect, by including the income (or technology) levels in our regressions. The empirical results below tend to confirm these observations.

Finally, the analysis above has ignored the possible positive feedback effects from technology or income growth to the level of education. If educational levels tend to increase with incomes, growth rates may also diverge.

## 4. - Growth Accounting with Human Capital Stocks Entering into Productivity

The alternative model presented above provides two mechanisms by which levels of human capital stocks can influence per capita income growth along the transition path. First, the endogenous growth component, $g(H_i)$ has an influence on relative growth rates of technology directly. Second, the catch-up component, which is specified as dependent upon the stock of human capital possessed by a country in the spirit of Nelson and Phelps, also allows levels of human capital to enter into per capita income growth.

It follows that the current model allows for human capital effects to enter in levels, at least in transition before the growth rates of $A_i$ catch up to that of the leader nation. To incorporate this possibility, we introduced human capital stocks in levels into the growth accounting equations run above (8).

Table 3 reports the results of ordinary least squares estimation using White's heteroskedasticity correction method. Model 1 simply introduces human capital in levels into the basic factor accumulation specification. It can be seen, as was found above, that physical capital accumulation and population growth enter significantly with their predicted signs. However, since initial income levels needed to capture catch-up effects are not included, the performance of human capital appears disappointing. Both in levels and in growth rates, human capital fails to enter significantly, and the point estimates are of incorrect sign.

However, as pointed out above, the human capital rich country need not always be the high growth country because of the catch-up factor. To account for differences in technology levels across countries, we introduce initial income levels, which will capture the role of the catch-up effect. As soon as initial income levels are introduced, human capital enters significantly in levels with the predicted positive sign. This result suggests that catch-up remains a significant element in growth, and that countries with higher education tend to close the technology gap faster than others. The transition towards a common growth rate set by the leading country may be quite long, and stochastic technological innovations by the leader can set countries on new transition paths. Furthermore, the growth in human capital still is highly insignificant and enters with the wrong sign. The results suggest that the role of human capital is indeed one of facilitating adoption of technology from abroad and creation of appropriate

(8) We also ran the same regressions with the log of the human capital stock and obtained essentially identical results. The results of this alternative specification are available upon request.

*Jess Benhabib · Mark M. Spiegel*

TABLE 3

GROWTH ACCOUNTING REGRESSIONS (1965-1985) (*)
(human capital enters into productivity factor)

| Dep var | dGDP 1965-1985 | dGDP 1965-1985 | dGDP 1965-1985 | dGDP 1965-1985 | dGDP 1965-1985 |
|---|---|---|---|---|---|
| Constant ........ | 0.017 (0.008) | 0.120 (0.035) | 0.090 (0.038) | 0.160 (0.039) | 0.127 (0.043) |
| dK ............ | 0.255** (0.039) | 0.239** (0.038) | 0.239** (0.045) | 0.226** (0.041) | 0.229** (0.049) |
| dPOP .......... | −0.470* (0.202) | −0.464* (0.196) | −0.466* (0.208) | −0.532** (0.192) | −0.498* (0.204) |
| HA 1965-1985 .. | −0.0004 (0.001) | 0.005** (0.002) | 0.004* (0.002) | 0.006** (0.002) | 0.004* (0.002) |
| dHK .......... | −0.027 (0.015) | −0.001 (0.023) | — | — | — |
| LGPO .......... | — | −0.017** (0.005) | −0.012* (0.005) | −0.021** (0.006) | −0.016** (0.006) |
| PIQ ............ | — | — | −0.002 (0.003) | | |
| INWARD........ | — | — | — | −0.006 (0.005) | −0.008 (0.005) |
| Obs ............ | 80 | 80 | 70 | 78 | 69 |
| F-stat .......... | 36.463 | 37.527 | 26.719 | 37.889 | 22.016 |
| R-squared ...... | 0.660 | 0.717 | 0.676 | 0.725 | 0.681 |

(*) 1965-1985. Capital stock estimated by iterative method with 7% assumed depreciation rate.

domestic technologies rather than entering on its own as a factor of production (9).

Initial income enters significantly and negatively in all the specifications. This implies some support for the convergence hypothesis. However, given the model above, a negative coefficient estimate on initial income levels may not be a sign of convergence due to diminishing returns, but of catch-up from adoption of technology from abroad. These two forces may be observationally equivalent in simple cross-country growth accounting exercises.

(9) One caveat is again the possibility of a bias in these coefficient estimates as discussed in Section 2 and in the appendix. However, the coefficient estimates on physical capital are close to its expected factor share and do not indicate a significant upward bias.

The ancillary variables are introduced in Models 3 through 5. The parameter estimates on the factor accumulation variables are robust to the introduction of various combinations of these ancillary variables, which enter with the expected negative sign. However, none of the ancillary variables are statistically significant at the 5% significance level. Relatively, the exchange rate overvaluation variable does better, entering at the 15% level of significance.

Table 4 reports the results of regressions run from 1970 through 1985. It can be seen that the results are quite similar. Physical capital accumulation and population growth enter highly significantly with their expected signs and plausible coefficient magnitudes. Human capital does not enter significantly, either in levels or in growth rates, until one corrects for initial income levels. Subsequent to this correc-

TABLE 4

GROWTH ACCOUNTING REGRESSIONS (1970-1985) (*)
(human capital enters into productivity factor)

| Dep var | dGDP 1970-1985 | dGDP 1970-1985 | dGDP 1970-1985 | dGDP 1970-1985 | dGDP 1970-1985 |
|---|---|---|---|---|---|
| Constant ........ | 0.019 (0.011) | 0.125 (0.035) | 0.094 (0.041) | 0.116 (0.043) | 0.082 (0.049) |
| dK ........... | 0.277** (0.039) | 0.279** (0.032) | 0.247** (0.034) | 0.289** (0.041) | 0.257** (0.042) |
| dPOP ......... | −0.620** (0.190) | −0.714** (0.192) | −0.580** (0.200) | −0.621** (0.209) | −0.466* (0.213) |
| HA 1970-1985 .. | −0.001 (0.001) | 0.005* (0.002) | 0.004* (0.002) | 0.003* (0.002) | 0.002 (0.002) |
| dHK ......... | −0.053 (0.038) | −0.029 (0.024) | — | — | — |
| LGPO ......... | — | −0.017* (0.005) | −0.013* (0.006) | −0.014* (0.006) | −0.009 (0.007) |
| PIQ ........... | — | — | 0.000 (0.004) | — | — |
| INWARD........ | — | — | — | −0.011 (0.006) | −0.011 (0.006) |
| Obs ........... | 89 | 89 | 77 | 87 | 76 |
| F-stat ......... | 33.889 | 34.828 | 23.031 | 35.332 | 20.063 |
| R-squared ...... | 0.617 | 0.677 | 0.619 | 0.686 | 0.636 |

(*) 1965-1985. Capital stock estimated by iterative method with 7% assumed depreciation rate.

tion, human capital enters robustly with a positive coefficient in levels, although it fails to enter significantly in Model 6. Initial income again tends to enter significantly negative, as expected. Finally, the ancillary variables again fail to enter at the 5% level. However, the exchange rate overvaluation variable does consistently enter at the 10% level of significance, so its importance has improved relative to the 1965 to 1985 growth accounting results.

In addition, we used likelihood ratio tests to examine whether human capital in levels should be added to a regression which included growth rate of population and physical and human capital as well as initial per capita income. For both the 1965 through 1985 and 1970 through 1985 periods, the likelihood tests indicated that human capital in levels should be included in the specification at the 1% confidence level.

## 5. - Determinants of Physical Capital Accumulation

In this section, we examine an alternative way that human capital may indirectly contribute to growth: human capital may not enter directly as a factor in the aggregate production function, but may encourage accumulation of other factors necessary for growth, particularly physical capital. Lucas [12] has suggested that one reason that physical capital does not flow to poor countries may be that these countries are poorly endowed with factors complementary to physical capital, so that the marginal product of physical capital in developing countries may not actually be that high, despite its apparent scarcity relative to the developed countries (10).

Similarly, the poor performance of the ancillary political in-stability variable in the growth-accounting equations may understate the importance of the stability of political regime in the determination of economic growth. A variety of studies (Alesina *et* Al. [1]) have

---

(10) However, both in the BENHABIB - SPIEGEL [4] and the smaller SUMMERS - HESTON [18] data set for which physical capital figures are reported, income-to-capital ratios are negatively related to income levels at a 5% confidence level. Therefore, using a Cobb-Douglas or *CES* specification, poorer countries would seem to have higher returns to physical capital inputs.

shown in models which do not include factor accumulation levels that political instability is negatively correlated with economic growth. This suggests the possibility that while political instability does not directly affect growth, it may have a positive effect on factor accumulation which does measurably enter into the growth equation. Kormendi and Meguire [8] have argued that political instability will be negatively correlated with physical capital accumulation because of lack of faith in the assignment of property rights within countries exhibiting political instability. Empirically, they have demonstrated a negative correlation between proxies for political instability and gross investment as a share of income.

If we assume that adjustment of physical capital stocks is costly in the short run, one would expect to find some cross-country differences in marginal products of capital which were not immediately removed through capital flows. However, one would also expect that rates of capital accumulation, or $I/K$, would tend towards equating these differences in marginal product, holding all else equal. Under a standard adjustment process, it follows that $I/K$ should be positively correlated with the current national marginal product of capital, which in turn depends on the current stocks of labor and physical and human capital.

Similarly, it follows that ancillary determinants of the expected return on investment, such as political instability, may also enter into investment as a share of the capital stock if stock adjustments are costly.

We examine the determinants of physical capital accumulation in Table 3. We regress the ratio of gross investment to capital stock on factor stocks: human capital, physical capital and the population, as well as two ancillary variables; political instability as measured by the Gupta index and overvaluation of the real exchange rate as measured by the Dollar index.

Note that ex-ante, the expected sign on the degree of economic distortion due to exchange rate overvaluation is unclear. This stems from the possibility that overvalued exchange rates and government policies may distort prices in favor of capital-intensive activities. This scenario seems particularly plausible for some developing countries which pursued capital-intensive import-substituting policies rather than export-oriented labor intensive policies. Although such policies should lower the value of total output, they may result in increased physical capital accumulation.

Table 5 reports regressions run for 1965, 1970 and 1975. From the 1965 regressions, it can be seen that physical capital consistently enters with the predicted negative sign at a 1% level of significance. Similarly, population enters positively, although not always significantly, as would be predicted.

Human capital stocks are positively correlated with physical capital accumulation and are significant at a 5% level for all specifications except Model 6. This implies that the role for human capital as an agent in attracting physical capital is vindicated for the 1965 regressions.

Among the ancillary variables, the oil-exporting dummy is highly insignificant for this period, and the regional dummies are insignificant as well, although they enter with their expected negative signs. Political instability consistently enters with the predicted negative sign, although the variable does not enter significantly at the 5% level. The exchange rate overvaluation variable enters insignificantly and changes sign with the inclusion of the political instability index. The poor performance of this ancillary variable may reflect economic policies which favor capital-intensive import-substituting industries.

The regression results for 1970 are similar, although both population variables and human capital stocks now fail to enter significantly at a 5% level of significance. Human capital fares better than the population variable, consistently entering positively and entering with 10 and 5% levels of significance in Models 1 and 5 respectively. The results are quite similar for the ancillary variables as well.

Lastly, the regression results for 1975 data are similar, with the troubling exception that population levels now enter consistently with the wrong sign, although never significantly. Human capital again enters consistently positively, and significantly at the 5% level in Models 1 and 5. The ancillary variables, with the exception of the oil dummy, continue to perform poorly. Political instability now enters with the wrong sign, although it is highly insignificant.

As a first pass at this data, the regressions above provide some interesting results: First, we see that physical capital stocks are

TABLE 5

DETERMINANTS OF INVESTMENT
AS A SHARE OF THE CAPITAL STOCK:
1965, 1970 and 1975 (*)

| Dep var | I/K | I/K | I/K | I/K | I/K |
|---|---|---|---|---|---|
| | | | *1965* | | |
| Constant ........ | 0.084 | 0.099 | 0.099 | 0.092 | 0.106 |
| | (0.007) | (0.012) | (0.014) | (0.018) | (0.022) |
| K .............. | −1.68E-8** | −1.56E-8** | −1.74E-8** | −1.59E-8** | −1.64E-8** |
| | (3.69E-9) | (4.34E-9) | (3.65E-9) | (3.81E-9) | (3.69E-9) |
| POP............ | 6.28E-8* | 3.50E-8 | 1.03E-7* | 5.24E-8 | 1.03E-7* |
| | (3.08E-8) | (3.66E-8) | (4.46E-8) | (3.12E-8) | (4.26E-8) |
| H .............. | 0.007** | 0.005* | 0.005* | 0.007** | 0.004 |
| | (0.002) | (0.002) | (0.002) | (0.002) | (0.003) |
| OIL ............ | 0.005 | −0.001 | 0.005 | 0.013 | 0.013 |
| | (0.014) | (0.014) | (0.014) | (0.015) | (0.014) |
| AFRICA ........ | — | −0.014 | — | — | — |
| | | (0.012) | | | |
| LAAMER........ | — | −0.012 | — | — | — |
| | | (0.008) | | | |
| PIQ ............ | — | — | −0.010 | — | −0.012 |
| | | | (0.008) | | (0.008) |
| INWARD........ | — | — | — | −0.005 | 0.002 |
| | | | | (0.010) | (0.010) |
| Obs ............ | 82 | 82 | 71 | 80 | 70 |
| F-statistic ...... | 4.743 | 3.563 | 3.711 | 3.756 | 2.970 |
| R-squared ...... | 0.198 | 0.222 | 0.222 | 0.202 | 0.220 |

(*) 1970-1985. Capital stock estimated by iterative method with 7% assumed depreciation rate. Gross investment figures calculated from Summers Heston data set.

*Jess Benhabib · Mark M. Spiegel*

TABLE 5 *continued*

| Dep var | $I/K$ | $I/K$ | $I/K$ | $I/K$ | $I/K$ |
|---|---|---|---|---|---|
| | | | *1970* | | |
| Constant ........ | 0.107 | 0.116 | 0.112 | 0.107 | 0.111 |
| | (0.009) | (0.013) | (0.014) | (0.017) | (0.022) |
| $K$ .............. | $-1.09E\text{-}8^*$ | $-1.17E\text{-}8^*$ | $-1.01E\text{-}8$ | $-1.12E\text{-}8^*$ | $-9.57E\text{-}9^{**}$ |
| | (5.30$E$-9) | (5.14$E$-9) | (5.22$E$-9) | (5.22$E$-9) | (5.22$E$-9) |
| $POP$ ........... | 4.21$E$-8 | 2.85$E$-8 | 3.12$E$-8 | 4.20$E$-8 | 2.76$E$-8 |
| | (3.84$E$-8) | (4.13$E$-8) | (3.73$E$-8) | (3.92$E$-8) | (3.84$E$-8) |
| $H$ .............. | 0.003 | 0.003 | 0.003 | 0.004* | 0.003 |
| | (0.002) | (0.002) | (0.002) | (0.002) | (0.002) |
| $OIL$ ........... | 0.010 | 0.007 | 0.011 | 0.018 | 0.016 |
| | (0.010) | (0.010) | (0.010) | (0.009) | (0.009) |
| $AFRICA$ ........ | — | $-0.008$ | — | — | — |
| | | (0.012) | | | |
| $LAAMER$........ | — | $-0.015$ | — | — | — |
| | | (0.008) | | | |
| $PIQ$ ........... | — | — | $-0.005$ | — | $-0.005$ |
| | | | (0.005) | | (0.005) |
| $INWARD$........ | — | — | — | $-0.001$ | 0.002 |
| | | | | (0.010) | (0.010) |
| $Obs$ ........... | 91 | 91 | 78 | 89 | 77 |
| $F$-statistic ...... | 1.111 | 1.120 | 1.004 | 1.206 | 0.878 |
| $R$-squared ...... | 0.049 | 0.074 | 0.065 | 0.068 | 0.070 |

TABLE 5 *continued*

| Dep var | I/K | I/K | I/K | I/K | I/K |
|---|---|---|---|---|---|

*1975*

| | | | | | |
|---|---|---|---|---|---|
| Constant ........ | 0.102 | 0.104 | 0.110 | 0.100 | 0.116 |
| | (0.007) | (0.017) | (0.011) | (0.016) | (0.018) |
| K .............. | −1.14E-8** | −9.89E-9** | −7.93E-9* | −1.21E-8** | −8.40E-9** |
| | (3.49E-9) | (3.80E-9) | (3.29E-9) | (3.48E-9) | (3.31E-9) |
| POP............ | −8.56E-9 | −1.06E-8 | −5.11E-9 | −2.99E-9 | −2.91E-9 |
| | (2.59E-8) | (2.63E-8) | (2.44E-8) | (2.31E-8) | (2.43E-9) |
| H .............. | 0.003* | 0.002 | 0.001 | 0.003* | 0.001 |
| | (0.001) | (0.002) | (0.002) | (0.001) | (0.002) |
| OIL ............ | 0.116** | 0.116** | 0.113** | 0.106** | 0.106** |
| | (0.019) | (0.021) | (0.020) | (0.020) | (0.021) |
| AFRICA ........ | — | −0.003 | — | — | — |
| | | (0.014) | | | |
| LAAMER........ | — | 0.009 | — | — | — |
| | | (0.010) | | | |
| PIQ ............ | — | — | 0.001 | — | 0.002 |
| | | | (0.004) | | (0.004) |
| INWARD........ | — | — | — | 0.012 | −0.005 |
| | | | | (0.092) | (0.009) |
| Obs ............ | 108 | 108 | 89 | 106 | 88 |
| F-statistic ...... | 20.124 | 13.588 | 16.526 | 12.661 | 10.895 |
| R-squared ...... | 0.439 | 0.447 | 0.499 | 0.388 | 0.447 |

consistently negatively correlated with investment as a share of income, which argues against scale economies in physical capital. Second, human capital stocks always enter positively, and usually significantly, in determining rates of physical investment. However, the results for population levels were relatively mixed, as were the performances of the ancillary variables.

The data lends support to the conjecture that human capital may be an important feature in attracting physical capital. Since we know from the growth equations that physical capital accumulation rates play a very important role in determining the rates of per capita income growth, the importance of this role is apparent.

The ancillary variables, particularly *OVER*, seem to have performed somewhat better as determinants of growth in the previous section than in explaining $I/K$. This may suggest that their effect on determining growth rates may work in more subtle ways than through stifling aggregate physical capital accumulation (11). We should be careful to note that human capital levels are highly negatively correlated with political instability and exchange rate overvaluation. This implies the possibility that multicollinearity may be precluding these ancillary variables from entering into the determination of cross country investment shares. When human capital is omitted from the regression, political instability enters with the predicted negative sign and is statistically significant. The coefficient on exchange rate overvaluation also enters with a negative sign, although the parameter still fails a 5% confidence interval test (12).

The impact of multicollinearity is particularly striking when one observes the impact of removing African nations from the sample, which diminishes the correlation between human capital and the political instability variable. When the African nations are removed

---

(11) In a previous study (BENHABIB - SPIEGEL [4]), we found that political instability does have a statistically significant negative impact on levels of investment, both gross and net. However, the dependent variable in the current specification determines the rate of physical capital accumulation, which is the relevant term in the growth accounting equations.

(12) These regressions are available upon request. We also ran similar specification tests for the growth accounting regressions reported in the previous sections. However, omission of human capital, in both levels and growth rates, failed to have a significant impact on the performance of the ancillary variables in explaining per capita income growth.

from the 1965 investment specification, political instability enters significantly with a negative sign at a 1% confidence level, while human capital is highly insignificant and enters with the incorrect sign (13). The coefficients on physical capital and labor are basically unchanged and enter significantly with the expected signs. It appears that this multicollinearity problem precludes distinguishing between the contribution of human capital and political instability to physical capital accumulation rates.

## 6. - Conclusion

Human capital accumulation has long been considered an important factor in economic development. The results obtained in our initial set of regressions are therefore somewhat disturbing: when one runs the specification implied by a standard Cobb-Douglas production function which includes human capital as a factor, human capital accumulation fails to enter significantly in the determination of economic growth, and even enters measurably negatively in some specifications.

When we introduce a model in which human capital influences the growth of total factor productivity we obtain more positive results. In this model, human capital affects growth through two mechanisms. First, human capital levels directly influence the rate of domestically produced technological innovation, as in Romer [17]. Second, the human capital stock affects the speed of adoption of technology from abroad, in the spirit of Nelson and Phelps [14]. The significance of this alternative model in terms of its empirical implications is that human capital stocks in levels, rather than their growth rates, now play a role in determining the growth of per capita income.

The growth accounting results with human capital introduced in levels were quite promising. Human capital consistently entered positively in the determination of economic growth, and usually significantly at a 5% confidence level. In addition, this alternative specification proved relatively parsimonious; an *R*-squared of 72% was

---

(13) This regression is available upon request.

achieved for an extremely heterogeneous group with a specification of only four variables: physical capital accumulation, population growth, initial income per capita, and average human capital levels. Likelihood ratio tests also indicated that human capital in levels belonged in the specification at a 1% confidence level.

The results vindicate the observations made by Nelson and Phelps [14]. Treating human capital as a factor of production implies that in the growth accounting regressions human capital should enter in growth rates. However, the standard growth accounting regression fails to deliver this result. We introduce two alternative avenues through which human capital can play a role in economic growth: both as an engine for attracting physical capital and as determinant of the magnitude of a country's Solow residual, it appears that a positive role does exist for human capital accumulation in the economic development process.

## 1. - Estimation of Aggregate Physical Capital Stocks (14)

Investment flow data is now available for a large number of countries from the Summers-Heston [18] data set. However, calculation of capital stocks using this data set requires some mechanism by which initial capital stocks can be estimated. In a simple two-factor neoclassical aggregate production function with constant returns, $Y = K^\alpha L^\beta$, the ratio of the log of capital to the log of output will be negatively related to the ratio of the log of the country's labor endowment to the log of output:

*(A.1)*        $(\log K / \log Y) = a + b (\log L / \log Y) + \varepsilon$

where estimates of $a$ and $b$ provide direct estimates of $\alpha$ and $\beta$ in the neoclassical production function: $\hat{\alpha} = 1/\hat{a}$, and $\hat{\beta} = \hat{b}/\hat{a}$.

Estimation of $\hat{a}$ and $\hat{b}$ in equation 1 requires an estimate of $K$. Therefore, we estimate $\hat{a}$ and $\hat{b}$ using two distinct methods. First, capital stocks in 1985 are available for 29 countries in the 1991 Summers and Heston data set (15). Using this data, we estimate the magnitude of $\hat{a}$ and $\hat{b}$ for this small sample of countries. The regressions results are:

*(A.2)*        $(\log K / \log Y) = 1.203 - 0.306 (\log L / \log Y)$
                         (0.014)    (0.027)

---

(14) Much of this section has been taken from BENHABIB - SPIEGEL [4], in which the estimation methodology is discussed in greater detail.

(15) The countries for which capital stock data is available include Kenya, Zimbabwe, Canada, Dominican Republic, Guatemala, United States, Argentina, Chile, Colombia, India, Israel, Japan, Korea, Philippines, Thailand, Austria, Belgium, Denmark, Finland, France, Germany, Greece, Ireland, Italy, Norway, Spain, Sweden, United Kingdom and Australia.

where capital is measured in dollars and labor is measured in thousands of units. The numbers in the parentheses represent standard errors. The *R*-squared for the regression is 31%, which is relatively large considering that we do not adjust for differences in human capital and natural resource endowments.

We use these coefficients to estimate initial capital stocks for countries in the Summers and Heston data set. Capital stock estimates for subsequent years are then directly attainable according to the equation:

$$(A.3) \qquad K_t = K_0 (1 - \delta)^t + \sum_{i=1}^{t-1} I_i (1 - \delta)^{i-t+2}$$

where $\delta$ represents the rate of physical capital stock depreciation and $K_0$ represents the estimated initial capital stock according to equation (2).

Note that the methodology above relies on the assumption that the dependence of capital-output ratios on capital-labor ratios are constant across both countries and time. Once this assumption is made, however, an independent methodology for estimating national capital stocks becomes possible: this methodology consists of positing that such a relationship exists and is constant across time, and then estimating the capital stock series which most closely satisfies this assumption.

Specifically, we use an iterative method for estimating aggregate capital stocks. We start an initial estimate of $\log K_0 / \log Y_0$ which satisfies $K_0 / Y_0 = 3$ for the United States. This starting value is consistent with many estimates for this country. Then, using discounted investment flows, we find the implied series of capital stocks, and calculate $\hat{a}$ and $\hat{b}$ in equation *(1)* by regressing capital-output ratios on capital-labor ratios. These estimated $a$ and $b$ coefficients are used to update our $K_0$ estimates and recalculate the capital stock series. The process is repeated until convergence is achieved, i.e. until the likelihood function associated with a given $\hat{a}$ and $\hat{b}$ used is maximized.

The estimation was conducted using 4, 7 and 10% rates of depreciation. Convergence was achieved under the 10% and 7% depreciation rate estimates in 8 iterations, and under the 4% depreciation rate estimate in 10 iterations. The final estimated values of *a* and *b* satisfied:

*(A.4)*     $(\log K/\log Y) = 1.225 - 0.327 (\log L/\log Y)$
                            (0.018)   (0.007)

under the assumption of 10% depreciation:

*(A.5)*     $(\log K/\log Y) = 1.229 - 0.317 (\log L/\log Y)$
                            (0.017)   (0.007)

under the assumption of 7% depreciation and:

*(A.6)*     $(\log K/\log Y) = 1.227 - 0.300 (\log L/\log Y)$
                            (0.016)   (0.006)

under the assumption of 4% depreciation with *R*-squares of 0.32, 0.34 and 0.35 respectively.

Both the series estimated using the implied *a* and *b* from the Summers-Heston data set and the series estimated from the iterative methodology yield well-correlated magnitudes using any of the 4%, 7% or 10% depreciation rates. Under a 7% depreciation rate estimate, for example, the correlation coefficient between the two series is 98.7%. In addition, the correlation coefficient between the small set of capital stock series available directly from Summers-Heston and those estimated using our iterative method under the assumption of a 7% depreciation rate is 97.7%. In table 6, we provide the capital stock estimates using the iterative methodology under a 7% depreciation rate assumption for five-year intervals. This is the physical capital stock series which was used in the reported results below (16).

## 2. - Estimation of Human Capital Stocks

Human capital stock data was obtained from Kyriacou [9]. Kyriacou estimates human capital levels from the Psacharopoulos — Ariagada [15] data set. Psacharopoulos — Ariagada have measures

---

(16) All the results remain essentially the same if we use 4% or 10% depreciation rates. The entire set of capital stock estimates is available upon request.

of years of schooling in the labor force for 99 countries. However, these measures are from a wide variety of years, from the 1960s through the 1980s. From this large set, Kyriacou identifies 42 countries for which average years of schooling in the labor force is available for the mid-1970s: 1974-1977. He estimates the following relationship between average years of schooling in the labor force and past enrollment ratios:

$$(A.7) \qquad H75 = 0.0520 + 4.4390\ PRIM60 + \\ + 2.6645\ SEC70 + 8.0918 HIGH70$$

where $H75$ represents average years of schooling in the labor force, $PRIM60$ represents the 1960 primary schooling enrollment ratio, $SEC70$ represents the 1970 secondary schooling enrollment ratio, and $HIGH70$ represents the 1970 higher education enrollment ratio. His regression has an $R$-squared of 82% and primary and higher education enrollment ratios enter significantly at a 5% confidence level. Kyriacou then uses these estimated coefficients to extrapolate human capital indexes for other time periods based upon past enrollment ratios. These extrapolated human capital indexes are used in the current study as human capital stock estimates.

## 3. - Estimation of the Bias (17)

A well-known difficulty with estimating aggregative production functions is the possibility of a correlation between the error term and the regressors which would yield biased coefficient estimates. For example, a stochastic shock to the production function would typically be expected to result in the faster growth of accumulated inputs in that period. If shocks are also persistent, this will induce a positive correlation between future shocks and future levels of physical and human capital. Looking at average growth rates over long periods does not eliminate these positive correlations (Benhabib and

---

(17) Much of this section is taken from BENHABIB - SPIEGEL [4] which provides a more detailed discussion of the bias issue.

Jovanovic [3]). Here, we attempt to identify the sign of the biases on the estimated coefficients. If we can show that the biases on the estimated coefficients are likely to be positive, our estimates will represent upper bounds.

For example, given the following specification:

$$(A.8) \qquad \Gamma Y = c + \alpha \Gamma K + \beta \Gamma L + \gamma \Gamma H + \varepsilon$$

and that $H$ and $K$ are likely to be correlated with the error term while $L$ follows an independent process, *OLS* estimation is expected to yield biased estimates for the constant term, $\alpha$, $\beta$ and $\gamma$ equal to:

$$(A.9) \qquad \begin{bmatrix} \hat{b}_c \\ \hat{b}_K \\ \hat{b}_H \\ \hat{b}_L \end{bmatrix} = \begin{bmatrix} n & \bar{K} & \bar{H} & \bar{L} \\ \bar{K} & a_{kk} & a_{kh} & a_{kl} \\ \bar{H} & a_{hk} & a_{hh} & a_{hl} \\ \bar{L} & a_{lk} & a_{lh} & a_{ll} \end{bmatrix}^{-1} \begin{bmatrix} \bar{a} \\ a_{k\varepsilon} \\ a_{h\varepsilon} \\ 0 \end{bmatrix}$$

where $\hat{b}_j$ is the expected bias on the estimate of coefficient $j$, $n$ is the number of observations in the sample, the $a_{ij}$ are the raw moments defined above, and bars represent mean growth rates, for example:

$$\bar{K} = \Sigma_{i,\,t} T_{it}^{-1}(K_{i,\,t+T_{it}} - K_{i,t})$$

As the sample size $n$ gets large, it is easy to show by partitioning the inverse matrix that the biases will tend towards:

$$(A.10) \qquad \begin{bmatrix} \hat{b}_k \\ \hat{b}_h \\ \hat{b}_l \end{bmatrix} = \begin{bmatrix} a_{kk} & a_{kh} & a_{kl} \\ a_{hk} & a_{hh} & a_{hl} \\ a_{lk} & a_{lh} & a_{ll} \end{bmatrix}^{-1} \begin{bmatrix} a_{k\varepsilon} \\ a_{h\varepsilon} \\ 0 \end{bmatrix}$$

The determinant of the matrix, $D$, will be positive since the matrix is positive semi-definite. Inverting the matrix, the bias on the physical and human capital coefficients are expected to equal:

(A.11a)
$$\hat{b}_k = D^{-1} [(a_{hh} a_{ll} - a_{hl}^2)(a_{k\varepsilon}) + \\ + (a_{kl} a_{hl} - a_{kh} a_{ll})(a_{h\varepsilon})]$$

(A.11b)
$$\hat{b}_h = D^{-1} [(a_{kk} a_{ll} - a_{kl}^2)(a_{h\varepsilon}) + \\ + (a_{kl} a_{hl} - a_{kh} a_{ll})(a_{k\varepsilon})]$$

(A.11c)
$$\hat{b}_L = D^{-1} [(a_{KH} a_{KL} - a_{KL} a_{HH})(a_{k\varepsilon}) + \\ + (a_{KH} a_{KL} - a_{KK} a_{HL})(a_{H\varepsilon})]$$

where $\hat{b}_j$ ($j = K, H, L$) represents the estimated bias, $D$ represents the determinant of the covariance matrix, which can be signed as positive because the matrix is positive definite, and the $a_{ij}$'s represent the raw moments (18).

Given that $a_{j\varepsilon} > 0$ ($j = K, H$) we can sign the first terms of both expressions as positive since the covariance matrix is positive semi-definite. However, both expressions contain the second term which has sign equal to that of the expression:

(A.12)
$$a_{LL} a_{HL} - a_{KH} a_{LL}$$

Since $a_{KH}$ may well be non-negative, and $a_{JL}$ ($J = H, K$) may also be positive because $H$ and $K$ are accumulated factors while $L$ is assumed to follow an independent stochastic process, the sign of *(A.12)* is indeterminate, and the sign of the expected bias cannot be obtained analytically. We therefore turn to econometric evidence to obtain information concerning the degree of severity of the potential bias.

Using a bootstrap (Efron [6]) procedure, we estimated the value of the covariance coefficients in equation *(8)* by creating 1.000 samples from the original sample and computing the covariances of the coefficients in these created samples as population estimates of the population covariances (19).

---

(18) For example: $a_{KL} = \Sigma_{i,t} T_{it}^{-2} (K_{i,t + Tit} - K_{it})(L_{i,t + Tit} - L_{i,t})$

(19) Note that a bootstrap procedure is desirable because of its ability to estimate the covariance matrix in the presence of heteroscedasticity, which is clearly a problem in this sample.

Our estimate for $a_{HK}$ was 0.0019 with a standard error of 0.0024, so we cannot statistically reject the possibility that $a_{HK}$ is either very small or zero, either of which would allow us to unambiguously sign the bias on the human and physical capital coefficients as positive by *(A.11a)* and *(A.11b)*. Nevertheless, we continued by attempting to estimate all the observables in the bias equation. The estimated bias under *OLS*, was expected to equal:

*(A.13a)*
$$\hat{b}_K = \underset{(79.45)}{71.57\ a_{K\varepsilon}} - \underset{(172.53)}{3.06\ a_{H\varepsilon}}$$

*(A.13b)*
$$\hat{b}_H = \underset{(1.406,23)}{226.61\ a_{H\varepsilon}} - \underset{(172.53)}{3.06\ a_{K\varepsilon}}$$

*(A.13c)*
$$\hat{b}_L = \underset{(924.02)}{141.01\ a_{K\varepsilon}} - \underset{(4,913.72)}{594.27\ a_{H\varepsilon}}$$

where estimated standard errors are in parentheses. Note that the values of $a_{j\varepsilon}$ $(j = H, K)$ are unobservable and hence cannot be estimated.

The large standard errors generated by estimation make strong inferences concerning the sign of the bias unattainable. The point estimates generated by the data clearly suggest a positive bias on the physical and human capital coefficient estimates, and a negative bias on the estimated labor coefficient provided the magnitudes of $a_{H\varepsilon}$ and $a_{K\varepsilon}$ are not wildly different. The point estimate of $\hat{b}_H$ will be positive if $a_{K\varepsilon}/a_{H\varepsilon} < 74$ and the estimate of $\hat{b}_K$ will be positive if $a_{K\varepsilon}/a_{H\varepsilon}/1/23$. Moreover, recall that the first component in *(A.13a)* and *(A.13b)* can be analytically signed as non-negative because the covariance matrix is positive semi-definite. None of these coefficient estimates are measurably different from zero, and furthermore one cannot reject the null of a non-negative bias on human and physical capital in favor of a negative bias.

TABLE 6

CAPITAL STOCK ESTIMATES:
ITERATIVE METHOD 7% DEPRECIATION RATE
SUMMERS-HESTON [18]

| Country | 1960 | 1965 | 1970 | 1975 | 1980 | 1985 |
|---|---|---|---|---|---|---|
| 1. Algeria | 14,408.71 | 17,547.6 | 24,104.97 | 50,980.42 | 103,316.8 | 164,694.4 |
| 2. Angola | 7,745.638 | 7,907.863 | 10,695.02 | 12,836.72 | 12,532.9 | 12,248.14 |
| 3. Benin | 2,799.485 | 2,292.67 | 2,079.515 | 2,261.272 | 2,806.734 | 3,270.098 |
| 4. Botswana | 332.7617 | 348.9764 | 697.6954 | 2,134.358 | 3,328.167 | 4,536.327 |
| 5. Burkina Faso | na | 2,016.905 | 2,479.971 | 4,182.116 | 5,453.741 | 6,577.449 |
| 6. Burundi | 1,443.313 | 1,185.643 | 1,058.404 | 1,086.973 | 1,594.455 | 2,366.46 |
| 7. Cameroon | 4,859.19 | 5,006.093 | 5,874.408 | 7,387.124 | 10,955.76 | 17,397.49 |
| 8. Cape Verde | 324.1363 | 434.7673 | 599.913 | 666.5976 | 867.6477 | 1,235.391 |
| 9. Central A. | 1,771.025 | 1,836.589 | 1,946.18 | 1,987.987 | 1,766.515 | 1,822.525 |
| 10. Chad | 2,779.333 | 3,779.393 | 4,566.377 | 5,035.908 | 5,566.051 | 4,486.041 |
| 11. Comoros | na | na | na | na | na | 406.4848 |
| 12. Congo | 1,025.267 | 1,179.179 | 1,543.155 | 2,336.888 | 2,640.943 | 4,618.504 |
| 13. Egypt | 9,411.55 | 11,355.74 | 12,777.99 | 17,214.71 | 30,160.24 | 47,446.41 |
| 14. Ethiopia | 2,813.866 | 3.444 | 4,415.468 | 5,124.954 | 5,586.569 | 6,641.107 |
| 15. Gabon | 973.1432 | 1,642.477 | 2,402.895 | 7,159.64 | 13,323.09 | 16,334.15 |
| 16. Gambia | 180.5004 | 133.8638 | 102.5347 | 92.35979 | 139.7236 | 254.9916 |
| 17. Ghana | 7,983.82 | 9,270.68 | 9,670.849 | 10,000.94 | 9,895.351 | 8,972.265 |
| 18. Guinea | 1,926.163 | 2,531.005 | 3,071.012 | 3,604.561 | 3,992.423 | 4,457.605 |
| 19. Guinea-Bissau | 404.0345 | 678.2856 | 956.9493 | 1,123.788 | 1,289.994 | 1,423.687 |
| 20. Ivory Coast | 4,601.084 | 4,995.211 | 6,381.431 | 8,657.37 | 15,381.93 | 16,496.17 |
| 21. Kenya | 10,209.6 | 10,231.35 | 12,733.48 | 16,749.23 | 21,450.08 | 24,663.53 |
| 22. Lesotho | 249.7331 | 258.4236 | 334.1906 | 540.2341 | 1,258.633 | 1,934.104 |
| 23. Liberia | 1,828.627 | 4,742.654 | 5,422.448 | 5,883.718 | 6,859.774 | 5,870.94 |

TABLE 6 *continued*

| Country | 1960 | 1965 | 1970 | 1975 | 1980 | 1985 |
|---|---|---|---|---|---|---|
| 24. Madagascar | 7,158.635 | 7,125.221 | 7,922.213 | 8,581.684 | 8,954.27 | 8,205.207 |
| 25. Malawi | 1,348.737 | 1,681.552 | 2,815.64 | 4,323.346 | 4,951.84 | 4,612.975 |
| 26. Mali | 2,388.118 | 2,106.695 | 2,165.358 | 2,223.061 | 2,452.919 | 2,672.343 |
| 27. Mauritania | 1,137.395 | 1,074.784 | 1,004.46 | 1,496.664 | 2,524.905 | 3,199.97 |
| 28. Mauritius | 2,048.805 | 2,213.841 | 2,160.925 | 3,219.838 | 4,292.976 | 4,553.583 |
| 29. Morocco | 9,659.954 | 10,463.95 | 13,562.99 | 19,280.82 | 30,121.46 | 39,053.35 |
| 30. Mozambique | 13,444.61 | 15,477.98 | 21,270.3 | 26,495.25 | 26,304.02 | 23,735.16 |
| 31. Niger | 2,130.663 | 2,449.928 | 2,744.303 | 3,244.723 | 4,105.638 | 4,248.374 |
| 32. Nigeria | 27.484 | 34,725.6 | 44,187.07 | 89,583.84 | 163,230.4 | 168,819.9 |
| 33. Rwanda | 1,602.791 | 1,276.443 | 1,145.742 | 1,227.117 | 1,546.277 | 2,228.009 |
| 34. Senegal | 5,301.897 | 5,018.317 | 4,931.231 | 5,493.763 | 5,883.277 | 6,217.595 |
| 35. Seychelles | na | na | na | na | 391.167 | 505.9897 |
| 36. Sierra Leone | 2,752.878 | 2,206.001 | 1,980.544 | 1,683.803 | 1,471.15 | 1,388.569 |
| 37. Somalia | 2,707.599 | 2,360.35 | 2,295.24 | 2,460.682 | 4,260.2 | 6,139.601 |
| 38. South Africa | 99,117.65 | 132,541 | 189,850.4 | 269.957 | 327,759.2 | 386,570.4 |
| 39. Sudan | 5,901.024 | 4,978.988 | 4,352.671 | 4,056.982 | 4,462.588 | 4,678.206 |
| 40. Swaziland | 714.6564 | 1,106.852 | 1,391.904 | 2,155.107 | 3,512.291 | 3,845.972 |
| 41. Tanzania | 2,876.536 | 4,613.614 | 8,231.311 | 12,616.53 | 16,805.84 | 18,479.73 |
| 42. Togo | 748.2511 | 1,028.782 | 1,441.412 | 2,197.361 | 3,829.433 | 4,098.925 |
| 43. Tunisia | 7,522.284 | 10,463.11 | 13,313.63 | 16,796.6 | 21,985.54 | 28,189.22 |
| 44. Uganda | 878.9259 | 989.1082 | 1,248.144 | 1,309.56 | 1,140.204 | 1,416.85 |
| 45. Zaire | 4,978.236 | 4,929.679 | 5,936.752 | 9,149.665 | 12,051.01 | 15,596.08 |
| 46. Zambia | 12,356.02 | 15,127.49 | 21,694.96 | 28.611 | 24,251.68 | 19,331.06 |

TABLE 6 *continued*

| Country | 1960 | 1965 | 1970 | 1975 | 1980 | 1985 |
|---|---|---|---|---|---|---|
| 47. Zimbabwe | 7,635.986 | 8,365.351 | 10,103.51 | 14,591.46 | 14,778.31 | 16,943.13 |
| 48. Bahamas | na | na | na | na | 3,104.18 | 3,933.76 |
| 49. Barbados | 1,298.625 | 1,439.065 | 1,782.18 | 2,222.178 | 2,740.817 | 3,225.507 |
| 50. Canada | 273,898.1 | 335,356.9 | 424,086.1 | 543,032.6 | 704,622.3 | 861.698 |
| 51. Costa Rica | 2,954.757 | 3,989.656 | 5,346.22 | 7,683.772 | 11,908.04 | 12,909.53 |
| 52. Dominica | na | na | na | na | na | 449.1569 |
| 53. Dominican Republic | 4,779.369 | 5,430.756 | 7,168.667 | 12,867.91 | 19,406.33 | 23,345.92 |
| 54. El Salvador | 3,101.151 | 3,712.169 | 4,382.711 | 5,775.696 | 8,080.049 | 7,746.236 |
| 55. Grenada | na | na | na | na | na | 555.5458 |
| 56. Guatemala | 7,136.033 | 7,677.985 | 9,117.987 | 11,485.37 | 15,971.71 | 16,771.38 |
| 57. Haiti | 4,464.109 | 3,591.167 | 3,045.666 | 3,301.584 | 4,586.944 | 5,685.013 |
| 58. Honduras | 2,322.076 | 2,751.264 | 3,771.387 | 4,582.95 | 6,604.475 | 7,251.933 |
| 59. Jamaica | 6,418.269 | 8,344.153 | 11,987.06 | 15,243.7 | 14,141.31 | 13,291.78 |
| 60. Mexico | 149,568.4 | 209,329.7 | 309,522.9 | 458,248.3 | 670,447.5 | 834,106.5 |
| 61. Nicaragua | 4,605.079 | 6,564.962 | 9,484.29 | 12,865.1 | 13,554.88 | 15,972.29 |
| 62. Panama | 2,979.013 | 4,301.851 | 7,223.259 | 12,401.56 | 15,020.99 | 17,046.81 |
| 63. St. Lucia | na | na | na | na | 787.5294 | 1,089.257 |
| 64. St. Vincent | na | na | na | na | 402.7187 | 530.6937 |
| 65. Trinidad | 5,018.216 | 6,654.338 | 7,102.415 | 10,021.66 | 18,200.96 | 23,024.31 |
| 66. Usa | 2,878.770 | 3,472.026 | 4.266.544 | 5,135.914 | 6,178.962 | 7,194.880 |
| 67. Argentina | 86,681.04 | 100,717.1 | 120,762.1 | 151,603.4 | 186,591.4 | 178,589.5 |
| 68. Bolivia | 6,303.226 | 7,853.099 | 10,724.44 | 15,290.77 | 18,930.7 | 17,995.66 |
| 69. Brazil | 187,875.9 | 263,346.5 | 367,589.4 | 623,017.6 | 900,525.2 | 991,676.5 |

TABLE 6 *continued*

| Country | 1960 | 1965 | 1970 | 1975 | 1980 | 1985 |
|---|---|---|---|---|---|---|
| 70. Chile ........... | 35,690.5 | 46,135.17 | 57,790.78 | 61,915.27 | 66,696.29 | 67,986.92 |
| 71. Colombia ..... | 52,775.91 | 65,035.14 | 81,862.62 | 102,126.2 | 124,894.7 | 151,312.7 |
| 72. Ecuador ...... | 12,790.22 | 16,432.1 | 22,094.35 | 33,037.93 | 52,450.31 | 61,868.88 |
| 73. Guyana ....... | 2,139.408 | 2,972.834 | 4,151.663 | 4,921.943 | 5,173.1 | 4,655.229 |
| 74. Paraguay ..... | 2,195.726 | 2,289.46 | 2,785.651 | 3,883.078 | 7,143.027 | 10,411.51 |
| 75. Perú.......... | 32,299.61 | 41,432.29 | 50,867.21 | 69,335.09 | 84,892.91 | 97,907.69 |
| 76. Suriname ..... | 1,456.457 | 1,855.869 | 2,089.217 | 2,553.785 | 3,022.444 | 3,092.972 |
| 77. Uruguay...... | 22,029.8 | 22,277.6 | 22,202.11 | 22,973.34 | 31,804.75 | 33,962.61 |
| 78. Venezuela .... | 44,393.36 | 49,329.55 | 57,790.43 | 90,973.29 | 160,636.8 | 173,968.3 |
| 79. Afghanistan ... | 8,430.532 | 8,155.631 | 7,681.827 | 7,581.741 | 9,329.702 | 10,708.1 |
| 80. Bahrain ...... | na | na | na | 4,978.477 | 11,291.15 | 15,208.62 |
| 81. Bangladesh.... | 26,555.63 | 29,129.53 | 35,463.98 | 31,569.79 | 32,612.48 | 41,508.22 |
| 82. Burma ....... | 7,985.933 | 10,604.15 | 12,933.66 | 14,487.93 | 19,773.82 | 26,480.8 |
| 83. China ....... | 356.322 | 465,506.7 | 765,375.6 | 1,370.767 | 2.184.267 | 3,426.360 |
| 84. Hong Kong ... | 10,276.73 | 17,163.3 | 22,926.01 | 34,126.06 | 57,836.86 | 85,445.61 |
| 85. India ........ | 274,610.8 | 375,164.4 | 499,050.3 | 632,309.8 | 763,685.5 | 908.275 |
| 86. Indonesia .... | na | 58,524.32 | 75,107.77 | 145,640.3 | 276,764.8 | 546.390 |
| 87. Iran ......... | 31,749.81 | 47,910.89 | 75,856.28 | 131,906.5 | 192,281.5 | 266,937.2 |
| 88. Iraq ......... | 27,269.88 | 33,484.86 | 40,540.09 | 80,221.59 | 199,252.6 | 252,620.1 |
| 89. Israel ....... | 16,202.03 | 27,374.09 | 38,280.64 | 62,411.36 | 75,801.03 | 85,194.93 |
| 90. Japan........ | 361,381.7 | 718.172 | 1,428.702 | 2.386.275 | 3,158.946 | 3.741.429 |
| 91. Jordan........ | 1,491.208 | 1,893.327 | 2,700.855 | 4,326.18 | 9,928.203 | 18,073.84 |
| 92. Korea, South... | 4,419.27 | 33,557.06 | 76,185.05 | 143,845.3 | 257,985.3 | 352,887.5 |

TABLE 6 continued

| Country | 1960 | 1965 | 1970 | 1975 | 1980 | 1985 |
|---|---|---|---|---|---|---|
| 93. Kuwait | 44,716.39 | 33,851.21 | 27,491.82 | 25,578.48 | 37,810.4 | 54.501 |
| 94. Malaysia | 20,400.61 | 31,394.91 | 45,298.88 | 72,867.98 | 121,206.6 | 205,316.5 |
| 95. Nepal | 5,615.533 | 5,384.545 | 5,452.183 | 6,828.02 | 10,647.71 | 15,193.55 |
| 96. Oman | na | na | na | na | 11,768.01 | 21,960.7 |
| 97. Pakistan | 48,445.36 | 84,595.67 | 114,333.9 | 133.008 | 137,291.7 | 140,923.9 |
| 98. Philippines | 41,825.74 | 58,742.14 | 84,455.86 | 117,620.6 | 177,200.5 | 210,610.8 |
| 99. Saudi Arabia | 18,423.61 | 14,285.87 | 12,793.87 | 18,964.29 | 65,978.52 | 185,831.2 |
| 100. Singapore | 7,151.14 | 8,524.085 | 14,290.82 | 29,684.23 | 47,719.47 | 77,589.61 |
| 101. Sri Lanka | 18,154.42 | 21,749.3 | 28,284.19 | 36,096.28 | 50,826.59 | 67,207.52 |
| 102. Syria | 10,515.33 | 13,658.47 | 17,807.37 | 28,540.48 | 54,521.65 | 81,948.6 |
| 103. Taiwan | 10,088.78 | 16,839.62 | 33,565.63 | 69,978.62 | 123,730.7 | 168,075.8 |
| 104. Thailand | 23,093.71 | 33,754.64 | 60,114.12 | 88,401.53 | 126,043.2 | 163,926.8 |
| 105. United Ar. | na | na | 15,924.67 | 20,405.53 | 42,008.17 | 60,220.77 |
| 106. Yemen, N. | na | na | 2,540.664 | 3,879.36 | 9,756.272 | 13,255.94 |
| 107. Austria | 54,999.63 | 79,328.23 | 112,065.7 | 154,716.6 | 196,124.8 | 225,039.9 |
| 108. Belgium | 99,064.7 | 129,319.7 | 169,759.6 | 217,357.9 | 263,109.2 | 268,564.9 |
| 109. Cyprus | 4,338.583 | 5,537.565 | 7,462.594 | 8,695.998 | 10,378.54 | 12,603.32 |
| 110. Denmark | 61,859.52 | 89,949.89 | 124,889.7 | 157,902.7 | 173,185.8 | 170,429.3 |
| 111. Finland | 56,662.3 | 80,314.75 | 105,159.2 | 140,596.4 | 160,039.9 | 180,064.7 |
| 112. France | 443,032 | 642,048.4 | 944,543 | 1,303.559 | 1,580.024 | 1,720.749 |
| 113. Germany | 670,980.1 | 1,002.829 | 1,334.263 | 1,625.870 | 1,872.654 | 2,000.910 |
| 114. Greece | 22,886.74 | 39,978.37 | 64,382.07 | 100,016.4 | 127.570 | 139,386.1 |
| 115. Hungary | na | na | 49,761.13 | 96,081.7 | 147,179.4 | 169,969.4 |

TABLE 6 continued

| Country | 1960 | 1965 | 1970 | 1975 | 1980 | 1985 |
|---|---|---|---|---|---|---|
| 116. Iceland | 2,030.654 | 2,702.156 | 3,546.898 | 4,832.809 | 5,955.847 | 6,921.546 |
| 117. Ireland | 18,606.14 | 24,261.44 | 32,923.05 | 45,616.33 | 58,306.7 | 66,359.43 |
| 118. Italy | 473,116 | 713,339.3 | 959,261.1 | 1,204.506 | 1,424.894 | 1,595.186 |
| 119. Luxembourg | 6,658.882 | 8,165.508 | 9,021.268 | 10,335.06 | 11,207.46 | 12,531.93 |
| 120. Malta | 1,210.868 | 1,609.83 | 2,445.43 | 2,837.72 | 3,518.546 | 4,834.557 |
| 121. Netherlands | 136,547.1 | 188,958.6 | 266,975.2 | 332,432.5 | 371,777.6 | 381,171.4 |
| 122. Norway | 54,290.04 | 69,988.54 | 90,712.42 | 119,341 | 145,003.4 | 169,652.5 |
| 123. Poland | na | na | na | na | 225,014.4 | 367,901.2 |
| 124. Portugal | 23,102.44 | 34,300.84 | 50,218.65 | 73,940.14 | 95,878.17 | 113,136.4 |
| 125. Spain | 158,967.7 | 259.761 | 400,623.4 | 562,682.7 | 666,445.8 | 684.300 |
| 126. Sweden | 105,998.7 | 140.575 | 180,924.9 | 217,000.7 | 234,281.3 | 242,629.3 |
| 127. Switzerland | 103,321.2 | 153,423.2 | 201,896.4 | 253,085.1 | 275,001.5 | 306,870.4 |
| 128. Turkey | 57,465.47 | 79,943.72 | 120,458.8 | 191,901.8 | 274,382.3 | 336.954 |
| 129. UK | 497,220.7 | 623,479.7 | 789,438.2 | 949,030.1 | 1,074.756 | 1,164.304 |
| 130. Yugoslavia | 42,986.78 | 101,230.8 | 154,136.3 | 219,132.7 | 310.984 | 384,392.2 |
| 131. Australia | 187,537.4 | 245,344.7 | 327,320.8 | 404,946.9 | 473,280.4 | 545,000.8 |
| 132. Fiji | 1,755.152 | 2,279.558 | 2,913.423 | 3,923.615 | 5,334.069 | 6,003.707 |
| 133. New Zealand | 32,984.29 | 41,311.28 | 49,119.28 | 66,395.39 | 72,183.65 | 81,794.13 |
| 134. Papua N.G. | 3,311.205 | 4,581.001 | 9,349.055 | 13,337.43 | 15,080.03 | 16,868.1 |
| 135. Solomon I. | na | na | na | na | 853.603 | 1,130.079 |
| 136. Tonga | na | na | na | na | na | 463.2805 |
| 137. Vanuatu | na | na | na | na | na | na |
| 138. Western S. | na | na | na | na | 728.5696 | 771.6787 |

94     *Jess Benhabib - Mark M. Spiegel*

## BIBLIOGRAPHY

[1] ALESINA ALBERTO - OZLER SULE - ROUBINI NOURIEL - SWAGEL PHILIP: *Political Instability and Economic Growth*, mimeo, 1991.

[2] BARRO ROBERT: «Economic Growth in a Cross Section of Countries», *Quarterly Journal of Economics*, n. CVI, 1991, pp. 407-43.

[3] BENHABIB JESS - JOVANOVIC BOYAN: «Externalities and Growth Accounting», *American Economic Review*, n. LXXXI, 1991, pp. 82-113.

[4] BENHABIB JESS - SPIEGEL MARK M.: «Growth Accounting with Physical and Human Capital Accumulation», C.V. Starr Center, *Working Paper*, n. 91, 66-1992.

[5] DOLLAR DAVID: *Outward Oriented Economies Really Do Grow More Rapidly: Evidence from 95 LDC's, 1976-1985*, World Bank, mimeo, 1990.

[6] EFRON BRADLEY: *The Jackknife, the Bootstrap, and Other Resampling Plans*, Society of Industrial and Applied Mathematics, England, J. Arrowsmith, 1982.

[7] GUPTA D.K.: *The Economics of Political Violence: The Effect of Political Instability on Economic Growth*, 1990.

[8] KORMENDI ROGER C. - MEGUIRE PHILIP G.: «Macroeconomic Determinants of Growth», *Journal of Monetary Economics*, n. XVI, 1985, pp. 141-63.

[9] KYRIACOU GEORGE: «Level and Growth Effects of Human Capital», C.V. Starr Center, *Working Paper*, n. 91-26, 1991.

[10] LEVINE ROSS - RENELT DAVID: «A Sensitivity Analysis of Cross-Country Growth Regressions», forthcoming, *American Economic Review*, 1992.

[11] LUCAS R.E.: «On the Mechanics of Economic Development», *Journal of Monetary Economics*, vol. 22, n. 1, 1988, pp. 3-42.

[12] — —: «Why Doesn't Capital Flow From Rich to Poor Countries?», *American Economic Review*, n. LXXX, 1990, pp. 92-6.

[13] MANKIW N. GREGORY - ROMER DAVID - WEIL DAVID N.: «A Contribution to the Empirics of Economic Growth», forthcoming, *Quarterly Journal of Economics*, 1992.

[14] NELSON RICHARD R. - PHELPS EDMUND S.: «Investment in Humans, Technological Diffusion, and Economic Growth», *American Economic Review: Papers and Proceedings*, vol. 61, n. 2, 1966, pp. 69-75.

[15] PSACHAROPOULOS G. - ARIAGADA A.M.: «The Educational Attainment of the Labor Force: An International Comparison», *International Labor Review*, n. CXXV, 1986.

[16] ROMER PAUL M.: *Cross Country Determinants of the Rate of Technological Change*, mimeo, University of Chicago, 1989.

[17] — —: «Endogenous Technological Change», *Journal of Political Economy*, vol. 98, n. 5, 1990, pp. S71-S102.

[18] SUMMERS ROBERT - HESTON ALAN: «The Penn World Table (Mark 5): An Expanded Set of International Comparisons, 1950-1988», *Quarterly Journal of Economics*, n. CVI, 1991, pp. 327-36.

# Allocation of Time, Human Capital and Endogenous Growth

**Mario Baldassarri** · **Paolo De Santis** · **Giuseppe Moscarini**
Università «La Sapienza», Roma          Ocsm-Luiss, Roma          Università «La Sapienza», Roma

## 1. · Introduction

In the second half of the 80s widespread attention has again been paid to growth theory, after the "wave" of business cycle studies.

This renewed interest originates from the pioneering work of Romer [9] and from the following papers by Rebelo [8], Lucas [6] and Barro [3].

This new line of research succeeds in explaining some stylized facts that a neoclassical growth theory (1) model could not deal with. Basically these stylized facts are: 1) long-run growth of per capita values; 2) non convergence among economies having the same structural parameters (2); 3) relevance of the savings rate in affecting the rate of growth of the economy.

With regard to the first stylized fact, a neoclassical model predicts zero rate of growth of per capita income, capital and consumption, due to decreasing returns in the reproducible factors; therefore in steady state the rate of growth of the economy is exogenously determined by the rate of growth of population. The observed in-

---

(1) Thrughout the paper we will refer to neoclassical model, meaning the Ramsey-Cass-Koopmans model.

*Advise:* the numbers in square brackets refer to the Bibliography in the appendix.

(2) By structural parameters we mean: 1) intertemporal elasticity of substitution; 2) discount rate; 3) labor and capital share.

creases in per capita values are explained by exogenous technical progress.

With regard to the second stylized fact, the neoclassical model says that if a rich and a poor (3) economy have the same structural parameters, they will converge to the same steady state, the poorer country growing faster due to the higher marginal productivity of its capital.

The last fact is strictly connected to the first one; as the rate of growth of the economy is determined solely by that of population, the savings rate has no role in affecting it. A one-time increase in the savings rate will simply augment per capita values; only in the transition to the new steady state will the rate of growth of the economy be temporarily higher, while in the new steady state it will again be determined by the exogenous demographic growth.

These three predictions are clearly counterfactual and furthermore strongly limit the role of economic policy in determining the growth path of an economy.

The crucial hypothesis needed to obtain self-sustained ("endogenous") growth, i.e. per capita growth explained by the model itself, and to account for the stylized facts mentioned above, is that of constant returns on the reproducible factors (4).

Given this, a great effort of investigation has been devoted to offering plausible explanations for nondecreasing returns to capital, meant as the complex of reproducible factors.

Among the researchers who have contributed most to this branch of the literature, Rebelo offers no explanation, Romer considers technological externalities and Barro public expenditure externalities; finally Lucas turns labor as well into a reproducible factor by allowing for human capital accumulation.

All these different explanations ensure constant returns to scale (CRS) to capital considered in a broad sense; all models argue that such a technology feature constitutes a sufficient condition for endogenous growth.

---

(3) Given two economies, the one with a lower stock of capital is poor.

(4) As long as the production function includes also non-reproducible factors, it exhibits overall increasing returns to scale. For problems concerning the existence of a set of prices supporting a general competitive equilibrium see the survey of SALA-I-MARTIN [10].

On the other hand, we have observed that all these models share not only such a description of technology, but also the hypothesis that a fixed proportion of the available time of economic agents is in some way devoted to accumulating some kind of capital. In all models but Lucas', time devoted to accumulation is not under choice. Only Lucas allows for an optimal allocation of time between studying and working, but these two activities in any case accumulate reproducible factors, human and physical capital respectively. Hence what matters is the sum of studying and working time, which is actually a fixed proportion of total time. Whatever the individual decides to do, he always spends the same hours of his day accumulating!

In this paper we simply mean to demonstrate that a technology with CRS on reproducible factors is not by itself a sufficient condition for endogenous growth. We want to show that it needs to be accompanied by the afore-mentioned condition on the allocation of time, taken for granted in all models, as far as we know. In other words, if we allow for an endogenous choice of the total time devoted to accumulation, it happens that, despite the CRS technology, we come back to exogenous neoclassical growth.

In order to prove this assertion we take into account the individual choice concerning the optimal allocation of time at any instant among leisure, studying and working. This aspect represents the key issue we addressed in our previous research on human capital accumulation and saving behavior in the life-cycle. In two papers we formulated two different optimization problems, a simple two-period stochastic model (Baldassarri, De Santis, Moscarini, Piga [1]) and a deterministic dynamic continuous time model (Baldassarri et Al. [2]). The explicit consideration of the optimal allocation of time allowed us to endogenously determine labor supply and income, human capital accumulation, career evolution, consumption and savings.

The natural extension of this framework to optimal growth theory led us to the endogenous growth literature and similarly permitted us to highlight some of its unexplored features. In particular, the possibility of choosing leisure brings us to the argument of this paper, the interpretation of which is straightforward; if the individual is not compelled to accumulate at a constant rate reproducible factors with CRS, endogenous growth is no longer a granted result.

Endogenous labor supply through intertemporal substitution with leisure has received considerable attention in business cycle literature, where it has been considered a major source of fluctuations in output. Yet, its role has been widely neglected in long-run growth theory.

We shall prove our assertion for two classes of models (5): endogenous growth with human capital accumulation (Lucas [6], section 2) and endogenous growth with externalities (Romer [9], section 3) (6). In section 4 we shall explain the mathematical conclusions reached in the other sections and section 5 offers a conclusion.

## 2. - Lucas' Model with Leisure

We now consider Lucas' model [6] of endogenous growth the "engine" of which is human capital accumulation. The social planner maximises:

$$(1) \qquad \underset{\{c_t, l_t, u_t\}}{\text{Max}} \int_0^\infty \frac{N_t \left[ c_t^{(1-\sigma)} + l_t^{(1-\sigma)} \right]}{1 - \sigma} e^{-\pi t}\, dt$$

s.t.

$$(2) \qquad \frac{dH_t}{dt} = \delta\, H_t (1 - l_t - u_t)$$

$$(3) \qquad \frac{dK_t}{dt} = A K_t^\beta (u_t\, H_t)^{(1-\beta)} H_t^\gamma - N_t\, c_t$$

---

(5) We omit a similar treatment to the *AK* Rebelo model, although it represents a common benchmark and all other models are simple microfoundations of its CRS technology. Actually, the introduction of leisure, and consequently of endogenous working time, obviously requires that labor be explicitly considered. In the *AK* model, however, all factors are reproducible and exhibit overall CRS; hence labor has also to be taken as a reproducible factor (which is stated by Rebelo himself), i.e. as human capital, and this can be simply accounted for in Lucas' framework, which seems to us a more general reference.

(6) The analysis carried out on the Romer's framework is valid for any externality based endogenous growth model, including Barro [3].

Small letters represent values in per capita terms, the utility function is a standard *CRRA*, $\sigma$ is the inverse of the intertemporal elasticity of substitution, equal for the two arguments, $\pi$ is the subjective rate of discount, $K_t$ is physical capital, $N_t$ is the size of population, $c_t$ is per capita consumption, $l_t$ and $u_t$ are leisure and working time respectively, both expressed as a share of the unit of time $dt$, $H_t$ is aggregate human capital (7), $\delta$ is the maximum rate of accumulation of human capital, $\gamma$ is the externalities parameter, $\beta$ and $(1 - \beta)$ are the capital and labor share respectively and $A$ is a constant parameter.

In order to solve this problem, set the following current Hamiltonian value:

$$R = \frac{N_t \left[ c_t^{(1-\sigma)} + l_t^{(1-\sigma)} \right]}{1 - \sigma} +$$

$$+ \theta_{1t} \left[ AK_t^\beta (u_t H_t)^{(1-\beta)} H_t^\gamma - N_t c_t \right] + \theta_{2t} \delta (1 - l_t - u_t) H_t$$

The necessary conditions for an interior maximum are:

(4) $$c_t^{-\sigma} = \theta_{1t}$$

(5) $$N_t l_t^{-\sigma} = \theta_{2t} \delta H_t$$

(6) $$\theta_{1t} A (1 - \beta) K_t^\beta H_t^{(1-\beta)} u_t^{-\beta} H_t^\gamma = \theta_{2t} \delta H_t$$

(7) $$\frac{d\theta_{1t}}{dt} = \pi \theta_{1t} - \theta_{1t} A\beta K_t^{(\beta-1)} (u_t H_t)^{(1-\beta)} H_t^\gamma$$

---

(7) With regard to Lucas' model, here we have introduced a slight modification. As a matter of fact in Lucas' model human capital is considered in per capita terms, while the other reproducible factor, physical capital, is in aggregate terms. This asymmetry is reflected in the first order condition that equalizes the marginal benefits from studying and working; in Lucas' model such a condition sets equal the aggregate gain from the last instant of working to the individual gain from the last instant of studying. Allowing for leisure, if $H_t$ were in per capita terms in capita, the necessary condition on leisure would equalize the aggregate marginal benefit from leisure to the individual marginal benefit from studying eq. *(5)*. In any case our results of zero per capita growth rates would not be affected, if we worked with per capita human capital.

(8) $\quad \dfrac{d\theta_{2t}}{dt} \quad = \pi\theta_{2t} - \theta_{1t} A (1 - \beta + \gamma) K_t^\beta H_t^{(\gamma-\beta)} u_t^{(1-\beta)}$

$$- \theta_{2t} \delta (1 - l_t - u_t)$$

(2) $\qquad\qquad\qquad \dfrac{dH_t}{dt} = \delta H_t (1 - l_t - u_t)$

(3) $\qquad\qquad\qquad \dfrac{dK_t}{dt} = AK_t^\beta (u_t H_t)^{(1-\beta)} H_t^\gamma - N_t c_t$

(9) $\qquad\qquad\qquad \lim_{t\to\infty} K_t \theta_{1t} e^{-\pi t} = 0$

(10) $\qquad\qquad\qquad \lim_{t\to\infty} H_t \theta_{2t} e^{-\pi t} = 0$

Define $\lambda$ as the rate of growth of population, $\chi$ as the rate of growth of per capita consumption, $\xi$ as the rate of growth of aggregate capital and $\gamma$ as the rate of growth of aggregate human capital.

Equation *(4)* says that at the margin the individual is indifferent the between consumption and investment, equations *(5)* and *(6)* set as equal the marginal benefits derived from the allocation of time that is equality between the aggregate gain from the last instant of leisure and the one from the last instant of studying and equality between the aggregate gain from the last instant of working and the one from the last instant of studying.

Equation *(7)* equalizes the marginal gain in utility from investing in physical capital to the gain from postponing the accumulation which is equal to the difference between the cost of the foregone consumption and the change in the shadow price of physical capital.

Equation *(8)* equalizes the marginal gain in utility from investing in human capital, in terms of both production of goods and new human capital, to the gain from postponing its accumulation which is equal to the difference between the cost of the foregone leisure and the change in the shadow price of human capital.

We now describe a solution imposing constant rates of growth.

Consider *(4)*, take logs and derivatives with respect to time, to obtain:

(11) $$-\sigma\chi = (d\theta_{1t}/dt)/\theta_{1t}$$

Divide both sides of *(7)* by $\sigma_{lt}$ and substitute from *(11)*; rearranging terms, we obtain:

(12) $$(\pi + \sigma\chi)/\beta = AK_t^{(\beta-1)}(u_tH_t)^{(1-\beta)}H_t^\gamma$$

Now divide both sides of *(3)* by $K_t$ to get:

(13) $$\xi \equiv (dK_t/dt)/K_t = AK_t^{(\beta-1)}(u_tH_t)^{(1-\beta)})H_t^\gamma - N_tc_t/K_t$$

Substitute from *(12)* to get:

(14) $$\xi = (\pi + \sigma\chi)/\beta - N_tc_t/K_t$$

bringing all the constants on the LHS, taking again logs and derivatives, we obtain:

$$0 = \xi - \lambda - \chi$$

that is:

(15) $$\xi = \lambda + \chi$$

In simple words the rate of growth of per capita consumption and per capita physical capital are equal.

Now, consider again *(12)*, take logs and derivatives, to get:

$$0 = (\beta - 1)\xi + (1 - \beta + \gamma)\upsilon$$

Now substituting from *(15)*, we obtain:

(16) $$\upsilon = (\chi + \lambda)(1 - \beta)/(1 - \beta + \gamma)$$

Clearly, per capita consumption and per capita human capital growth rates differ only because of the externality.

Now take logs and derivatives in *(6)* and substitute from *(11)*, to get:

$$- \sigma\chi + \beta\xi + (1 - \beta) v + \gamma v = v + (d\theta_{2t}/dt)/\theta_{2t}$$

Substituting from *(15)*, one obtains:

*(17)*          $$(d\theta_{2t}/dt)/\theta_{2t} = \chi (\beta - \sigma) + \lambda\beta + v (\gamma - \beta)$$

Finally from *(5)*, taking logs and derivatives, we get:

*(18)*          $$(d\theta_{2t}/dt)/\theta_{2t} = \lambda - v$$

Therefore we have to solve the following system:

*(16)*          $$v = (\chi + \lambda) (1 - \beta) / (1 - \beta + \gamma)$$

*(17)*          $$(d\theta_{2t}/dt)/\theta_{2t} = \chi (\beta - \sigma) + \lambda\beta + v (\gamma - \beta)$$

*(18)*          $$(d\theta_{2t}/dt)/\theta_{2t} = \lambda - v)$$

the three unknowns being $(d\theta_{2t}/dt)/\theta_{2t}, \upsilon, \chi$.

Substituting for $\upsilon$ from *(16)* in *(17)* and *(18)*, equalizing the two equations and rearranging their terms, we obtain:

$$\chi [1 - \beta + (\beta - \sigma)/(1 + \gamma - \beta)] = 0$$

it follows that:

*(19)*          $$\chi = 0$$

*(20)*          $$v = \lambda (1 - \beta)/(1 + \gamma - \beta)$$

*(21)*          $$(d\theta_{2t}/dt)/\theta_{2t} = \lambda\gamma/(1 + \gamma - \beta)$$

Hence endogenous growth does not occur. From *(17)* the rate of growth of aggregate capital is equal to the exogenous rate of growth of population.

Since: $$\upsilon = \lambda (1 - \beta)/(1 + \gamma - \beta)$$

from eq. *(2)* we obtain:

$$\delta (1 - l_t - u_t) = \lambda (1 - \beta) / (1 - \beta + \gamma)$$

which represents the steady state optimal value of studying time $s_t$

*(22)* $$s^*_t = \lambda (1 - \beta)/(1 + \gamma - \beta) \delta$$

Insert *(6)* in *(8)*, to obtain:

$$(d\theta_{2t}/dt)/\theta_{2t} = \pi - u_t \delta \gamma / (1 - \beta) - \delta (1 - u_t - l_t)$$

Substituting from eq. *(21)* and *(22)* we obtain the steady state values for leisure and working time

*(23)* $$u^*_t = [(\pi - \lambda) (1 - \beta)]/\delta(1 + \gamma - \beta)$$

*(24)* $$1^*_t = 1 - \pi (1 - \beta)/\delta(1 + \gamma - \beta)$$

Apart from the externality $\gamma$, the interpretation of the optimal steady state values of the variables concerning the allocation of time is simple. Studying time is equal to $\lambda / \delta$ : the individual must study only to provide the newborns with the same per capita human capital stock and the higher $\delta$ (the maximum rate of feasible accumulation of human capital) the lower is the needed investment in human capital. Note also that, since the flow of human capital (studying time) is independent from the rate of time preference, the same holds for its steady state level, for any initial known value.

Working time is positively related to $\pi$ : the higher the rate of time preference, the lower the steady state physical capital per unit of labor (via the modified golden rule). In other words, a higher $\pi$ induces a substitution of working for physical capital in production, implying lower leisure *(24)* for any given human capital.

Finally we look at the two transversality conditions. Both equation *(9)* and *(10)* are verified as long as $\pi > \lambda$ (8).

In Lucas' model, optimisation with respect to leisure causes the system to grow at the exogenous rate of growth of population.

The equation that makes the point is the optimality condition on leisure *(5)*, which then implies eq. *(18)*.

## 3. - The Romer Model with Leisure

Allowing for leisure, the Romer model of 1986 can be formalized as follows.

First of all we define the aggregate production function in the presence of endogenous working time.

$$Y_t = [(1 - l_t) N_t]^{(1-\beta)} K_t^{\beta} \kappa^{\eta}$$

dividing both sides by $N_t$, we get the per capita production function,

$$y_t = (1 - l_t)^{(1-\beta)} k_t^{\beta} \kappa^{\eta}$$

For the sake of simplicity, we work with stationary population (as in Romer) and furthermore we normalize it to one.

Hence the planner maximises:

$$(25) \qquad \underset{\{c_t, \, l_t\}_0^{\infty}}{\text{Max}} \int_0^{\infty} \frac{[c_t^{(1-\sigma)} + l_t^{(1-\sigma)}]}{1 - \sigma} e^{-\pi t} \, dt$$

s.t.

$$(26) \qquad dk \, / \, dt = (1 - l_t)^{(1-\beta)} \kappa_t^{\beta} \kappa^{\eta} - c_t$$

---

(8) As a matter of fact, in equation *(9)* $\theta_{1t}$ is constant and $K_t$ grows at the rate $\lambda$ and therefore the transversality condition is verified if and only if $\pi > \lambda$. Analogously, in eq. *(10)* the sum of the rates of growth of $H_t$ and $\theta_{2t}$ is equal to $\lambda$ and again eq. *(10)* is verified if and only if $\pi > \lambda$.

As usual, small letters are for per capita values and $\kappa^\eta$ is the technological externality, where $\kappa$ is defined as aggregate knowledge. Furthermore, equilibrium in the capital markets requires

$$\kappa = N_t \, k_t = K_t \, ,$$

In our case:

$$\kappa_t = k_t$$

Let us write the standard current Hamiltonian value:

$$R = [c_t^{(1-\sigma)} + l_t^{(1-\sigma)}] / (1-\sigma) + \theta_t [(1-l_t)^{(1-\beta)} k_t^\beta \kappa^\eta - c_t]$$

The first order conditions for an interior maximum are.

(27) $$c_t^{-\sigma} = \theta_t$$

(28) $$l_t^{-\sigma} = \theta_t (1-\beta) (1-l_t)^{-\beta} k_t^{\beta+\eta}$$

(29) $$d\theta_t / dt = \pi \theta_t - \theta_t (\beta+\eta) k_t^{(\beta+\eta-1)} (1-l_t)^{(1-\beta)}$$

(30) $$dk / dt = (1-l_t)^{(1-\beta)} k_t^\beta \kappa^\eta - c_t$$

(31) $$\lim_{t->\infty} e^{-\pi t} k_t \theta_t = 0$$

In order to find solutions with constant rates of growth proceed, as usual, as follows; take logs and derivatives of *(27)*, to get:

(32) $$[(d\theta_t / dt)] / \theta_t = -\sigma \chi$$

Now divide both sides of *(29)* by $\theta_t$ and substitute from *(32)*, to obtain:

(33) $$\pi + \sigma \chi = (1-l_t)^{(1-\beta)} (\beta+\eta) k_t^{(\beta+\eta-1)}$$

Now dividing both sides of *(30)* by $k_t$, one obtains the rate of growth of per capita capital:

$$\gamma_k = (1 - l_t)^{(1-\beta)} k_t^{(\beta+\eta-1)} - c_t / k_t$$

Substituting for $(1 - l_t)^{(1-\beta)} k_t^{(\beta+\eta-1)}$ from (33), bringing all the constants on the LHS and taking logs and derivatives, one obtains

$$0 = -\chi + \gamma_k$$

that is:

(34)                                  $\chi = \gamma_k$

in simple words, the rate of growth of per capita consumption and per capita capital are equal.

From (28) taking logs and derivatives we get:

(35)                  $0 = [(d\theta_t / dt)] / \theta_t + (\beta + \eta) \gamma_k$

$$[(d\theta_t / dt)] / \theta_t = -(\beta + \eta) \gamma_k$$

Therefore we have to solve the system of equations (32), (34) and (35).

(32)                        $[(d\theta_t / dt)] / \theta_t = -\sigma\chi$

(34)                                  $\chi = \gamma_k$

(35)                    $[(d\theta_t / dt)] / \theta_t = -(\beta + \eta) \gamma_k$

As long as $\sigma \neq \beta + \eta$, which is true since $\beta + \eta = 1$, $\chi$ and $\gamma_k$ are equal to zero and therefore once again we are back to the neoclassical world (9).

---

(9) The same results hold for the market economy. In this case the maximization problem is the same as the one solved by the social planner, thanks to the production function, which is CRS, $\kappa^\eta$ being considered as given by the individuals. The FOC for a maximum are all the same but eq. (30). Individuals do not derive with respect to $\kappa$ hence $\eta$ does not appear on the r.h.s. as coefficient, but only as exponent. The following analysis proceeds on the same lines and the final results of zero per capita growth rates are not altered. The technological externalities obviously still play a role, affecting the steady state levels of per capita values, not their rates of growth.

Finally, looking at the transversality condition of eq. *(31)* we see that, since $k_t$ and $\theta_t$ are constant, the condition is satisfied as long as $\pi > 0$.

## 4. - Why Does Leisure Lead us Back to Exogenous Growth?

We now intend to provide a simple interpretation of our mathematics. The key equation leading to exogenous growth is the optimality condition ruling the choice of leisure. Examining the FOC for a maximum in our version of the Romel model, we clearly have to equate over time the weighted marginal utilities of consumption and leisure. If there were endogenous growth, per capita consumption would grow unbounded and its marginal utility would tend to zero. As leisure must be constant in steady state, having an obvious upper limit, the growth of capital should increase leisure's opportunity cost (marginal benefit from working) in order to make up for the decrease in the marginal utility of consumption and keep the equality of marginal benefits *(28)*. Remembering that the growth of per capita capital is always equal to the growth of per capita consumption, $\theta$'s dynamics should follow the preferences ($\sigma$, eq. *(27)*) and the technology ($\beta + \eta$, eq. *(28)*). But there is no reason for preferences and technological parameters to be consistent in order to make up for the scarcity of time, which then causes exogenous growth.

Careful attention must be paid to the scarcity of resources. It is well known that, in the marginalistic tradition, decreasing returns originate from the existence of fixed production factors. This constraint is avoided by endogenous growth models thanks to the reproducibility of a number of factors sufficient to ensure constant returns. Such a reproducibility stems from the use of the resource "time", the fraction of which devoted to market activities is a production factor; for example, in Lucas, market activities, studying and working time, accumulate human and physical capital respectively.

All endogenous growth models, however, make two strong assumptions about the resource "time":

1) The reproduction of each factor occurs at constant return:

i.e., each instant of studying and working becomes steadily more and more productive;

2) The opportunity cost of the complex of "market activities" is zero, as leisure is neglected in the preferences; consequently, time is a free resource. The fixed fraction of time devoted to market activities does not affect the growth rates of the variables but only their levels; in other words, this fraction is a parameter of the model, exactly as the savings rate (the fraction of income saved) in the original Solow [11] growth model.

The explicit consideration of leisure gives the market activities a positive opportunity cost, thus turning time into an economically significant resource. Now it is clear that a new, unavoidable scarcity is at work; either leisure or market activities, once endogenously determined, cannot exceed the extent of the current period, whatever its length. Since leisure is a normal good, a positive steady growth of consumption generates an income effect which induces a reallocation of time from market activities to leisure. But, limiting the analysis to the steady state, leisure must be constant because of its upper bound, i.e. because of the scarcity of "time".

Thus, the scarcity of a relevant production factor reintroduces a sort of decreasing returns in this class of models: it follows that, as in the standard neoclassical model, despite the CRS technology, in equilibrium there is no room for balanced paths with per capita income growth.

## 5. - Conclusions

In this paper we have tried to show that a CRS technology on reproducible factors is not, by itself, a sufficient condition for endogenous growth. The literature has always relied on the CRS hypothesis and it has implicitly assumed that accumulation activity was not under choice. Actually the entire time optimally allocated, either by the planner or by the individuals, is dedicated to accumulating reproducible factors, which have CRS: the endogenous growth is therefore a necessary result. In other words, CRS is a sufficient condition if and only if the allocation of time is never affected by the rates of growth or by the levels of the variables.

In order to release such an implicit hypothesis, we have re-examined some representative endogenous growth models with the explicit introduction of leisure as a source of welfare for the individuals. This gives an opportunity cost to "market activities" (working + studying time), turning time into a production factor and making its scarcity relevant. The analysis leads back to exogenous growth, notwithstanding CRS on reproducible factors, confirming our argument.

A further development of our idea should address the behavior of the system without the hypothesis of constant growth rates. The structure of the model readily suggests the possibility of positive per capita growth, something that we showed to be unfeasible only at constant rates. The hypothesis of constant rates of growth seems to add a further constraint to the optimisation problem. As a matter of fact, in the neoclassical model it is shown that the steady state solution, investigated for analytical convenience, is stable and furthermore is the only one to satisfy all the optimality conditions: hence it does not take us away from the first best. On the other hand, the role of this hypothesis is not well understood in the endogenous growth literature, there being no complete stability analysis around an increasing growth path. Our presumption is that, once the traditional saddle paths around the steady state have been abandoned, there could be no more equivalence between the first best growth path and constant rates of growth. In such a case further investigation should give up the traditional exponential paths (10).

---

(10) We have been supported in this respect by R. Solow, who read an earlier version of this paper.

## BIBLIOGRAPHY

[1] BALDASSARRI M. - DE SANTIS P. - MOSCARINI G. - PIGA G.: «An Attempt to Model a Tobin-Modigliani Approach to Savings», *Rivista di politica economica*, Roma, October 1990.

[2] —— . —— . —— . —— :*Earnings and Human Capital in a Deterministic Life-Cycle Model; a Tobin-Modigliani Approach to a Spring-Saving Behavior*, paper presented at Annual Meeting of the AEA, New Orleans, January 1992.

[3] BARRO R.J.: «Government Spending in a Simple Model of Endogenous Growth», *Journal of Political Economy*, October 1990.

[4] CASS D.: «Optimum Growth in an Aggregate Model of Capital Accumulation», *Review of Economic Studies*, n. 32, July 1965.

[5] KOOPMANS T.C.: «On the Concept of Optimal Growth», in *Econometric Approach to Development Planning*, Amsterdam, North Holland, 1965.

[6] LUCAS R.E.: «On the Mechanics of Economic Development», *Journal of Monetary Economics*, n. 22, 1988.

[7] RAMSEY F.P.: «A Mathematical Theory of Saving», *Economic Journal*, n. 38, 1928.

[8] REBELO S.: «Long Run Policy Analysis and Long Run Growth», NBER, *Working Paper*, April 1990.

[9] ROMER P.: «Increasing Returns and Long Run Growth», *Journal of Political Economy*, n. 94, 1986.

[10] SALA-I-MARTIN X.: «Lecture Notes on Economic Growth», vols. I e II, NBER, *Working Paper*, nos. 3563, 3564, 1991.

[11] SOLOW R.: «A Contribution to the Theory of Economic Growth», *Quarterly Journal of Economics*, n. 70, 1956.

# II - EXPLAINING GROWTH

# Infrastructure and Growth

**David Canning - Marianne Fay - Roberto Perotti** (*)

Columbia University

## 1. - Introduction

The aim of this project is to investigate the macroeconomic impact of infrastructure on economic growth and development. The static impact of infrastructure is that it raises a country's level of output. The dynamic impact is that the level of infrastructure may increase the growth rate of the economy. There are two routes by which infrastructure could have a major impact on growth rates. Firstly, by raising the productivity of capital so that the economy experiences more private investment and this investment is more productive. Secondly, and perhaps more importantly, the infrastructure may allow specialization in sectors, or technologies, which give rise to technical progress. A model of how this can happen is set out in section two.

The main effort of this paper is to undertake an empirical study to find if the level of infrastructure at the beginning of a period has a measurable effect on the growth rate of GDP per capita over the period. The infrastructure measures we use are telephones (or telephone lines) per capita, electricity generating capacity per capita and length of road and railway, divided by area. In addition, some quality measures are used, in particular the percentage of roads which are paved.

(*) We would like to thank Ezra Bennathan, Gordon Hughes and Ruby Taylor, for their helpful discussion and help in providing data from World Bank data sources. We would also like to thank Alberto Alesina and Paul Swagel for providing a data set of political variables.

*Advise*: the numbers in square brackets refer to the Bibliography in the appendix.

Two methods of investigation are employed. Firstly we carry out cross section regressions attempting to explain growth rates of per capita GDP over the period 1960-1985 using infrastructure stock levels in 1960. To allow direct comparison with the work of Barro [3] we simply add our infrastructure variables to his cross section data set and regressions. The results of these regressions are that the coefficients on our infrastructure variables have a positive sign; percentage roads paved, electricity generating capacity and telephones per capita appear to have a positive, and statistically significant, effect on the rate of economic growth.

Secondly, we use a panel data approach regressing growth rates of GDP per capita for the periods 1960-1970, 1970-1980, 1980-1988 on explanatory variables from the beginning of each period. This has the advantage of allowing for country fixed effects in growth rates which may correct, to some extent, for bias caused by missing explanatory variables in the cross section regressions (Hsiao, [12]). With the panel approach both telephones and electricity have a positive effect (at the 99.95% confidence level). Percentage paved roads is still significant and positive, and length of railways, divided by area, do have a significant impact on growth rates provided we interact them with GDP per capita. Both telephones and electricity also seem to have a significant interactive effect with GDP per capita indicating that infrastructure has more of an effect on growth rates at high GDP per capita levels.

Despite the revival of interest in growth theory of the last few years, the role of infrastructure capital in the growth process still seems to be a relatively neglected topic.

Our contribution is mainly empirical. We are interested in exploring the intuitive idea that the stock of infrastructure capital may affect the rate of growth of an economy. Thus, our contribution takes a different perspective than a recent strand of literature, starting with Aschauer [1], that focuses (indirectly) on the relation between growth and infrastructure accumulation.

Empirically, this infrastructure accumulation is essentially based on the estimation of a production function (see e.g. Aschauer [1], Munnell [16], Hulten - Schawb [10]) in which infrastructure capital appears as an input. Alternatively, infrastructure capital is used to explain multifactor productivity (Munnell [15], Hulten - Schwab [11]). Much of the work following Aschauer [1] has been devoted to extending his approach by using different data (especially using data from US states rather than a time series on the whole US) and correcting for the implausibly high values of the marginal productivity of public capital that he obtains (see Ebert [8] for a brief survey).

The theoretical implication of all these studies is that what matters for growth of multi-factor productivity (*MFP*) is the growth of infrastructure. This is an almost unavoidable consequence of the growth-accounting nature of the exercise. In such models the stock of infrastructure capital is associated with a particular level of output; creation of new infrastructure is required if we wish to have a contribution to growth.

However, the idea that the stock of infrastructure is also important for growth has a long tradition in economics. Recently, Barro [2] and Barro-Sala-Y-Martin [4] have discussed endogenous growth models where over some ranges an increase in the provision of government services increases the rate of growth of the economy. The government services are provided through taxation of income, and have therefore the dimension of a flow variable. In Clarida-Findlay [5] the stock of infrastructure has a positive external effect on the productivity of private factors of production. Public capital is used to produce itself with a constant marginal productivity that depends positively on the amount of the fixed factor employed in this production. In equilibrium the rate of growth of the economy depends on the proportion of the fixed factor devoted to the production of infrastructure, and therefore on the rate of growth of the latter. Our model is most closely related to Hercowitz - Huffman [9]. As in Clarida-Findlay [5] public capital enhances the productivity of the other factors of production and both private and public capital are state variables. However, now public capital is accumulated, as in Barro [2], by taxing income.

## 2. - Theory

We begin by setting out a simple model that will form the basis of our statistical analysis.

The aim here is to examine the mechanism by which infrastructure levels can affect growth rates and to determine what other factors should be important; we shall not try to impose a particular theoretical functional form on the relationship.

The central requirements for an adequate model of economic growth are to explain the long run growth of output per capita and why this growth varies so much across countries. Two main answers have been put forward to the first question; firstly, technical progress and secondly, constant, or increasing, returns to reproducible factors of production. The stock of infrastructure can affect economic growth by either of these routes. To meet the second requirement the theory must allow for factors which cause growth rate to vary across countries and do so in a way that is testable. Here we shall construct a model with such endogenous technical progress and increasing returns. The alternative, constant returns, approach to growth and convergence is set out and examined empirically in Mankiw, Romer and Weil [14].

Firstly, suppose that the rate of technical progress depends on the rate of investment, both in private and public capital. The idea behind this is that there is a stock of technical progress waiting "on the shelf" that can be incorporated in production when new investment takes place. Infrastructure may be important for technical progress by several routes. Transportation infrastructure may improve communication, increasing the extent of the market and allowing specialization. This specialization may allow access to high volume, high technology, production techniques. Electricity may be essential to some technologies and the provision of an electricity supply may allow access to these techniques; De Long and Summers [6] emphasize investment in electrical machinery as an observed source of growth.

For simplicity let us assume that the total factor productivity level changes in response to investment. That is:

$$\frac{\Delta \lambda_{it}}{\lambda_{it}} = \beta^t \frac{\Delta K_{it}}{K_{it}} + \gamma^t \frac{\Delta G_{t-1}}{G_{t-1}}$$

where $it$ is firm $i$'s productivity level at time $t$. The growth in firm $i$'s productivity at time $t$ depends on its investment (change in its capital stock, $K$) and time $t$ and the change in the public stock of infrastructure capital to which it has access, $G$. The public capital stock is lagged by one period since we assume there is a lag between its creation and its availability for use.

We suppose the production function for firm $i$ at time $t$ is of the form:

$$Y_{it} = \lambda_{it}\, L_{it}^\alpha\, K_{it}^\beta\, \frac{G_{t-1}^\gamma}{D_t}$$

where $Y$ is its output, $L$ its labor input, $K$ its capital input, $G$ the stock of public capital and $D$ a congestion deflator for this stock. The effect of public capital is assumed to depend on the previous period's stock; this period's new public capital not having had time to come into operation. The congestion deflator $D$ measures how much the presence, or activity, of other economic agents reduces access to the public capital.

The congestion deflator, $D$, can take several forms. For example, if the public service is non-rival each firm has access to the full amount $G$. If it is rival then each worker gets an amount $G/L$. If it is non excludable then total output may congest use, for example, more use of the road system may increase travel times, it may be that each firm gets an amount of services $G/Y$ where $Y$ is aggregate output. A general formulation of the congestion externality is

$$D_t = L_t^\delta\, Y_t^\varepsilon$$

The values $\delta = \varepsilon = 0$ give the case of a pure, non rival, excludable, public good; the total amount provided enters each firm's production function. The case where $\varepsilon = 0$ and $\delta = \tau$ gives the case of a pure rival good.

Integrating our technical progress equation gives:

$$y_{it} = \lambda_0\, L_{it}^\alpha\, K_{it}^{\beta + \beta^t}\, \frac{G_{t-1}^{\gamma + \gamma^t}}{D_t}$$

If we assume constant returns to scale then making technical progress depend on investment implies that the firm output behaves "as if" it has increasing returns to scale; expansion is associated with increased productivity. We could follow Barro [2] and assume increasing returns directly though this alternative technical progress interpretation seems more appealing. In what follows we normalize $\lambda^0$ to one and assume that $\beta' = \tau' = 0$ though it is important to realize that our "increasing returns" coefficients on our inputs can be interpreted as coming from endogenous technical progress. The point is that at the aggregate level the technical progress and the increasing returns explanations of growth of per capita GDP may be observationally equivalent.

We assume $\beta + \beta = 1$ so that private sector activity enjoys constant returns to scale. In the section on long run growth we shall assume that $\beta + \tau = 1$ so that for fixed labour inputs we have constant returns in private and public capital given together. This is necessary for the existence of a balanced growth path along which capital inputs and output per capita grow at a constant rate.

Under our assumption that $\alpha + \beta = 1$, so that, given the public capital stock, the private sector has constant returns to scale, we can aggregate the production function to give output per capita:

$$ y_t = k_t^{\frac{\beta}{1+\varepsilon}} G_{t-1}^{\frac{\gamma}{1+\varepsilon}} L_t^{\frac{-\delta}{1+\varepsilon}} $$

where $k$ is private capital per capita. If $\delta = \tau$, output per capita depends on the private and public capital stocks per capita. If $\delta = 0$, the public good is non rival output per capita depends on the private capital stock per capita and the aggregate public capital stock. Note that the congestion externality due to non-excludability ($\varepsilon > 0$) has the effect of depressing the GDP/input ratio as the amount of inputs rise.

Now suppose the economy consists of overlapping generations. Agents are endowed with one unit of labor and work when young, saving some of their income in the form of private capital in order to consume when old. Their utility function over first and second period consumption is given by:

$$ U(C_t,\ C_{t+1}) = \log c_t + d \log c_{t+1} $$

which they maximize subject to subject to the budget constraints:

$$c_t + s_t = w_t(1 - \tau), \quad c_{t+1} = s_t r_{t+1}(1 - \tau)$$

where $w$ is the wage, $r$ is the gross rate of return on capital, $s$ is their savings (held as capital), and $\tau$ is the tax rate. Assuming that labor and capital earn their marginal products this gives an optimal aggregate level of saving $S_t$ which also serves as the next period's stock of capital:

$$K_{t+1} = S_t = \frac{d\alpha(1 - \tau)Y_t}{1 + d}$$

Note that we assume 100% depreciation of private capital. The advantage of this overlapping generations framework over the infinite horizon model is that it makes the private sector's decision making very simple. Since agents only live one period into the future and capital only lasts one period there is no need for them to look into the distant future when making their decisions. This means that they do not need to form expectations of Government policy in the distant future. The cost of this is that we assume that private capital is relatively short lived.

We can now derive the growth rate of output per capita between period $t$ and period $t + 1$:

$$g_{t+1} = \frac{\beta}{1 + \varepsilon} \log \frac{d\alpha(1 - \tau)}{1 + d} + \left(\frac{\beta}{1 + \varepsilon} - 1\right) \log y_t +$$

$$-\frac{\beta}{1 + \varepsilon} n_{t+1} + \frac{\gamma - \delta}{1 + \varepsilon} \log G_t + \frac{\delta}{1 + \varepsilon} \log g_t$$

where $n_{t+1}$ is the growth of population between the two periods and $g_t$ is the public capital stock per capita. Note that the growth rate is falling in the tax rate, the previous period's GDP per capita and the growth rate of population. If $\delta = 0$ the public capital is non rival and the growth rate is rising in public capital stock, but if $\delta = \tau$ then public capital is rival and it is only the stock of public capital per capita that matters.

This equation holds no matter how the public capital stock is being accumulated. The point is that the overlapping generations framework allows us to solve for the level of investment and the future private capital stock once we know the tax rate and the existing level of output. A more complex utility function for the agents might allow them to save more when the marginal productivity of capital was higher, this is easy to add to the model and gives the public capital stock extra effectiveness. However, even in this case investment decisions depend only on the current and next period conditions; agents do not have to consider the entire future stream of returns to capital as they do in a model with long lived private capital. It would be attractive to construct a model with both long lived private and public capital; but this gives an exceedingly complex dynamic model with two state variables.

The reason that public sector capital increases the growth rate is that it leads to higher output and investment. This investment increases productivity, either through increasing returns, or by inducing technical progress. In our framework we have "cumulative causation"; a high level of output tends to raise growth rates.

Note that our growth rate is always increasing with the quantity of public capital. This contrasts with Barro [2] who finds an optimal quantity of public capital which maximizes the growth rate. However, Barro imposes a balanced budget condition so that the infrastructure services must be financed by taxation; as we shall see in the next section, once we do this, higher levels of infrastructure may require higher tax rates and may lead to lower growth. However, our short run equation is able to capture the possibility that infrastructure capital is inherited and may bear little relationship to existing tax rates.

Our equation for growth between two periods holds no matter what future path the stock of public capital takes; it holds both on a balanced growth path and during disequilibrium adjustment. Its usefulness in estimation follows from this. It is interesting however to investigate the implications of our model for long run growth rates.

Let:

$$G_t = G_{t-1} + \tau \, Y_{t-1}$$

so that the public capital stock does not depreciate and all taxes are used to finance new public sector capital. Now we consider balanced growth paths. Let:

$$\frac{G_t}{G_{t-1}} = 1 + x \qquad \frac{Y_t}{G_t} = R_t$$

for all $t$, so that $x$ is the growth rate of the public capital stock and $R$ is the ratio of private output to public capital. On a steady state growth path the growth of public capital is constant at the rate $x$, as is the growth rate of private capital and output per capita. The tax rate is constant and the ratio of output to public sector capital is constant.

For simplicity assume we have no population growth and that $\delta = \gamma$, so that the public capital stock per capita is what matters for output and growth. Note that we also require our assumption that $\beta + \tau = 1$ for balanced growth in per capita output to be possible.

Along the steady state path the tax rate must be set so as to finance the growth of the public capital. This gives:

$$x = \tau R$$

Note that rates go up faster than the desired rate of growth of public capital. This is because, as the tax rate rises, the capital stock falls and the tax base declines.

The ratio of output to public capital is given by:

$$R = \frac{Y_t}{G_t} = \left[ \frac{\alpha d}{(1 + d)} (1 - \tau) \right]^{\frac{\beta}{1-\beta}}$$

Note that the ratio $R$ falls with the tax rate. A high tax rate reduces disposable income and private investment, reducing the ratio of private to public capital.

An interesting special case is to set $x = 0$, so that public capital is fixed at some initial level $G_0$ indefinitely. This means the tax rate is set at zero and the long run equilibrium output/public capital stock ratio is given by:

$$R = \left( \frac{\alpha d}{d+1} \right)^{\frac{\beta}{\beta-1}}$$

Notice that, in the long run, two countries with different, but fixed, public capital stocks will both have zero growth. The one with the higher public capital stock will have proportionately higher income but no higher growth rate. However, our short run growth equation still holds in this steady state; growth rates increase with public capital if we control for initial GDP per capita. Once GDP per capita reaches its equilibrium level the two effects cancel out.

More importantly, outside the steady state, our short run growth equation still holds. It is easy to show that for the case $x = 0$ the system is stable with output converging to its steady state level given the public capital stock, the growth rate in each period being given by our short run growth equation. For two countries with the same fixed public capital stock the one with the lower GDP per capita will grow faster in the short run (which may still be several decades) before both converge to the same income level.

In general our two equations in the three variables $x$, $\tau$ and $R$, allow one to be set as a policy variable. The nature of our equations implies that there may be multiple balanced growth paths associated with the same growth rate. The relationship between growth rates and the tax rate is given by:

$$x = \left[ \frac{\alpha d}{1+d} \tau (1 - \tau) \right]^{\frac{\beta}{1-\beta}}$$

so that there is a maximum growth rate possible, given by a tax rate of $\tau = 1 - \beta$ and for any lower growth rate there are two possible tax rates that can sustain it; one less than $\gamma$ and one greater than $\gamma$. Given a tax rate however there is only one solution for the growth rate.

Given a fixed tax rate the balanced growth paths are stable; if the output/public capital ratio is too high the stock of public capital grows at a rate faster than the steady state while the stock of private capital grows more slowly. We can therefore think of economies being on their balanced growth path or moving towards it. More generally the tax rate may be varying over time and the economy moves in response to these changes. The important point is that in any of these cases or short run growth equation holds and can be estimated.

In the above analysis we implicitly assumed that the private sector did not pay for access to the public sector capital. This is usually true for roads but for other infrastructure, which is both rival and excludable, such as electricity, telephones and railways, users pay charges. We consider the effect on our short run growth equation of three charging systems: 1) users pay running costs for the service and the Government pays capital costs 2) users are rationed but pay a fee per unit consumed 3) the rental price of public capital is set to make demand equal supply.

We argue that user charges do not change our basic equation if such charges are considered as "taxes". The key point is that our model depends only on the production function we have employed. It follows that charging for public capital will have no effect on output and growth providing it does not alter the microeconomic allocation of resources; the number of firms or the inputs which each of the firms employ.

1) Suppose capacity is set up by the Government who then allow consumers to purchase the good at average cost net of capital inputs. We can regard each agent as being given $1/L$ of the capital stock for free and being allowed to combine it with other inputs (including inputs which make up running costs). The public capital stock behaves exactly as in our model.

2) Under rationing each agent gets a fraction $1/L$ of the stock of capital. He has to pay for this, but given that the rationing constraint is biting this works just like a lump sum tax; it does not change his marginal decisions. If we replace our income tax with a lump sum tax it makes no difference in our model since we assume that labour is supplied inelastically.

3) The stock of public capital is fixed within the period. If the increasing returns are external to the firm the only effect pricing can have is to have it allocated more efficiently, but given our assumption of identical firms pricing leads to exactly the same equal allocation as does equal allocations. A problem emerges if we take the view that there are increasing returns at the level of the firm. In a market

system this will lead to oligopoly or monopoly as firms expands to take advantage of the scale economies. However, Canning, 1989, shows that under free entry with a Cobb-Douglas production function the zero profit condition gives a number of firms which depends only on the degree of returns to scale ($\alpha + \beta + \gamma$) and not on relative prices. It follows that the number of firms in the economy is fixed over time, growth coming in the form of increases in the size of firms. Since firms are assumed identical it follows that pricing leads to the same allocation as an equal allocation.

The effect of this pricing of the public sector good is exactly the same as a tax on output; it transfers income from the private sector to the public sector and so lowers private sector investment. These two effects need not cancel however. Under increasing returns each factor earns less than its marginal product (marginal products exceed average products) so even if public capital is hired out at its market clearing price the effect on output will still increase with its level.

While the short run equation holds with user charges the long run evolution of the system may be very different depending on how the user charges are spent. In particular we do not assume optimal user charges and optimal accumulation of public capital.

## 3. - The Data (1)

In the cross section regressions we use data provided by Barro [3] and add our infrastructure variables; details of these are given below.

---

(1) Data *Sources*: *a) Telephones, primary source is: ATT: The World's Telephones*, various issues. (1961, 1971, 1981, 1989); secondary source: INTERNATIONAL TELECOMMUNICATIONS UNION: *Yearbook of Common Carrier Statistics*, Geneva, 1975: GATT: *Statistical Yearbook*.

*b) Electricity*, UNITED NATIONS: *Energy Statistics Yearbook*, various years, New York.

*c) Roads*, Main source: INTERNATIONAL ROAD FEDERATION: *World Road Statistics*, various issues, Washington, (DC). Also. UN: *Statistical Yearbook for Asia and the Pacific*; UN: *Statistical Yearbook for Latin America*; UN: *Statistical Yearbook for Africa*; UN: *Annual Bulletin of Transport Statistics for Europe*.

*d) Railways*, Main sources: MITCHEL B.: *Historical Statistics for Europe*; *Historical Statistics for Africa and Asia*; *Historical Statistics for Latin America*; other

In the panel data regressions we construct our own data set. GDP figures are from the Summers and Heston ICP project, and measured in 1985 international prices. Since our interest is to measure the contribution of infrastructure to growth it is natural to use as a dependant variable a measure of productivity, such as GDP per worker, rather than GDP per capita. To avoid the endogeneity problem associated with the growth of GDP per worker (numbers working may respond to productivity and wages), we use GDP per person of working age, deflating the Summers and Heston measures by the series of population between the ages of 14 and 65 taken from the World Bank social indicators. The growth rates represent average yearly growth, in percentage terms, over the relevant decade (1960-1970, 1970-1980, 1980-1988).

We used both a stock and a flow measure for education as a proxy for human capital. EDT measures the average years of education of the population of working age, as calculated by the 1991 *World Development Report*. It is only available for 68 developing countries. *PRIM* and *SEC* measure the proportion of the relevant age group enrolled in primary and secondary schools. Because of repeaters, these rates can exceed 100%.

Our infrastructure measures fall under three categories: telecommunication, electricity, transportation.

Total number of telephones per person (or person of working age in panel regressions), *TEL*, is our main measure of the level of telecommunication infrastructure. Although there is an argument in favor of using main lines as the basic measure of infrastructure capital, the relation between receivers and main lines is reasonably linear, and the data coverage is much more complete for numbers of telephones. Telephones per capita seems the correct measure since access to a telephone is a rival good. However, once we have access there are network externalities due to other people being linked up to

sources, THE ECONOMIST: *The World in Figures*, London, 1982; UN: *Statistical Year Book for Africa*; *Statistical Yearbook for Asia*.

  *e)* Other, GDP: SUMMERS R. - HESTON A. [18]; *COUP, ASSASS*: ALBERTO ALESINA and PAUL SWAGEL (Harvard University); *POP*, WORLD BANK; *PPPIDEV*: calculated from *International Comparison Project Data*; *PRIM, SEC, EDT*: BARRO [3] and WORLD BANK; Population of working age: WORLD BANK; *Area*: WORLD BANK; *ZOIL*: UN: *Energy Statistics Yearbook*, New York.

the system and congestion externalities   due to others using the system. In our panel data analysis we try to capture these effects.

In 1960 our sample of countries had an average of just under 5 telephones per 100 people with a standard deviation of around 8 (the maximum was in the USA with 41 telephones per 100 people). The number of telephones per capita tends to rise with GDP per capita as shown in the following regression for 1960:

$$\log TEL = -\ 4.810\ +\ 1.762\ \log GDP$$
$$(0.087)\quad (0.085)$$
$$R^2 = 0.84\quad N = 87$$

Standard errors in all cross section regressions use White's hetroscedasticity adjustment to give robust standard errors.

Telephones per capita rise with income per capita, but faster than proportionately; doubling income per capita tends to raise telephones per capita by a factor of about three.

Given the close relationship between all our infrastructure variables and GDP per capita there is the possibility that our measures simply act as proxies for GDP; in our analysis we shall try to control for this effect.

Total electricity generating capacity, *EGC*, measures the net installed capacity of electric generating plants per person (in panel regressions we use people of working age). It is measured in kilowatts per person. The sample mean for 1960 was 0.18 and the standard deviation 0.32. Regressing log electricity capacity per capita on log GDP per capita gives similar results as for telephones:

$$\log EGC = -\ 3.462\ +\ 1.681\ \log GDP\quad R^2 = 0.66\quad N = 83$$
$$(0.131)\quad (0.114)$$

For our transportation measures we use road length divided by effective area, *RD*, and railroad line length divided by effective area, *RR* (units of both are km per km$^2$) as a measure of transportation infrastructure. Total road measurement is somewhat problematic as measurement appears to vary across countries and over time. Many countrics show an absolute decline in total roads reported between 1960 and 1970 as they stopped including unpaved rural ways and/or urban roads as part of stated total road stock. Using the percentage of total road that is paved, *PPV*%, attempts to adjust for quality differences in road stocks.

The relationship between roads and the GDP per capita is quite weak. However, the following regression, which shows the relationship between road length, *R*, area of country, *A*, density of population, *D*, and *GDP* per capita seems to provide quite a good fit:

$$\log R = -\ 3.820\ +\ 0.930\ \log A\ +\ 0.689\ \log D\ +\ 0.928\ \log GDP$$
$$(0.905)\quad (0.058)\qquad\quad (0.077)\qquad\qquad (0.126)$$

$$R^2 = 0.84\quad N = 62$$

This regression suggests that road length is linear in country area and increases with GDP per capita and density of population. Our basic measure of the provision of road services is road density; roads divided by area. This assumes that access to places is what firms want and that there are no congestion externalities in the use of roads. This fails to work very well and the equation above suggests that this may be because the road density simply acts as a proxy for population density once we have controlled for the level of GDP per capita. Various other methods of measuring provision of road services were attempted (dividing by population or GDP) but none made roads have a significant effect. It may be that road services depend not only on density of roads but also on the distribution of population (e.g. percentage urbanized) in ways that we have been unable to capture.

Our main political variable, *COUP*, measures the average yearly number of successful and unsuccessful coup attempts over the decade. It is a proxy for political stability, which can be interpreted as a broad measure of property rights protection. It is similar to Barro's coup and revolution measure. Another political variable, also used by Barro, is the number of political assassinations, *ASSASS*. Since this is harder to interpret, and does not seem to play an important role in our panel regression we dropped it and limited our analysis of the importance of political factors to *COUP*.

As a measure of market distortion we follow Barro and use *PPPIDEV*, the country's absolute deviation from the sample mean price of investment goods measured at purchasing power parity exchange rates.

## 4. - Cross Section Results

We begin, for comparison purposes, by running the regression used by Barro [3] to explain growth rates of per capita GDP over the period 1960-1985 in a cross section of 98 countries, but adding our infrastructure variables. One advantage of this is that it allows direct comparison with his results. Another is that by fixing, *a priori*, a specification of the regression equation the hypothesis tests on the coefficients on our infrastructure variables do not suffer from the bias induced by "data mining"; the trying a large number of rival specifications and searching for significant results. The results are shown in regressions $C1$ to $C5$ which appear in table 1*a*.

In regression $C1$, we replicate Barro's equation 1 (2). *GDP*60 is GDP per capita in 1960 and has a negative effect on growth rates over the period. *SEC*60 and *PRIM*60 are secondary and primary school enrolment rates in 1960 respectively; these proxy for human capital. Each has a positive effect on growth rates. *HSGOV* is the average share of Government consumption in GDP over the period; we can think of this as a proxy for the average tax rate. *REV* and *ASSASS* are political variables measuring the number of revolutions (or coup d'etat) and political assassinations over the period. *PPPIDEV* measures the absolute deviation of the real price of investment goods in the country relative to the sample average and proxies for distortions in the economy. Standard errors are given in parentheses (these are calculated using White's hetroskedastic robust method); the number of observations and adjusted $R^2$ are given below each regression.

---

(2) The results are slightly different from those reported by Barro due to the fact that the data we used for Government spending includes education and defence, while his Government spending variable excludes these components.

TABLE 1*a*

CROSS SECTION REGRESSIONS
(dependent variable: annual average percentage growth rate 1960-1985)

| | Regression number | | | | |
|---|---|---|---|---|---|
| | $C1$ | $C2$ | $C3$ | $C4$ | $C5$ |
| $C$ .............. | 3.027 (0.808) | 2.680 (0.839) | 3.174 (0.870) | 2.889 (1.115) | 2.939 (0.828) |
| $GDP$........... | −0.666 (0.110) | −0.874 (0.162) | − 0.800 (0.134) | −0.741 (1.154) | −0.606 (0.119) |
| $SEC$ ........... | 3.221 (0.852) | 2.721 (0.859) | 3.080 (0.771) | 4.204 (1.414) | 3.316 (0.791) |
| $PRIM$ ......... | 2.433 (0.613) | 2.956 (0.617) | 2.595 (0.631) | 1.696 (1.050) | 1.870 (0.659) |
| $G/Y$........... | −8.083 (2.586) | −8.242 (2.898) | −10.223 (3.127) | −9.681 (2.974) | −7.611 (2.593) |
| $REV$........... | −1.997 (0.667) | −1.835 (0.616) | − 1.619 (0.631) | −0.501 (0.627) | −1.806 (0.678) |
| $ASSASS$ ........ | −0.312 (0.208) | −0.272 (0.211) | − 0.274 (0.212) | −0.603 (0.267) | −0.226 (0.213) |
| $PPPIDEV$ ...... | −1.459 (0.523) | −0.839 (0.733) | − 1.316 (0.555) | −0.336 (0.650) | −1.316 (0.623) |
| $TEL$........... | — | 5.441 (2.645) | — | — | — |
| $EGC$........... | — | — | 1.015 (0.452) | — | — |
| $ROAD$ ......... | — | — | — | 0.150 (0.321) | — |
| $PAV\%$ ......... | — | — | — | 0.0125 (0.006) | — |
| $RAIL$ ......... | — | — | — | — | 3.889 (3.180) |
| $N$.............. | 96 | 88 | 83 | 55 | 85 |
| $R^2$ ........... | 0.465 | 0.471 | 0.503 | 0.419 | 0.414 |

In regression $C2$ we add telephones per capita, $TEL$; in regression $C3$ we add electricity generating capacity per capita, $EGC$; in $C4$ our road variables, road length divided by area, excluding wilderness, $ROAD$, and percentage roads paved, $PPV\%$; and in $C5$ we add railway length divided by area, $RAIL$. All these variables relate to 1960 levels. The telephone and electricity levels are deflated by total population to make them comparable with the dependant variable which is growth of GDP per capita. Note that adding these variables tends to reduce the sample size; infrastructure date is not available for all 98 countries (the base regression, $C1$, is run for the 96 countries for which at least one infrastructure measure is present).

The results suggest that the infrastructure variables have the right sign (positive) and are statistically significant. The coefficient on telephones per capita in regression $C2$ has a $t$-statistic of 2.01, which means that the hypothesis that the effect of telephones on growth is positive cannot be rejected at the 95% significance level. The coefficient on telephones per person is 5.4 indicating that increasing telephone coverage to an additional 10% (just over 1 standard deviation for the sample) of the population raises the growth rate of per capita GDP by 0.5% a year. The advantage the USA has gained from its telephone stock as compared to a country with no telephones in 1960 (e.g. Nepal) is estimated to be around 2% growth per year.

The coefficient on electricity per capita in regression $C3$ has a $t$-statistic of 2.24 which indicates that we cannot reject the hypothesis that electricity generating capacity has a positive impact on growth rates at the 95% confidence level. An increase in the level of electricity generating capacity per capita by 1 standard deviation of the sample distribution raises the growth rate by about 0.3% per year.

In regression $C4$, road length divided by area has a positive coefficient but is statistically insignificant; however, the $t$-statistic on the coefficient of $PPV\%$ is 2.14, which means the hypothesis that percentage road paved increases growth rates cannot be rejected at the 95% significance level. The coefficient of 0.012 indicates that paving all of a country's roads increases its growth rate of GDP per capita by about 1.2% a year.

As we mentioned above there is a possibility that our infrastructure variables are merely proxying for GDP per capita. Indeed, given the unreliability of the GDP estimates for some developing countries the infrastructure measures may be better proxies than the GDP figures. The first argument against this is that the coefficients on our infrastructure variables are the wrong sign; if they merely proxy GDP we would expect them to have a negative effect on growth rates.

However, a second possibility is that they are picking up a non-linear GDP effect. Barro [3] finds that if a GDP squared term is added to the regression it has a positive sign, indicating that the effect of higher GDP in reducing growth becomes less pronounced at high levels of GDP. Since our infrastructure variables do tend to rise faster than GDP (in fact almost as fast as GDP squared) we could be picking up a spurious result due to this correlation. In order to avoid this possibility we use constructed the deviation of our infrastructure levels per capita from the predicted levels, given GDP, from our log equations. The results are reported in table 1*b* which shows that the deviations of infrastructure levels from those predicted given GDP levels remain significant explanatory variables for growth rates.

TABLE 1*b*

CROSS SECTION REGRESSIONS
(dependent variable: annual average percentage growth rate 1960-1985)

|  | Regression number | |
|---|---|---|
|  | C6 | C7 |
| C .......................... | 2.603 | 3.123 |
|  | (0.823) | (0.861) |
| GDP ..................... | −0.674 | − 0.675. |
|  | (0.111) | (0.105) |
| SEC....................... | 2.532 | 3.032 |
|  | (0.890) | (0.779) |
| PRIM ..................... | 2.880 | 2.536 |
|  | (0.601) | (0.633) |
| G/Y....................... | −8.282 | − 10.224 |
|  | (2.888) | (3.102) |
| REV....................... | −1.785 | − 1.592 |
|  | (0.614) | (0.629) |
| ASSASS ................... | −0.307 | − 0.293 |
|  | (0.212) | (0.212) |
| PPPIDEV ................. | −0.803 | − 1.297 |
|  | (0.733) | (0.558) |
| DIFTEL ................... | 6.403 | — |
|  | (2.880) |  |
| DIFEGC ................... | — | 1.045 |
|  |  | (0.433) |
| N......................... | 88 | 83 |
| $R^2$ ....................... | 0.472 | 0.503 |

## 5. - Cross Section Versus Panel Data

Most of the work that has been carried out in this area has relied on cross section data from a number of countries. We have reported results of this type using growth rates for the period 1960-1985. We also use the panel data approach, splitting the time period into three sub-periods, 1960-1970, 1970-1980, 1980-1988. The panel data approach has two major advantages; it adds to our data set, more than tripling our number of observations, and, more importantly, it allows us to take into account, to some extent, the problem of missing explanatory variables. For example, technical progress may be linked to a country's protection of intellectual property rights. The Government's anti-trust policy may determine the degree of monopoly power in the economy and may have implications for the rate of innovation. If these missing explanatory variables are correlated with the variables we use, our parameter estimates will be biased. The evidence for missing explanatory variables in cross section growth regressions is strong; in particular, Barro [3] finds large and significant coefficients on continent dummies in his regressions, while Durlauf and Johnson [7] argue that different countries may have different intercept terms reflecting different long run equilibrium positions. The panel data approach may, therefore, overcome some of the criticisms voiced by Levine and Renelt [13] who argue that many existing cross section studies of growth suffer from misspecification bias, and their results are sensitive to the inclusion of extra explanatory variables.

Using panel data we can think of country $i$'s growth rate at time $t$, $g_{it}$, as being determined by:

$$g_{it} = a_i + d_t + b' X_{it} + \varepsilon_{it}$$

where: $a_i$ is a country fixed effect, $d_t$ is a time period dummy, $X_{it}$ is a vector of exogenous variables, $b'$ is a vector of parameters, and $\varepsilon_{it}$ is an independent, identically distributed, normal, error term.

The great advantage of this formulation is that the country fixed effect controls for any missing exogenous variables that affect the growth rate that are constant in the country over the time period being considered. To take a simple example, suppose we run a cross section regression on growth rates using only initial GDP as an explanatory variable. As Barro notes, there is little correlation between growth rates and initial GDP and we get an insignificant $t$-statistic in our regression. However, when Barro adds education and political variables to the regression, the effect of GDP is significant and negative; leaving out these variables biases the coefficient on GDP upwards because of the positive effect of education on growth and the positive correlation between initial GDP and education levels.

Regressions *P1* and *P2* give some simple results using panel data. The regressions were run on 342 data points representing 3 data points on 115 countries (3 countries having missing data for 1960). The dependent variable is the annual average percentage growth rate of per capita GDP over the period (this is Barro's variable *GR6085*, multiplied by 100 to give a percentage). The independent variables are *GDP*, the GDP per capita at the beginning of the period, $D_{60}$ a dummy representing the period 1960-1970 and e $D_{70}$ a dummy representing the period 1970-1980. The term *Fix* indicates that 114 country specific dummies, representing fixed effects, were included in the regression; these are not reported though country fixed effects are large and significant for many countries in all of our panel data regressions. Standard errors are given in parentheses.

$$(P1) \quad GR = -0.048 + 0.0870\ GDP + 2.98\ D_{60} + 2.65\ D_{70}$$
$$\quad\quad (0.319) \quad (0.0463) \quad\quad\quad (0.37) \quad\quad (0.36)$$
$$R^2 = 0.19 \quad N = 342 \quad DF = 338$$

$$(P2) \quad GR = Fix - 0.5278\ GDP + 1.83\ D_{60} + 2.01\ D_{70}$$
$$\quad\quad (0.1450) \quad\quad\quad (0.43) \quad\quad (0.35)$$
$$R^2 = 0.58 \quad N = 342 \quad DF = 224$$

When we run our panel data regressions using only intial GDP levels as our exogenous variable, and without the fixed effects, the coefficient on GDP is insignificant and positive (i.e. the wrong sign). Once we add the fixed effects, however, the coefficient on GDP becomes significant and negative and has a coefficient similar to that found by Barro.

The education variables are reasonably steady within each country over the period and their effect is, to a large extent, picked up by the country fixed effect, removing the bias on the parameter estimate on GDP. Later in our analysis we will add human capital variables, but we shall see that they add little to the country fixed effects. Note that the country fixed effects improve the fit of the equation significantly. The time period dummies tend to be significantly positive for both the 1960s, and the 1970s, relative to the 1980s, indicating that both these periods had higher average growth rates than the 1980s. The 1980s were indeed a period of slow growth worldwide, with an average growth rate of per capita GDP across countries of 0.3% per annum, compared with 3.1% in the 1960s and 2.9% in the 1970s. Again these time dummies can be thought of as allowing for missing exogenous variables, variables which are constant across countries within a time period. These might be variables such as international interest rates, commodity prices, or general international demand conditions.

While the panel data approach has the advantage of correcting for missing explanatory variables, it suffers from the problem that 10 years may not be long enough for supply side effects to dominate the demand side disturbances countries suffer. For example, if 1970 is the peak of a boom in a country, the growth rate will appear high for the period 1960-1970 and low for the period 1970-1980. Measuring short run growth rates peak to trough or trough to peak gives quite different results. These demand side disturbances will bias our parameter estimates; our estimates might be consistent in the sense that in a very large sample (in the sense of many time periods), we would expect no correlation between the demand side shocks and the supply side explanatory variables, but in small samples chance correlations will be present. To some extent, our time dummies will capture the demand side disturbances which are international, but this leaves open the possibility that there are cross sectional correlations between supply side variables and the demand shocks; e.g. the effect of international demand shocks may be correlated with our measure of openness to international trade.

To a large extent, it is a matter of judgement whether the increased bias due to demand side effects in panel data outweighs the reduction in bias due to correcting for omitted country specific explanatory variables.

## 6. - Panel Data Results for Telephones and Electricity

We begin by trying to find an appropriate "base" equation to which we will add our infrastructure variables. Table 2 shows a number of regression run on our panel data. The dependent variable is average annual percentage growth of GDP per person of working age. As argued above, this is more appropriate than per capita measures. In regression *P3* the varible GDP, the beginning of period GDP per capita of working age, has a significant and negative effect. *PPPIDEV* is the absolute size of the percentage deviation of the investment price in the country from the period average of the sample which Barro argues picks up price distortions within the economy. This has a robustly significant and negative effect on growth rates in our panel equations. We tried several political variables but only the political variable *COUP*, average number of coups per annum, seemed robust. *ZOIL* is the value of a country's oil production at the end of the period, minus its value at the beginning of the period, divided by its initial total GDP. This is a proxy for the contribution to growth of GDP over the period which comes from oil, either in the form of higher oil prices or increased oil production.

This variable tends to be positive for oil producers in the 1970-1980 period but negative for the 1980-1988 period, due to the rise in the real oil price over the 1970s and its fall over the 1980s, though a few countries do go against the trend due to depletion, or discovery, of oil reserves. Adding this variable as exogenous implies that we treat oil revenues as an exogenous "gift" to a country. This variable proved significant in all our panel regressions. The time period dummies $D^{60}$ and $D^{70}$ are always significant and positive.

Equation *P3* shows that the beginning of period human capital, proxied by average years of schooling of the work force, *EDT*, is insignificant in the regression including country fixed effects. In regression *P4*, without the country fixed effects, it has a significant positive coefficient. Using the flow variables *PRIM* and *SEC* give

TABLE 2

PANEL REGRESSION: BASE REGRESSIONS
(dependent variable: decade average percentage annual growth rates)

| | Regression number | | |
|---|---|---|---|
| | P3 | P4 | P5 |
| C .................... | fixed effects | − 0.613 (0.617) | fixed effects |
| GDP .............. | − 1.664 (0.518) | − 0.129 (0.258) | − 0.899 (0.210) |
| GDP² .............. | 0.066 (0.031) | 0.008 (0.020) | 0.017 (0.006) |
| PPPIDEV ........... | − 1.510 (0.495) | − 0.182 (0.245) | − 1.400 (0.479) |
| COUP .............. | − 2.091 (0.811) | − 1.211 (0.664) | − 1.695 (0.698) |
| EDT................. | − 0.096 (0.403) | 0.285 (0.124) | — |
| ZOIL .............. | 2.581 (1.711)ʳ | 6.054 (1.570) | 6.080 (1.156) |
| $D_{60}$ ................. | 1.210 (0.946) | 3.237 (0.501) | 1.568 (0.466) |
| $D_{70}$ ................. | 1.373 (0.609) | 2.054 (0.479) | 1.337 (0.354) |
| N .................... | 178 | 178 | 317 |
| DF ................. | 110 | 169 | 202 |
| $R^2$ ................. | 0.65 | 0.29 | 0.64 |

similar results, they tend to have a positive effect without the country dummies, but this effect becomes insignificant, or even significantly negative, when the country fixed effects are added.

Our interpretation of these results is that the human capital variable is slow moving and most of its effect is already captured by the country specific fixed effects. Similarly, the education flow variables have much more cross sectional than time series variability. In addition, the negative results on the impact of primary education can be explained by standard human capital theory. The long run level of education in a country is captured by the fixed effect. Increases in primary or secondary education enrollment rates within a particular country represent mainly an investment in the future which have costs in terms of increased expenditure and reduced labor availability today. It is these changes in education levels which our model is picking up once the fixed effect has taken account of the cross sectional differences in the level of education. For these reasons, we omit the education variables and rely on the fixed effects in our regressions.

Similarly, the share of Government GDP, which shows up significantly in cross section regressions, becomes insignificant in panel data regression with our fixed effects included. Again this share variable is relatively slow moving and its cross sectional explanatory power is picked up by the fixed effect.

In all the regressions a term $GDP^2$, the square of GDP per capita of working age, proves to have a significant and positive effect on growth rates. The idea of this term is that the effect of GDP per capita on growth may be non-linear. The significant coefficient on this square term suggests that raising the GDP per capita level does slow growth, but that this effect is most marked at low levels of GDP per capita. This is compatible with both the technology catchup story, and the diminishing productivity of capital story; technology catchup may be faster the further behind a country lags in technology, and the marginal productivity of capital falls with GDP per capita, but at a decreasing rate. This squared term is retained though its significance is marginal in some of our regressions with infrastructure.

In regressions *P3* and *P4* the inclusion of the human capital term, *EDT*, restricts our sample to developing countries. Regression *P5* reports our base equation, the absence of the *EDT* variable gives it a much wider coverage than *P3* and *P4*. Our theory suggests that we add the growth of population of working age; more workers dilute the capital stock per person and tend to reduce output per capita. Including this variable in the regression did produce significant and negative effects on growth rates with a coefficient of just below one. However, rerunning our infrastructure regressions including the growth rate of working age population did not change the results significantly and introduces to possibility of endogeneity; growth of per capita income may cause population growth (though population of working age should be less sensitive to current growth rates than total population).

TABLE 3

ELECTRICITY AND TELEPHONES PANEL REGRESSIONS
(dependent variable: decade average percentage annual growth rates)

| | Regression number | | | |
|---|---|---|---|---|
| | P6 | P7 | P8 | P9 |
| GDP | −1.085 | −0.855 | −1.516 | −1.726 |
| | (0.218) | (0.243) | (0.234) | (0.278) |
| $GDP^2$ ......... | 0.020 | −0.005 | 0.021 | 0.021 |
| | (0.008) | (0.013) | (0.006) | (0.007) |
| PPPIDEV ...... | −1.844 | −1.908 | −1.575 | −1.521 |
| | (0.463) | (0.460) | (0.460) | (0.457) |
| COUP ......... | −1.754 | −1.768 | −2.252 | −2.365 |
| | (0.675) | (0.674) | (0.724) | (0.724) |
| ZOIL ......... | 6.108 | 5.004 | 3.953 | 3.319 |
| | (1.220) | (1.305) | (1.463) | (1.474) |
| EGC........... | 1.354 | −0.413 | — | — |
| | (0.475) | (1.250) | | |
| EGC*GDP...... | — | −0.250 | — | — |
| | | (0.111) | | |
| $EGC^2$ ......... | — | −0.360 | — | — |
| | | (0.195) | | |
| TEL........... | — | — | 11.490 | 10.144 |
| | | | (2.161) | (5.780) |
| TEL*GDP ...... | — | — | — | 0.861 |
| | | | | (0.407) |
| $TEL^2$ ......... | — | — | — | −11.897 |
| | | | | (5.253) |
| $D_{60}$ ........... | 1.978 | 2.016 | 1.338 | 1.141 |
| | (0.477) | (0.483) | (0.496) | (0.498) |
| $D_{70}$ ........... | 1.492 | 1.601 | 1.588 | 1.519 |
| | (0.340) | (0.342) | (0.373) | (0.371) |
| N.............. | 294 | 294 | 292 | 292 |
| DF ........... | 180 | 178 | 176 | 174 |
| $R^2$ ........... | 0.70 | 0.70 | 0.70 | 0.71 |

Table 3 shows the results of adding electricity and telephone variables to our base equation *P5*. Equations *P6* and *P7* analyze the effect of electricity generating capacity per capita. As in the cross section regressions, electricity per capita has a significant effect on growth rates (it's *t* value is 2.85). This variable also improves the fit of the equation significantly. Adding our interactive term with GDP per capita and a squared term in electricity capacity per capita shows that both these terms are significant (with $t$ values 2.25 and 1.84 respectively), but the linear term becomes insignificant.

Regression *P6* shows the results of adding *TEL*, telephones per person of working age, to our base equation. The telephone variable is significant (with a $t$-statistic of 5.32) and there is a significant improvement of fit in the equation. The coefficient on *TEL* of 11.49 indicates that increasing the coverage of telephones by an additional 10% of people of working age increases a country's growth rate by about 1.1% per annum. This is almost exactly the same as the coefficient found in the cross section regressions, since the population of working age is around half of total population. In equation *P7*, we add a squared term in telephones per capita and an interactive term with GDP per capita. The interactive term with GDP per capita is significantly positive (a $t$-statistic of 2.12), indicating that telephones contribute more to growth at higher levels of GDP. However, the squared term is significantly negative ($t$-statistic of 2.26), indicating diminishing marginal effect of telephones per capita on growth. The effect of the level of telephones remains significantly positive at the 95% level ($t$-statistic of 1.76). Telephones appear to be able, to some extent, to raise growth rates on their own, even at low levels of GDP per capita, though effectiveness increases with GDP. On the other hand electricity capacity appears to work as a source of growth only if a country has a reasonably high level of GDP per capita.

One problem with interpreting these results is the possibility that our infrastructure variables are merely better measures of GDP than the official GDP figures and are therefore simply proxies for GDP per capita of working age rather than infrastructure per capita. We expect GDP per capita to have a negative effect on growth, so the positive effects we find with our infrastructure variables appear to undermine this view. However, the term in GDP squared turns our to be positive and significant in equation *P5*. It may be the case that our infrastructure variables vary non-linearly with GDP per capita and therefore amount to adding another non-linear GDP per capita term to our regression. That is, we pick up a spurious correlation due to omitting the correct non-linear GDP term.

In order to investigate this possibility, we regressed the log of our infrastructure variables against the log of GDP per capita of working age.

*(P10)*          $\log TEL = -\ 5.932\ +\ 1.863 \log GDP$
                    $(0.080)\quad (0.048)$
                    $R^2 = 0.83\quad N = 310$

*(P11)*          $\log EGC = -\ 11.104\ +\ 1.712 \log GDP$
                    $(0.094)\quad (0.058)$
                    $R^2 = 0.74\quad N = 311$

The results are in equations *P10* and *P11*. The results for telephones are in line with those reported by Saunders, Warford and Wellenius [17] (3). These regressions show that the infrastructure variables and GDP per capita do move together; the fit of the equations seems quite good. The relationship is non linear; the coefficients on GDP per capita indicate that infrastructure levels rise more than proportionately with GDP but not quite as fast as GDP squared. It is therefore possible that these variables are merely picking up a non-linear GDP term; though the inclusion of $GDP^2$ in our regressions should largely correct for this effect.

In order to further investigate the possibility of spurious correlation, we used the predicted values from equations *P10* and *P11* to create the difference between actual infrastructure levels and those expected given GDP per capita and then used these deviation measures, *DEVEGC* and *DEVTEL* as explanatory variables in regressions *P12* and *P13*. These show that deviations of actual infrastructure levels from the expected levels, given GDP per capita of working age, of both telephones and electricity do have a significant effect on growth rates (*t*-statistics of 3.21 and 6.13 respectively). The coefficients are very similar to those found in the regressions *P6* and *P8*. This is not surprising since regressions *P6* and *P8* give the effect of our infrastructure variables that is orthogonal to both GDP and $GDP^2$; these correct for the dependence of infrastructure on GDP. However, regressions which omitted $GDP^2$ would seriously overestimate the

---

(3) Regressions of this type have been used to predict the demand for telephones and electricity.

TABLE 4

ELECTRICITY AND TELEPHONE RESIDUALS PANEL REGRESSION
(dependent variable: decade average percentage annual growth rates)

|  | Regression number | |
|---|---|---|
|  | *P*12 | *P*13 |
| *GDP* ..................... | − 1.264 | − 1.650 |
|  | (0.243) | (0.231) |
| *GDP*$^2$ ..................... | 0.034 | 0.046 |
|  | (0.008) | (0.007) |
| *PPPIDEV* ................. | − 1.924 | − 1.629 |
|  | (0.473) | (0.462) |
| *COUP* .................... | − 1.775 | − 2.364 |
|  | (0.689) | (0.729) |
| *ZOIL* .................... | 10.000 | 5.100 |
|  | (1.700) | (2.200) |
| *DEV TEL* ................. | — | 12.807 |
|  |  | (2.089) |
| *DEV EGC* ................. | 1.551 | — |
|  | (0.482) |  |
| *D*$_{60}$ ...................... | 1.838 | 1.246 |
|  | (0.493) | (0.501) |
| *D*$_{70}$ ...................... | 1.559 | 1.653 |
|  | (0.348) | (0.373) |
| *N* ......................... | 294 | 292 |
| *DF* ....................... | 180 | 176 |
| *R*$^2$ ....................... | 0.68 | 0.69 |

effect of infrastructure on growth rates, since, by regressions *P12* and *P13*, infrastructure variables are a reasonable proxy for *GDP*$^2$ which, from regression *P5*, has a positive effect on growth rates.

## 7. - Panel Data Results for Roads and Railways

The analysis of the previous section on the effects of infrastructure on growth rates can also be carried out for railways and roads. However, there is a problem in choosing the right deflator to measure the "quantity" of railways and roads per person in a country. We analyze the case of roads.

Large countries, with low population densities may have more roads per capita, merely to cover the extra distance between communities and households. These roads are required to overcome the extra need for roads; they do not provide more "road services" in terms of added communication between agents. In terms of the effects on growth rates, it is the "road services" per capita we wish to measure since this measures communication between agents and it is this communication, and note the roads themselves, which causes growth. Note that this implies that a densely populated country has a natural advantage since with fewer roads it can provide as good a transportation system as a large, low population density, country.

Regression *P14* suggests that our cross section equation for roads also fits the panel data reasonably well:

$$(P14) \quad \log R = -\ 3.540 + 0.909 \log A + 0.688 \log GDP +$$
$$(0.446) \quad (0.030) \qquad (0.049)$$
$$+\ 0.612 \log D$$
$$(0.040)$$

with: $\qquad\qquad\qquad R^2 = 0.81 \quad N = 277$

where $R$ is the total length of roads. Controlling for GDP per capita of working age, *GDP*, and population density, *D*, roads are approximately linear in area, *A* (in fact we use "effective" area, removing wilderness regions).

Applying this analysis of railroads suggests that it too should be measured as rail length divided by area. However, few countries are building railways; the length of line declines in almost all countries which have railways over the period. This suggests that the marginal social value of railways is less than their current cost of construction, the stock is simply an inheritance that is being run down. A regression like *P14* does not fit very well; railways appear to be historical accident rather than response to current needs. Assuming that roads and railways are substitutes, we might combine them into an aggregate transport infrastructure variable. Here, however, we treat them separately but in the same way as roads in terms of deflators.

TABLE 5

RAILWAYS AND ROADS PANEL REGRESSION
(dependent variable: decade average percentage annual growth rates)

| | Regression number | | | |
|---|---|---|---|---|
| | *P*14 | *P*15 | *P*16 | *P*17 |
| *GDP* | −1.076 | −1.217 | −0.724 | −0.831 |
| | (0.214) | (0.223) | (0.281) | (0.307) |
| *GDP*$^2$ ......... | 0.023 | 0.023 | 0.010 | 0.010 |
| | (0.006) | (0.006) | (0.007) | (0.007) |
| *PPPIDEV* ...... | −1.305 | −1.163 | −2.103 | −2.092 |
| | (0.482) | (0.492) | (0.502) | (0.500) |
| *COUP* ......... | −1.778 | −1.807 | −1.642 | −1.662 |
| | (0.683) | (0.680) | (0.883) | (0.882) |
| *ZOIL* ......... | 8.413 | 7.927 | 4.088 | 3.940 |
| | (1.368) | (1.378) | (1.118) | (1.118) |
| *RAIL* ......... | −41.298 | −107.297 | — | — |
| | (29.520) | (66.939) | | |
| *RAIL* * *GDP* .... | — | 4.562 | — | — |
| | | (2.146) | | |
| *RAIL*$^2$ ......... | — | 327.310 | — | — |
| | | (341.935) | | |
| *ROAD* ......... | — | — | 0.015 | −3.907 |
| | | | (1.449) | (2.743) |
| *ROAD* * *GDP* .... | — | — | — | 0.124 |
| | | | | (0.128) |
| *ROAD*$^2$ ........ | — | — | — | 0.464 |
| | | | | (0.705) |
| *PPV%* .......... | — | — | 0.025 | 0.017 |
| | | | (0.014) | (0.015) |
| $D_6 0$ ............ | 1.490 | 1.432 | 2.005 | 1.586 |
| | (0.467) | (0.465) | (0.690) | (0.728) |
| $D_7 0$ ............ | 1.220 | 1.224 | 1.670 | 1.504 |
| | (0.348) | (0.346) | (0.392) | (0.401) |
| *N* .............. | 303 | 303 | 233 | 233 |
| *DF* ............ | 187 | 185 | 119 | 117 |
| $R^2$ ............ | 0.67 | 0.68 | 0.75 | 0.75 |

We take *RAIL* and *ROAD*, railroad line length and total road length, each divided by area, as our basic transport variables, and add *PPV%*, percentage of roads that are paved, as an extra variable to adjust for road quality. Regressions *P14* to *P17* in table 5 show our results. The only statistically significant positive results are achieved by railways interacting with GDP in regression *P15* and percentage paved roads in regression *P16*. The fit in the regression using roads is improved markedly over the base regression *P5*, but this may be due to the smaller sample; road data availability is correlated with level of development so regression *P16* is missing some of the poorest countries.

## 8. - Conclusions and Directions for Further Research

Our infrastructure variables, particularly telephones and electricity, have a significant positive effect on growth rates. The effectiveness of roads and railways is more problematic. The results found here are promising. However, a great deal remains to be done.

1) *Data.* More disaggregated data on infrastructure is available and should be used. The failure of roads in our regressions may be due to measurement problems. Roads should be further broken down by quality; this varies greatly and "total" roads appear to have significantly different quality cutoff points in different countries ("new measurement" methods can change a country's "total" road length by a factor of 3 (Canada 1989-1990)). Railway tracks (not just lines), and rolling stock, should be included as railway infrastructure capital. The number of vehicles on the road system and the number of passage miles and ton miles of goods travelled on railways can be included as capacity utilization measures for transport. Electricity generating capacity can be split up by type (coal oil nuclear etc.) and a natural capacity utilization measure, power actually generated is available. We tried using this variable in our panel regressions but it was always insignificant. Telephone main lines, as opposed to number of telephones, are available; when we used main lines, they did not change our results and reduced country coverage considerably. In addition, calls per person are available as a measure of capacity utilization.

2) *Aggregation.* Regressions using our infrastructure variables simultaneously proved to be disappointing. The *t*-statistic levels drop substantially due to multicollinearity between the infrastructure variables. This implies that caution must be used when interpreting the

size of our coefficients on infrastructure, when each is entered independently into regressions; each may be proxying for a wider class of infrastructure, implying that balanced increase in infrastructure is required to achieve the estimated effect. One way around this multicollinearity is to aggregate the infrastructure variables into an infrastructure index. This can be done on the basis of relative prices, which are collecting. Certainly, railways and roads should be aggregated into a transport index.

3) Here we only report replication of Barro's cross section regressions adding our infrastructure variables. We have tried to improve on the Barro regression, both by increasing the data set and specification of the model. In particular moving to GDP per person of working age and including the oil variables improved the fit.

4) *Statistical Issues.* The panel data approach should be tested. The independence of the residuals can be tested. Hetroskedasticity of the residuals in the panel regressions should be tested for and, if found, corrected. Preliminary investigation of the effect of splitting the sample into developed and developing countries indicates that our parameter estimates in the panel equation are robust. Further investigation of varying parameters with different samples is required, but the fixed effects approach appears to be robust to sample selection; the fixed effects already correct for any unobserved exogenous variables that may be correlated with a country's level of development.

5) *Panel versus Cross Section.* We should test the panel data approach against the cross section model; in practice these are the models we must choose from rather than an unspecified alternative hypothesis. We are working on a method of testing the gain from using panel data against the loss it introduces from misspecification due to omitting demand side effects. The similarity of our results, particularly the coefficients found on infrastructure, using the two approaches suggests that our results are robust, however we decide to estimate the relationship.

6) *Investment.* We report only results from growth rate regressions. We need to find the mechanism through which infrastructure works. Preliminary regressions explaining the investment ratio using panel data suggest that without our fixed effects, higher infrastructure levels increase the investment ratio. However, the relationship ap-

pears to be reversed when fixed effects are included. This area requires more work and thought. In addition, sectoral disaggregation, to investigate which sectors respond most to the presence of infrastructure, is required if we are to understand the mechanism by which infrastructure works.

## BIBLIOGRAPHY

[1] ASCHAUER DAVID A.: «Is Public Expenditure Productive?», *Journal of Monetary Economics*, n. 23, 1989.

[2] BARRO ROBERT J.: «Government Spending in a Simple Model of Endogenous Growth», *Journal of Political Economy*, n. 98, 1990.

[3] — —: «Economic Growth in a Cross Section of Countries», *Quarterly Journal of Economics*, vol. 106, May 1991, pp. 407-44.

[4] BARRO ROBERT J. - XAVIER SALA-Y-MARTIN: *Public Finance in Models of Economic Growth*, Harvard University, 1991.

[5] CLARIDA RICHARD H. - RONALD FINDLAY: *Optimal Endogenous Growth, Public Capital, and the Dynamic Gains from Trade*, Columbia University, 1992.

[6] DE LONG J.B. - SUMMERS L.H.: «Equipment Investment and Economic Growth», *Quarterly Journal of Economics*, vol. 106, May 1991, pp. 445-503.

[7] DURLAUF S.N. - JOHNSON P.A.: «Local Versus Global Convergence Across National Economics», LSE Financial Markets Group, *Discussion Paper*, n. 131, 1992.

[8] EBERT RANDALL W.: «Public Infrastructure and Regional Economic Development», *Federal Reserve Bank of Cleveland Economic Review*, 1990.

[9] HERCOWITZ ZVI - GREGORY W. HUFFMAN: *Infrastructure and Growth*, Tel Aviv University, 1990.

[10] HULTEN CHARLES R. - ROBERT M. SCHWAB: *Is There Too Little Public Capital? Infrastructure and Economic Growth*, University of Maryland, 1991.

[11] — — - — —: *Public Capital Formation and the Growth of Regional Manufacturing Industry*, University of Maryland, 1991.

[12] HSIAO C.: «Analysis of Panel Data», *Econometric Society Monograph*, n. 11, Cambridge, Cambridge University Press, 1986.

[13] LEVINE R. - RENELT D.: «Cross Country Studies of Growth and Policy: Methodological, Conceptual and Statistical Problems», World Bank, PRE, *Working Paper*, n. 608, 1991.

[14] MANKIW G.N. - ROMER D. - WEIL D.N.: «A Contribution to the Empirics of Economic Growth», NBER, *Working Paper*, n. 3541, 1990.

[15] MUNNELL ALICIA H.: «Why Has Productivity Growth Declined? Productivity and Public Investment», *New England Economic Review*, January-February 1990.

[16] — —: «How Does Public Infrastructure Affect Regional Economic Performance», *New England Economic Review*, September-October 1990.

[17] SAUNDERS R.J. - WARFORD J.J - WELLENIUS B.: *Telecommunications and Economic Development*, World Bank Publication, Baltimore, John Hopkins University Press, 1983.

[18] SUMMERS ROBERT - HESTON ALAN: «The Peen World Table (Mark 5): An Expanded Set of International Comparisons, 1950-1988», *Quarterly Journal of Economics*, n. CVI, 1991, pp. 327-36.

# Quality, Trade
# and Endogenous Growth

**Luigi Paganetto - Pasquale L. Scandizzo**
Università «Tor Vergata» and Ispe, Roma

## 1. - Introduction

The large differences in the growth rates of productivity among the industrial countries in the 70s have caused a rethinking of the theory of economic growth. Such a rethinking has started from the consideration that the neoclassical theory of growth based on the law of decreasing returns is in contradiction with experience.

If capital goods were free to move, they should go where greater returns are possible, i.e. to the less developed economies, which have higher marginal productivities of capital (Lucas [10]) (*). As a consequence, if countries were similar with respect to the fundamental parameters on preferences and technology the lowest income countries should grow at higher rates than the higher income ones (Barro [4]).

To overcome the difficulty given by the fact that lower income countries in general show a less advanced technology than the more developed ones, the *New Growth Theory* has assumed that growth can be characterized by some form of increasing returns to scale.

Even though the diffusion of knowledge encounters many obstacles, experience shows that those lower income countries that have invested in research and development, have also achieved high and sustained growth rates (Baumol [5]). Technological spillovers, therefore, appear to be able to provide the less developed countries with an opportunity to close the gap with the more developed ones. Their

---

(*) *Advise*: the numbers in square brackets refer to the Bibliography in the appendix.

consumption patterns and their investments, therefore, will have to be accompanied by the introduction of technical progress capable of ensuring increasing returns to scale.

The internationally observable tendency of growth rates not to decline, already mentioned by Kaldor [8] among the "stylized" facts of the economy, depends on the fact that knowledge has a tendency to spread. Moreover, growth rates may not fall because of the circumstance, stressed by Romer [11], that technology spillovers create effects that refer not only to innovative activities, but, in general, to the stock of knowledge.

In his pioneering work Arrow [3] had already showed how, through the learning-by-doing mechanism, the effect of knowledge upon growth is characterized by the capacity to generate increasing returns. Since then, it has been clear that the presence of increasing returns, linked to knowledge accumulation and spillovers, is compatible with a competitive equilibrium with externalities.

The externalities, in fact, are linked to the knowledge spillovers and this permits the analysis of conditions of dynamic competitive equilibrium. On one hand, in fact, we can assume that individual agents solve their maximization problems under conditions of decreasing returns in competitive markets. On the other hand, the individual solutions, once put together, may generate external effects that may cause increasing returns for the whole economy.

The utilization of the Marshallian idea of externalities with increasing returns, therefore, appears an appropriate response to the need to explain the empirical observations on growth rates of productivity and income, the spatial allocation of economic activities, international trade and capital and labour movements.

The role of increasing returns in the interpretation of growth processes, which found its first proposer in A. Smith and was subsequently stressed by Ally Youry [2] was maintained somewhat underground, as recalled by Kaldor [9], by the difficulty of reconciling the hypothesis of increasing returns with competitive equilibrium.

A recent discovery of the *New Growth Theory* is the finding that increasing returns of physical capital and decreasing marginal productivity of knowledge (Romer [12]) allow the interpretation of growth processes within the model of dynamic competitive equilibrium. The idea that knowledge is not completely appropriable, and thus is largely available for anybody's use, appears to be fruitful for explaining a whole series of growth processes based on accumulation of knowledge, spillovers and innovation. In these processes increasing returns arise from self reinforcing loops between the allocation of resources to research and other knowledge producing activities, knowledge spillovers and accumulation, as well as human capital and overall technical progress.

International investment in research and development, in particular, gives rise to a wide variety of new products and technologies, whose effects are much greater than those generated by the individual research projects from which they originate.

This phenomenon, viewed at international level, leads to models of the product cycle, where products originally developed in the North are subsequently transformed in the South (Grossman - Helpman [6]), through processes of learning and imitation. In this perspective, the way in which knowledge is distributed and appropriated at the international level is strongly related to the long term trends of trade and growth.

International trade, in fact, may be seen as way to efficiently re-allocate the employment of resources for research and development, avoiding the overlapping between the various activities. In this context, the role of trade appears crucial with respect to endogenous growth. Imported and exported goods, in fact, may have different knowledge and innovation contents, or they may be expression of specific technologies.

In this paper we present a model, where innovation and knowledge are assumed to be transferred in improvements of product quality, with consequences both on the volume of trade and on technical progress.

The literature on the relationship between quality and exports has underlined the importance of competition for technological supremacy through research and development. The cyclical nature of the processes through which products are born has led to models where, through the analysis of patents, innovations are analyzed, inducing repetitive improvements in product quality. The problem emerging, however, is to represent in a systematic way the sequence through which the innovative process occurs, both at industry and economy-wide level (Grossman - Helpman [7]).

In our model, quality is considered to be an output that competes for resources with quantity, and thus is not independent of the process that produces it. As such, it determines a degree of success in exporting products, that is related to the market power that the new products secure. The quality effect in turn yields increasing returns through the increase in knowledge that is accomplished in the process of innovation. At the same time it stimulates the introduction of innovative technologies that determine economy-wide increases in the productivity of capital.

The paper is organized in three more sections. In the next one, a simple model is proposed that looks at the core of the question of why trade in general, and an export surplus in particular, may be valuable for growth. In the third section, a more complete model of trade and growth is developed with the objective of considering the effects of a more general endogenous loop between quantity, quality, trade and development. Finally, a fourth section proposes some concluding observations.

## 2. - Why Are Exports Valuable?

We first try to clarify what could be the possible value of developing a trade surplus in a growth context, with a very simple model. Consider a country where the $i$-th firm faces a linear homogeneous production function:

$$(1) \qquad Q_i(t) = F_i(K_i(t), L_i(t)) \qquad i = 1, 2,..., N$$

where $K_i$ denotes capital and $L_i$ labour.

Because of scale economies external to the firm, however, the aggregate production function contains a term (for example, a multiplicative shifter) representing an effect arising from the aggregate behaviour of all firms:

$$(2) \qquad Q(t) = A(t) F(K(t), L(t))$$

We assume that the growth of $A(t)$, indicated for short as "technical progress", is, inter alia, function of the country per capita trade surplus, such a relationship depending on the fact that experience in the export markets helps building human capital in a uniquely productive way:

(3)                    $\dot{A}(t) = h(x(t))$        $\delta h/\delta x > 0$

where $\dot{A}$ denotes the derivative with respect to time and $x(t)$ is the per capita net trade surplus, which is constrained by the dynamic relationship:

(4)                    $x(t) = \dot{g}(t) - (\rho - n)g(t)$

where $g(t)$ denotes accumulated credits (or debts if it is negative) with the rest of the world, $\dot{g}$ is its variation over time, $\rho$ the international interest rate and $n$ the growth rate of the labour force $L$.

Equation (4) states that the country in question can freely lend or borrow at the international interest rate $\rho$. In the case of lending, $x(t)$ simply adds in every period to the stock of credits that can be extended to the rest of the world, i.e. the trade surplus is given out against a promise to pay, to be exercised later. In the case of borrowing, the trade surplus is used to reduce the debt burden. The value of the trade surplus, therefore, is to make possible either the postponement or the anticipation of consumption in exchange for an interest payment, given the No Ponzi Game condition:

(5)                    $\lim_{t\to\infty} e^{-\rho t}g(t) = 0$

i.e. given the understanding that the present value of the credits (or the debts) be zero for a sufficiently long time horizon.

Using a basic national accounting identity, we can also write:

(6)        $A(t)f(k(t)) = c(t) + \dot{k}(t) = nk(t) + x(t)$

where lower case letters denote per capita magnitudes. Expression (6) shows that the trade surplus is just a component of final demand and, as such, would have no particular value in an aggregate economy. Equation *(4)*, however, implies that it can be used to change the mix between present and future consumption (first source of value) and equation *(3)* suggests that it generates an externality that accelerates technical progress (second source of value).

At this point we can formulate an intertemporal maximization problem and ask ourselves what are the consequences of these two distinct sources of value on the optimal path of the economic variables. Assume that the intertemporal problem consists in maximizing the present value of the utility of consumption:

(7)  $$\text{Max } U_0 = \int_0^\infty e^{-\rho t} U(c(t)) \, dt$$

where $U(c(t))$ is a concave social welfare function and the maximization is performed under the constraints specified in *(3)*, *(4)*, *(5)* and *(6)*.

Forming the Hamiltonian, we find:

(8)  $$H(t) = e^{-\rho t}[U(c) + p(Af(k) - c - nk - x) + \\ + \lambda((\rho - n)g + x) + \mu h(x)]$$

Necessary and sufficient conditions for a maximum are:

(9)  $$U_c - p = 0 \quad \text{where: } U_c = \delta U/\delta c$$

(10)  $$-p + \lambda + \mu h_x = 0, \quad \text{where: } h_x = \delta h/\delta x$$

(11)  $$\dot{p} = -(A f_k - \rho - n) p$$

(12)  $$\dot{\lambda} = (n - \rho' g) \lambda \quad \text{where: } \rho' = \delta \rho/\delta g < 0$$

or

$$\dot{\lambda} = (n + \varepsilon) \lambda \quad \text{where: } \varepsilon = |\rho'| \frac{g}{\rho}$$

(13)  $$\dot{\mu} = \rho \mu - p f(k)$$

Of these conditions, equation *(9)* is the usual equality between the marginal utility of consumption and the shadow price of investment. Equation *(10)*, which incorporates some of the consequences of the assumption on the "value" of exports for growth, requires that, along the optimum path, the shadow price of investment be equal to the shadow value of the marginal productivity of exports in fostering technical progress plus (minus) the shadow price of foreign credits (debts). Equation *(9)* and *(10)* together, therefore, indicate that consumption, investment and exports should be chosen in such a way as to insure that their marginal values are always equal.

As for the conditions on the time path of shadow prices, equation *(11)* states that the shadow price of investment should fall at a rate equal to the marginal productivity of capital minus the rate of interest minus the rate of population growth. Equation *(12)*, on the other hand, states that the shadow price of foreign credits (debts) should rise at a rate equal to the sum of the rate of population growth and the rate of interest corrected for the absolute value of its elasticity with respect to the size of the credits (debts) extended.

Finally, equation *(13)* states that the shadow price of human capital increases at a rate equal to the difference between the product between the interest rate and the same shadow price, which represents debt servicing per unit of technical progress achieved, and the average value of output per unit of the human capital stock accumulated. In other words, the marginal value of investment in human capital $\dot{A}$ rises with the interest rate and falls with the average product of human capital, evaluated at the shadow price.

By differentiating *(9)* w.r.t. $c$, and using *(9)* and *(11)*:

$$(14) \qquad U_{cc} \cdot c + (A f_k - \rho - n) U_c = 0$$

Defining as:
$$\eta = - \frac{U_{cc}}{U_c} c$$

the elasticity of marginal utility of income, we can solve:

$$(15) \qquad \frac{\dot{c}}{c} = \frac{1}{\eta}(A f_k - \rho - n)$$

This is the same solution as in the traditional neoclassical model of growth except that the marginal productivity of capital is not condemned to fall below $\rho + n$ by the law of decreasing marginal returns, since the technical progress term $A$ can continuously lift it above this limit.

Differentiating *(10)* w.r.t. $x$ and using *(9)* *(13)*, we obtain:

$$(16) \quad \frac{\dot{x}}{x} = \frac{1}{\theta(U_c - \lambda)} \left[ U_c \left( Af_k - n - f(k) \, h_x \right) + \lambda \left( \rho \left( i - \varepsilon \right) - n \right) \right]$$

Where: 
$$\theta = -\frac{h_{xx}}{h_x} x$$

is the elasticity of the marginal productivity of net trade surplus, a local measure of the curvature of the function that links technical progress to the trade surplus.

Expression *(16)* indicates that the optimal growth rate for exports, because the shadow price of foreign exchange $\lambda$ is lower than the shadow price of domestic consumption, (see *(10)*), is proportional to the sum of two terms: 1) the differential between the marginal productivity of capital and the marginal productivity of exports plus the population growth rate evaluated at the shadow price of domestic consumption $U_c$, and 2) the differential between the international interest rate, corrected for monopoly power, and the population growth rate, evaluated at the shadow exchange rate $\lambda$. The first term represents the net pro capite benefit from accumulating domestic capital, rather than using the same amount of goods to export, while the second term represents the net pro capite benefit from receiving the interest payment from abroad.

In order to obtain further insights on the nature of the export path suggested, we simplify *(16)* by assuming $n = 0$, a condition fairly common to industrialized countries nowadays, and $\varepsilon = 0$, i.e. absence of monopoly power in the international capital markets. In this case expression *(16)* can be written as follows.

$$(17) \quad \frac{\dot{x}}{x} = \frac{U_c}{\theta \left( U_c - \lambda \right)} \left[ A f_k - f(k) \, h_x - \frac{\lambda}{U_c} \rho \right]$$

If the shadow price of investing at home ($U_c$) is higher than the shadow price of investing abroad ($\lambda$), a condition that can be expected to prevail by virtue of *(10)*, the role of exports will be to exploit the difference between the marginal value of the trade surplus (technical progress plus interest payments from abroad) and the marginal cost of domestic capital. If this difference is negative, therefore, exports will be postponed, i.e. future exports will exceed present exports, and the rate of growth will be higher the higher the same negative difference.

On the other hand, as the trade surplus rises, its marginal product in increasing human capital accumulation will fall, while the marginal product of domestic capital may experience a net increase because of technical progress induced by trade. If the interest rate remains constant, therefore, the growth rate of the trade surplus along the optimum path will tend to accelerate.

From *(17)*, assuming that the same expression applies for the rest of the world, we can also compute the equilibrium rate of interest, which in this case represents the international terms of trade, i.e. the rate at which the country and the rest of the world exchange the single aggregate good against promises to pay back in kind in the future. Indicating with stars the values for the rest of the world, imposing the equilibrium condition: $\dot{x}/x = -\dot{x}^*/x^*$, and solving for $\rho$ yields:

$$(18)\check{\rho} = w\left[\frac{U_c}{\lambda}(Af_k - f(k)h_x)\right] + (1-w)\left[\frac{U_c^*}{\lambda^*}(A^*f_k^* - f^*(k)h^* = h^*)\right]$$

Where $w$ is a weight defined as follows:

$$(19) \qquad w = \frac{\dfrac{\lambda}{U_c}\theta^*(U_c^* - \lambda^*)}{\dfrac{\lambda^*}{U_c^*}\theta^*(U_c - \lambda) + \dfrac{\lambda}{U_c}\theta(U_c^* - \lambda^*)}$$

Thus, the equilibrium rate of interest along the optimum path is a weighted average of the values of the marginal productivity differentials of physical capital and exports (in terms of human capital) respectively in the country and in the rest of the world. Intuitively, this result is based on the fact that the minimum interest rate $r$ that the exporting country will be willing to accept to be convinced to export will be higher, the higher the net opportunity cost (output foregone minus technical progress) from exports. Viceversa, the maximum interest rate $\bar{r}$ that the rest of the world is willing to pay will be higher, the higher its net advantage from running a trade deficit. If $\bar{r} > r$, trade will occur with the equilibrium value of the interest rate set at $r < \hat{\rho} < \bar{r}$ as indicated in the text.

For a given differential between marginal productivities, exports will grow (imports will fall) for the countries with higher productivity, while they will decrease for the countries with the lower one. The growth rate of trade, on the other hand, will be higher, the higher the difference in marginal productivity of capital, net of the effects on technological progress, between each country and the rest of the world.

Since commodities increasingly move from the country with the higher marginal productivity of capital to the country with the lower one, therefore, if exports were of no consequence for technical progress, the country with the higher rate of growth of exports would experience also the higher rate of capital accumulation and growth. The marginal productivity of capital would thus gradually come down in the faster growing country and gradually grow up in the rest of the world, with the flow of trade acting as an equalizer. Eventually, the values of the marginal productivities would be the same both at home and abroad, the interest rate would equate this common value and no further growth in trade would occur.

The introduction of technical progress and the link with exports, however, modify this framework, since the exporting country will see a coeteris paribus rise in the marginal productivity of domestic capital because of the human capital accumulation caused by the export activities. At the same time, the marginal productivity of exports in technical progress will fall. As trade grows, therefore, the net flow of goods from the exporting to the importing country may not bring together the two differentials (and, consequently, $r$ and $\bar{r}$) as fast as in the case where exports have no impact on accumulation. Eventually, however, once the net rates of return to capital are equalized in the two countries, trade will show no further growth.

Have we reached the steady state? Not quite, as we see by substituting the no trade value of

$$\rho = \frac{U_c}{\lambda}(A f_k - f(k) h_x)$$

in the expression for $\dot{c}/c$ in *(15)*. When the country reaches the no-trade condition, by *(15)*:

(20)
$$\frac{\dot{c}}{c} = \frac{1}{\eta}(\lambda f(k) h_x + (U_c - \lambda) A f_k)$$

As a consequence, consumption will continue to grow both at home and abroad and so will domestic accumulation of capital, so that the no growth point for trade, once reached, will be soon abandoned since the productivity differentials in the country and in the rest of the world will start diverging again. Trade will thus be characterized by cycles, and in each period the flow of exports will invert itself with respect to the previous period. This alternate pattern of trade will be the consequence of the fact that exports increase the productivity of capital in the exporting country, thereby tending to eliminate the original reason for developing a trade surplus. Only when the productivity of exports will be drawn to zero both at home and abroad, a full steady state will be reached and consumption, capital accumulation and trade will remain constant.

Graph 1 shows the phase diagram for trade in the exporting country. The trajectory of export growth in this diagram is a spiral.

In a first phase, exports affect technical progress, thereby increasing the gap between the net marginal productivity of capital and the interest rate. As a consequence, trade growth rates will increase as trade increases. In a second phase, the increase in technical progress will be overpowered by the decrease in marginal productivity, the process of growth rate decline will take place and the terms of trade will gradually turn against the exporting country, until a point is reached where exports will show no further growth. In a third phase, growth rates will become negative, and the trade surplus will gradually turn into a trade deficit. The growth of productivity caused by

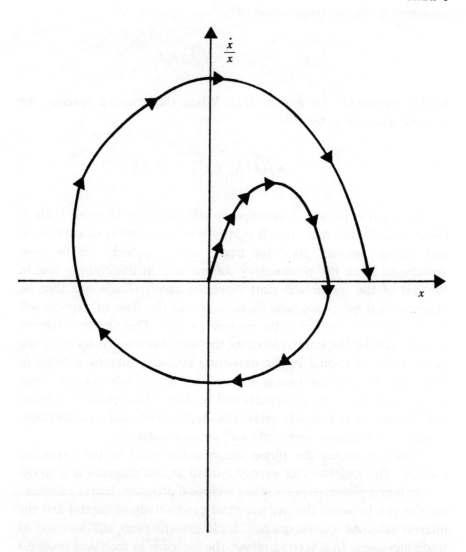

exports will stop, but because the rest of the world is now undergoing the export-led phase, trade will continue according to the same pattern and the country will alternate periods of trade surpluses with periods of trade gaps. The process of endogenous technical progress described, on the other hand, will insure that the spiral will never close and trade will expand forever.

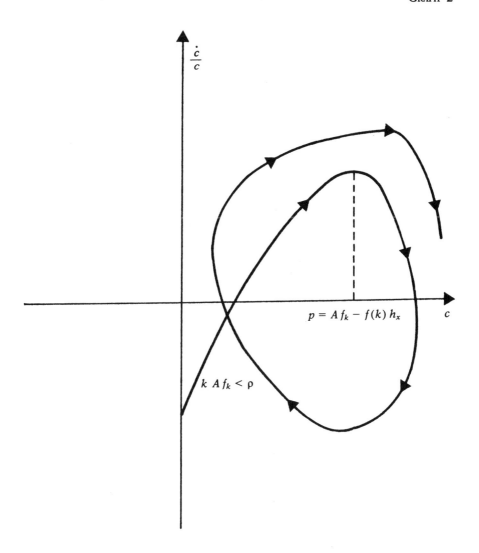

Graph 2 shows the corresponding phase diagram for consumption, also characterized by a spiral. Consumption growth goes through a first phase where growth increases both because the marginal productivity of capital increases and because the interest rate falls (both because of exports), a second phase where the growth rate falls in correspondence of the inversion of the trade pattern, a third phase where consumption falls because the rate of interest is above the marginal productivity of capital, and a fourth phase where a new cycle of development starts, bringing a higher level of growth and consumption.

## 3. - A More General Model of Trade and Endogenous Growth

In order to generalize our simple model, consider the case where the production of the home country can be multiplicatively decomposed into a quantity component and a quality index. In per capita terms, maintaining the assumption of linear homogeneity, this entails rewriting expression *(6)* as follows:

$$(21) \qquad A(t) f(k(t)) = z(t) \cdot q(t) + k(t) + nk(t) + x(t)$$

where $z(t) \cdot q(t) = c(t)$, stands for "quantity" per head and $q(t)$ is an index of product quality, a bundle of desirable characteristics whose production competes with quantity (the number of "pieces" of standard production) for the allocation of capital.

Assume further that increases in human capital $\dot{A}(t)$, which we consider tantamount to technological progress, depend on accumulated human capital $A(t)$, the total stock of physical capital per head $k(t)$, and the index of product quality $q(t)$:

$$(22) \qquad\qquad \dot{A}(t) = h(A(t), k(t), q(t))$$

Product quality is assumed to be an endogenous, positive factor entering the per capita export function:

$$(23) \qquad\qquad x(t) = x(q(t))$$

In other words, an increase in product quality will enhance, coeteris paribus, the country export capacity.

As before, the country is assumed to maximize the present value of national welfare:

(24) $$\text{Max } U_0 = \int_0^\infty e^{-\rho t} U(c(t)) \, dt$$

subject to: *(21)*, *(22)*, *(23)* and the two B.O.P. conditions *(4)* and *(5)* on current and capital accounts.

Forming the Hamiltonian, we obtain:

(25) $$H(t) = e^{-\rho t} [U(c(t)) +$$
$$+ \, p(A(t)f(k(t)) - c(t) - hk(t) - x(t)) +$$
$$+ \, \lambda((\rho - n)g(t) + x(t)) + \mu h(A(t), k(t), q(t))]$$

Deriving the necessary and sufficient conditions for a maximum yield:

(26) $$\frac{\partial H}{\partial z} = (U_c - p) q = 0$$

(27) $$\frac{\partial H}{\partial q} = (U_c - p) z - p x_q + \lambda x_q + \mu x_q = 0$$

where:        $U_c = \partial U / \partial c$, $x_q = \partial x / \partial q$ and: $h_q = \partial h / \partial q$.

(28)        $\dot{p} = - (A f_k - \rho - n) p$        as in *(11)*

(29)        $\dot{\lambda} = (n + \varepsilon \rho) \lambda$        as in *(12)*

(30)        $\dot{\mu} = (\rho - h_a) - p f_k$

where:

$$h_a = \partial h / \partial a$$

For $z > 0$, equation *(26)* states the usual condition that the marginal utility of consumption be equal to the shadow price of investment. Given this condition, equation *(27)* can be restated as:

(31) $$(\lambda - U_c)\, x_q + \mu\, h_q = 0$$

which states that quality should be increased until the net marginal benefits resulting from the expansion of the trade surplus and from technical progress fall to zero. Note that the increase in exports arising from quality improvements have both a benefit, as a consequence of the foreign credits earned, and a cost, as a result of the domestic consumption foregone.

By differentiating *(31)* w.r.t. time and using the maximization conditions, we obtain:

(32) $$\frac{\dot{c}}{c} = \frac{1}{\eta}\left[ (A f_k - c - n) + x_q \frac{h_k}{h_q}\left(\frac{U_c - \lambda}{U_c}\right) \right]$$

In addition to the difference between the marginal productivity of capital and the "gross" rate of interest $\rho + n$, consumption growth is now affected by quality improvements, export growth and technological progress. For $\lambda > U_c$, this effect will be negative and will equal the rate of substitution between exports and capital in producing technological progress. Applying the chain rule to the second term in the square brackets in *(32)*, in fact, yields:

(33) $$\frac{x_q\, h_k}{h_q} = \left( \frac{\partial x}{\partial q}\frac{\partial q}{\partial h}\frac{\partial h}{\partial k} \right) = \frac{\partial x}{\partial k}$$

For quality growth, on the other hand, we find:

(34) $$\frac{\dot{q}}{q} = \frac{1}{\sigma(U_c - \lambda)}\left[ U_c\left( A f_k - \frac{h_q}{x_q} f(k) - n - h_a - \frac{\partial x}{\partial k} \right) + \right.$$
$$\left. + \lambda\left( \frac{\partial x}{\partial k} + n x_q - \rho\,(1 - \varepsilon) - h_a \right) \right]$$

where $\sigma$ is the difference between the elasticity of the marginal productivity of quality for technical progress and the elasticity of its marginal productivity in promoting exports. If $\sigma > 0$, which seems the most reasonable assumption to make, we are operating in a regime of decreasing returns to quality. In this case, expression *(34)* tells a story that is very similar to the simpler story of equation *(16)* of the previous section of this paper. Being an export enhancer, quality will in fact behave as a proxy for export. As such, it should grow for the exporting country in proportion to the sum of a term indicating total net domestic gain from diverting resources to human capital rather than physical capital accumulation, and a term accounting for the net gain earned from the export activities.

Making again the simplifying assumptions $n = 0$ and $\varepsilon = 0$, we obtain the following expression, corresponding to *(17)*:

*(35)*
$$\frac{\dot{q}}{q} = \frac{U_c}{\sigma(U_c - \lambda)}\left[\left(A\,f_k - \frac{h_q}{x_q}f(k) - h_a - \frac{\partial x}{\partial k}\right) - \left(\frac{\lambda}{U_c}\,\rho - h_a - \frac{\partial x}{\partial k}\right)\right]$$

The growth rate of quality will be proportional to the balance between the net benefit from abroad (interest payments minus the opportunity cost due to the diversion of resources that could have been used to increase human capital or exports), and net opportunity cost at home (the marginal product of physical capital plus the increase in technological progress due to quality improvement, minus the increase in technical progress because of human capital accumulation and the increase in exports).

Again, the story is similar to the one of the simple model, except that the chain of effects to account for is more complex. Given the two differentials in *(35)*, however, the equilibrium interest rate can be expressed as:

*(36)*
$$\dot{\rho} = w\,\Delta + (1 - w)\,\Delta^*$$

where:
$$\Delta = \frac{U_c}{\lambda}\left(A\,f_k - \frac{h_q}{x_q}(k)\right) - \left(h_a + \frac{\partial x}{\partial h}\right)\left(\frac{U_c - \lambda}{\lambda}\right)$$

$\Delta^*$ is the same expression for the rest of the world and $w$ and $(1 - w)$ are defined as in *(19)*.

The rate of interest will thus lie between $\Delta^*$ and $\Delta$, and quality will grow for the country with the higher marginal productivity of domestic capital causing exports to flow increasingly to the country with the lower one. In this process, the differentials between the two countries will increase at first, because quality improvements have the effect of increasing the productivity of capital in the exporting country. Only when this effect becomes lower than the decrease in marginal productivity due to the accumulation of capital stock in the exporting country, will the two differentials in *(36)* come together.

When the two differentials are equated, the rate of interest will exactly match the net productivity difference in *(35)* so that all quality improvements will stop. Consumption, however, will not stop growing and productivity differentials at home and abroad will again diverge. Cycles of trade will again develop, and trade and growth may go on indefinitely if both the country and the rest of the world correctly optimize and both take into account the externalities arising from quality and trade.

## 4. - Some Conclusions

The model presented in this paper is based on the idea that exports may be associated with an important externality in the process of endogenous growth. Such an externality may be summarized by the chain: quality, export markets, technological progress, that is likely to be at the base of the success of outward oriented economies in permanently raising their rates of growth.

If the model of neoclassical growth is modified to account for a virtuous circle between trade and technical progress, however, a number of striking consequences follow. First, as expected, the process of growth is not condemned to end in the neoclassical steady state, but may go on forever, since technical progress allows the decline of the marginal productivity of capital to be overcome.

Second, however, and contrary to our expectations, such an indefinite process of growth is necessarily a cyclical one. Because technical progress is engendered by trade, through quality improvements and innovations, the process of growth has necessarily to come to a temporary halt if the incentive to trade is gradually reduced by the convergence of the two trading economies. In order to provide an incentive to trade, in fact, the marginal productivity of the exporting country, "net" of the effects of the exports on growth, will have to be higher than the corresponding variable of the importing country. But trade will increase the productivity of the exporting country, thereby slowing down convergence and mantaining the incentive to trade. Only if the originally importing country becomes in turn the exporting one and viceversa, therefore, can trade be the source of a permanent impulse to grow.

Third, the cyclical pattern implies that integration of the two economies would be preferable to pure commodity trade. If some of the technical progress created by exports in one country did spill over to its trading partners, each cycle of trade-led growth would last longer with mutual benefits both for exporting and importing countries.

Fourth, the cyclical pattern also entails that a period of expansion led by trade is somewhat inevitably followed by a period of retrenchment, lower and possibly negative growth, as the dynamic force of export growth is quenched first by the gradual reduction and then by the inversion of the incentives to trade. Of course, in the real world, the stimulus to grow may shift from exports to other endogenous sources, but nevertheless it appears that one should expect that export oriented economies can only go that far without modifying their model of growth.

Fifth, and with special reference to Italy, export, quality and technology appear to be a list of ingredients that our country has not yet fully tried, in spite of its heavy reliance on international markets. In this respect, the model suggests that quality improvements, divorced from the accumulation of human capital and technical progress, even though they may be a temporary source of market power, are not capable of generating the self reinforcing chain of events that could generate a real momentum of growth.

BIBLIOGRAPHY

[1] ABRAMOVITZ M.: «Catching up, Forging Ahead and Falling Behind», *Journal of Economic History*, n. 1096, pp. 385-486.

[2] ALLY YOURY: «Increasing Returns and Economic Progess», *Economic Journal*, December 1928.

[3] ARROW K.: «The Economic Implications of Learning by Doing», *Review of Economic Studies*, n. 29, June 1962.

[4] BARRO R.J.: «Economic Growth in a Cross Section of Countries», *Journal of Economics*, May 1991.

[5] BAUMOL W.: «Productivity, Growth, Convergence and Welfare: What the Long-Run Data Show», *American Economic Review*, vol. 76, n. 5, p. 1986.

[6] GROSSMAN G.M. - HELPMAN E.: «Endogenous Product Cycles», *Economic Journal*, September 1991.

[7] —— · —— : «Quality Ladders in the Theory of Growth», *Review of Economic Studies*, vol. 58, n. 1, 1991.

[8] KALDOR N.: «Capital Accumulation and Economic Growth», in LUTZ F. (ed.): *Theory of Capital*, Macmillan, London, 1961.

[9] —— : «What is Wrong with Economic Theory», *Quarterly Journal of Economic*, August. 1975.

[10] LUCAS R.E.: «Why Doesn't Capital Flow from Rich to Poor Countries», *American Economic Rewiew*, May 1990.

[11] ROMER P.A.: «Endogenous Technical Change», *Journal of Political Economy*, vol. 98, n. 5, 1990.

[12] ROMER P.M.: «Increasing Returns and Long-Run Growth», *Journal of Political Economy*, vol. 94, n. 5, 1986.

# Explaining Growth:
# Competition and Finance (1)

Joseph E. Stiglitz
Stanford University

One major set of events have transpired since the formulation of neoclassical growth theory in the 1950s and 1960s: the success of Japan, the Asian tigers, and more recently, of Thailand, Malaysia, Singapore, and Indonesia. The growth rates experienced by these countries over a span of several decades has put new meaning into the concept of "rapid growth". Annual growth rates in excess of 15%, and average growth rates in excess of 7%, were not uncommon. To some economists, this experience provided a refutation of neoclassical growth theory: where was the evidence of diminishing returns which that theory would have led one to expect? Could growth feed upon itself? Could there be increasing returns, so that the marginal return to investment actually increased as the economy grew? Or was there something about technical progress which meant that its pace increased as the marginal product of capital decreased?

The "new growth" economics of the 1980s attempted to provide answers to these questions, and more broadly to find better, or at least more complete, explanations of the determinants of economic

(1) This paper is based on joint research projects undertaken with Bruce Greenwald, Andrew Weiss, Thomas Hellmann and Andrés Rodríguez, to all of whom I am greatly indebted. Earlier versions of some of the ideas presented here were presented to conferences on growth theory at Vail and Buffalo, to the CEPR Conference on *Finance and Development in Europe*, Santiago de Compostela, Spain, and to the ABCDE meeting at the World Bank, April, 1992. Financial support from the Ford Foundation, the Sloan Foundation, and the Hoover Institution are gratefully acknowledged.

*Advise*: the numbers in square brackets refer to the Bibliography in the appendix.

growth, from which one could draw useful policy implications about what those countries whose growth is lagging might do to enhance it.

This paper has three objectives: to clarify (what should be) the objectives of the growth research programme, to provide a critique of the vision embodied in several common versions of the new growth economics, and to emphasize the role played by one set of factors-financial markets-that has, to date, received, in my judgement, insufficient attention.

## 1. - What is to be Explained

In this section, I want to call attention to several "facts" and theoretical " puzzles" that a theory of growth needs to come to terms with. The growth theory of the 1950s was motivated by a mixture of theoretical and empirical puzzles: the theoretical puzzles presented by the Harrod-Domar growth model - the difficulties of reconciling the warranted and natural rates of growth as well as the empirical puzzles of explaining such stylized facts as the constancy of factor shares, the real rate of interest, and the capital output ratio. So, too, the recent resurgence of interest is motivated by a combination of theoretical and empirical puzzles.

These puzzles include: *a)* why have the Asian tigers been able to sustain such a high rate of growth for so long; and *b)* why does growth seem to be so often concentrated - both in time and in location; even within a country, certain regions may remain persistently backward. The earlier neoclassical literature predicted a convergence in rates of growth, and, in a world of free capital mobility (2), even of factor prices and per capita outputs. While there is some debate about whether or not there has been convergence (3), there is little doubt that, if it is occurring, it is occurring at a remarkably slow speed, requiring sophisticated econometric techniques to detect; and income

---

(2) Capital mobility is sufficient, but not necessary. Under some conditions, free trade in goods could substitute for factor mobility (the factor price equalization theorem), though in dynamic models, specialization was not an unlikely outcome. See STIGLITZ [49].

(3) See, e.g. BAUMOL [9] and DURLAUF-JOHNSON [18].

disparities remain enormous. Moreover, there is little evidence of marked differences in returns to capital that one should see associated with the marked differences in capital labor ratios (4).

In constructing a growth model, one has to be clear about what phenomenon one wants to explain. There is a strong presumption that the determinants of growth in the most developed countries are different from those in the less developed countries, and even from those in the middle income countries. In this paper, in Section I, I shall be mainly concerned with the rapid growth of the middle income countries, not the determinants of the growth of the most advanced. The discussion of Section II focuses on the more advanced countries.

Underlying the debate over the determinants of growth, in particular the success of the East Asian tigers, lie three different perspectives concerning what has happened (and is happening).

*(i) The Factor Accumulation Hypothesis.* The one approach in which there is the greatest similarity between growth in developed and less developed countries sees growth as the result of a rapid increase in inputs, in human and physical capital; in this view, the less developed countries are on the same production function as the more developed; they only have fewer inputs.

*(ii) The Catching up Hypothesis.* The second sees the less developed economies (including the Asian tigers) as *on* a "different" production function. For the most part, the countries produce different goods and use different techniques of production than do the more developed countries. Many LDCs have a "dual" structure, in which part of their economy uses technologies similar to those employed in more developed countries, and others use quite different technologies and produce quite different products. In this perspective, then, growth entails shifting more resources into the advanced sectors and shifting out the production function of the less advanced, in an attempt to "catch up" with the more developed countries.

[Sometimes it is argued that there is a common production function (as in the factor accumulation hypothesis), but that the LDCs operate below that common production function. Growth entails

---

(4) See STIGLITZ [55]. Indeed, as noted there, may of the LDCs seem to use their capital less intensively than do the more developed countries.

moving out towards the production frontier. But this seems to be semantic quibbling (5)].

*(iii) Returns to Scale.* The final approach sees the countries as *on* the *same* production function, and growth entails taking advantage of increasing returns to scale. Higher levels of input simply imply higher outputs per unit input.

The principal arguments of this paper can be summarized as follows:

1) the most reasonable (and logically consistent) interpretation of the cross section growth observations, in particular, the rapid growth of the countries of East Asia, is that it entails a process of catching up to the technology of the more advanced countries;

2) while imperfect competition *may* not give rise to significant distortions in the efficiency of the growth process, if different sectors face similar learning functions and similar elasticities of demand, if the labor supply elasticity is zero, and if there are no credit constraints, credit constraints may impede the economy's ability to engage in as rapid growth (learning); and if the labor supply increases with the real wage, not only is the level of learning (the rate of growth) in the market equilibrium likely to be too low, but it is quite possible that, with learning-by-doing, there may be multiple equilibria; in one equilibrium the rate of growth is higher than in others; and it may even be possible to Pareto rank the growth equilibria;

3) capital market imperfections affect many aspects of the growth process; they limit, for instance, the rate of growth of individual firms, restricting their ability to avail themselves of the advantages of returns to scale or learning by doing, and they affect the

---

(5) Formally, the distinction is that between saying that the country has its own production function:

$$Q^j = F^j(x^j)$$

where $Q$ is output and $x$ is the vector of inputs; that there is a common production function, but the country's state of knowledge, $A^j$ is low:

$$Q^j = F(A^j, x^j)$$

and that there is a common production function, but that the country simply produces below that common production function, without specifying what determines the relationship between inputs and output.

ability to reallocate funds to their most productive use. Growth is affected not only by the level of savings, but the form; equity may be particularly "high powered". Policies of limited financial repression may have a negligible effect on the level of savings, but a substantial effect on the amount of equity capital;

4) most analyses of recent growth experiences identify the importance of one of several market imperfections (increasing returns, externalities, capital market imperfections, imperfect competition), which provide the basis of a role for government beyond that of simply "getting the prices right".

We now look at one of the central puzzles, the persistence of high growth rates, from these alternative perspectives.

## 1.1 *Capital Accumulation and Economic Growth*

We begin our discussion with the standard restatement of the high growth puzzle, as it is usually posed in the context of a more developed country.

The NICs have had high savings rates and rapid rates of capital accumulation. The question is, can these by themselves account for their growth? And why, given their persistently high rates of capital accumulation, hasn't diminished returns set in?

If the production function did not shift, we would observe diminishing returns as capital accumulation proceeded. Thus, graph 1$a$ shows country $J$, which increases its capital labor ratio from $k_0$ to $k_1$, and then from $k_1$ to $k_2$; it shows a smaller increase in output (a lower growth rate) during the second period than in the first.

Solow's analysis ([43], [44]) — both his empirical and theoretical results — seemed to denigrate the importance of capital accumulation. Most of the growth in output per capita could be interpreted as a result of technological progress. In the long run, the savings rate made no difference for the rate of growth. In the short run, an increase in the saving rate had only a limited effect on growth rates, because of the relatively small share of capital. (An increase in the savings rate from 15% to 20%, a large increase, would increase the growth rate by only one percentage point, if the share of capital was 0.2%).

Later work tried to find a larger role for capital accumulation, at least in the short run; new techniques were embodied in new capital, so that capital accumulation was required in order to bring into production new technologies. But the magnitude and duration of these effects seemed limited (Solow [46]). In this interpretation, the high savings rates of the NICs played a relatively minor role in their success.

By contrast, much of the *New Growth Theory* has stressed the importance of capital accumulation. To see how these theories differ from that of Solow, we need to return to Solow's basic growth accounting equation. Of course, Solow's growth accounting equation does not depend on either constant returns or competitive theory. It simply says that if we can relate outputs to inputs by a production function of the form

(1) $$Y = AF(K, L)$$

then, differentiating:

(2)    $$d\ln Y/dt = d\ln A/dt + F_K K/F \times g_K + F_L L/F \times g_L$$

when $g_K$ is the rate of growth of capital and $g_L$ is that of labor. Disagreements about the role of capital accumulation thus arise either from disagreements about the magnitude of capital accumulation or about estimates of $F_K K/F$. Both are possible.

The literature growing out of the Griliches-Jorgenson ([26]) studies showed how difficult, important, and problematic corrections for capital quality were. They argued that if capital quality was correctly accounted for, the residual was almost eliminated, and capital accumulation, rather than technical progress, became the main engine of growth. Critics worried that their procedures basically attributed the gains from technical change which were embodied in machines to the machines which embodied them, giving no credit itself to the technical change. The question was posed: which do we believe more, our eyes or our statistical adjustment procedures? Do we really believe that technical change did not occur, and that it does not account for a significant fraction of growth. At the very least, however, the Griliches-Jorgenson work should make us cautious of taking *too* seriously econometric work in this area, particularly if not carefully done.

These measurement problems are relevant for our current discussions: if we have mismeasured capital, there may be no empirical puzzle at all; perhaps the success in growth can simply be accounted for by the high rates of capital accumulation, and the failure of diminishing returns to set in by offsetting changes in the *true* rates of capital accumulation. For instance, on-going work at the World Bank suggests that total factor productivity growth in several of the Asian countries, such as Singapore, has not been extra-ordinary; though that in other countries, such as Korea, has been truly impressive.

Putting aside for the moment these measurement-of-capital problems, if we are to reconcile the patterns of growth observed by the Asian tigers with the Solow growth equation *(2)*, we must either postulate extra-ordinary high rates of total productivity increase (easy to understand, if one believes one is in a process of catching up), or that the observed share of capital underestimates $F_K K/F$ (6). If we take the latter tack, we need to ask, why might market prices differ from marginal productivities? The fact that they do — as in the models of increasing returns and externalities to be discussed below — raises, of course, immediate questions concerning the scope of public policy.

---

(6) Some data suggest a high share of capital in some of the East Asia countries-much higher than the shares observed in the United States and other developed countries. There are a number of reasons to suspect that these data do not accurately reflect $F_k K/F$. For one, the US and Europe had capital shares not much different from their current shares, when their capital labor ratios were comparable to those in the East Asian countries today. Secondly, if we assume a roughly constant capital output ratio, and if, say, Hong Kong's per capita income is roughly 0.75 that of the US, then a share of capital of 0.5 (compared to, say, 0.2 in the US) would imply an elasticity of substitution of 0.4, considerably smaller than most cross sectional or time series estimates of the elasticity of substitution. The share of capital may be overestimated because returns to factors other than capital (such as returns to land, or entrepreneurship), or pure profits are included. In the case of countries such as Singapore, the hypothesis that factor prices are determined as part of a competitive equilibrium is hard to take seriously.

## 1.2 *Technological Change*

If the production function shifted, then the extent of diminishing returns would be much less marked. The criticism put forward by endogenous growth theory is that if the shift in the production function were exogenous and fixed — and the same for all countries — as postulated in standard neoclassical growth theory, then countries that grew more rapidly would experience relative diminishing returns, as illustrated in graph 1*b*.

The only conditions under which this would not be observed is if the country whose capital were accumulating more rapidly experienced a larger shift in its production function. Endogenous growth theory attempts to explain why this might be so.

GRAPH 1

DIMINISHING RETURNS (*)

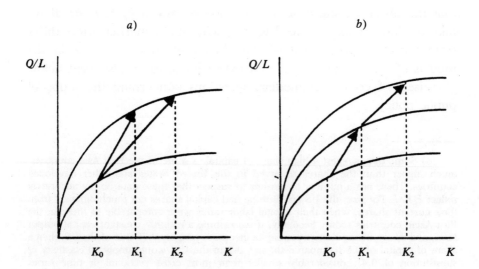

(*) With a given technology, the economy faces diminishing returns. Even with technological change, so long as the rate is fixed, independent of the rate of capital accumulation, countries that accumulate capital faster will exhibit diminishing returns.

The remarkable successes of the Asian tigers does not, in itself, call into question standard neoclassical growth theory, except if one believes that, at the start of the period of growth, these countries were on the international production frontier, that is, if one believes that initially, these countries were on the same production as the United States and Western Europe, with the only difference being differences in scale and capital labor ratio. Beginning with that hypothesis, some versions of endogenous growth theory then try to explain the persistently high growth rates of the Asian tigers by such natural hypotheses as that the country which invested more in physical capital invested more in R & D, or had more learning by doing, and thus shifted its production function more.

There is a certain logical inconsistency in this position. For it attempts to explain differences in performance in terms of differences in shifts in their production functions; and yet it assumes that all countries are on the same production function. If technological knowledge flows freely across countries, then expenditures on research are unrelated to shifts in their production function. If technological knowledge does not flow freely across countries, the underlying hypothesis that countries are on the same production function cannot be maintained.

Indeed, the hypothesis that they are on the same production function — that they have access to the same technology — seems patently absurd: even within a country within an industry, we know that there are remarkably large differences in productivity; we know that knowledge about best practices does not diffuse instantaneously. It seems clear that there are barriers to the free flow of knowledge across countries, particularly between the North and the South, and such barriers would clearly result in differences in productivity (7). Micro-studies confirm these differences.

If the Asian tigers were initially (and continue to be) on a different production function, then explaining their growth success is, in

---

(7) And indeed, there is some evidence that these barriers are becoming larger, as companies in the more developed countries take more seriously the potential competition that firms in the developing countries (in particular, East Asia) may pose. They are becoming increasingly reluctant to sell state-of-the-art technology, precisely because these countries can absorb that technology quickly, and go on from there to improve it.

principle, an easier matter. In this perspective, then, the movement of
the Asia tigers can be thought of as a movement from a low level of
capital intensity far below the international best practices production
frontier to a point closer to the frontier at a high level of capital
intensity. It is not just a movement along a production function. As
graph 2 illustrates, there is nothing in this movement which would
imply that we should expect diminishing returns to set in, as we would
expect if we were moving along a production function.

GRAPH 2

CATCHING UP (*)

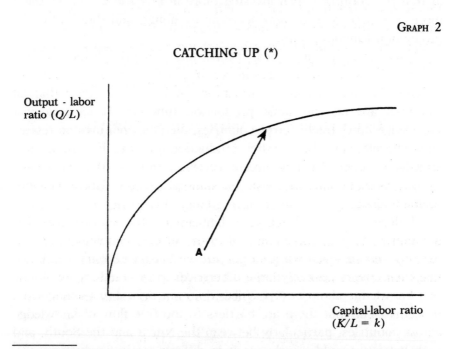

(*) If initially the country is below the world's best practice production possibilities schedule, it
can experience a period during which no diminishing returns is exhibited.

Indeed, in this perspective, there is even an argument for why,
for some periods, there may be increasing returns. An important part
of development is "learning to learn", (Stiglitz [53]), that is,
developing the capabilities that allow a country to *(i)* determine which
of the foreign technologies are most suitable for the conditions of that

country; *(ii)* absorb and adapt the technology (8). Then, if as before we represent the LDC's production function as (9):

$$Y = AF(K, L)$$

then:

$$g_A = d \ln A/dt = \Psi (A^*/A, R)$$

where $A^*$ represents the state of the "best practices" technology, and $R$ the ability to learn. It is natural to postulate that:

$$\Psi_1 > 0$$

i.e. other things being equal, the greater the gap between the country's technology and best practice technology, the faster the improvement of technology; and the higher the learning capabilities of the economy, the higher the rate of technological change. Normally, countries with low $A$ also have low $R$, so that in spite of a large gap between their technology and best practices, learning occurs at a slow rate. On the other hand, one can argue that part of the development strategy of the successful NICs was an explicit effort to increase $R$; in the earlier years of their growth spurt, increases in $R$ dominate the decrease in the "gap", i.e.:

$$d \ln \frac{g_A}{dt} = \gamma_1 \left( \frac{A^*}{A^*} - g_{A^*} \right) + \gamma_2 \, g_R > 0$$

---

(8) For instance, the non-tradeable intermediate inputs within a country may differ in important respects from those of the country where the technology was originally developed. Sometimes traded intermediate substitutes can be obtained, but at a higher cost. The importer of the new technology must make judgments concerning which intermediate inputs will have to be imported from abroad and which can be purchased domestically; in either case, there may have to be adaptations of the product or the production process.

(9) There is no reason, of course, to assume Hicks neutral technological changes; while the constancy of capital output rates suggests Harrod neutrality, i.e.:

$$Y = F(K, AL)$$

Kim and Lau's [33] and Boskin and Lau's [10] more recent econometric work suggests that technical change may be capital augmenting.

so long as:

$$\frac{\Psi_2}{\Psi_1} \geq \frac{g_A - g_{A^*}}{g_R}$$

where:

$$\gamma_1 = \frac{\Psi_1}{\Psi} \frac{A^*}{A} , \quad \gamma_2 = \frac{\Psi_2 R}{\Psi}$$

Of course, eventually, the gap will be narrowed sufficiently, and increases in learning abilities will presumably be limited, that the rate of growth of technology will slow down; it eventually must asymptote to $g_{A^*}$ (10).

## 1.3 *The Common Production Function Hypothesis*

While we dismissed the hypothesis that the LDCs and the more developed countries are on a common production function as patently absurd, there is a sense in which the issue is almost beside the point: as we noted earlier, the technologies that the LDCs are employing — corresponding to their lower level of capital per worker — are so markedly different that one cannot make a direct comparison. To put it another way, the developed countries do not embrace the factor prices — and therefore the techniques of production — associated with the less developed countries. Firms in the more developed countries that use the same technologies are presumably "off the production function" and therefore, they do not tell us the extent of the technology gap between the developed and less developed economies. Moreover, to a large extent, the products produced in the

---

(10) As the country approaches the best practices in any sector, continual rapid growth will require a switch from imitation to innovation. As the experience of Japan demonstrates, a country can be an innovator in some sectors while an imitator in others, a distinction which is lost in our simple aggregative, one sector framework. As we noted earlier, the issues and models relevant for an analysis of innovators are considerably different from those of the imitators, upon which we are focusing in this section.

different countries are different, making comparisons between production technologies of even more dubious value.

What is at issue here is closely related to some of the long-standing criticisms of production functions. Kaldor, for instance, emphasized that one only knew how to translate inputs into output with the particular array of inputs that one conventionally used. Outside that array, it would take research (engineering) to know how to translate inputs into outputs. We can think of the production function as well-defined at current arrays of inputs, and only conjectural at others. Thus, it is only by an act of heroic extrapolation that one can extend the data describing the relationships between inputs and outputs for the more developed countries to the circumstances relevant for the LDCs.

There is a tautological sense in which one can "force" all countries to be on the same production function: if seemingly the same levels of input produce lower levels of output, one simply says that the "effective" inputs are smaller. But like most tautologies of this sort, intended to save a clearly inadequate paradigm, it obfuscates more than it clarifies (11).

## 1.4 *Disaggregation and Differences in Technologies*

Underlying this aggregative analysis is a great deal of microeconomic detail. There is not a store to which the LDCs can go, to get the technology of the more advanced countries. The process of technology transfer goes on on a sector by sector, industry by industry, product by product basis. To be sure, what is learned in one industry, or in connection with the purchase of one technology, may diffuse to other industries and sectors.

It is important to recognize this, because the differences in the aggregate level of technology reflects an amalgam: some sectors in which technology differences may be relatively small, next to other sectors in which technology differences may be large.

---

(11) We should note the similarity between this position, and those which seek to "correct" capital input data referred to earlier. Both approaches seek to find new ways of measuring the inputs to resolve the growth puzzle.

A static version of this perspective can be captured in graph 3, where we have two technologies, one reflecting the capital intensity of the more developed countries, the other of the less developed. At the aggregate level we can obtain any linear combination of these two, simply by mixing the two technologies, as illustrated by the dotted line *AB*. We have drawn some intermediate technologies, represented for instance by the point *C*. These lie below the line *AB*.

The theory of localized technical change (Atkinson and Stiglitz [8]) provides an explanation of why this should be so. Learning — whether as a result of explicit R & D expenditures or as a consequence of production (learning by doing) — shifts the production function at a particular point, as illustrated in graph 4; there are, to be sure, spill-overs to neighboring technologies, but these spill-overs are limited. Thus the production function does not shift out uniformly, but rather in a "bumpy" manner, yielding a production function of the form illustrated in graph 4.

This formulation has three important implications. First, for such a country, the aggregate production function simply cannot be represented by the Cobb Douglas production function so loved by the new growth theorists.

Secondly, the process of capital accumulation, involving the economy moving from a capital labor ratio of $k_0$ to $k_1$, results simultaneously in a shift in resources (including labor) from the low technology (represented by the point *A* of graph 3) to the high technology (represented by the point *B*). The average productivity of labor in these two sectors are markedly different.

And thirdly, during the "transition" period, diminishing returns does not set in. There is a linear relationship between output per capita and the capital output ratio.

Thus, two of the familiar characterizations of the development process — that it entails a shift out of low productivity agriculture to high productivity industrial activities, and that it entails capital accumulation — are but two sides of the same process.

(It is perhaps worth noting that the same form of aggregate production depicted in graph 3 arises in a world of free trade; the linear segment arises in the interval of capital labor ratios corresponding to non-specialization, in which the factor price equalization

GRAPH 3

## DIFFERENT TECHNOLOGIES AND LOCALIZED LEARNING (*)

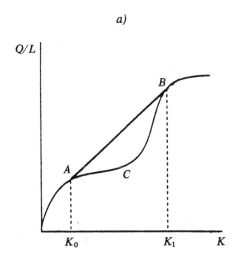

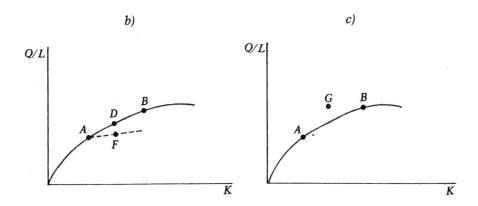

(*) With localized learning, technologies *A* and *B*, and linear combinations of those technologies will dominate intermediate technology *C*. Then as the economy accumulates capital, no diminishing returns will be evidenced. One could decompose the movement from *A* to *D* as movement along the "old" production function, from *A* to *F*, and an improvement in technology, a movement from *F* to *D*. There may exist technologies in the more developed countries, such as *G*, which dominate those available to the LDC, but the more developed countries may charge a sufficiently high price to reap the rents associated with the improved technology.

Graph 4

## LOCALIZED LEARNING LEADS TO
## DOMINATING TECHNOLOGIES (*)

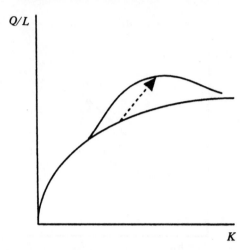

(*) When learning is localized, then the production function shifts out at points around which the economy is operating; these technologies then become dominant.

theorem holds. Thus, if a cross country regression were dominated by countries with not too dissimilar capital labor ratios, we would expect to observe no diminishing returns; and certainly, as Japan's capital labor ratio approached that of the more advanced Western countries, diminishing returns would not be expected to set in (12). For a variety of reasons — the same reasons discussed below that one can reject the perspective that all of these countries are operating on the same production function — I find this explanation unconvincing) (13).

(12) There are strong arguments to expect that countries should be within the non-specialization region: all that is required is that one of the factors (e.g. capital) be mobile.

(13) Note that the presence, or even dominance, of intra-industry trade, does not refute the relevance of these arguments; the fact that countries of the same capital-labor ratio trade, because of the gains from increasing returns (as in the HELPMAN-KRUGMAN [28] and DIXIT-STIGLITZ [17]) models) is perfectly consistent with the existing *patterns* of "relative" specialization associated with differences in capital labor ratios (that is, the capital rich countries produce relatively more of the capital intensive products) *and* with factor prices being equalized.

### 1.4.1 Ambiguous Interpretations of the Data

The movement from *A* to *D* in graph 3*b* can be interpreted in several different ways. The interpretation that we gave was that there were two technologies, one associated with lower levels of development (*A*) and the other with the more developed countries (point *B*). Development consisted of capital accumulation which was used to produce more output using the higher technology. In this perspective, technological improvement and capital accumulation are inextricably linked.

We might artificially break the two down by extrapolating the primitive technology along the dotted line in graph 3*b*. In that case, in the absence of the acquisition of the new technology, the country would have been at point *F*. Then, the movement from *A* to *F* is the result of capital accumulation, and from *F* to *C* the result of technological progress.

Graph 3*c* represents still another possible interpretation. Assume that there are two capital intensive technologies available in the world. The LDC has a technology *B* as described earlier. But the more developed countries have a technology depicted in the graph as *G*, yielding the same output per man at a lower level of capital costs. But they do not costlessly transfer this new technology to the LDC. They charge a cost of transfer, equal to the difference between the capital cost of *G* and that of *B*. That is, they essentially extract all the rents associated with their superior technology. Then, the movement from *A* to *D* does entail an improvement of technology - indeed, the country is purchasing the best available technology. But it will show up not as a shift in the production function, but as an increase in capital. They have purchased the new technology, and therefore the increase in output comes from an increase in inputs (expenditures).

Thus, the difficulties in differentiating the role of capital accumulation from the role of technological change arise not only because capital accumulation may be required to implement new technologies, but also because new technologies may be purchased, and thus show up as the consequence of an increase in inputs. What is at issue here, however, is more than an econometric identification problem. If the country has purchased new technology, which permanently shifts its capabilities of transforming inputs into outputs, then while in the short run, it appears as if the increase in output is "attributable" to capital expenditures, in the long run its production function has shifted out. (Indeed, depending on how much it pays for the new technology, it may even appear in the short run as if there has been a backward shift in the technology).

## 1.5 *External Economies*

Earlier, we outlined three alternative resolutions of the "growth" paradox: *a)* there was no growth paradox - only a mismeasurement of capital; *b)* the Asian tigers were below the world frontier production function, and they thus could experience rapid technological change in the process of catching up; or *c)* the share of capital underestimated the return to capital. So far, we have discussed the first two possibilities. We now turn to the third.

The possibility that prices do not reflect marginal returns has profound implications: for it means, in particular, that the economy will not be Pareto efficient; there will be scope for government intervention.

There are a variety of market failures which can result in observed market prices differing from social marginal returns (14). Two such market failures will be discussed in section 2 and section 3: imperfect competition and imperfect capital markets. In this and the next subsection, we focus on two other market failures.

Much of the more recent literature has focussed on a third explanation: externalities, benefits to accumulation (15) that are external to the firm. The reason that this approach has drawn such

(14) There are also several reasons why the observed share of capital may overestimate the return to capital: *a)* with imperfect competition (see prg. 2), there are pure profits; it is hard to distinguish pure profits from the return to capital, and the standard statistics often include monopoly rents as part of the returns to capital; *b)* the observed statistics reflect average returns to capital, and these may exceed the marginal returns; it is the marginal returns which are relevant for the Solow growth equation. Thus, some profits represent a return to R & D expenditures; these represent a return to winning the patent race (or the return to being first in a market); but the private returns to winning the patent rate exceed the social marginal returns.

(15) Of course, there are many returns to R & D which are not appropriated by firms doing the research.

attention is that under some circumstances — the case of Marshallian externalities — one can preserve the hypothesis of a competitive equilibrium, even though there are aggregate increasing returns. To be sure, at the same time, one of the great virtues of competitive markets, their efficiency, is lost (16).

There are two fundamental criticisms of this approach. First, as I noted, what made it attractive was that one could preserve the hypothesis of competition; but under closer investigation, it turned out that one could do so only under extreme assumptions. Presumably much, or most, of these externalities are internal to the industry; but if that were the case, strong market forces would be at work to "internalize" the externalities, that is, to have a single firm dominate each industry.

Even without such "mergers", Dasgupta and Stiglitz [16] had shown that unless all of the learning that results from production or investment spills over to other firms, industries with learning by doing would be imperfectly competitive.

Equally importantly, while there may be some externalities, it is hard to believe that they are sufficiently large to account for at least some of the observed patterns, as reflected, for instance, in the Solow growth equation (17). (Many of the more recent theoretical models attempting to explain the observed patterns have suggested that the aggregate production function is linear in $K$, in which case, private returns are a fifth of total returns!)

## 1.6 *Rent Based Theories*

The assumption underlying standard neoclassical growth theory, that all factors are allocated efficiently across sectors, seems inconsistent with many characterizations of the growth process, which emphasize the reallocation of resources from less productive to more productive sectors. Earlier, we used our theory of localized tech-

---

(16) AOKI [2] formalized the notion of Marshallian external economies, economies which were external to the firm but internal to the industry, and it was this approach that Romer used in his often cited 1986 paper.

(17) There are, however, some other phenomena for which externalities (and increasing returns) provide an explanation, as we comment below.

nological change to provide one way of reconciling these alternative perspectives.

But there is another fact which seems inconsistent with both that approach and conventional characterizations of the growth process. We emphasized earlier that capital accumulation allowed the shift from sectors where the average product of labor was low to those where it was high. Yet, the earlier model implicitly had the *marginal productivities*, and hence wages, equated. But typically, as workers move out of agriculture to industry, their wages rise. The discrepancy between wages has been both a theoretical puzzle and a cause of concern, because of the high rates of urban unemployment to which it often gives rise.

While the simplest explanations (which may have considerable validity) are based just on lags of adjustment, the phenomenon has given rise to a large literature on efficiency wages; wages are kept high because doing so increases profits, either because it results in a higher quality labor force, lower turnover, or greater effort. Industrial wages thus contain an element of rent.

The important growth consequence is that the social return to increasing capital is greater than the private return. The social return includes an increase in the welfare of the worker who gets the new industrial jobs; saver/investors do not take into account this welfare gain when determining their savings rate.

Moreover, since the magnitude of these rents differs across sectors, the patterns of allocation of investment will not be socially optimal.

Rents are associated not only with the labor market, but also the capital market, as we shall see in section 3.

But if there are rents associated with capital accumulation, then the social marginal return to investment may well exceed the private return, and thus the appropriate value of $F_K K/F$ to use in the growth accounting equation is *greater* than the market share of capital.

### 1.7 *Increasing Returns*

The Solow growth equation, with which we began this paper, does not require that there be constant returns to scale, though the competitive interpretation of marginal products encounters problems when there are not constant returns. And indeed, it is well known when there exist increasing returns, there is unlikely to be perfect competition, so that factor prices may well differ from marginal returns. Yet, it is hard to believe that they differ enough to fully resolve the growth paradox.

In spite of this, the hypothesis that increasing returns could account for the persistently high growth rates of the «Asian miracle» countries has received widespread attention. This is partly because the hypothesis of increasing returns may be helpful in accounting for some of the other phenomena to which we referred in the beginning of the paper, for instance, the fact that diminishing returns does not seem to have set in the way that one would have predicted with standard neoclassical theory (18).

There is, to be sure, other evidence that is consistent with externalities and increasing returns to scale which extend beyond the firm. Growth often seems to occur in spurts and, at least initially, the spurts leave some regions within the country behind. In some cases, the growth spurts are highly localized. Thus, in the United States, the South remained a relatively backward region until the 1930s. The gap between Sao Paulo and the northeast of Brazil is dramatic. Recent developments in China have likewise been highly concentrated. This concentration of growth suggests the importance of several themes stressed in the earlier development literature, such as Hirschman's [2], *Theory of Linkages* or, in modern parlance, the importance of non-convexities and externalities, themes which have been taken up once again in the *New Growth* literature (19).

---

(18) Though we need, once again, to recall the caveats: the failure to observe diminishing returns only presents a problem if we believe that the NICs are on the same production function.

(19) Much of this literature, unfortunately, has not bothered to study the older growth literature. It is simply wrong to say (as advocates of this new growth literature claim) that the older growth literature took the rate of technological change as exogenous. Indeed, there were at least two strands of literature attempting to endogenize technological change (beyond the well known work of ARROW [3]).

The volume of essays edited by SHELL [42]represents perhaps the most well known set of studies undertaken by the students of Uzawa (see also UZAWA'S own work [60]), but there were others; the issues, both the economic problems and the modelling difficulties, were hotly discussed at all the major centers of research, including Chicago,

There can be little question that there are important elements of increasing returns in the economy. The theories of imperfect competition developed in the 1930s by Young [61], Robinson [36] and Chamberlain [11], and extended in the 1970s by Dixit and Stiglitz [17], Spence [47] and others were developed, in part, explicitly to provide a micro-theory of the firm in the presence of increasing returns.

The critical issue is moving from increasing returns to scale at the level of the firm to increasing returns at the aggregate level; and in identifying the nature and source of the increasing returns. Increasing returns at the industry and firm level can explain patterns of specialization, but they may not be able to explain patterns of growth. As in the familiar models of *U*-shaped cost curves, there can exist increasing returns at the firm level (and even at the industry level), but still, not increasing returns at the aggregative level.

Empirically, even at the industry level, the hypothesis of significant increasing returns appears to be problematic. If there were significant increasing returns, we would expect each industry to be dominated by a single firm.

More generally, both non-convexities and externalities may be and indeed are likely to be, localized, both geographically and by sector. Indeed, a disturbing defect of much of the new growth literature is an unconvincing account of the "units" over which the non-convexities and externalities arise. Countries consist of many regions. Is it the size of the region or the size of the country which determines the relevant "scale?" Does it make a difference whether the goods produced are traded or not? Presumably, for many traded goods, full advantage of economies of scale can be attained even in a relatively small economy such as Singapore.

The problem can be put in another way: there is no natural metric for measuring distances in modern economies, and accord-

---

Yale, and MIT. The second major strand was in Cambridge, represented most notably by the KALDOR-MIRRLEES [32] article. My own early work on endogenous growth with TONY ATKINSON [8] was influenced by both of these strands.

Similarly, the importance of non-convexities was also recognized in the earlier literature. Not only did Nicky Kaldor stress the importance of increasing returns in manufacturing, he successfully advocated the introduction of the selective employment tax in Britain to take advantage of these returns to scale.

ingly, no obvious unit over which agglomeration economies arise. Thus, with telephone and fax communication, some types of activities at some geographical distances from each other may participate in the benefits of agglomeration economies.

Thus, the challenge is not to construct aggregative models assuming increasing returns, but to identify the locus of these non-convexities and externalities, and in the latter case, to identify those that are not internalized by markets. Coase [14] went too far when he (or his disciples) asserted that all externalities could be internalized; yet many can. Indeed, a major theme of Chandler's [12] classic study is that firms are an alternative to markets, and succeed in internalizing certain externalities, in solving coordination failure problems. «US Steel», in constructing its major mill on the Southern shores of lake Michigan in 1906, solved the coordination problem of bringing together iron ore, limestone, coke, coal, and workers, and transportation facilities to bring inputs to the firm and the output to markets (20).

We know from conventional economic theory that if there are increasing returns to scale, but they are sufficiently limited relative to the scale of the market (that is, there are $U$ shaped cost curves, with demand at a price equal to the minimum average cost being many times that of the output at the minimum average cost), then increasing returns causes no problems; the industry supply curve can even be approximated as horizontal. With free international trade, the relevant market is the world market.

By the same token, if there are locational increasing returns, but again, because of congestion or other reasons, these increasing returns are limited, there will be geographical concentration; but as a large economy such as the United States grows, the growth will take the form of the formation of successive locational clusters; at the aggregative level, there will be no increasing returns. (And if regional agglomeration economies are more important for different kinds of production, and correspondingly, the optimal community size differs across products, then in equilibrium, with free migration (21) we will

---

(20) For instance, SAH - STIGLITZ [40] identify "diffuse externalities" as being relatively unamenable to internalization.

(21) Free mobility of capital, and/or free trade can substitute for free migration.

find communities of different sizes, each with equal utility for individuals of comparable skills) (22).

The success of some small countries, such as Taiwan, Hong
Kong, Singapore, and Switzerland, provides perhaps the most convincing support to the perspective being advanced here, that aggregative economies of scale are not important (23). Perhaps it is not that
these economies are large, but that big countries are composed of
many smaller economies.

The presence of increasing returns (and externalities) may be able
to account for two important phenomena: the presence of growth
spurts, and the failure of economies to converge. It has long been
recognized that with increasing returns and externalities, there may
be multiple equilibria, and indeed, growth may be path dependent
(24). Thus, an economy could be trapped in a low level equilibrium,
there would be a failure to converge (25) and once the economy is
moved out of the low level equilibrium (say by some form of
government intervention) there may be an extended period of high
growth before it converges to the high level equilibrium.

Still, many of the models constructed to date which give rise to
multiple equilibria seem unconvincing. They are critically dependent
on the economy being closed. Some of them (such as that of
Rosenstein-Rodan) entails a coordination failure, the failure of say a
market for steel to exist, because the market for products which use
steel does not exist; and the failure of the market for products which
use steel to exist, because the market for steel does not exist. But
international trade resolves many of these coordination failure problems: if steel is not available domestically, it can be purchased abroad.
Final users to not have to wait until intermediate goods producers
develop; and intermediate goods users do not have to wait until final

---

(22) The efficiency of the resulting world equilibrium is more problematic, as the
extensive literature in the *Theory of Local Public Goods* suggests. See, e.g. STIGLITZ
[51], [52].

(23) The counterargument, that in terms of the size of their economy, these
countries are large, is hardly convincing; first, they remain minuscule compared to the
largest economies in the world; second, they grew rapidly even when they were small.

(24) See STIGLITZ [59], DAVID, 1987, ARTHUR [4], [5], [6] ROSENSTEIN-RODAN [39]
or MURPHY - SHLEIFER - VISHNY [34].

(25) Even in growth rates, as in the model of STIGLITZ [53].

goods producers develop. In many cases, multinational firms can provide the critical coordination. In other models, the multiplicity of equilibrium arises from demand effects: with a low scale of production, incomes will be low; and with low incomes, the level of demand will be low, sufficiently low that the country cannot take advantage of the returns to scale. Again, this problem disappears when there is an open economy: the scale of production is not limited to domestic demand.

## 1.7.1 Open Economies

Returns to scale may be important even in open economies, but we have to be careful in locating its source. Andres Rodriguez' recent work [37] provides the first attempt to do so. He has shown how a small open economy may be caught in a low level equilibrium, one in which there are no incentives for capital to flow into the country, and in which both skilled and unskilled laborers receive lower wages (26). It rests on the reasonable hypothesis that there are non-convexities in the production of intermediate goods, some of which (like services) are essentially non-tradeable, and that the range of these intermediates that are available depends on the pattern of production of final goods. Countries that produce to their current comparative advantage (based on their current supply of these intermediate goods), may produce final goods which never generate the demand for the wide range of intermediate goods which form the basis of industrialization and which permit the production of more complex final goods (27).

---

(26) That is, the rate of return to capital in the poor country is no higher than in the rich country. An important implication of his analysis is that marginal rates of return to capital may not be a monotonically decreasing function of the aggregate capital labor ratio. The fact that (across steady states) interest rates were not monotonically declining in the value of capital was one of the central issues in the reswitching controversy.

(27) Capital accumulation may affect even the existence of this dominated equilibrium; at sufficiently high levels, only the efficient equilibrium survives. If the government cannot shift the economy by other means from the low level equilibrium to the high level equilibrium, this may provide another rationale for government intervention to encourage savings.

### 1.7.2 Technical Change

Once we introduce R & D (or learning by doing), there is implicitly some returns to scale, as has long been recognized (28). If the production fuction is constant returns to scale in conventional factors of production, and if the state of technology is a function of inputs into R & D, then the aggregative production function:

$$Q = A(K_R, L_R) F(K_P, L_P)$$

where subscript $R$ denotes factors used in research and subscript $p$ denotes factors used in production, exhibits increasing returns in total factor inputs. This argument applies as much to the expenditures required to adapt and absorb pre-existing technologies, as it does to expenditures for developing new products. (Countries like Korea spent considerable amounts of resources acquiring and adapting new technologies).

At the same time, there is no *a priori* reason to believe that diminishing returns will not set in in either the research or adaptation process. In the context of the laggard countries, an argument can be made for a logistics curve. As we noted earlier, in the early stages the countries have to "learn to learn" (Stiglitz [53]). In the later stages, there is less to learn.

For those countries at the frontier, research may enhance their ability to learn learning to learn may remain important. But, at any time, there is only a limited stock of unexploited ideas; the "easiest" ideas — those most easily translated into productive opportunities — get exploited first, leaving the harder problems. Basic research replenishes this stock of ideas, but the rate at which fundamental ideas are discovered is hard to predict, and though undoubtedly related to the levels of expenditures, the relationship is neither simple, nor necessarily stable over time. Thus, it is perfectly plausible that diminishing returns may set in R & D. To be sure, one can write down functional forms where this does not happen, and one can explore the consequences; but writing down these functional forms, unsupported by empirical research, provides us with little insight into the growth

---

(28) See, for instance, STIGLITZ [54].

process: it simply says what it assumes that if there is no diminishing returns, then we will not see diminishing returns (29).

Technical change is important for reasons beyond its implications for the aggregate production function: at the micro-economic level, the increasing returns which is associated with it gives rise to imperfect competition. The implications of imperfect competition for efficiency and growth are somewhat subtle, and are the subject of section 2.

In addition, as Schumpeter emphasized, financing R & D may be more difficult than financing the construction of a building, because of problems of collateralization. The relationship between finance and growth is the subject of section 3. But before turning to these issues, there is one more aspect of the growth process to which we wish to call attention.

## 1.8 *The Role of Government*

The second major difference in policy implications concerns the potential role of government. In the standard neoclassical models, there are no market failures. In virtually all of the models we have discussed so far, there are market failures: increasing returns leads to imperfect competition; it is impossible for all factors to receive their marginal products, since were they to do so, by Euler's equation, total returns would be more than exhausted; externalities - including the externalities associated with unappropriated returns from R & D, obviously mean that market economies may not be efficient; and we have just detailed the variety of ways in which market allocation of resources will not be efficient if there are important elements of rent.

## 1.9 *Concluding Remarks*

In this section, we have presented three alternative perspectives on recent growth experiences; in the process, we have commented on

---

(29) This characterization is actually slightly unfair; for it takes some care to specify exactly the nature of the functional forms which can give rise to steady states. At the same time, the lack of robustness of many of the results of most of the models, which appear quite sensitive to minor changes in the parameterization, is a disturbing feature of much of this literature.

a variety of models attempting to interpret those growth experiences. Models which assume that different countries are on the same constant returns production function are fundamentally implausible - in many less developed countries, wages of both skilled and unskilled workers seem below that in the more developed countries, yet returns to capital seem higher (30). We argued that aggregate increasing returns to scale provides an unconvincing explanation of differences in productivity, partly because it is hard to think that they are of the required magnitude.

But saying that different countries are on different production functions opens up a whole new set of questions: Why? and, What can be done about it? Part of the reason is knowledge, the access to information concerning best practice techniques, and the lack of human capital to make the technology transfer. A central part of the success of many of the Asian countries is that they recognized this, and allocated large amounts of resources to the formation of relevant forms of human capital.

And part of the reason may be economic organization, the efficiency with which resources are allocated. We have identified a number of reasons why resources may not be efficiently allocated - imperfect competition, rents, externalities. Less developed countries also have less developed markets; more broadly, the institutions whose function it is to ensure that resources are efficiently allocated work less well. This is a real *market* failure. The remainder of the paper is devoted to examining two of the market failures, imperfect competition and financial market constraints. We will argue that the former is likely not to be very important, but the latter is.

## 2. - Imperfect Competition

Though imperfect competition normally results in economic inefficiency, it does not necessarily result in too slow a rate of technical progress. Indeed, a central result of standard monopoly theory is that

---

(30) There are many pieces of evidence for this, besides those directly relating to the flow of capital. For instance, in LDCs capital is often used fewer shifts. For a fuller discussion of this point, and references, see STIGLITZ [56].

such firms are productively efficient. The monopolist can be viewed as producing output in different periods. Expenditures on R & D can be viewed as purely "technological" the firm decides how much to invest in capital goods, how much to spend on current inputs, and how much to spend on R & D; *given* the level of output, it makes all of these decisions efficiently.

This kind of argument would suggest that conditional on the levels of output produced by the monopolist, the level of expenditures of R & D should be optimal.

Some years ago, Lerner argued that the levels of output produced in a monopolistic equilibrium by each firm would be optimal, provided only that there were no monopolists of intermediate goods, provided the elasticity of demand facing each monopolist was the same and that the elasticity of labor supply was zero. The argument was simple. Assume that there is a single input, labor; firms will hire labor to the point where:

$$(2.1) \qquad p_i^m = w \left[ \frac{1}{\left(1 - \frac{1}{\varphi}\right)} \right] / f_i' \, [L_i^m]$$

marginal revenues equal marginal costs, where:

$p_i^m$ = price of ith good (produced by ith firm) in monopolistic equilibrium;

$L_i^m$ = employment in ith firm;

$\varphi$ = elasticity of demand;

$w$ = wage, and

$f_i$ = is the production function of the ith firm.

Market equilibrium is defined by the solution to *(2.1)* and the market clearing equation

$$(2.2) \qquad \Sigma \, L_i = L^*$$

where $L^*$ = total labor supply.

By constrast, the competitive market equilibrium is described by the solution to *(2.2)* and the equations:

*(2.3)*                         $p_i^c = w/f_i'[L_i^c]$

where $p_i^c$ = price of ith good in competitive equilibrium.

It is clear that if $L^*$ does not depend on real wages (and the composition of demand does not depend on the distribution of income), and the number of firms is fixed, the solutions to these sets of equations involve:

*(2.4a)*                         $L_i^c = L_i^m$

and:

*(2.4b)*                 $w/p^m = \left(1 - \dfrac{1}{\varphi}\right)w/p^c$

i.e. real wages are reduced as a result of imperfect competition, but the levels of output of each sector are unchanged.

Dixit-Stiglitz [17] extended the Lerner result to the case where the number of products produced was endogenous and where, because of fixed costs, there could not be a perfectly competitive equilibrium without government intervention; they showed that the market solution was constrained Pareto efficient, where the government was restrained not to provide lump sum subsidies to firms.

In this part of the paper, we develop a set of models in which we ask, «are markets which are imperfectly competitive and in which there is learning by doing (as a concrete form of increasing returns) efficient, in some sense?».

The prevailing wisdom, that there will be too little production, is based on the similarity between R & D and learning by doing. Arrow [3] argued that with imperfect competition that would be too little expenditure on R & D. First, he argued that competitive firms would spend too little on R & D, since competitive firms failed to capture the consumer surplus associated with improved technology on new products. Secondly, he argued that monopolists would produce less than competitors, and since the incentive to innovate increases with the level of production, the incentive to innovate would be lower with monopoly than under competition.

With learning by doing, at the margin, one can view the decision to produce as partially an investment in improved technology. Thus, if incentives to make conventional investments in improved technology are too low under imperfect competition, so too are those investments associated with production. In this view, with learning by doing there is underproduction with imperfect competition, for a new reason, beyond the traditional one of marginal revenue being less than price.

But the arguments given above suggest that Arrow's reasoning is too partial equilibrium in nature. In a general equilibrium model with all firms facing the same constant elasticity demand curve, production with monopoly is not less than under competition. Moreover, R & D is essentially like a fixed cost, and the Dixit-Stiglitz analysis suggests that if the government were constrained not to provide lump sum subsidies to firms, the market equilibrium might still be (constrained) Pareto efficient. In an earlier study, I showed that these conjectures are in fact correct; that is, market equilibria with imperfect competition may entail a constrained Pareto efficient level of expenditures on R & D.

Thus, below we extend these results to an economy with learning by doing, establishing an analogous constrained Pareto efficiency result.

The results on constrained Pareto efficiency require, however, two rather stringent assumptions. The first is that credit markets are perfect, the second is that the labor supply elasticity is zero. If either assumption is violated, there is scope for government intervention.

## 2.1 *Imperfect Capital Markets*

With learning by doing, in many cases it will be desirable for firms to produce a sufficiently large amount in earlier periods that price will be less than average costs (Dasgupta and Stiglitz [15]). The losses can only be financed by borrowing or government grants. (The earlier arguments began with the presumption that lump sum subsidies were precluded) (31).

But as section 3 below discusses, capital markets are notoriously imperfect. Work in the economics of information over the past fifteen years has explained why both equity and debt markets are imperfect: there is both credit and equity rationing (32).

But if firms cannot borrow, they will produce too little. And hence the level of technological progress will be less than desirable. It is the capital market imperfection which leads to too low a rate of technological progress. Elsewhere, Stiglitz [58] develops a model in which this second intuition is explored, and confirmed (33). In doing so, we identify a new category of imperfect information - imperfect capital market failures, arising when lenders cannot commit themselves to borrow from the same lender in succeeding periods.

## 2.2 *Inefficiency with Wage Sensitive Labor Supplies*

We now show that the assumption of a zero elasticity of labor supply is quite critical in the above analysis. In earlier work (Stiglitz [50]) we identified two kinds of inefficiencies, what we refer to as marginal and structural inefficiencies. The economy may have multiple equilibria which may be Pareto ranked. An economy is said to have a problem of structural inefficiency if it is trapped in a Pareto dominated equilibrium. Government policy is then aimed at shifting the economy from one equilibrium to another. Each of the equilibrium might, however, be improved upon by limited government interventions, e.g. taxes and subsidies. Such inefficiencies are referred to as marginal inefficiencies. Both of these can occur when there is learning by doing.

Earlier, we noted that the economy will be efficient, conditional

---

(31) The motivation for this assumption was that if the subsidy was not related to output, every individual could claim to be a firm, and collect the lump sum subsidy; while, of course, if the subsidy were related to output, it is not lump sum, and distorts the level of production.

(32) Not only are these markets imperfect, but the market equilibrium is constrained Pareto inefficient, GREENWALD-STIGLITZ [20], [22].

(33) For a more extensive discussion on the growth context, see STIGLITZ [57].

on the level of output. But if as a result of imperfect competition, real wages are lower than they otherwise would have been, labor supply, and hence aggregate output, will be lower (assuming an upward sloping labor supply curve). Because future output is lower, the value of learning will be lower, and current output will be lower on two counts: imperfect competition has the effect of driving down the real wage, and the value of learning is lower, and this too drives down the demand for labor. Because current output is lower, there will be less learning. Thus, imperfect competition in the presence of learning by doing and a positively sloped labor supply curve reduces the rate of technological progress. (Increasing the level of competition may, on that account, not only have a one time effect of increasing the level of efficiency, but may actually increase the rate of technological progress).

## 2.3 *Efficiency Without Capital Constraints*

### 2.3.1 The Basic Model

Throughout this section, we use a two period model. There are a fixed number of products; each product is produced by a single producer. Demand curves for each product have the same constant elasticity. For notational convenience, we drop the subscripts i referring to the specific commodities, whenever there is no resulting ambiguity. Output the first period, $Y_{oi}$, is proportional to labor input, $L_{oi}$, and we choose units so we can write:

$$(2.5) \qquad\qquad Y_{oi} = L_{oi}$$

Output the second period is proportional to labor input the second period, with the proportionality constant depending on the level of production the first period (learning by doing):

$$(2.6) \qquad\qquad L_{1i} = c_{1i}(Y_{oi})\, Y_{1i}$$

with:

$$c'_{1i} < 0, \ c'' > 0$$

For simplicity, we assume two classes of individuals, workers who live for only one period, and capitalists who own the firms and receive the profits. We assume that they all have utility functions which are time separable, with constant discount rate equal to unity:

$$u = \Sigma_t \Sigma_i (Y_{ti}^{1-\sigma}/1 - \sigma) \quad \sigma > 1$$

so that, using symmetry:

$$\frac{p_{0i}}{p_{1i}} = \frac{Y_{1i}^{-\sigma}}{Y_{0i}^{-\sigma}} = \left[ c\frac{L_0}{L_1} \right]$$

In subsection 1 we assume that there is zero marginal disutility of labor up to some critical level $L^*$, and infinite disutility beyond that. In subsection 2, we assume that the labor supply is a function of the real wage.

Capitalists have the same indirect utility function for goods that workers have.

## 2.3.2 Inelastic Labor Supply

*a) Myopia.* We first consider the possibility of myopic firms, that fail to take into account the consequences of learning by doing. They simply set marginal revenue equal to marginal cost. (We let the wage be the numeraire, and set $w = 1$). Thus firms set:

(2.7)
$$p_{0i} = 1/\left[ 1 - \frac{1}{\varphi} \right]$$

(2.8)
$$p_{1i} = w_1\left[ 1/\left( 1 - \frac{1}{\varphi} \right) \right] c_1 (L_{0i})$$

*b) Perfect Foresight.* We contrast this with the case where firms do take into account the value of learning. Now, the first period, they set (34):

$$(2.9) \qquad p_{i0}\left(1 - \frac{1}{\varphi}\right)\left(1 - \frac{p'_{1i} L_i}{p'_{0i}} \frac{c'_{1i}}{c_{1i^2}}\right)$$

Now we use the facts that 1) labor supply is inelastic; 2) all firms are symmetric to establish that labor allocations in the two situations are identical. But that means that the amount of learning is identical.

What then are we to make of the fact that in the non-myopic world, firms take into account that if they produce more, they learn more, and costs are lower? The recognition of these learning benefits does nothing more than to drive up the wage (lower the price the first period). The recognition of the importance of learning by doing has distributional effects, but not (in this simple model) allocative effects.

*c) Constrained Pareto efficiency.* Now assume that the government can allocate labor directly. How does the resulting resource allocation compare with that just described? The answer is again trivial: given the symmetry of the problem, it allocates 1/Nth of the

---

(34) *(2.9)* is derived as follows. The firm:

$$\max_{\{Y_{0i}, Y_{1i}\}} p_{0i} Y_{0i} - L_{0i} + p_{1i} Y_{1i} - Y_{1i} c (L_{0i}) w$$

where we recognize that $p_{1i}$ depends on output, and where $L_{0i} = Y_{0i}$. Thus, maximizing with respect to $Y_{0i}$, we obtain:

$$p_{0i} + \frac{\partial p_{0i}}{\partial Y_{0i}} - 1 - wY_{1i} c' = 0$$

or, using *(2.8)* and *(2.6)*:

$$p_{0i}\left(1 - \frac{1}{\varphi}\right) = 1 + wY_{1i} c'$$

$$= 1 + p_{1i}\left(1 - \frac{1}{\varphi}\right) L_{1i} \frac{c'_i}{c^2_i}$$

labor each period to each sector, total labor supply each period is the same as in the earlier case; and accordingly output is the same.

### 2.3.3 Wage Sensitive Labor Supplies

We now assume that the labor supply the ith period is a function of the real wage that period. Given the symmetric nature of our model, we can write:

$$L_0 = L(p_0), \quad L_1 = L_1(p_1/w_1)$$

Our utility function is now:

$$\Sigma_t \Sigma_i u(Y_{ti}) - v(L_0) - v(L_1)$$

The equations describing firm behavior remain unchanged. Now, however, we note that in general, there are real resource consequences from the increased demand for labor that results when firms recognize the dependence of future productivity on current output.

In particular, the higher wage results in greater or less labor supply depending on whether the labor supply curve is upward sloping or backward bending.

With backward bending supply curves, the recognition that future productivity depends on current output leads to a lower level of output and productivity improvement.

Rewriting the first order condition for first period production, and making use of the imperfect competition pricing equations, we obtain:

(2.10)
$$p_0(1 - 1/\varphi)$$

$$\left[ 1 - \frac{c_1'\left(\dfrac{L_0(p_0)}{n}\right) L_0^\sigma(p_0) L_1^{1-\sigma}\left(C_1\left(\dfrac{L_0(p_0)}{n}\right) / (1 - 1/\varphi)\right)}{n\, c_1^{2-\sigma}(L_0(p_0)/n)} \right] = 1$$

Any value of $p_0$ for which this equation holds is a general equilibrium. Differentiating with respect to $p_0$, we obtain:

$$(2.11) \qquad \frac{1}{p_0} - \frac{p_0\left(1 - \frac{1}{\varphi}\right)}{n^2} \, L_0' L_0^{\sigma}$$

$$\left[ \frac{C_1'' L_1^{1-\sigma}}{c_1^{2-\sigma}} + \frac{(1-\sigma)\,C_1'^2\,L_1'}{L_1^{\sigma}\left(1 - \frac{1}{\varphi}\right)c_1^{2-\sigma}} + \frac{\sigma\,c_1'\,L_1^{1-\sigma}}{L_0 c_1^{2-\sigma}} - \frac{(2-\sigma)\,c_1'^2\,L_1^{1-\sigma}}{c_1^{3-\sigma}} \right]$$

Because there may be more than one solution to *(2.10)*, *there may be multiple equilibria*. The intuitive reason for this is simple. With higher levels of output today, real wages next period will be higher (prices lower) because of the increased productivity. With higher levels of real wages, employment will be higher with an upward sloping labor supply curve; with higher employment, the benefits of learning will be higher; and with higher benefits to learning, firms will bid up the current real wage; and with higher real wages, output this period — and hence learning — will be higher.

Heuristically, the result we have just described can be put illustrated in graph 5, where we put output next period on the vertical axis and output this period on the horizontal axis. Higher levels of expected output next period mean that the value of learning is higher, so that output this period is higher.

On the other hand, higher levels of output this period mean that there is more learning, so that the marginal cost of production is lower, and actual output next period is higher. Both curves are upward sloping, and whenever they intersect, actual output next period equals the output that was expected: there is an equilibrium.

When there exists multiple rational expectations equilibria, they can be Pareto ranked provided the labor supply response is sufficiently great: equilibria with higher real wages may be unambiguously better than equilibria with lower real wages.

It is obviously the case that the workers are better off the lower $p_0$. Hence, all we need to consider is profits.

GRAPH 5

## MULTIPLE EQUILIBRIA WITH LEARNING BY DOING

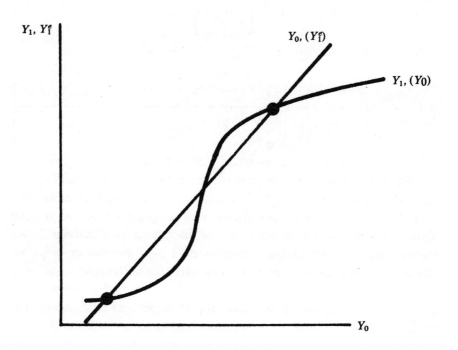

First period profits can be written as:

(2.12) $$\pi_0 = (p_0 - 1) L_0$$

Similarly, dropping subscripts $i$'s:

(2.13) $$\pi_1 = p_1 Y_1 - w_1 L_1 = p_1 \frac{L_1}{c_1} - w_1 L_1$$

(2.13a) $$= L_1 = \frac{p_1 L_1}{c_1} \left( 1 - \left( 1 - \frac{1}{\varphi} \right) \right)$$

(2.13b) $$= L_1 p_1 / \varphi$$

With an upward sloping labor supply curve, $\pi_0$ is greater the greater is the real wage provided the elasticity of labor is large enough (35). Thus, the higher rate of technological progress leads to higher real wages, which, by itself lowers profits in later periods. But if the labor supply response is large enough, it offsets the fact that on each unit of labor, the firm makes less profits.

Note, of course, that equilibria with higher real wages always have higher total output and the gains to the workers more than offset (under the compensation principle) the losses to the capitalists, since the direct effect of the real wage increase is just distributional, while the workers, in deciding on how much labor to supply, do not take into account the increased profits generated by higher labor supply to capitalists.

Not only are the multiple Pareto rankable equilibria, each of the equilibria is locally inefficient. To see this, consider the direct control problem where we maximize:

$$u = \frac{Y_{\tau i}^{1-\sigma}}{1-\sigma} - v(L_0) - v(L_1)$$

we obtain:

$$u'(Y_{0i}) - v'(L_0) - \frac{u'(Y_{1i}) L_{1i} c'}{c^2} = 0$$

Letting:

$$\frac{u'(Y_0)}{v'(L_0)} = \hat{p}_0$$

---

(35) Formally, we require:

$$\left[ -\frac{P_0}{L_0} \frac{dL_0}{dP_0} \right] > \frac{P_0}{P_0 - 1}$$

$\pi_1$ is greater provided only that:

$$\left[ -\frac{p_1}{L_1} \frac{dL_1}{dp_1} \right] > 1$$

efficiency requires:

$$(2.14) \quad \hat{p}_0 - \left[ 1 + \frac{L_1 \left( c_1 \left( \frac{L_0 \left( \hat{p}_0 \right)}{n} \right) \right) c_1' \left( L_0 \left( \hat{p}_0 \right)/n \right)}{n \, c_1^{2-\sigma}} \right] = 1$$

Clearly, *(2.14)* and *(2.10)* coincide only when $\varphi = 0$.

## 3. - Financial Markets

The last two decades has seen large advances in our understanding the role of, and limitations in, financial markets.

### 3.1 *Role of Financial Markets*

Financial markets, broadly defined to include an array of financial institutions, perform a number of functions, which we can briefly summarize as *a*) facilitating the accumulation of capital; *b*) reallocating capital; and *c*) monitoring the usage of capital. Much of the development literature has focused on *a*), and on the basis of this, governments which have restricted interest rates have been criticized for "financial repression". This, it is contended, has reduced savings rate. Yet, econometric studies have shown little evidence of a large interest elasticity of savings, and savings rates have been very high even in some countries with relatively low interest rates.

Equally, or perhaps more important than the interest rate *promised* is the security of the assets, avoiding the possibility of large negative returns, which result from bankruptcies of financial institutions. Note that excessive competition in the banking industry may, without government regulation and support, actually increase the financial fragility of particular financial institutions, and thus have a deleterious effect on savings, at least savings intermediated through financial institutions. By the same token, reduced interest rates may increase the financial viability of these institutions, and this effect may more than offset the direct effect from the lower return (36).

The fact that so many countries have obtained low returns on their investment that incremental capital output ratios have been so high suggests that at least as important as the magnitude of the savings is the efficiency with which it is allocated. We now recognize that central planning bureaus simply did not get at the essence of the allocation problem: more important than determining the sector of the economy is determining the precise project and managing that project; and given that, the choice of who is to manage a project is crucial.

While one of the central functions of financial institutions is precisely that looking at particular projects and firms (37), and selecting which get loans they do this imperfectly: because information is costly, screening among projects is never done with perfect accuracy.

That is why they have to rely on "indirect control mechanisms." They know that the mix of applicants that they get, and the extent of risk taking is affected by the interest rates which they charge, and other non-price terms of the loan contract. Thus, expected returns may be reduced even when the firm increases the interest rate charged. As is by now well known, this may lead to credit rationing.

Credit rationing, in turn, has one consequence which is important for our purposes: interest rates do not reflect the marginal productivity of capital. The social return to savings (in forms which get lent in credit markets) exceeds the private return. Given that credit is rationed, it is natural to look to other forms of capital, in particular, to equity markets. But equity markets are, if anything, even more imperfect than credit markets. While equity has marked advantages over credit (from the borrowers perspective) in that it entails risk sharing and avoids the threat of bankruptcy which the fixed obligations associated with credit entail, equity remains a relatively unimportant source of funds, even in the more developed countries (tables

---

(36) Obviously, maintaining a stable macro-economic policy is among the most important policies which governments can pursue to enhance the stability of the financial system.

(37) The choice of a firm can be thought of as a decision about who should "manage" the funds.

1 and 2). Recent work has provided an explanation of this: on average, when firms issue shares, there is a marked decline in the price of each share (See, e.g. Asquith and Mullins [7]). And we have good theoretical reasons for why this should be so, based on models of adverse selection (Greenwald, Stiglitz, and Weiss [25] and Myers and Majluf [35] and agency (Jensen [30]).

TABLE 1a

GROSS SOURCES OF FINANCE 1970-1989
(weighted average, undepreciated, revalued)

|  | France | Germany | Japan | UK | US |
|---|---|---|---|---|---|
| Internal ............... | 42.2 | 62.4 | 42.2 | 61.1 | 62.7 |
| Bank finance........... | 37.7 | 18.0 | 34.1 | 23.5 | 14.7 |
| Bonds ................. | 2.7 | 0.9 | 3.3 | 1.4 | 12.8 |
| Equity................. | 14.1 | 2.3 | 3.1 | 7.4 | −4.9 |
| Trade credit ........... | 2.9 | 1.8 | 14.9 | 1.9 | 8.8 |
| Capital transfers ........ | 3.4 | 6.6 |  | 2.3 |  |
| Other ................. | 0.3 | 8.0 | 2.4 | 2.4 | 5.9 |
| Notes ................. | 1970-1985 | 1970-1989 | 1970-1987 | 1970-1989 | 1970-1989 |

*Source:* Unpublished flow of funds figures from the CEPR: *International Study of the Financing of Industry.* Data courtesy of Tim Jenkinson and Colin Mayer.

TABLE 1b

NET SOURCES OF FINANCE, 1979-1989
(weighted average, undepreciated, revalued)

|  | France | Germany | Japan | UK | US |
|---|---|---|---|---|---|
| Internal ............... | 66.3 | 80.6 | 71.7 | 98.0 | 91.3 |
| Bank finance........... | 51.5 | 11.0 | 28.0 | 19.8 | 16.6 |
| Bonds ................. | 0.7 | 0.6 | 4.0 | 2.0 | 17.1 |
| Equity................. | − 0.4 | 0.9 | 2.7 | − 8.0 | − 8.8 |
| Trade credit ........... | − 0.7 | − 1.9 | − 7.8 | − 1.6 | − 3.7 |
| Capital transfers ........ | 2.6 | 8.5 |  | 2.1 |  |
| Other ................. | − 14.9 | 1.5 | 1.3 | − 4.1 | − 3.8 |
| Statistical adj. .......... | − 5.1 | 0.0 | 0.1 | − 8.2 | − 8.7 |
| Notes ................. | 1970-1985 | 1970-1989 | 1970-1987 | 1970-1989 | 1970-1989 |

*Source:* Unpublished flow of funds figures from the CEPR: *International Study of the Financing of Industry.* Data courtesy of Tim Jenkinson and Colin Mayer.

TABLE 2

## SOURCES OF FUNDS BY THE CORPORATE SECTOR KOREA
### (in percent)

| | 1963-1965 | 1966-1971 | 1972-1976 | 1977-1981 | 1982 | 1984 | 1986 | 1987 |
|---|---|---|---|---|---|---|---|---|
| Internal funds ......... | 47.7 | 25.4 | 32.9 | 23.3 | 27.0 | 33.3 | 39.9 | — |
| External funds ......... | 52.3 | 74.6 | 67.1 | 76.7 | 73.0 | 66.7 | 60.1 | — |
| Total ............. | 100.0 | 100.0 | 100.0 | 100.0 | 100.0 | 100.0 | 100.0 | 100.0 |
| External funds ......... | 100.0 | 100.0 | 100.0 | 100.0 | 100.0 | 100.0 | 100.0 | 100.0 |
| Borrowings from Monetary institutions .. | 48.4 | 41.8 | 51.1 | 53.7 | 55.4 | 60.5 | 44.8 | 46.4 |
| Banks ........... | 33.5 | 32.8 | 34.3 | 32.6 | 30.0 | 21.6 | 33.6 | 21.2 |
| Nonbanks ........... | 15.0 | 9.0 | 16.8 | 21.1 | 25.5 | 38.9 | 11.2 | 25.2 |
| Securities (direct finance) ...... | 27.6 | 14.3 | 21.8 | 24.8 | 31.8 | 32.1 | 24.7 | 40.5 |
| Debts ............ | 1.2 | 0.7 | 2.5 | 4.2 | 18.3 | 11.5 | 9.6 | 8.1 |
| Stocks ........... | 21.4 | 11.8 | 18.1 | 14.4 | 10.4 | 20.6 (*) | 15.1 (*) | 32.4 (=) |
| Capital paid in | 5.0 | 2.7 | 1.3 | 1.9 | 3.2 | — | — | — |
| corporate bills ........ | — | — | 1.8 | 5.5 | 7.7 | — | 100.0 | − 2.3 |
| Government and curb market loans ......... | 8.5 | 7.8 | − 0.3 | 0.8 | 1.0 | 3.2 (**) | 5.3 (**) | 17.0 (=*) |
| Borrowing from abroad ......... | 15.4 | 36.2 | 26.6 | 15.2 | 4.1 | − 5.1 | 15.2 | − 1.6 |

(*) Stocks and capital paid in.
(**) Others included.

*Source:* The BANK OF KOREA: *Annual Report,* various issues, AMSDEN - EUH [1].

## 3.2 *Implications of Imperfect Capital Markets*

These limitations on financial markets in turn have important consequences:

*a*) firms may be limited by their retained earnings in the amount which they can invest; the marginal return to firms' savings may be very high. More generally, the marginal returns to capital in different firms may differ (38);

*b*) with even small degrees of increasing returns (such as associated with learning by doing) markets will be dominated by a single firm in the absence of capital market imperfections. With capital market imperfections, this will not be true: financial market imperfections provide an alternative to imperfect competition as a resolution of the problem of increasing returns (39);

*c*) when firms have access to credit markets, retained earnings have a further effect in providing the collateral which gains them access to the credit market; on the other side, the more "equity" (retained earnings) they have, the more willing they are to undertake the risks associated with borrowing, i.e. the lower the probability of default at any level of economic activity, and the lower the *marginal* probability; thus, the "marginal cost" of producing more and of investing more is reduced, leading to higher levels of these activities. Moreover, the greater their "wealth", the greater their willingness to engage in more risky activities, such as associated with investments in R & D (40). Accordingly, there may be higher returns to savings; we can think of this equity as "high powered" capital;

*d*) the ability and willingness of banks and other financial institutions to lend depends too on their financial position, including their

---

(38) For example, large firms may obtain a higher return because there are increasing returns associated with obtaining information; it pays them to spend more to screen among alternative projects. Moreover, larger firms may be able to diversify risks better, and thus be willing to undertake higher risk-higher return projects.

(39) Actually, the two theories are, in many cases, complementary, with the financial constraints playing a more important role in some markets (particularly when there are many small firms, as in the computer industry) and imperfect competition in others.

(40) In GREENWALD - STIGLITZ [21] we describe the portfolio theory of the firm, in which we show how the various actions of a firm can be thought of as a portfolio, the mix of which affects the probability distribution of final values of the firm.

net worth; banks too are equity constrained. Their willingness and ability to borrow funds (recruit deposits), which they then lend out is affected by their net worth. (A bank can simply be thought of as a firm whose activity is to make loans). A reduction in their net worth thus reduces the amount they are willing to lend.

## 3.3 *Role of Government*

This perspective has quite different implications with respect to the growth process and the consequences of a variety of forms of government intervention. In particular, policies which increase the financial strength of firms or of financial institutions may reap large dividends. By contrast, in neoclassical growth theory, the corporate veil is easily pierced: only real factors matter. Indeed, in the simplistic models of much of the new growth theory, there is a representative agent, who simply maximizes his intertemporal utility. The distribution of wealth among individuals, or between households and firms, is of absolutely no consequence.

Enhancing firm profits increases the potential for retained earnings, thus increasing firm's equity base, and their ability and willingness to invest and take risks. Since the social returns to investment may well exceed the private returns, government, by imposing high taxes on distributed profits, can encourage firms to retain a larger fraction of their profits. (In rapidly growing economies, the returns to retained earnings noted earlier are sufficiently high that no further encouragement from the government may be needed).

Profits will be high if wages remain low. Here we see an alternative mechanism for why surplus labor facilitates growth. Traditional theory has focused on the fact that it enables growth to proceed without large increases in wages. Increases in wages, it was thought, slowed down the growth process presumably because savings rates out of wages were smaller than savings rates out of profits. In a sense, our analysis provides a theoretical rationale for these differences in savings rates, a rationale related to differences in returns to savings (since household saving is largely mediated through credit institutions, and the interest rates they pay depositors are typically far lower than the return to capital). Our analysis emphasizes that it is not just the amount of savings, but the form. If it were just the amount of savings, the deficiency could be made up through government borrowing abroad.

### 3.3.1 Government Regulations

Lowering interest rates charged to borrowers has ambiguous effects. On the one hand, it increases the profitability of firms; it induces firms to borrow more; it increases their retained earnings; and through these channels has, in the long run, a possibly large multiplicative effect.

The effects on financial institutions depends on whether they can "pass on" the reduced interest rates in the form of reduced deposit rates. If they can, then there may a slight deleterious effect on household savings. But this is likely to be far outweighed by the positive effects from increased corporate savings. (And indeed, the lower interest rates result in lowered default probabilities, again enhancing the financial stability of financial institutions, which, we suggested, has a positive effect on savings).

If they cannot pass on these lowered interest rate charges to their depositors (say because of competition from an unregulated financial intermediary), then the strength of financial institutions will be weakened, and this will have adverse effects on their ability and willingness to lend.

This analysis also suggests that government actions restricting competition in the banking sector may have more ambiguous effects than has previously been thought. Reduced competition may not lead to higher interest rates charged if interest rates charged are determined in a manner described by standard credit rationing models. Reduced competition may lead to lower interest rates paid to depositors, but the net effect on savings may be small; and the increased net worth of the financial institutions may result in increased lending activities (and may lead banks to be willing to lend to higher risk-higher expected returns projects).

Restrictions on competition always represent (at best) a two edged sword: isolated from competition, bank managers may become slack; rather than the increased profits being used to facilitate increased lending, the funds may be used to increase managerial perks.

### 3.3.2 Regional Lending

Earlier, we noted evidence of agglomeration economies, and posed the problem of identifying the sources and extent of these economies. Banks, we have argued, are essentially in the information business. Much of the information which they acquire is very particular, very localized, by-products of other activities. A lending officer can get often more reliable information about how a store is doing by randomly checking on the store, looking at inventory on the shelf, the number of customers, etc. than by looking at financial accounts. Localized hearsay information often yields important clues as to what is going on.

Similarly, venture capital firms tend to specialize not only with respect to the industries to which they provide finance, but also with respect to the locale. They want to be able, at low costs, to make on-site inspections.

It is thus not surprising that financial centers are often linked closely with production centers.

### 3.3.3 Industrial Organization

While we have emphasized the role of banks in financial intermediation, they are not the only institutions involved in that activity. We have already mentioned venture capital firms. These often serve an intermediary role; they receive capital (often from large institutional investors) which they reinvest in new ventures. They are specialized in screening and monitoring.

But intermediation is more pervasive: the nexus of production relations which characterized modern industrial economies gives rise to complicated patterns of information flows. A firm knows much about its suppliers and customers; if they are slow in delivering products, if product quality is variable, if customers are slow in making payments, questions about managerial or financial strengths of the firms are raised. Firms are, thus, often in a better position to monitor the firms with whom they have relationships than are banks, and it is accordingly not surprising that the nexus of production relationships is associated with a nexus of financial relationships, with firms supplying credit to each other. A large firm may simultaneously borrow funds from its bank and lend both to its suppliers and customers. It is acting as a financial intermediary.

Large conglomerates also can facilitate the flow of capital. Just as earlier literature stressed the importance of an internal labor market, there may be an internal capital market. A major lesson to emerge from the US experience with conglomerates is that these internal capital markets may not work very well; or at least that the diseconomies of scope may outweigh any gains from the improved reallocation of capital. This may not be surprising: the information flows among the disparate parts of conglomerates engage in relatively unrelated economic activities may not have been much, or any, better than those available to an unrelated bank.

What then accounts for the seeming success of the Korean conglomerates, or the analogous institutions in Japan? Answering this question would take us beyond the scope of this paper, but a suggestion is that "better" governance structures, which prevented or limited the abuse of managerial discretion, as occurred in the United States (41): the closely held nature of the Korean firms, and the role of the main bank (which often held equity interests in the firms to which they lent) in Japan.

## 3.3.4 Infant Industry Arguments

We have seen that financial market imperfections (arising naturally out of the fact that information is imperfect and costly) mean that there is a discrepancy between private and social returns, a discrepancy which may differ across industries. While this in itself would provide a rationale for an industrial policy, it is worth noting that financial market constraints may, in particular, provide a rationale for

---

(41) For theoretical analyses explaining the rationale for these managerial "abuses" see SHLEIFER - VISHNY [41] or EDLIN - STIGLITZ [19].

"infant industry" arguments. The classical criticisms of infant industry arguments is that if, in the long run, a firm will gain a comparative advantage by producing, then it should pay it to borrow, to sell below its current marginal costs. (With learning, production should be related to the long run marginal cost; that is, the marginal return to producing more is not just today's increased profits, but the decreased costs of production in the future). If the interest rate is zero, then the relevant marginal cost is simply the asymptotic value (Spence [48]). In the absence of externalities, it is socially profitable to enter an industry if and only if it is privately profitable to do so. But this analysis assumes that the firm can have easy access to capital. If it cannot, there may be high social returns to "investing" in learning, yet private firms simply cannot afford to do so.

### 3.3.5 Collateralization

This is particularly true because this form of investment cannot be collateralized; the "investment" is not like an investment in a building or a machine. Because the costs of information imperfections are greater for investments which cannot be collateralized, the market will have a "bias" towards collateralizable investments, and against investments in "learning by doing", or R & D, which cannot be collateralized.

### 3.3.6 Macro-Stability

Theories emphasizing the importance of financial constraints also emphasize the importance of macro-economic stability for growth. In the older, neoclassical models, technical change was exogenous, so that any short term disturbance that might move the economy below its production possibilities curve would have only temporary effects; it might slow down the process of capital accumulation, and thus delay slightly the approach to the steady state, but that is all.

In models with endogenously determined expenditures on R & D, but with no financial constraints, cyclical fluctuations should have little effect on the pace of R & D. Investment in R & D is driven by long run considerations — say the savings from lower costs of production — and neither long run real wages, interest rates, or output is, in this perspective, likely to be affected much by a short term downturn in the economy, and therefore neither are incentives to invest in R & D or learning.

By contrast, models with financial constraints argue that short term macro-fluctuations have marked effects on R & D and learning, so that the growth path of the economy may be *permanently* lower, as illustrated in graph 6. The reason for this is that stated earlier: with lower "net worth" firms are less willing or able to make these investments; with major downturns, in spite of the higher adjustment costs often associated with R & D, firms cut back on R & D expenditures, since it has an immediate positive effect on net cash flow, and its long run effects on profitability will not be felt for some time. Greenwald, Salinger and Stiglitz, 1992, provide empirical evidence in support of this contention, and Greenwald, Kohn and Stiglitz [24] provide a theoretical model extending this analysis to the case of learning by doing.

GRAPH 6

## AN ECONOMIC DOWNTURN HAS A LONG RUN EFFECT ON OUTPUT

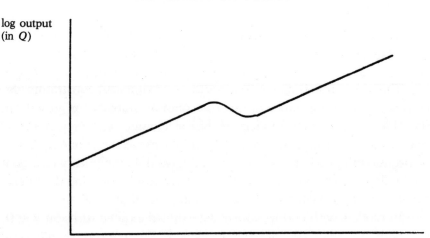

log output
(in *Q*)

time

Thus, in economies in which financial constraints are important, achieving macro-stability has distinct long-run benefits. Indeed, they are even greater than we have suggested, since one of the main sources of information imperfections concerns the ability of firms to withstand cyclical shocks. Reducing the magnitude of the cyclical shocks reduces, in this sense, the extent of information imperfections in the economy (42).

### 3.4 A Simple Model

The complexity of the relationships that we have described cannot be fully captured in any single model (43). The following simple model illustrates several of the themes we have emphasized. Assume that, as in Stiglitz and Weiss 1981, projects either are successful and yield a return of $R$, or are a failure, and earn a return of zero. ($R$ may itself be a function of the wage rate). For simplicity, we assume all entrepreneurs have projects yielding the same $R$, but differ in the probability of success, $p$. Entrepreneurs know their probability of success, but lenders do not. We assume there are no functioning equity markets. Each project costs 1 (a normalization). Lenders can observe the wealth, $w$, of entrepreneurs. They require entrepreneurs to invest all of their wealth in the project, and they lend the difference, $1 - w$. The interest rate charged is such as to yield an expected return on all of those borrowing equal to the safe rate of interest $r$. Let $F(p)$ be the distribution function of $p$, $N$ the number of entrepreneurs, and define:

(3.1)
$$K(\hat{p}) = \int_{p}^{1} p \, dF(p)$$

(3.2)
$$H(\hat{p}) = K(p)/(1 - F(p))$$

---

(42) This argument has to be qualified by the observation that in the presence of more stable macropolicies, firms may be induced to borrow more, thus exacerbating the effects of any economic downturn.

(43) For several models attempting to capture various aspects of the equity-growth relationship, see GREENWALD - KOHN - STIGLITZ [24].

the mean probability of success of all projects with success probabilities greater than or equal to $\hat{p}$. An individual with wealth $w$ has a choice of borrowing at an interest rate $i$, or investing his wealth in the safe asset. Thus, he will borrow so long as:

$$(3.3) \qquad p\left[R - (1 + i)(1 - w)\right] \geq (1 + r)w$$

Define $\hat{p}$ as the marginal person borrowing. Then:

$$(3.4) \qquad \hat{p}\left[R - (1 + i)(1 - w)\right] = (1 + r)w$$

$\hat{p}$ can be expressed as a function of $w$ and $1 + i$:

$$(3.5) \qquad \hat{p} = \Phi(w, 1 + i) \equiv \frac{(1 + r)w}{R - (1 + i)(1 - w)}$$

$i$ is set so as yield the same expected return as the safe asset:

$$(3.6) \qquad H(\hat{p})(1 + i) = 1 + r$$

The above two equations can be solved simultaneously for $i$ and $p$; e.g. substituting $(3.6)$ into $(3.4)$ we obtain:

$$(3.7) \qquad \hat{p}R - \hat{p}(1 - w)(1 + r)/H(\hat{p}) = (1 + r)w$$

We denote the solution for the rate of interest charged by $i(w)$.

It is apparent that an increase in $w$ lowers the nominal interest rate charged and increases $\hat{p}$:

$$\frac{w\,d\hat{p}}{\hat{p}\,dw} = -\frac{w\left(1 - \dfrac{1}{H}\right)}{w + \hat{p}(1 - w)h/H^2} > 0$$

where:

$$h \equiv H' = \frac{f(p)}{1 - F}\{-\hat{p} + H(\hat{p})\} > 0$$

Hence:

$$\frac{di}{dw} = -\frac{(1 + r)}{H^2} h \frac{d\hat{p}}{dw} < 0$$

Net social expected returns from the lending activity to those with wealth $w$, $S$, is:

(3.8)     $$S = N K(\hat{p}) R - N(1 - F(\hat{p})) (1 + r)$$

differentiating with respect to $\hat{p}$, we obtain:

(3.9)     $$\frac{\partial S}{\partial \hat{p}} = N f(\hat{p}) [(1 + r) - R \hat{p}]$$

But from (3.7):

$$\hat{p} R - (1 + r) = (1 - w)((1 + i)\hat{p} - (1 + r)) =$$
$$= (1 - w)(1 + i)(\hat{p} - H) < 0$$

Thus, an increase in $w$ increases the net social return from the lending activities.

Consider now a two period model in which no one begins with any wealth; but in which those who are successful the first period accumulate a wealth of:

$$w = R - (1 + i)$$

The first period, all potential entrepreneurs borrow ($\hat{p} = 0$), while the second period,

$$p^* = \Phi (R - (1 + i(0)), 1 + r(R - (1 + i(0))))$$

assuming that the probabilities of success each period are independent. We can now see that lowering the interest rate charged the first period may increase net social product:

$$dS/di = [dS/dp^*] [dp^*/dw] [dw/di] < 0$$

Financial "repression" may increase net national product.

Similarly, we can show that lowering the wage (even below the market clearing level) may result in increased net national product.

## 4. - Concluding Remarks

Much of growth policy is predicated on the economists' basic competitive model. Governments are advised simply to let markets work, or as the expression goes, "get the prices right". Yet many observed aspects of the growth process seem inconsistent with the competitive model. Almost all recent theorizing about growth processes — whether based on externalities, learning by doing, increasing returns, or financial market imperfections — identifies significant departures from the standard competitive paradigm as being central. It has become commonplace for economists, at this juncture, to sound the caveat that the existence of market failures does not in itself provide a justification for government intervention. One must show that the government can, and is likely, to intervene in ways which are welfare enhancing. In many of the East Asian countries governments seem to have taken an active role; they have intervened, not in the manner envisaged by the now thoroughly discredited central planning paradigm, but in more subtle, if no less pervasive ways. They have helped not only create markets, they have used markets: they have helped make them work in ways which may well have enhanced the success of these countries. How they have done this, and the extent to which the lessons we can learn from their experiences are replicable in other countries, is a matter for future research (44) (45).

---

(44) A major World Bank project examining these questions is presently underway.

(45) AMSDEN - EUH [1] provide an interesting description of the interventions of the Korean government in their financial markets, interventions which are remarkably similar to those which the theories we have described above might suggest.

The Korean government did a great deal to encourage the development of equity markets, including putting limits on the debt equity ratios; they kept interest rates charged low, with evidently no significant adverse effects on savings.

BIBLIOGRAPHY

[1] AMSDEN A.E. - EUH Y.D.: «South Korea's 1980s Financial Reform: Goodbye Fiancial Repression (Maybe), Hello New Institutional Restraints», *World Development*, forthcoming, 1992.

[2] AOKI M.: «A Note on Marshallian Process Under Increasing Returns», *Quarterly Journal of Economics*, vol. 84, n. 1, February 1970, pp. 110-2.

[3] ARROW K.J.: The Economic Implications of Learning by Doing, *Review of Economic Studies*, n. 29, June 1962, pp. 155-73.

[4] ARTHUR W.B.: *Competing Techniques and Lock-in by Historical Events. The Dynamics of Allocation under Increasing Returns*, Stanford University, mimeo, 1985.

[5] — — : «Competing Technologies: an Overview», in DOSI G. *et* AL. (eds.): *Technical Change and Economic Theory*, London, Pinter Publishers, 1988.

[6] — — : «Competing Technologies, Increasing Returns and Lock-in by Historical Events», *Eeonomic Journal*, n. 99, 1989, pp. 116-31.

[7] ASQUITH P. - MULLINS D.W.: Equity Issues and Stock Price Dilution, *Journal of Financial Economics*, n. 13, 1986, pp. 296-320.

[8] ATKINSON A.B. - STIGLITZ J.E.: A New View of Technological Change, *Economic Journal*, vol. 59, n. 2, May 1969, pp. 46-49.

[9] BAUMOL W.: «Productivity Growth, Convergence and Welfare: What the Long Run Data Shows», *American Economic Review*, n. 76, 1986, pp. 1072-85.

[10] BOSKIN M. - LAU L.J.: «Capital Formation and Economic Growth», in *Technology and Economics: a Volume Commemorating Ralph Landau's Service to the National Academy of Engineering*, Washington (DC), National Academy Press, 1990, pp. 47-56.

[11] CHAMBERLIN E.H.: *Theory of Monopolistic Competition*, Cambridge (MA), Harvard University Press, 1933.

[12] CHANDLER A.: *The Visible Hand*, Cambridge, The Belknap Press, 1977.

[13] CHENERY H. - SRINIVASAN T.N. (eds.): «Economic Organization, Information, and Development», in *Handbook of Development Economics*, Elsevier Science Publishers, 1988, pp. 94-160.

[14] COASE R.: The Problem of Social Cost, *Journal of Law and Economics*, n. 3, 1960, pp. 1-44.

[15] DASGUPTA P. - STIGLITZ J.E.: «Uncertainty, Market Structure and the Speed of R&D», *Bell Journal of Economics*, vol. 11, n. 4, 1980, pp. 1-28.

[16] — — : «Learning by Doing, Market Structure & Industrial & Trade Policies», *Oxford Economic Papers*, vol. 40, 1988, pp. 246-68.

[17] DIXIT A. - STIGLITZ J.E.: «Monopolistic Competition and Optimal Product Diversity», *American Economic Review*, vol. 67, n. 3, June 1977, pp. 297-308.

[18] DURLAUF S. - JOHNSON P.A.: *Local Versus Global Convergence Across National Economies*, mimeo, Stanford University, 1992.

[19] EDLIN A. - STIGLITZ J.E.: «Discouraging Rivals: Managerial Rent Seeking and Economic Inefficiencies», read at the conference of the Centre for Economic Policy Research on *Corporate Governance*, Stanford University, May 1992.

[20] GREENWALD B.C. - STIGLITZ J.E.: «Externalities in Economies with Imperfect Information and Incomplete Markets», *Quarterly Journal of Economics*, n. 101, May 1986, pp. 229-64.

[21] GREENWALD B.C. - STIGLITZ J.E.: «Money Imperfect Information and Economic Fluctuations», in KOHN M. - TSIANG S.C. (eds.): *Finance Constraints Expectations and Macroeconomics*, Oxford, Oxford University Press, 1988, pp. 141-65.

[22] —— : «Pareto Inefficiency of Market Economies: Search and Efficiency Wage Models», *American Economic Review*, vol. 78, n. 2, May 1988, pp. 351-5.

[23] —— : «Asymmetric Information and the New Theory of the Firm: Financial Constraints and Risk Behavior», *American Economic Review*, vol. 80, n. 2, May 1990, pp. 160-5.

[24] GREENWALD B.C. - KOHN M. - STIGLITZ J.E.: «Financial Market Imperfections and Productivity Growth», *Journal of Economic Behavior and Organization*, n. 13, 1990, pp. 321-45.

[25] GREENWALD B.C. - STIGLITZ J.E. - WEISS A.: Informational Imperfections in the Capital Markets and Macro-Economic Fluctuations, *American Economic Review*, vol. 74, n. 1, May 1984, pp. 194-9.

[26] GRILICHES Z. - JORGENSON D.W.: «The Explanation of Productivity Change», *Review of Economic Studies*, 1967, pp. 229-48.

[27] HALL R.E. - JORGENSON D.W.: «Tax Policy and Investment Behavior», *American Economic Review*, n. 57, June 1976, pp. 391-414.

[28] HELPMAN E. - KRUGMAN P.: *Innovation and Growth in the Global Economy*, London, MIT Press, 1991.

[29] HIRSCHMAN A.O.: *The Strategy of Economic Development*, New Haven, Yale University Press, 1958.

[30] JENSEN M.: Agency Costs of Free Cash Flow, Corporate Finance and Takeovers, *American Economic Review*, n. 76, May 1986, pp. 323-9.

[31] KALDOR N.: «A Model of Economic Growth», *Economic Journal*, n. 68, December 1967, pp. 591-624.

[32] KALDOR N. - MIRRLEES J.A.: «A New Model of Economic Growth», *Review of Economic Studies*, vol. XXIX, June 1962, pp. 174-92.

[33] KIM J.I. - LAU L.J.: *The Sources of Economic Growth of the Newly Industrialized Countries on the Pacific Rim*, mimeo, Stanford, Stanford University, 1992.

[34] MURPHY K.M. - SHLEIFER A. - VISHNY R.W.: «Industrialization and the Big Push», *Journal of Political Economy*, vol. 97, n. 5, 1989, pp. 1003-1-26.

[35] MYERS S. - MAJLUF N.: «Corporate Financing and Investment Decisions When Firms Have Information that Investors do not Have», *Journal of Financial Economics*, n. 13, 1984, pp. 187-221.

[36] ROBINSONS J.: *Economics of Imperfect Competition*, London, 1933.

[37] RODRIGUEZ A.: *The Big Push in a Small Open Economy*, mimeo, 1992.

[38] ROMER P.: «Increasing Returns and Long-Run Growth», *Journal of Political Economy*, vol. 94, n. 5, 1986.

[39] ROSENSTEIN-RODAN P.N.: «Problems of Industrialization in Eastern and Southeastern Europe», *Economic Journal*, n. 53, June-September 1943, pp. 202-11.

[40] SAH R. - STIGLITZ J.E.: Sources of Technological Divergence Between Developed and Less Developed Countries, in CALVO G. *et* AL. (eds.): *Debt, Stabilizations and Development: Essays in Memory of Carlos Diaz-Aleiandro*, Oxford, Basil Blackwell, 1989.

[41] SHLEIFER A. - VISHNY R.: «Management Entrenchment: the Cast of Manager-Specific Investments», *Journal of Financial Economics*, n. 25, November 1989, pp. 123-39.

[42] SHELL K. (ed.): *Essays on the Theory Optimal Economic Growth*, Cambridge (MA), MIT Press, 1967.

[43] SOLOW R.M.: «A Contribution to the Theory of Economic Growth», *Quarterly Journal of Economics*, n. 70, 1956, pp. 65-94.

[44] ——: «Technical Change and the Aggregate Production Function», *Review of Economics and Statistics*, n. 39, August 1957, pp. 312-20.

[45] ——: «Investment and Technical Progress», in ARROW K.J. - KARBIN S. - SUPPES P. (eds.): *Mathematical Methods in the Social Sciences*, Stanford, Stanford University Press, 1959.

[46] ——: *Growth Theory - An Exposition*, Oxford, Oxford University Press, 1970.

[47] SPENCE A.M.: «Production Selection, Fixed Costs, and Monopolistic Competition», *Review of Economic Studies*, n. 43, June 1976, pp. 217-35.

[48] ——: The Learning Curve and Competition, *Bell Journal of Economics*, vol. 12, n. 1, Spring, 1981, pp. 49-70.

[49] STIGLITZ J.E.: Factor Price Equalization in a Dynamic Economy, *Journal of Political Economy*, vol. 78, 1970, pp. 456-89.

[50] ——: «On the Optimality of the Stock Market Allocation of Investment», *Quarterly Journal of Economics*, vol. 86, n. 1, February 1972, pp. 25-60.

[51] ——: «Theory of Local Public Goods», in FELDSTEIN M.S. - INMAN R.P. (eds.): *The Economics of Public Services*, New York, Macmillan Publishing Company, 1977, pp. 274-333.

[52] ——: «The Theory of Local Public Goods Twenty-Five Years After Tiebout: a Perspective», in ZODROW G.R. (eds.): *Local Provision of Public Services: the Tiebout Model After Twenty-Five Years*, New York, Academic Press, 1983, pp. 17-53.

[53] ——: «Learning to Learn, Localized Learning and Technological Progress», in DASGUPTA P. - STONEMAN P. (eds.): *Economic Policy and Technological Performance*, Centre for Economic Policy Research, Cambridge, Cambridge University Press, 1987, pp. 125-53.

[54] ——: «On Microeconomics of Technical Progress», in KATZ J.M. (ed.): *Technology Generation in Latin American Manufacturing Industries*, Hampshire, Macmillan, 1987, pp. 56-77.

[55] ——: «Economic Organization, Information, and Development», in CHENERY H. - SRINIVASAN T.N. (eds.): *Handbook of Development Economics*, New York, Elsevier Science Publishers, 1988, pp. 94-160.

[56] ——: «Market, Market Failures and Economic Development», *American Economic Review*, vol. 79, n. 2, May 1989, pp. 197-203.

[57] ——: «Some Retrospective Views on Growth Theory», in DIAMOND P. (ed.): *Growth, Productivity, Unemployment: Essays to Celebrate Bob Solow's Birthday*, Cambridge (MA), IT Press, 1990, pp. 50-68.

[58] ——: *Notes on Learning, Capital Constraints, Growth and Efficiency*, paper read at the conference held by the Institute for the Study of Free Enterprise Systems, New York, Buffalo, May 1990.

[59] ——: «Social Absorption Capability and Innovation», paper for the *Symposium for the Twentieth Birthday of the Korean Development Institute*, Seoul, July 1991, forthcoming, 1992.

[60] UZAWA H.: «Optimal Technical Changes in an Aggregative Model of Economic Growth», *International Economic Review*, n. 6, 1965, pp. 12-31.

[61] YOUNG A.: «Increasing Returns and Economic Progress», *Economic Journal*, n. 39, 1928, pp. 527-42.

# Economic Convergence and the Theory of Factor Price Equalization Areas

**Robert A. Mundell**

Columbia University

## Introduction

The subject of economic convergence has received considerable attention in the past decade (1). Do incomes, wealth and/or growth converge internationally, and if so, why? The answers encompass virtually every field of economic theory.

There are three types of interaction that can affect the extent of convergence: 1) atmospheric effects, like climate, war, and general knowledge, which affect all countries simultaneously; 2) exchange effects, including international trade, factor movements and the technology transfers, which operate through the mechanism of exchange; and 3) policy effects, which enhance or discourage saving, technology, trade, factor movements and monetary, fiscal and exchange-rate stability.

It is important to distinguish between two different types of convergence. Convergence of per capita incomes, or growth rates of per capita incomes, must be distinguished from convergence of factor prices or their growth rates. Whereas progress towards equal factor prices represents a movement toward efficiency, progress toward equality of incomes may be a step away from integration and efficiency. Two completely integrated economies may have complete equality of factor prices but substantially different per capita incomes.

---

(1) See MADDISON [34], [35], for long run analyses of income levels and growth rates.

*Advise:* the number in square brackets refer to the Bibliography in the appendix.

This paper discusses the subject from the standpoint of the theory of international trade. It examines the extent to which theories of trade and factor movements elucidate the various forces affecting convergence of per capita incomes or factor prices, paying special attention to the commodity composition of trade and factor endowments.

The classical model of trade postulated differences in comparative costs as the foundation of international trade and emphasized the gains from trade and the extent to which asymmetries of size and tariff policies affect the division of the gains from trade. Elaborations of the classical theory showed how the benefits of growth in one country would be divided between that country and its partners, including the exceptional case of "damnifying" or "immiserizing" growth. The classical economists paid little attention to the factors determining differences in comparative costs.

By contrast, Ely Heckscher and others developed a theory of comparative advantage based on differences in factor endowments. Trade is a substitute for movement of the factors of production and it leads to the convergence of factor prices. At first the idea seemed remote from reality, but in recent decades there has been an unmistakable tendency toward convergence of factor prices among certain groups of countries. The economic integration has been manifested both in freer trade and in greater factor mobility, especially the mobility of capital.

As already noted, the idea of factor price convergence is not the same as income or growth-rate convergence. Heckscher's multifactor model of trade predicts factor price convergence but it does not predict income convergence; instead, incomes per capita are proportionate to the ratios of the endowments of non-labor factors to the stock of labor (2). Even though the rewards of all the factors of production are the same all over the world, incomes per capita would differ according to the distribution of factor endowments, high in countries with relatively large endowements of land and capital, and low in other countries.

---

(2) This suggests that one-sector models, which fail to distinguish between income and factor-price convergence, may be seriously misleading.

Of course, factor price convergence has by no means been complete in the real world. On the contrary, disparities between the richest and poorest countries may even have increased over the four decades. What has occurred is an unmistakable tendency toward factor price equalization in specific economic spaces. Factor prices have converged throughout much of the OECD area, excepting the regions of Southern Europe. Convergence also seems to have occurred to some extent in other areas of the world, but at different levels. The tendency toward convergence of factor prices has therefore been highly selective, giving rise to the question: Why has factor price convergence occurred in some economic spaces but not in others?

It will be convenient to use the term factor price equalization (or convergence) areas (*FPEAs*) to describe those areas within which factor process seem to converge. What are the characteristics distinguishing *FPEAs* that have led to convergence within, but prevented convergence between areas? What characteristics, if any, do *FPEAs* share with the economic concept of regions or even currency areas?

The theory of economic policy can also contribute to the subject of convergence. What are the normative characteristics of *FPEAs*? What policies should govern the formation of an *FPEA*? This question has relevance to a world undergoing political transformation where regions are seeking to create new economic spaces in the formation of free trade areas, customs unions, economic unions and even monetary unions. What policies should individual countries, seeking admittance to a favorable factor-price equalization area, follow, and what entry requirements, related to *FPEAs*, if any, should be imposed on countries seeking entry into an economic union? Finally, would the creation of a system of *FPEAs* around the world be desirable for the world as a whole?

## 1. - The Classical Theory

The classical theory of international trade developed almost accidentally as a by-product of a mistake in the classical theory of value. Values in the classical theory were determined by relative costs of production, sometimes simplified to labor costs. Although this one-sided approach to the theory of value ignored demand, it had its place in a Malthusian world where population and the labor force were endogenously determined by living standards within areas of factor mobility. In international trade, however, where factors were assumed to be immobile between countries, the classical theory of value broke down. Because countries were likely to have different relative costs of production, it could no longer be said that values, in this case international values, were determined by costs of production. Ricardo had no theory of the forces determining the equilibrium terms of trade between the comparative cost ratios of the two countries (3).

Pennington (4), Longfield, Torrens, Mill and others supplied the missing theory required to solve the problem of the terms of trade: Demand. This, however, was an exception that created a bizarre dichotomy between the theories of domestic and international values: Whereas value was supply-determined on the home front, it was demand-determined on the foreign front. Despite Marshall's integration of supply and demand in the theory of value, he nevertheless clung to the unnecessary distinction between the two theories in his privately-circulated unpublished pamphlet, *Pure Theory of Foreign and Domestic Values;* whereas he used supply-demand curves to determine domestic values, he used offer curves to determine international values (5). To be sure, the technique of supply-and-demand

---

(3) Ricardo assumed that the terms of trade would settle approximately at the midpoint between the comparative cost ratios of the two trading countries: In England 1 unit of cloth would be produced by 100 units of labor, and 1 unit of wine by 120 units of labor; whereas in Portugal, 1 unit of cloth would be produced by 90 units of labor and 1 unit of wine by 80 units of labor. Ricardo assumes that the terms of trade will settle at 1 unit of cloth = 1 unit of wine, compared to the midpoint, which is 1 cloth = 47/48 wine.

Mill had dealt with the problem in his *Essays on some unsettled questions,* published in 1844, but first written in 1829-1930; these essays were incorporated and improved in his *Principles of Political Economy,* where he recognizes that it is possible that the terms of trade may settle at one of the limiting ratios, in which case all the gains go to the other country. See VINER ([63] ch. 8) for a historical development of the classical model.

(4) James Pennington (1777-1862) was, according to VINER ([63], 447), the first to point out in print that comparative costs set maximum and minimum rates for the terms of trade and that within these limits they would be determined by reciprocal demand.

(5) Marshall's pamphlet was published by the London School of Economics in 1930.

offer curves, when correctly interpreted and integrated, put international trade theory on a general equilibrium footing, making it a
powerful engine for determining the effects of policy changes on
general equilibrium. But this development did not occur until long
after the reign of Alfred Marshall (6).

## 1.1 *Large and Small Countries*

There are several propositions of international trade theory relevant to the subject of income convergence. One is the conclusion
about the division of the gains from trade between large and small
countries. Nicolson (1897, p. 302) and Bastable [5] pointed out, in the
framework of the two-country two-commodity model, that the relative sizes of the two countries would affect the equilibrium terms of
trade, settling nearer the comparative cost ratio of the larger country.
Small countries tend to be price takers in the world economy and thus
trade at given international prices, in the limit capturing the entire
gains from trade.

The converse of this proposition is that small countries have little
scope for improving the terms of trade; in the limit, the elasticity of
the foreign offer curve is infinite and the small country's optimum
tariff is zero. The obverse of this proposition is that a large country has
considerable scope for "exploiting the foreigner" because the terms of
trade will improve by almost the full extent of the large country's
tariff.

Considerations of relative size have importance for small countries bordering on large economic spaces such as the United States or
the Economic Community. The economic power in the large country,
with its potential for bilateralism, is manifested in the difference in the
elasticities. Indeed the mere formation of an area of discrimination
tends to turn the terms of trade against the outside countries (7).

Differences in the size of countries in integrating areas do not

---

(6) A complete integration of supply and demand factors, even in the two-country
model, was not made until MOSAK'S [43] and MEADE'S [40], works.

(7) See MUNDELL [46] for a multiple-country analysis of the effect of discriminatory
tariffs and the terms of trade.

necessarily make for convergence in living standards, but there is a presumption to that effect. Other things equal, it is true that a large trading area promotes a broader division of labor, economies of scale and higher incomes. Insofar as the outside country can gain entry to the market area of the larger customs union, it has a chance to eliminate this disadvantage, and thus to achieve convergence. The same argument holds for the wider access to knowledge that inclusion in an economic union makes possible.

Other things, of course, may not be equal. Technocratic economies of scale may be offset by organizational diseconomies of scale; perhaps this has already occurred in some of the populous giants of Asia. Integration of the small countries peripheral to China and India with those giants might lead to convergence downward (8).

## 1.2 *Economic Growth*

Another area where the classical theory impacts on convergence theory is in the division of the gains from growth. A country can reap the entire gains from economic growth if its terms of trade remain constant. But this is likely only in the case where expansion takes place in a country whose industry commands only a small share of the market. Otherwise, the direction of change in the terms of trade depends on whether the growth takes place in export or in import-competing industries. Growth in export industries reduces the growing country's terms of trade and thus transfers abroad some of the benefits of growth. Growth in import-competing industries, on the other hand, has the opposite effect, worsening incomes in the rest of the world and allowing the growing country to gain more than the increase in its output.

In an important exception, where the foreign elasticity of demand is less than unity, export-biassed growth may make the growing country worse off. If foreign demand were exactly unit-elastic, further exports would not provide any extra real income, and if foreign

---

(8) It is, for example, hard to see how Hong Kong as a whole will benefit from its expected integration with China in 1997.

demand were inelastic, a growing country would get fewer imports for more exports. The criterion, however, must also take into account the benefit to home consumption of export goods due to the fall in their price; when this is done, the condition for immiserizing growth is that the foreign elasticity of demand be less than the domestic marginal propensity to consume (9). The exports of primary products is a typical example where exporting countries can lose by greater production.

The immiserizing growth possibility is nevertheless not as important as it may at first appear. It requires a country to face an inelastic demand for its own products in the rest of the world; and if a country faced such a demand, it would gain by restricting trade by trade taxes; at the optimum tariff point the foreign elasticity must be greater than unity.

In none of these cases does the theory of trade suggest any necessary tendency toward or away from convergence. Starting at international equality of incomes, growth in one country at constant terms of trade would lead to a divergence. When changes in the terms of trade are taken into account, this may not occur, especially when the growth takes place in the export industries. Increases in productivity and expansion of output of, say oil, would make the exporting countries worse off, in effect exporting more than the entire gains from growth to the rest of the world. In this case growth by the exporting countries creates divergence but in an unexpected direction.

Even if immiserizing growth does not take place, the terms of trade may turn in either direction, depending on whether growth occurs in the export or the import industries. Growth in the export industries (but without immiserization) of a country produces less

---

(9) MILL [42] was aware that an increase in productivity in export industries would worsen the commodity and even the factorial terms of trade if foreign demand were inelastic. Edgeworth interpreted Mill's passage as indicating that a country could be "damnified" by growth, supplying the necessary assumption to make Mill's analysis correct. The first derivations of the complete formula for the effect of changes in production of the export good were achieved by MEADE ([39] e.g., 153); their importance has been brought out by JOHNSON [21], [22], CORDEN [13] and BHAGWATI [7], who first used the term "immiserizing growth". See MUNDELL [45] for a discussion of these and other propositions associated with the pure theory of international trade in both the two-country and multiple-country case.

divergence because part of the gains from growth is shared with the rest of the world through the terms of trade effect. But the opposite occurs if growth takes place in the import-competing industries; this aggravates the divergence due to growth itself. There are, therefore, no unambiguous generalizations from classical theory about the relation between growth and convergence.

Other mechanisms, however, may be relevant. Atmospheric effects such as in improvement in technology in one industry are likely to affect all countries at the same time. The tendency in this case is to aggravate the effects on the terms of trade. Suppose industry $X$, a product which both countries produce but which country $A$ exports to country $B$, is subjected to a productivity shock, affecting both countries equally. Output of $X$ increases in both countries; the productivity gains in the export industry in $A$ and the import industry in $B$ combine to aggravate the worsening of $A$'s terms of trade. Although the productivity gain at constant prices would be relatively more important to the exporting country than the importing country, the terms of trade effects would work against the exporting country and in favor of the importing country.

## 1.3 *Endogenous Growth*

Growth of the capital stock requires investment and investment depends on the rate of return to capital. Atomistic producers may be able to ignore the effect on rates of return of their own investment, but they would ignore at their peril the effect of expected industry-wide changes in output on their own terms of trade; survivors will incorporate such changes in their calculation of profit streams and rates of return. Export-biassed growth in a country would soon result in a falling marginal efficiency of capital in the export industries and a rising marginal efficiency in the import-competing industries, correcting the "externality" to individual producers provided by the deteriorating terms of trade.

Other factors, more long run in classical theory, concerned changes in population and the labor force. A country experiencing a falling terms of trade would suffer a reduction in living standards, inducing outward migration or, in the long run, a reduction in the rate of growth of population. Some of the classical economists, interested in the long run, made population growth an endogenous feature of economic analysis, an additional (but very long run) adjustment factor mitigating some otherwise harmful effects of excessive export-led growth.

### 1.4 *Factor Mobility*

Another factor that was outside the spirit of the classical model, but which was often taken into account in applying the theory to the real world, was factor mobility. The effects of factor mobility was never analyzed in detail by any of the classical economists, although Longfield, Cairnes and Sidgwick made contributions to analysis of some of its effects. Indeed, Sidgwick raised a question about the gains from trade in the presence of factor mobility. Sidgwick concluded that the "aggregate wealth of persons living in this country may be reduced" by a change from no trade to free trade because of the possibility that the production group squeezed out by the change emigrates or dies from starvation!

Sidgwick's proposition correctly illustrates the importance of defining precisely whether growth per capita refers to people living within a country before or after the change under analysis has occurred (10).

## 2. - Trade Theory and the Distribution of Income

The classical model abstracted from the effects of trade on income distribution, creating both a strength and a weakness. It was a strength because it greatly simplified analysis and was able to produce strong conclusions with respect to economic policy than would have been possible with a more complicated model. But it was at the same time a weakness, inasmuch as the abstraction oversimplified reality and neglected study of the determinants of comparative advantage.

---

(10) The theory of the optimum tariff should similarly distinguish between the utilities of the pre-tariff and post-tariff populations.

The marginal productivity theory of the functional distribution of national income was never fully integrated into the theory of international trade. It provided a framework for analysis, but, with one exception (11), it had no immediate impact on the theory of international trade. There was no direct connection made between international trade (or tariffs) and the distribution of income, nor between the terms of trade and factor prices.

## 2.1 *The Heckscher-Ohlin Model*

The development of the two-factor international trade model filled the vacuum; it introduced a model that suggested that trade leads in the direction of an international convergence of factor prices. In early 1919, Knut Wicksell had written a critical review of a book by Ely Heckscher. It was the ideas in Wicksell's review that inspired Heckscher to write his pathbreaking article, Heckscher [16]. Heckscher established the proposition that comparative costs were a function of the «different relative scarcity, i.e., different relative prices of the factors of production in the exchanging countries as well as different proportions between the factors of production in different commodities». He argued that trade must continue to expand until an equalization of the relative scarcity of the factors of production among countries has occurred. Assuming the same technique and the same prices of products, the absolute returns to the factors of production must also be equalized». Here then, in 1919, was the full apparatus of the Heckscher-Ohlin model and the factor price equalization theorem.

Heckscher's article, published in Swedish, did not become generally known to the rest of the world until its translation into English and its publication, by 1949, by the American Economic Association (Heckscher [16]). Meanwhile, Heckscher's pupil, Bertil Ohlin, had elaborated Heckscher's ideas in a doctoral dissertation published in 1924 and then more fully in Ohlin's book *Interregional and International Trade*, published in 1933. Ohlin's book, however, differed from

---

(11) The exception was the work of Stuart Wood who was not only a codiscoverer of the marginal productivity theory, but a pioneer in the analysis of two sector models of growth and trade.

Heckscher's work in that it denied the possibility that free trade could equalize factor prices, a formulation that invited the rediscovery of the factor price equalization theorem, by Abba Lerner (12) in 1933, and by Paul Samuelson [51] and [52]; these articles confirmed and generalized (for variable proportions) Heckscher's early proof that equalization of commodity prices could equalize factor prices.

As already noted, the idea was not completely new in the twentieth century. Even before Heckscher's seminal work, there were antecedents in the 19th century. Sismondi and Longfield had both elaborated theories of trade based on factor endowments. Perhaps more important, Stuart Wood, Harvard's first Ph.D. in economics, and a co-discoverer of the doctrine of marginal productivity, had outlined the assumptions for what became known as the Heckscher-Ohlin model including the conditions for factor price equalization.

That the earlier discoveries received insufficient notice was probably due to the inability of the economic profession to absorb the complications of a two-sector model when the full implications of one-sector models had not been worked out. The revolution in economic technique that was underway in the 1930s, 1940s and 1950s, however, paved the way for the more sophisticated theory and increased the receptivity of the economic profession to the collection of theorems that came to be associated with the two-sector trade model.

The discovery of the factor price equalization theorem initially turned out to be a two-edged sword. On the one hand, it created an integral link between the theories of trade and income distribution, at the same time resulting in a much-needed reformulation of the theory of general economic equilibrium linking commodity and factor prices. On the other hand, it seemed to push the Heckscher-Ohlin model into a *reductio ad absurdum*. Its implication that international factor prices would converge seemed so far from the mark in the real world that it cast doubt on the usefulness of the entire factor-proportions approach to the theory of trade and, by implication, on the two-sector model of economic growth.

---

(12) This was presented in an unpublished paper in Lionel Robbins' seminar at the London School of Economics in December 1933. Lerner's paper was finally published in *Economica* in 1952; see LERNER [33].

The world of the late 1940s and 1950s, when the major theorems were being worked out, did not seem hospitable to the predictions of the two-sector model, especially in the version that implied factor price equalization. In the post-war era, real wages in the United States so far outstripped those in the rest of the world that a model of international trade that predicted convergence seemed unrealistic, disproved by even casual evidence. There did not seem to be any evidence of the convergence of factor prices that Heckscher's analysis predicted.

There was, however, a remarkable change in the following decades. A tendency toward convergence could already be seen in the so-called growth miracles of several countries in the 1950s and 1960s. Decades later, by 1992, wages rates in Japan, and many countries in Europe, have approached or even exceeded wage rates in the United States; no longer does the US stand alone above the crowd in its living standards as it did in 1950. For parts of the world, Heckscher's prediction of convergence of factor prices no longer seems absurd.

## 2.2 *Trade Theorems and the Leontief Paradox*

The theoretical conditions for complete convergence of factor prices appeared at first to be rather restrictive. The assumptions were as follows: identical technology and factor qualities; constant returns to scale; systematic ranking of factor intensities; commodity price equalization (free trade and no transport costs); incomplete specialization; and as many traded goods as factors.

Proof of factor price equalization in the two-factor two-good two-country model followed readily from the assumptions. Identical production functions coupled with constant returns to scale means that marginal productivities, which, under competition, are equivalent to factor rewards, depend, in each industry, only on factor proportions. At every price ratio there is only one efficient set of factor proportions that minimizes costs and this is independent of the scale of output. There is therefore a one-to-one correspondence between factor and commodity prices. As long as both countries produce both goods and share the same commodity prices, they must have the same factor prices.

Although the simplifying assumptions are quite restrictive, it should not be thought that the theorem is irrelevant when the assumptions do not hold. First of all, factor price equalization is not restricted to two commodities. Extra commodities help rather than hinder if there are no impediments to trade. It is sufficient that there are at least as many mobile commodities as there are fixed factors.

Factor price equalization, in a restricted sense, may also apply in the presence of barriers to trade and domestic goods. Even if trade in some goods is subject to transport costs or tariffs, a localized factor price equalization can take place as long as there are no barriers to trade in at least two goods produced in common in the two countries; in this case marginal products, measured in terms of the two goods traded goods, will be equal. For example, if commodities gold and wheat were freely traded (without impediments) and produced in both countries, wage rates and rentals defined in terms of gold and wheat must everywhere be equalized. There would not, of course, be equalization in terms of commodities subjected to trade impediments.

Two major challenges confronted the set of ideas associated with the Heckscher-Ohlin model and the factor price equalization theorem, one theoretical, the other, empirical. James and Pearce [20] raised the argument that factor-intensity reversals provide an exception to the theorem. One good might be relatively capital intensive at one set of factor prices, but relatively labor intensive at another set of factor prices. If this were true, factor price equalization might not work. The theorem proved to be valid only for a restriction on the production function that ruled out reversals of factor intensity at different relative factor prices. It should be pointed out, however, that the theorem may still be true in a restricted sense provided only that two commodities whose production functions do not reverse their factor intensities are produced in common in both countries.

The other challenge, not only to factor price equalization but to the Heckscher-Ohlin theorem itself, came from Leontief's research [31], [32] on the factor-intensity of America's foreign trade. The conventional wisdom held that America was relatively abundant in capital and scarce in labor; according to the Heckscher-Ohlin theorem, American exports should be capital-intensive and her imports labor-intensive. Leontief's input-output studies, however,

shocked the economics profession (including himself!) with his finding
that American exports were more labor-intensive than American
imports. This analysis has since become known as the *Leontief
Paradox*.

Although many explanations have been offered for the "paradox", it has never completely resolved. Leontief had shown that a
million dollar's worth of representative American exports used more
labor and less capital than a million dollars of replacements for
American imports. Leontief tried to explain this paradox by the
greater innate productivity of American labor such that the productivity of one American worker was, on the average, equal to a multiple
of that of foreign workers.

Leontief's early attempt to deal with the human-capital content of
skill-intensity of labor, as well as other characteristics, would receive
more explicit and detailed treatment in the next decades by Kenen
[27], Keesing [25], Baldwin [2], [3], Branson and Monoyios [11],
Stern and Maskus [58] and others. These analyses tended to confirm
the proposition that US exports were skill-intensive relative to US
imports.

A second problem lay with Leontief's assumption that all non-
labor represented capital and his failure to distinguish between natural
resources and labor. When land and natural resources are included in
capital, raw materials would be capital-intensive, so that the imports
of any manufacturing country that imported its raw materials would
be relatively capital intensive. Correction for this limiting assumption,
however, would resolve the paradox only if America's imports, in
1947 (the date of Leontief's statistics), were relatively resource-intensive.

A third problem arose from Leontief's failure to specify the full
implication of the model he was testing. Relative factor abundance
could be defined in terms of factor scarcities, measured by relative
factor prices, as in Heckscher's early analysis, or by factor quantities,
as in some subsequent studies. However, the measurement of factor
abundance by relative factor quantities does not necessarily imply the
Heckscher-Ohlin theorem. Even if one country were relatively capital-
abundant, measured by quantities, it might be capital scarce,
measured by factor prices, if home demand were biassed toward

capital-intensive goods. Thus America's imports would be capital-intensive even if America were capital abundant if American demand were sufficiently biassed toward capital-intensive goods. Although this argument is probably not persuasive enough to account for the Leontief paradox, it did serve to clarify the basic proposition and to redirect attention back to Heckscher's original (and correct) definition of factor abundance in terms of factor scarcities.

## 2.3 *Changes in Factor Endowments and Factor Mobility*

Further development of the model widened its applicability. In 1955, Rybczynski [50] showed how changes in factor endowments would affect the production-possibility curve. An increase in the endowment of one factor would change the shape of a country's production possibility curve: at constant commodity prices an increase in the stock of, say, labor, would require an increase in the output of the labor-intensive good and a decrease in the output of the other good. Similar theorems were produced by Ronald Jones and Romney Robinson.

In 1957, I analyzed the connection between trade and factor mobility and showed that impediments to trade would stimulate factor movements, and vice versa. By the Stolper-Samuelson theorem, a tariff would raise the reward of the scarce factor, say capital. If capital were internationally mobile, its influx would alter production possibilities along the lines of the Rybczynski theorem. Under the precise conditions required for factor price equalization, capital would continue to move until trade was completely ended! The same conclusion would hold if the other (abundant) factor, say labor, were mobile; in this case the tariff-imposing country would export labor until trade ended. The conclusion holds up, somewhat surprisingly, even when account is taken of the changes in the production possibilities of the rest of the world. Regardless of the relative sizes of the two countries, impediments to trade eliminate trade provided only that both goods continue to be produced in the two countries.

The explanation for my conclusion lies in the dual routes to factor-price-equalization. Free trade without transport costs leads to commodity price equalization which, by the factor price equalization theorem, provides one route to factor price equalization; factor mobility provides another, more direct route. As long as there are constant returns to scale, mobility of a single factor is sufficient for factor price equalization.

With two equally good routes to factor prices equalization, an impediment in one route activates the other. Just as two lakes connected by two streams maintain equal levels, and damming up one stream enhances the levelling activity in the other; so cutting off one route to factor price equalization enhances the equalizing activity of the other route.

An apparent problem with my analysis was its razor's edge characteristic which implied that even slight impediments to trade would bring about a trade-eliminating rearrangement of factors. In a world of incomplete information, uncertainty and adjustment costs, this characteristic disappears. It is, however, useful to dwell on the broader implications for the theory of the location of factors implied by the existence of transactions costs.

## 2.4 *Geography, Location and Trade*

Countries do not exist in a world without transactions costs. If commodities and factors are completely mobile, it makes no difference where production takes place. there is no connection between industries and there is no geography. International or interregional trade depends on at least one fixed factor.

The fixed factor is usually taken to be land, which determines one element of location. The geography of the planet is the starting point for the economic analysis of countries. There is little practical alternative to people living on the global land space nature has thrown up. Land is the immobile factor (13).

Where people locate on this land space depends on trade and on labor mobility. Labor mobility depends on both the incentive to move and the barriers to movement. Labor is more mobile than land but

---

(13) Trade in raw materials and soil can, however, alter through depreciation and exhaustion the endowment of land.

less mobile than capital. If labor were completely mobile and homogeneous, competition would guarantee that wages are the same everywhere. With land as the only alternative factor, there will be a unique distribution of labor around the world, analogous to Ricardo's theorem of the unique distribution of the precious metals.

The real world, of course, throws up important barriers to factor mobility. When a new opportunity for migration opens up, it seems to matter who gets there first. When the Western Hemisphere was first discovered by Europeans, one of the first steps, after subduing the indigenous populations, was to erect barriers to migration from competing empires. The Portuguese, Spanish, Dutch, French and English monopolized their new conquests, with substantial restrictions on navigation and trade between empires. The role of migration was to equate wage rates within the imperial zones of labor mobility; there were no direct routes to equalization of wage rates between empires.

With two commodities produced by different quantities of factors, trade might be sufficient to equalize factor prices even between areas where barriers inhibit factor mobility. With factor price equalization assumptions and some factor mobility, however, there is no longer a unique distribution of labor around the world. Multiple solutions (14) exist for the geographical location of Earth's billions, with various combinations of trade or factor locations, all of which could be optimal from the standpoint of the maximization of global income implied by factor price equalization.

The indeterminacy of location ends, however, when we move to the case where the factors exceed the number of commodities produced in common. If, for example, there are four factors of production, land, labor, capital and enterprise, and only two commodities produced in common, factor price equalization could not take place unless one of the factors, say capital, were mobile. In general, factor price equalization requires that

$$n + m \geq r$$

---

(14) This indeterminacy was clearly recognized by Samuelson (1953-4:6-7) in his analysis of the general equilibrium implications of the multiple-country multiple-commodity case whenever the number of mobile goods exceeds the number of fixed factors.

where *n* is the number of commodities produced in common, *r* is the number of factors and *m* is the number of mobile factors.

If all four factors of production were fixed, factor price equalization would require four traded commodities produced with different factor intensities (15).

Mobility of goods or factors can be thrown into the instrument-target Tinbergenian approach to policy. Achievement of specified targets of economic policy requires at least as many instruments as there are targets. If equalization of factor prices are put in the position attributed to targets, free trade of commodities produced in common, or factor mobility, are in the position of instruments. Alternatively, factor movements can be thought of as instruments for achieving targets of commodity price equalization.

## 2.5 *Specialization and Factor Mobility*

In a world where trade is sufficient to produce factor price equalization without factor movements, what is the function of factor mobility? In the real world the answer is provided at least in part by transactions costs of various kinds. If, for example, there are risks of trade being shut off, a country would be safer to import the factor to produce at home what would otherwise be produced abroad. If, on the other hand, there are risks of nationalization or default of a country's capital located abroad, a country might be safer to trade rather than export capital. In the real world, transactions costs help to determine whether the mountain goes to Mahomet or Mahomet goes to the mountain.

In the absence of transactions costs, factor price equalization requires that specialization be incomplete. The degree of specialization, however, is itself a function of differences in factor endowments, and thus is not independent of factor mobility.

To study the role of specialization, suppose that factor endowments are distributed between countries in such a way as to ensure

---

(15) Difficulties arise with multiple goods and factors in achieving an unambiguous ranking of factor intensities. A selected bibliography would include TINBERGEN [60], MEADE [38], SAMUELSON [53], [54], [55]; MELVIN [41], VANEK [62], JONES [24], DEARDORFF [14] and BOWEN and SVEILKAUSKAR [10].

incomplete specialization and that the terms of trade, and therefore factor prices, of the small home country are tentatively fixed. In graph 1, let $AB = DC$ be the initial labor endowment of the home country and $AD = BC$ be its initial endowment of capital. Let the point $P$ denote the initial production equilibrium on the efficiency locus $APC$ with the slope of the straight line $AP$ extended indicating the capital-labor ratio in labor-intensive industry $X$, and the slope of $CP$ extended the capital-labor ratio in industry $Y$. If the conditions of factor price equalization are met, the factor proportion ratios in the home industries are the same as those in industries abroad.

GRAPH 1

ZONE OF FACTOR PRICE EQUALIZATION

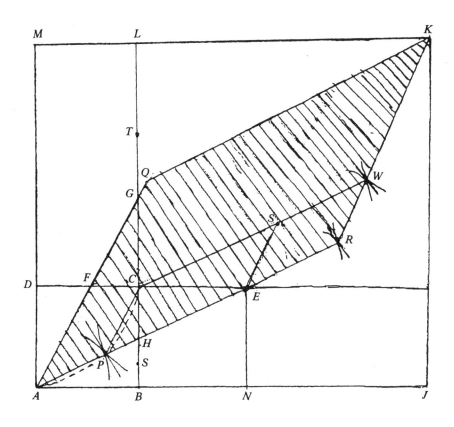

Now change the equilibrium by shifting labor from the rest of the world to the home country, relocating production, along the lines of the Rybczynski-Meade-Mundell theorem (16), without any change in factor prices. The point *C* travels to the east as the stock of labor in the home country increases, moving along the line *CE*

As labor continues to be shifted into the home country, a point is eventually reached where the ratio of labor to capital in the country as a whole is equal to the labor/capital ratio in the labor-intensive industry, *X*. At that point, *E*, the country becomes completely specialized in *X*. This point is one limit of the range of labor endowments where factor price equalization can take place.

The other limit for variations in labor occurs when labor emigrates from the home country, moving the endowment point along the line *CF*, and, at constant factor prices, reducing the output of the labor-intensive commodity, *X*, and increasing the output of the capital-intensive commodity, *Y*. The specialization point occurs when the national endowment ratio equals the ratio in the capital-intensive industry *Y*, at the point *F*. The variations of labor in which factor price equalization is possible are therefore given by the range *FE* (17).

---

(16) The Rybczynski-Mundell theorem refers to the propositon that, under the conditions required for factor price equalization, a *limited* shift of one factor of production from one country to another leaves global production, at unchanged commodity and factor prices, unchanged. The production component of the theorem is a corollary of the factor price equalization theorem, as SAMUELSON [54] and JONES [23] had shown. Prices would in fact remain unchanged if the factor movement does not alter tastes.

The theorem applies within the boundaries of the factor price equalization areas; eventually, migration of one factor would lead to specialization in either the emigrant or immigrant country.

In the case of labor migration, the immigrant workers consume the same collection of goods as before. In the case of capital movements (without migration of capitalists), the capital-importing country generates an export surplus equal to the interest payments on the imported capital, also equal to the difference between the change in the country's gross domestic product and its gross national product.

When account is taken of foreign-owned factors of production, a country may cease to export its abundant-factor-intensive commodity (defined by quantities rather than values); this is because international factor payments create a gap between expenditure and income that allows demand conditions to reverse the Heckscher-Ohlin theorem. The same argument applies for any situation in which trade is not balanced, as LEAMER *et* Al. [28] has shown.

(17) This applies precisely only to the situation where world commodity prices are unchanged. There is a different range *FE* for each distinct commodity price ratio.

Analogous conditions hold for changes in the stock of the capital. As capital is shifted from the rest of the world to the home country, the labor-capital endowment ratio declines, pushing the endowment point from *C* toward *G*, which indicates the same capita-labor ratio as the capital-intensive *Y* industry. Conversely, as capital leaves the home country, the endowment point moves from *C* to *H*, where specialization in the labor-intensive *X* industry takes place.

When either or both of the factors shift, corresponding changes in production take place in the rest of the world. In graph 1, *AJ = MK* represents the global stock of labor, and *AM = JK*, the global stock of capital; these are divided initially between the home country and the rest of the world (*ROW*) as indicated by the factor endowment point *C*. Production in *ROW* is indicated by the resource allocation point *W*.

The changes in production in *ROW* exactly match the changes in production in the home country. Thus when labor equal to *CE* is shifted from *ROW* to the home country (*H*), the contraction of production of *Y* in *H*, indicated by the ray *PC*, is exactly matched by the increase in the production of *Y* in *ROW*, equal to *WR*; similarly, the expansion of production of *X* in *H*, represented by *PE*, is exactly matched by the contraction in production of *X* in *ROW* by *CS*, as the small parallelogram *PCSE* indicates.

Within the shaded parallelogram *AQKR*, both *H* and *ROW* produce both goods and factor price equalization takes place. But incomplete specialization is too strict a condition; specialization is not per se inconsistent with factor price equalization. Any position on the lines forming the parallelogram itself is consistent with both factor price equalization and specialization. A division of resources between the countries indicated by the point *Q* would result in *H* being completely specialized in the production of the capital-intensive goods *Y*, and *ROW* being completely specialized in the labor-intensive good *X*. Similarly, the global division of endowments represented by the point *R* results in *H* being completely specialized in *X* and *ROW* in *Y*. Both these factor endowment points (*R* and *Q*) represent corner solutions of complete specialization in both countries consistent with factor price equalization.

There are other types of multiple situations, also consistent with factor price equalization, in which one country produces both goods and the other country is completely specialized. With resource divisions anywhere (except at the end points) on the parallelogram segments *AR* and *AQ*, *ROW* produces both goods, whereas *H* is specialized: in *X* on the segment *AR* and in *Y* on the segment *AQ*. Conversely, with resource divisions on the segments *KR* and *KQ*, the home country produces both goods whereas *ROW* is specialized: in *X* on the segment *KQ*, and in *Y* on the segment *KR*. Complete specialization in one or even both countries is not therefore incompatible with factor price equalization.

The borderline cases of "incipient specialization" are by no means unlikely situations. Once we move outside the classical factor price equalization world, where both countries produce both products, we encounter situations made to order for a revival of factor mobility. With a division of endowments outside the shaded parallelogram, factor prices will be different and there will be incentives for mobility.

Let us suppose, tentatively, that only capital is mobile, and that labor is divided between the two areas such that *H* has *AB* and *ROW* has *BJ* of the world's labor force. If capital is initially divided such that *H* has *BS* and *ROW* has *SL*, the wage rate in *H* will be lower than in *ROW* and the return to capital higher. Capital will then have an incentive to move to *H* until its return is the same as at home. In the absence of significant impediments to capital movements, this implies a move to the endowment point *H*, where the home country will be specialized in the labor-intensive good *X*, and the rest of the world will produce both goods, with *ROW* becoming the creditor, and *H*, the debtor, country. The "borderline" case of incipient specialization becomes the natural equilibrium as long as there are even tiny frictions associated with moving capital or supervising it once it has moved.

Similarly, at an initial endowment point like *T*, the wage rate is lower and the return to capital is higher in *ROW* than in *H*; capital will then move from *H* to *ROW*, until the borderline division of resources at *G* is reached; at this point *H* will be the creditor and *ROW* the debtor country.

Any division of endowments outside the zone would result in a failure of factor price equalization, providing an incentive for factor mobility until the border of the zone is again reached.

## 2.6 *Factor Price Equalization Parallelograms*

The parallelogram of factor price equalization is not, of course, independent of demand conditions. An increase in the demand for, and the price of the labor-intensive product, for example, would increase wages and raise the capital-intensity of both activities, twisting the factor-price-equalization parallelogram in a north-west direction. This means that a country which, before the price change, was completely specialized in capital-intensive products might, after the shift in demand, produce both products. A country that was outside the parallelogram before the price change might enter the factor price equalization area after the price change. Whether equalization takes place therefore depends on demand conditions.

The closer to one another are relative factor endowments, the more similar will be the economic structure, and the more likely is incomplete specialization, with countries producing the same products; the incentive for factor mobility will also be lower among countries with similar factor endowments. Conversely, the more diverse are factor endowments, the greater the likelihood of specialization and the greater the incentive for factor mobility.

In a two-country two-factor two-commodity world, there can be only one *FPEA*. With several countries and commodities, however, distinct *FPEA*s can appear, defined as follows: two or more countries within an area have the same factor prices, but different factor prices from countries in other areas.

Consider, for example, a world of four countries, *A*, *B*, *C* and *D*, ranked in decreasing order of their relative capital abundance; and four commodities, *w*, *x*, *y* and *z*, ranked unambiguously in decreasing order of their capital intensities at any given set of factor prices. There are now several possibilities, one of which is world-wide factor price equalization, in which *A* would tend to export *W*; *B* would tend to export *X*; *C* would tend to export *Y*; and *D* would tend to export *Z*. Universal factor price equalization is more likely to occur the closer to one another are factor endowments among countries and factor intensities among industries.

Now suppose that industries *W* and *X* are highly capital intensive relative to *Y* and *Z*; and that the capital-labor endowment ratios of countries $A$ and $B$ are a great deal higher than those of countries $C$ and $D$. Then factor price equalization may occur between $A$ and $B$, and between $C$ and $D$, but not between the two *FPEAs*.

In a multiple-country multiple-commodity context it is probable that several groups of countries produce goods in common with other members of the group, but not between groups, giving rise to the phenomenon of several *FPEAs*. A necessary condition for an *FPEA* is either that two countries produce two goods in common or that they fall into one of the borderline cases already alluded to.

One characteristic of an *FPEA*, therefore, is that factor endowments be not too dissimilar, either because the countries are initially in similar situations, or because factor movements have been sufficient to reduce any dissimilarity to the critical proportions.

Countries can change their *FPEA* by altering their factor endowments, either by capital formation and/or population policy, or by factor mobility. Factor mobility is the most effective measure to ascend the capital-endowment hierarchy in the short run. However, once a country enters an *FPEA*, it no longer gains by factor mobility; gains are restricted to movements from one *FPEA* to another.

## 2.7 *Knowledge and the Transfer of Technology*

Technology is another factor that determines the composition of *FPEAs*. Equalization can only be complete if countries have identical production functions. The implicit assumption of the Heckscher-Ohlin framework is that knowledge travels costlessly, without delay or friction. In the real world, however, there are significant barriers to the transfer of technology not only because technology is not a free good (even though it is a public good), but also because the absorption and exploitation of technology is not costless.

Within the long time-frame of the Heckscher-Ohlin model, innovations take place simultaneously in all countries. Thus an innovation that lowers the costs of production in industry $X$ will turn the terms of trade against the country that exports $X$. Alternatively, an innovation that increases the productivity of labor everywhere will worsen the terms of trade of the country that exports the labor-intensive product. The predictions of the Heckscher-Ohlin model in a world of different and changing technology should therefore be interpreted as the end point of what might be in reality a lengthy process of technology transfer.

Technology can be analyzed as an independent factor of production or as an improvement embodied in capital or labor.

Technological differentials take time to be evened out. Economic incentives may be lacking. There are both artificial and real impediments to technology transfer. The capacity to deliver or absorb technology may be limited. The speed with which technology can be moved between countries depends on the willingness and ability of the hi-tech country to export, and of the low-tech country, to import technology. Recent work (18) confirms that the ability of a country to absorb technology is a function of its educational level.

Human capital takes time to accumulate, and investment in human capital must be financed out of saving. Even if financial capital is mobile, there are definite limits to the rate at which domestic or foreign savings can be productively employed in human capital formation. Even if technology were easily transportable, its importation may not be very productive if the necessary complement of skilled labor is not there to utilize it efficiently. Acting on an idea of Nelson and Phelps [48], Benhabib and Spiegel [6] developed and tested a model of the growth catch-up process between countries, making its speed, in a world of heterogeneous technology levels, an increasing function of the level of education; an interesting feature of the model is that a country with a higher level of education, but an initially lower technology, could not only catch up but overtake the leading country (19).

The technology factor plays a role in the formation of *FPEAs*. Countries with very dissimilar endowments of technology will tend to produce a different product mix and thus occupy different *FPEAs*. The

---

(18) See BENHABIB - SPIEGEL [6].

(19) Nelson and Phelps rejected the notion of incorporating human capital simply as another input into the production function in favor of the idea that education facilitates the adoption and implementation of new technology that are continuously invented at an exogenous rate; and that the growth of technology depends on the gap between its level and the level of "theoretical knowledge". See BENHABIB - SPIEGEL [6].

integration of different *FPEA*s may therefore have to wait upon propinquity of the areas' technologies. The speed of convergence will itself, howevef, depend on levels of human capital. A country that is backward in technology but high in education may end up in a better position than a country that is advanced in technology but backward in education. The convergence of factor prices in the OECD area may be explained therefore not only by trade and factor mobility, but by the comparable levels of education that enabled the initially poorer countries to absorb the inventions of the technological leader. These factors probably play a role also in explaining the spectacular success of some of the countries in the East Asian nexus (20).

## 3. - Policy Systems and Economic Convergence

In the nineteenth century, *FPEA*s tended to coincide with the great European empires. Among the contributing factors were free trade (or some kind of imperial preference), a high degree of factor mobility (21), a common administrative system, a common trading tongue, a common central currency (or a currency board system), and a metropolitan financial market. Integration was achieved within the empire although, of course, nothing approaching equalization of wages took place between labor of different races or different endow-ments of human capital (22).

Between empires there was a growing tendency toward factor price equalization in the half-century preceding the outbreak of World

---

(20) There is obviously room for a short run as well as a long run theory of comparative advantage. Short run theories have been developed on the basis of factor immobilities *within* countries along the lines of the specific factors model; see SAMUEL-SON [56], JONES [24], MUSSA 1974, and MAYER 1974; or along the lines of monopolistic competition models involving economies of scale; see especially HELPMAN [17] and HELPMAN - KRUGMAN [18]. See BALDWIN [4] for a brief but insightful commentary on the literature and its implications for tests of the Heckscher-Ohlin model.

(21) Factor mobility, however, was never complete. In the case of labor, for example, it was usually restricted to the citizens and race of the imperial country, making it necessary to regard imperial and colonial labor as separate factors of production.

(22) The existence of discrimination (between races, creeds, caste, etc.) makes it necessary to treat discriminator and discriminatee as separate factors.

War I. Great Britain's move toward free trade, the extension of industrialization to the Continent of Europe, the gold standard, great advances in communication and transportation, and increased international mobility of capital all contributed to growing interdependence and economic integration among major powers and a tendency toward the equalization of factor prices.

World War I temporarily halted that convergence process, but at the same time it accelerated the growth and introduction of technology. There were two opposing forces at work in the 1914-1945 period. On the one hand, reinforced by continuing spectacular advances in transportation and communication, the real world moved closer to the Heckscher-Ohlin model! On the other hand, economic policy worked in the opposite direction; the three decades between 1914 and 1945 was a period characterized by higher tariffs, quotas, exchange control, inflation, depression, and international monetary instability.

In the post 1945 era, the Cold War created a split between the East and the West, while disimperialism created the Third World, largely located in the Southern hemisphere. The very persistence of the usefulness of these terms, West, East, and South, to characterize "three" worlds over the four decades 1946-1989 testifies to a substantive, if selective, homogeneity within each.

The "West" was very far from being a factor price equalization area at the time Samuelson wrote his famous articles, but it grew close to it by the time the international monetary system broke down in 1971, and even closer in the next two decades.

There were strong forces moving in the direction of integration. One factor was American technological and financial aid, which helped to put the former belligerent countries back on their feet; an important catalyst was the OEEC, which helped to weld the European countries into a joint decision-making framework that gave an impetus to European integration. The aid factor, however, important though it was in accelerating the achievements of Europe and Japan, was probably dwarfed by more persistent forces operating to integrate the richer countries.

The leadership role of the United States provided a focus for both emulation and envy. Imitation of the technology and the free-enterprise ethos of the leading technological power helped to reduce the disparity between the United States and the other countries. The inauguration of the European integration movements, starting with the Coal and Steel Community, Euratom, the European Payments Union and the *Treaty of Rome*, enabled Europe to gain the economies of scale associated with a great power, on a scale comparable to the United States itself. The formation of an orderly tariff-cutting procedure at what became the GATT laid the basis for what would become comparatively low levels of tariffs; inflation further eroded the burden of specific tariffs. Finally, and not less important, was the development of an international short and long term capital market, the enormous increase in capital mobility, and the emergence of a financial globalization process.

Up to 1971, the OECD area was also characterized by a stable international monetary system (23) built around the convertible dollar, a system that helped to unify international capital markets and provide an anchor for stability of other countries in addition to the United States.

In the light of these developments, it is not therefore surprising that those countries possessing an adequate level of educational capital would be able to exploit the technological catch-up necessary (but not sufficient) for convergence to US factor prices. Freer trade alone might not have been sufficient; but a high and growing level of capital mobility meant that excessive disparities between factor endowments could be eliminated quickly. With the possible exception of the countries of Southern Europe, the OECD countries may have come as close to factor price equalization as that which exists in an area of labor mobility like the United States.

The rest of the world did not share in the convergence of incomes at the high level of the leading power. To a certain extent, this can be blamed on the economic policies of these countrues, many of which did not create environments hospitable to the market economy. In the

---

(23) It might appear strange to characterize the gold-dollar system as a stable system in view of its subsequent breakdown in 1971. Only one feature of the system, however, was unstable. Exchange rates were stable, but the dollar price of gold, set in 1934, became obsolete as a result of World War II and post-war inflation, leading to a persistent gold scarcity.

first two decades before 1971, when there existed a reasonably stable international monetary system, policies in many countries of the South were characterized by inflationary finance, import-substitution policies, trade and exchange controls and systematic regulation of the economy by inefficient and even corrupt bureaucrats. After the international monetary system broke down, in 1971, the international monetary framework was no longer favorable to the non-oil developing countries. Soaring oil prices, excess liquidity, general inflation and negative real interest rates led to huge borrowing and a build-up of debt among the DCs. When the correction set in, with the disinflationary policies of the United States in the early 1980s, much of the third world found itself on the verge of bankruptcy. The fall of oil prices in the 1980s mitigated the problem somewhat, but it is only recently that the outlook appears again favorable. It is hopeful also that the failure of communism will have a favorable demonstration effect on economic policies of the developing world.

Not all the developing countries misbehaved. East Asian countries, following the Japanese model, engaged in systematic export-promotion policies that created the prospect of eventual entry into the OECD factor price equalization area. Inspired by the example of these countries, and discouraged by debt, Mexico has reversed its earlier policies; the widening of the US - Canada North American Free Trade Area to include Mexico and some other Western Hemisphere countries is a promising development in the right direction.

The Socialist countries fared much worse than the OECD area; they started at, and ended up at, a higher level than the South. The centralized economic system works best in a static world, but it fails in a dynamic world where a premium is put on decentralized competitive information systems. The countries of Eastern Europe and the CIS failed to keep up with pace of growth in the West, largely because of the organizational failure to exploit the magic bullet of economic freedom.

The dissolving of the Soviet bloc opens up the promise that a few of the Eastern European countries will be able to lock into the factor price equalization area of Western Europe early in the next century. It seems likely, however, that many of the Moslem countries of the former Soviet Union will form an independent factor price equalization area closer to that of Afghanistan, Iran, Pakistan and Turkey than to their Eastern European neighbors.

## 4. - Concluding Remarks

The concept of convergence of growth and income is elucidated by the Heckscher-Ohlin framework in which goods are distinguished by the factor intensities and countries by their factor endowments. Trade promotes convergence of factor prices in a wide range of cases, especially those in which factor endowments are not too unequal. In other cases, where factor endowments are very different from country to country, factor price equalization runs up against the barrier of specialization, which creates differences in factor prices and a stimulus to factor mobility. Factor mobility therefore is vital between areas with very diverse factor prices. The regionalization of the world economy that is currently proceeding requires substantial movements of factors to achieve efficiency through factor price equalization.

Two points need to be emphasized. It almost goes without saying that factor price equalization does not imply equality of wages of human beings in different countries. The human being is a complex entity, incorporating parts of each of the productive factors, labor being only the most important. Human beings with different levels of human capital or entrepreneurial abilities will be paid rents and profits as well as wages. The most striking difference between rich and poor countries is not that skilled professional people get paid more in rich than in poor countries (although that is often true), but that there is a higher proportion of skilled professional people in rich than in poor countries. Between countries in the same factor price equalization area, wage differentials reflect differential rents for human capital.

Second, it needs to be reiterated that equalization of factor prices, does not imply equalization of per capita incomes. Per capita incomes reflect payments to labor and other factors, and the larger the quantity of "other factors", relative to factor owners, the higher will be per capita income; in the two-factor (labor and capital) case, it is equal to the wage rate plus the product of the interest rate and the capital/labor endowment ratio. The difference between rich and poor countries may therefore be reflected, not in differences in factor rewards, but in differences in the ratio of other resources to the labor force. Of two countries in the same *FPEA*, the richer country, measured by per capita income, will be that with the largest ratio of non-labor factors to labor.

What insights can the theory of international trade and factor mobility make to history? What are the characteristics of *FPEA*'s in history? One insight is the dominating role, with given technology, of policy in creating the boundaries on factor price equalization spaces. The political structure created the boundaries of trade, migration and capital, whether in the ancient empires of Babylonia, Egypt or Persia, the city-states of classical Greece, or their successors. The great world empires tended to be integrating forces, creating wider economic spaces for trade and migration and capital mobility. Factor movements were generally possible only within security areas, i.e., spaces within which war is ruled out, but between which war and confiscation and imprisonment is possible. The imperial systems represented a means of securing political security and property rights throughout the empire.

Even in pre-historical times, trade must have been a substitute for factor movements, and been an alternative to war in cases where conquest provided the only outlet for migration and colonization. The development of the empires in the ancient world created zones of integration through both trade and factor mobility, whereas trade between empires, mainly in the form of scarce materials, was often a means of avoiding the alternative of war. In medieval times, factor-price equalization areas and civilization in general became centered around competing city-states, especially in Germany and Italy, but giving rise, in Spain, France, England and Poland, to the centralized nation-states that became the great powers of the Renaissance.

With the discovery of the Americas, itself a by-product of the search for gold, a sea change occurred in economic development. The new hemisphere opened up to European settlement, creating great opportunities for conquest, migration and trade. Over time, with competition for territory among the Atlantic powers, Portugal, Spain, France, England and Holland, diminishing returns set in, with productivity limited by heavy transportation, communications and organization costs. The creation of the railway, and later the telegraph, following on the heels of the industrial revolution, opened up the West in the nineteenth century. One of the most important facts of the nineteenth century was the rise of America as a world power on the basis of an *FPEA* of sub-continental proportions, growth that was fed by immigration capital imports.

With specialization and further migration, diminishing returns eventually set in, until a critical point was reached, the end of the frontier, when comparative advantages changed in favor of a wider range of products; at this point real wages are no longer higher (after allowing for location preferences) than in the country of emigration. After that point, further emigration, instead of changing factor prices, has the function of shifting the location of production from the emigrant to the host country. American protectionism probably had the effect of stimulating inward capital and labor movements as comparative advantages shifted from primary industries to labor-intensive manufacturing.

Meanwhile, as in ancient times, the European imperial systems created factor price equalization areas within the empires but not between them. Nevertheless, the fluid movement of technology in a rapidly changing world, as well as intense rivalries prevented great disparities in technological development from arising.

The two World Wars and the Cold War had the historical function of dismantling the system of European imperialism, forcing a reorganization of the international economy around independent states. The most recent example of disimperialism, involving the breakup of the Soviet Union and its Eastern European empire, is but the final nail in the coffin of a system that had outlasted its usefulness.

The multilateral system that replaced imperialism gave rise to a division of the world between North and South, roughly parallelling the division between rich and poor countries. The North, comprising largely the OECD area, has been in the process of completing the creation of an *FPEA*.

It is too early to say whether the creation of distinct trading blocs of continental size is a fundamental tendency or a transition phase to an alternative solution. Open questions include the possibility of widening the scope of the Economic Community to include the countries of Eastern Europe, and whether the special links of the Community to Africa will be increased. It may be that the global problems associated with re-introducing the "new" territories of Eastern Europe into the world economy will be a catalyst for creation of an improved multilateral liberal trading order.

The prospect of a widening of the North American Free Trade Area to include Mexico and perhaps other Latin American countries offers a fascinating experiment for study of wider relationships. Mexico on the one hand, and Canada and the United States on the other, are very far from being a *FPEA*. Because of the huge gap in wage rates between Mexico, and Canada and the United States, it will be interesting to see whether the creation of a commodity-price equalization area can contribute to the convergence of factor prices between such diverse countries. An analogous experiment in Europe would be the inclusion of Turkey and North Africa in the European Economic Space. For this reason, a widened North American Free Trade Area would provide a prototype for study of North-South relations in the world as a whole.

## BIBLIOGRAPHY

[1] Aw Bee-Yan: «The Interpretation of Cross-Section Regression Tests of the Heckscher-Ohlin Theorem with Many Goods and Factors», *Journal of International Economics*, n. 14, February 1983, pp. 163-7.

[2] Baldwin Roberts E.: «Determinants of the Commodity Structure of US Trade», *American Economic Review*, n. 61, March 1971, pp. 126-46.

[3] ——: «Determinants of Trade and Foreign Investment: Further Evidence», *Review of Economics and Statistics*, n. 61, February 1979, pp. 40-8.

[4] ——: «The Development and Testing of the Heckscher-Ohlin Model of International Trade», Siena, International School of Economic Research, *Issues in International Trade*, 1992.

[5] Bastable C.F.: *The Theory of International Trade*, 4th ed., London, 1903.

[6] Benhabib Jess - Spiegel Mark M.: «The Role of Human Capital and Political Instability in Economic Development», Paper presented at *IV Villa Mondragone International Economic Seminar*, June 30-July 2 1992.

[7] Bhagwati J.: «Immiserizing Growth: a Geometric Note», *Review od Economic Studies*, n. 25, June 1958.

[8] ——: «The Heckscher-Ohlin Theorem in the Multiple-Commodity Case», *Journal of Political Economy*, n. 80, 1972, pp. 1052-5.

[9] Bowen H.P. - Leamer E.E. - Sveiskauskas L.: «Multicountry, Multifactor Tests of the Factor Abundance Theory», *American Economic Review*, n. 77, December 1987.

[10] Bowen Harry P. - Sveiskauskas L.: «Judging Factor Abundance», National Bureau of Economic Research, *Working Paper*, n. 3059, August 1989.

[11] Branson W.H. - Monoyios N.: «Factor Inputs in US Trade», *Journal of International Economics*, n. 7, May 1977, pp. 111-31.

[12] Brecher R.A. - Choudhri E.U.: «The Leontief Paradox, Continued», *Journal of Political Economy*, n. 90, August 1982, pp. 820-3.

[13] Corden W.M.: «Economic Expansion and International Trade: A Geometric Approach», *Oxford Economic Papers*, n. 8, June 1956.

[14] Deardorff A.V.: «Weak Links in the Chain of Comparative Advantage», *Journal of International Economics*, n. 9, 1977, pp. 197-209.

[15] Edgeworth F.Y.: *Papers Relating to Political Economy*, Originally published in 1894, London, Macmillan, 1925.

[16] Heckscher E.: «The Effect of Foreign Trade on the Distribution of Income», *Economist Tidskrift*, n. 21, 1919, pp. 497-512; Reprinted in *Readings in the Theory of International Trade*, Philadelphia, Blakiston, 1949.

[17] Helpman E.: «International Trade in the Presence of Product Differentiation, Economies of Scale and Monopolistic Competition: a Chamberlin-Heckscher-Ohlin Approach», *Journal of International Economics*, n. 11, 1981, pp. 305-40.

[18] Helpman Elhanan - Krugman Paul: *Market Structure and Foreign Trade: Increasing Returns, Imperfect Competition, and the International Economy*, Cambridge, MIT Press, 1985.

[19] Hufbauer G.C.: «The Impact of National Characteristics and Technology on the Commodity Composition of Trade in Manufactured Goods», in Vernon R. (ed.): *The Composition Technology Factor in International Trade*, New York, Columbia University Press, 1970.

[20] JAMES S.F. - PEARCE I.E.: «The Factor Price Equalisation Myth», *Review of Economic Studies*, vol. 19 (2), n. 49, 1951-1952, pp. 111-20.

[21] JOHNSON H.G.: «Economic Expansion and International Trade», *Manchester School of Economic and Social Studies*, n. 23, May 1955, pp. 95-112.

[22] — —: *International Trade and Economic Growth: Studies in Pure Theory*, Cambridge, Harvard University Press, 1958.

[23] JONES R.W.: «The Structure of Simple General Equilibrium Models», *Journal of Political Economy*, n. 73, 1965, pp. 557-72.

[24] — —: «A Three-Factor Model in Theory, Trade and History», in BHAGWATI J.N. - JONES R.W. - MUNDELL R.A. - VANEK J. (eds.): *Trade, Balance of Payments and Growth*, Amsterdam, North-Holland Publishing Co, 1971.

[25] KEESING D.B.: «Labor Skills and Comparative Advantage», *American Economic Review*, n. 56, May 1966, pp. 249-58.

[26] — —: «The Impact of Research and Development on United States Trade», *Journal of Political Economy*, n. 75, 1967, pp. 38-48.

[27] KENEN P.B.: «Nature, Capital and Trade», *Journal of Political Economy*, n. 73, October 1965, pp. 437-60.

[28] LEAMER E.E. - BOWEN H.P.: «Cross-Section Tests of the Heckscher-Ohlin Theorem: Comment», *American Economic Review*, n. 71, December 1981, pp. 1040-3.

[29] LEAMER E.E.: *Source of Comparative Advantage, Theory and Evidence*, Cambridge, MIT Press, 1984.

[30] — —: «Testing Trade Theory», National Bureau of Economic Research, *Working Paper*, n. 3957, January 1992.

[31] LEONTIEF W.W.: «Domestic Production and Foreign Trade: The American Capital Position Re-Examined», *Proceedings of the American Philosophical Society*, September 1953, pp. 332-49.

[32] — —: «Factor Proportions and the Structure of American Trade», *Review of Economics and Statistics*, November 1956, pp. 386-407.

[33] LERNER A.P.: «Factor Prices and International Trade», *Economica*, vol. 19, n. 73, February 1952, pp. 121-2.

[34] MADISON ANGUS: *The World Economy in the Twentieth Century*, Paris, OECD, 1989.

[35] — —: *Dynamic Forces in Capitalist Development: A Long-Run Comparative View*, New York, Oxford University Press, 1991.

[36] MARSHALL ALFRED: *The Pure Theory of Foreign Trade*, 1879, reprinted by School of Economics, London, 1930.

[37] McKENZIE L.W.: «Equality of Factor Prices in World Trade», *Econometrica*, vol. 23, n. 3, July 1955, pp. 239-57.

[38] MEADE J.E.: «The Equalisation of Factor Prices: The Two-Country Two-Factor Three-Product Case», *Metroeconomica*, n. 2, 1950, pp. 129-33.

[39] — —: *The Balance of Payments Mathematical Supplement*, London, Oxford University Press, 1951.

[40] — —: *A Geometry of International Trade*, London, Oxford University Press, 1952.

[41] MELVIN J.R.: «Production and Trade with Two Factors and Three Goods», *American Economic Review*, n. 58, 1968, pp. 1248-68.

[42] MILL JOHN STUART: *Principles of Political Economy*, London, 1848.

[43] MOSAK JACOB L.: *General Equilibrium Theory in International Trade*, Bloomington, Indiana University Press, 1944.

[44] MUNDELL R.A.: «International Trade and Factor Mobility», *American Economic Review*, n. 47, June 1957, pp. 321-35, reprinted in MUNDELL [47], pp. 85-99.

[45] — —: «The Pure Theory of International Trade», *American Economic Review*, n. 50, June 1960, pp. 68-110, reprinted in MUNDELL [47], pp. 3-53.

[46] — —: «Tariff Preferences and the Terms of Trade», *The Manchester School of Economic and Social Studies*, n. 32, January 1964, pp. 1-13, reprinted in MUNDELL [47], pp. 54-64.

[47] — —: *International Economics*, New York, MacMillan. 1968.

[48] NELSON RICHARD R. - PHELPS EDMUND S.: «Investment in Humans, Technological Diffusion, and ·Economic Growth», *American Economic Review, Papers and Proceedings*, n. 61, May 1966, pp. 69-75.

[49] PEARCE I.F.: «A Note on Mr. Lerner's Paper», *Economica*, vol. 19, n. 73, February 1952, pp.16-8.

[50] RYBCZYNSKI T.M.: «Factor Endowment and Relative Commodity Prices», *Economica*, n. 22, November 1955, pp. 336-41.

[51] SAMUELSON PAUL A.: «International Trade and the Equalisation of Factor Prices», *Economic Journal*, n. 58, June 1948, pp. 163-84.

[52] — —: «International Factor Price Equalisation Once More», *Economic Journal*, n. 59, June 1949, pp. 181-97.

[53] — —: «A Comment on Factor Price Equalisation», *Review of Economic Studies*, vol. 19 (2), n. 49, 1951, 1952, pp. 121-2.

[54] — —: «Prices of Factors and Goods in General Equilibrium», *Review of Economic Studies*, vol. 21 (1), n. 54, 1953, 1954, pp. 1-20.

[55] — —: «Equalization by Trade of the Interest Rate Along with the Real Wage», in *Trade, Growth and the Balance of Payments: Essays in Honor of Gottfried Haberler*, Chicago, Rand McNally & Co., 1965, pp. 34-52.

[56] — —: «Ohlin Was Right», *Swedish Journal of Economics*, n. 73, 1971, pp. 365-84.

[57] SIDGWICK H.: *Principles of Political Economy*, London, 1887.

[58] STERN R.M. - MASKUS K.E.: «Determinants of the Structure of US Foreign Trade, 1958-1976», *Journal of International Economics*, n. 11, May 1981, pp. 207-24.

[59] STOLPER W.F. - SAMUELSON P.A.: «Protection and Real Wages», *Review of Economic Studies*, n. 9, November 1941, pp. 58-73, reprinted in *Readings in the Theory of International Trade*, Philadelphia, Blakiston, 1949.

[60] TINBERGEN J.: «The Equalisation of Factor Prices in Free Trade Areas», *Metroeconomica*, n. 1, July 1949, pp. 40-7.

[61] TRAVIS W.P.: *The Theory of Trade and Protection*, Cambridge, Harvard University Press, 1964.

[62] VANEK JAROSLAV: «The Factor Proportions Theory: the N-Factor Case», reprinted in *Program on Comparative Economic Development*, Cornell University, 1968.

[63] VINER JACOB: *Studies in the Theory of International Trade*, London, Allen & Unwin, 1937.

# III - THE IMPORTANCE
# OF ECONOMIC AREAS

# On the Importance of Joining the EC's Single Market: The Perspective EFTA Members

**Richard E. Baldwin**

Graduate Institute of International Studies, in Geneva and CEPR

## 1. - Introduction

In 1989 the European Free Trade Association (EFTA) and the European Community (EC) embarked on market opening negotiations which culminated in 1991 with the European Economic Area (EEA) agreement. The essence of the EEA agreement is to extend the reforms embodied in the EC's Single Market Program, widely known as the *1992 Program*, to the EFTA countries (1). Although the agriculture sector is explicity excluded, the EEA is intended to ensure the free movement of goods, services, capital and people among EFTA and EC nations. Moreover, Austria, Finland, Sweden and Switzerland have applied for full EC membership; Norway is likely to follow suit. This recent interest in closer integration with the EC contradicts a long tradition. Many analysts are quick to point out that the end of the cold war may explain the reversal of these countries' traditional aversion to EC membership. Most of the prospective members are neutral and the EC was viewed as firmly in the Western camp. I find this reasoning largely spurious. For most of its existence, the EC played almost no role in foreign policies or military policies. Indeed, France is not a member of NATO and Ireland is neutral. The current

---

(1) Sweden, Norway, Finland, Iceland, Sweden, Switzerland, and Liechtenstein. Most of the data in this paper comes from the EFTA Economic Affairs Department's publication entitled *EFTA Trade 1990*.

*Advise:* the numbers in square brackets refer to the Bibliography in appendix.

EC members had no unified response to the Persian Gulf conflict and have so far failed to arrive at a unified response to the break up of Yugoslavia. Moreover if history is any lesson, the fall of one particular set of regimes like the Soviet bloc will not end all conflicts between nations. It is quite probable, for instance, that sometime in the next 40 years, some sort of systematic hostility between the EC and some other country will re-emerge.

Be that as it may, this paper argues that the sudden interest of EFTA countries in joining the unified EC market is driven by the closer integration of the 12 EC nations — the *1992 Program* in particular. The *1992 Program* would lead to a significant economic loss in the EFTA countries if they do not join the EC's single market via the EEA agreement or some other institutional arrangement. If they do join the single market, the EFTA countries are likely to gain even more from the 1992 reforms than the existing EC members. Since the true benefit of joining is the sum of the loss that is avoided and the gains that are won, the economic logic of joining the single market is compelling. Another way to say this is that the *1992 Program* has forced the issue. EFTA nations no longer have the luxury of choosing between EEA membership and the *status quo*. The choice now is between EEA membership and a significant deterioration of the *status quo*.

Once the EFTA countries realize that they must join the single market via the EEA, the step to full membership is all but inevitable due to political factors. The major economic differences between EC and EEA membership can be boiled down to cash payments, agriculture, competition policy, the common external tariff structure and a relatively ill-defined concept of irreversibility. These economic differences, however, have little to do with the recent interest in EC membership. The desire to have a say in future policy formation is without a doubt the driving force behind the EFTA countries' membership bids. Under the EEA, EFTA countries have little or no say in the formulation of EC directives that may greatly affect their firms. Since the move to full membership has little to do with economics, this paper deals primarily with the economic rationale for EEA membership.

The paper is organized in four subsequent parts. The next looks at the classic trade diversion and trade creation analysis and its applicability to the case at hand. The next section looks at how 1992 would put EFTA firms at a strategic disadvantage if EFTA does not join the EEA. The following section examines quantification of static and dynamic gains. The final section presents a summary and conclusion.

## 2. - Trade Diversion and Trade Creation Analysis

To understand the classis trade diversion argument demands mastery of two simple propositions: 1) consumers care only about the prices that are inclusive of tariffs, but the price that the country as a whole pays is the price exclusive of tariffs, and 2) a country is harmed when it has to pay higher prices for its imports. The latter point is obvious — everyone would prefer to pay less for the things they buy. The first point is only slightly more subtle. Purchases by domestic consumers (this encompasses individuals buying final goods and firms buying industrial goods and raw materials) are guided by market prices which reflect tariffs as well as prices charged by producers. The prices that one country as a whole pays, however, depends only on the producer prices since tariffs are essentially a case of the left hand paying the right; the domestic government receives all indirect taxes paid by domestic consumers.

Eliminating tariffs on goods imported from members of a trading bloc but not on goods from other nations will alter the purchasing pattern of domestic consumers in an artificial manner. This is because home consumers only have to pay tariffs on imports from non-member countries. As a result consumers may find it in their interests to switch their purchases from non-member producers that charge a low producer price to a member country that changes a high production price. Although this is better for consumers — they get the goods at lower prices — it may worsen the situation for the country as a whole. The point is that the domestic government loses out on some tariff revenue when consumers switch. In fact if the loss in tariff revenue is greater than the reduction in price perceived by domestic consumers (this is the normal case), we know that the country as a whole is paying a higher price for its imports. This harms the country.

Offsetting this so-called trade diversion, is the possibility that the biased tariff reduction will lead some domestic consumers to stop buying from domestic producers that charge a high price and switch to imports from member countries that can make the same goods at a lower cost. In such cases the country as whole, as well as the consumers, would get the goods at a lower cost. This is called trade creation and it benefits the country.

These two effects of preferential trade liberalization, trade diversion and trade creation, are the traditional approach to evaluationg the economic benefit, or cost, of a particular country joining a preferential trade arrangement. If the trade creation outweighs the trade diversion the country gains, otherwise it loses. There are a couple of rules of thumb for evaluating which effect dominates. If joining a trading bloc leads a country to switch a large fraction of its imports from non-member countries to member countries, we suspect that a lot of trade diversion is going on. If the country switches a significant fraction of its purchases from home producers to producers in other member countries, we suspect a lot of trade creation is going on. Thus if the country's overall import/GDP ratio stays about the same but imports from the bloc replace imports from non-member suppliers, the arrangement has probably harmed the country. If the converse is true, joining the trading bloc probably benefits the country. In many cases, lots of trade creation and trade diversion occur, so we cannot use the rules of thumb to evaluate the impact. We must turn to more involved and detailed methods of measuring the importance of trade creation and trade diversion.

## 2.1 *Relevance to the EC Expansion*

This type of analysis, however, fails to capture the most important effects of the EEA agreement on the EFTA countries. First the scope for trade diversion is fairly small. Both the EC and the EFTA countries receive the vast majority (about 67% for the EC and 73% for EFTA) of their imports from other EEA countries, so the scope for diverting imports from third countries is modest. Moreover, the existing EC and EFTA tariffs on imports from non-EEA countries are fairly low — the average EC tariff on manufactures is about 4.2%, the EFTA average is even lower at 3.0% — so the amount of lost tariff revenue per dollar of diverted trade will be low. Moreover, the liberalization accompanying EC membership will involve removing non-revenue creating barriers. Things like border controls, complicated VAT refund processes, discriminatory industrial stand-ards and the like are what will be removed. When non-revenue raising barriers are removed, any switching of imports from non-members to members will increase the welfare of the joining country and the existing members. The point is now there is no tariff-revenue loss incurred by the government to offset the gain to private consumers.

There is, however, one sector where the trade diversion-trade creation analysis provides a bountiful harvest — agriculture. For-tunately, this is also one of those cases where the rules of thumb can be used. The level of protection on agriculture in the new members is even higher than it is in the EC, and the agricultural sectors in the EFTA countries are even less cost effective than those in the EC. Thus eliminating agricultural protection will lead the new members to buy less from their own high cost farmers and more from lower cost producers in the EC. This is trade creation. There will be a shift of resources in the EFTA countries away from agriculture and toward other sectors. Since it is clear that agriculture in these countries is highly inefficient, such a reallocation of resources will boost overall EFTA output. Of course, it would be even more beneficial for the expanded EC to buy more on the world market since EC farmers generally cannot match world prices.

Turning to the potential for trade diversion, it is important to note that the prospective members do not currently import much in the way of agriculture goods from non-EC members, so the scope for trade diversion in agriculture is limited. In 1990, EFTA countries imported a total of $12.8 billion in agricultural goods (SITC 0 and 1), with $8.4 billion of this coming from the EC or EFTA itself. In summary, the scope for trade creation is agriculture is great while the scope for trade diversion is relatively minor. In the agricultural sector, the new members are almost surely going to gain from preferential trade liberalization.

## 3. - Preferential Trade Cost Reductions
## with Imperfect Competition

We argued above that since 80% of trade between the EC and the new members was in manufactured goods (for which tariffs were a negligible consideration due to previous liberalizations) the classic trade creation versus trade diversion analysis was of limited use. Taking this line of reasoning to its extreme, we could say that the economic rational for EEA membership was rather weak. This section shows that such a conclusion misses a very important point.

The traditional analysis of preferential trade arrangements excludes consideration of imperfect competition and scale effects. A large body of research done since 1979 has shown that excluding the possibility of imperfect competition rules out an important class of effect. A useful analogy to illustrate the importance of imperfect competition is the contrast between the traditional analysis of a foreign export subsidy and the more recent analysis. A well-known comment attributed to Milton Friedman is that the proper domestic response to a foreign export subsidy is to send a letter of thanks to the foreign tax payers. The work of Jim Brander and Barbara Spencer, among others, has shown us that in some cases a foreign export subsidy could actually harm the domestic country by shifting rents to foreign firms.

The question facing the prospective members of the EEA is not simply that of whether to remove trade barriers with the EC. The EC's Single Market Program is projected to significantly improve the economic climate within the EC. For instance, a survey of 20,000 EC businesses (Nerb [8]) cited in the *Cecchini Report* found that on average, firms thought that the *1992 Program* would lower their total costs by something like 2%. Pelkman, Wallace and Winters [9] estimate the trade-cost reduction impact of 1992 to be between 1 and 3%. A survey reported in EFTA [4] broadly confirmed this finding for EFTA industry. This may not sound like much, but in a situation of imperfect competition, any cost reduction to your rival harms your profits. Thus, firms based in EFTA would face a significant loss if EFTA does not join the EEA. If these losses are great enough the firms may be forced to chose between going out of business and re-locating to the EC. In both cases, the EFTA countries would experience an output drop.

To illustrate the point, consider a simple partial equilibrium model of duopoly involving one firm located in an EC country and one located in a non-EC country. The two firms produce identical products and both sell in each other's markets (two-way trade in identical goods). Competition in both regions is Cournot, that is the firms play Nash in quantities. Production by both firms takes place at constant marginal production costs ($c$ for the non-EC firm, $c^*$ for the EC firm) subject to a fixed set-up cost $F$, and transport costs that are a constant *ad valorem* $\tau$. It turns out that even this simple set-up allows us to learn something about why the 1992 program might greatly step up EFTA countries' interest in joining the EEA. The first step is to pin down what the equilibrium would be for a given relative competitiveness of EC and non-EC firms. After that we ask what happens to profits, prices and sales of the non-EC firm when EC firms find their costs of doing business in the EC lowered thanks to the *1992 Program*.

Taking the demand elasticity to be constant at unity, the market share of the non-EC firm in the EC market will satisfy:

$$s = (1 + \Phi)^{-1}$$

where:

$$\Phi = c(1 + \tau)/c^*$$

that is to say $\Phi$ is the relative competitiveness of the non-EC firm. Clearly a decrease in the EC's firms costs lowers the non-EC firm's market share. It is easy to show that with a unitary demand, the level of operating profits earned by the non-EC firm in the EC market is simply the square of its market share, that is:

$$\pi = s^2$$

Putting the two formula together, it is plain that any lowering of the costs of the EC firm without a lowering of the non-EC firm's costs will harm the non-EC firm. Moreover, it turns out that the percentage drop in non-EC profits for a given percent drop in the EC firm's marginal costs is higher the lower is the non-EC market share. That is, if a non-EC firm has only a small share of the market in the first place, it will be harmed even more by a loss in competitiveness. To see this algebraically, note that:

$$(d\pi/\pi)/(dc^*/c^*) = 2(1-s), \quad \text{for } s > 0.$$

This same point can be seen graphically in Graph 1. Graph 1 shows the cost curves (*MC* is marginal cost; *AC* is average cost), residual demand (*RD*) and residual marginal revenue (*RMR*) curves for a non-EC firm selling in the EC market. The initial operating profit (profit gross of fixed costs) equals the area of the box *ABCD*. A lowering of the competitors marginal costs relative to those of the non-EC firm will result in a reduction of the non-EC firm's market share. In the graph this is shown as an inward shift of the *RD* to *RD'* and a corresponding shift of *RMR* to *RMR'* . The profit is reduced to *EFGH* , which is smaller than *ABCD* since the price is lower and sales are lower.

The last thing to do is to see how the drop in profits earned by the non-EC firm in the EC affects their overall profits. To keep things simple for the moment, suppose that 1992 lowers EC firms' cost of doing business in the EC, but has no effect on their export competitiveness. In this oversimplified case there is no change in market shares or profits of either firm in the non-EC market. Consequently all changes in total profits of the non-EC firm stem from their reduced operating profit in the EC. Clearly the more important the EC market for the non-EC firm, the larger will be the impact on total profits. In particular, the percent change in the non-EC firm's total profits equals the percent change in their earnings in the EC times the initial share that the EC profits constituted in their total profits.

Now let us revise the assumption of no change in EC export competitiveness. If in addition to lowering costs within the EC, 1992 also boosted export competitiveness of EC-based firms (say due to greater exploitation of economies of scale), the result would be even stronger. Non-EC firms — or more specifically — firms that do not

Graph 1

### THE EFFECTS OF 1992 FOR NON-EEC COMPANIES (*)

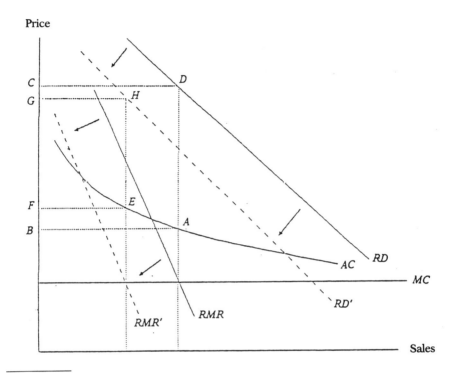

(*) *Project 1992* reduces the costs of companies which belong to and operate in the EEC, thus reducing the competitiveness of non-EEC companies. This leads to a reduction in the market share and profits of non-EEC companies.

benefit fully from the trade cost reducing aspects of 1992, will be harmed due to a loss of profits on their EC sales and a loss of profit on their home sales due to heightened EC competitiveness. Furthermore, the total drop in profits for the non-EC firm depends upon the share of profits coming from exports. If EC profits were a large enough share of total profits, a loss of relative competitiveness could force the non-EC firm out of business, or at least force it to relocate to the EC.

In summary, the *1992 Program* harms non-EC firms by boosting the competitiveness of EC firms relative to non-EC firms. The weight of this injury is greater the more important is the EC market to a given non-EC firm and the smaller is that non-EC firm's market share in the EC. A couple of fictional examples may help clarify the point. On one hand, think about a Swedish auto maker that has only a tiny fraction of the total EC market, yet this small market share is highly important to the firm's overall performance. Such a firm would be greatly harmed by the *1992 Program*, if Sweden does not join the EC. If Sweden does join the EEA, then presumably the Swedish firm would also benefit from the cost reduction, so there would be little or no change in relative competitiveness. On the other hand, think of a US computer producer who has a large share of the EC market, yet for whom the EC market accounts for only a fraction of total sales. Such a firm will experience some losses as a result of 1992, but its global performance will not be greatly affected.

## 4. - Static and Dynamic Effects of Trade Liberalization

The static gains from trade that have been estimated using computable partial and general equilibrium models are all pretty small. Indeed, until Rick Harris and David Cox introduced a model that allowed for economies of scales and imperfect competition, the standard estimates of even large-scale trade liberalization programs were extremely small, always less than 2% of GDP and often less than 1% of GNP. There is no secret about why this was true. Graph 2 shows the standard diagram used to look at the static effects of lowering tariffs and quotas. As is well-known, the area of the two Harberger triangles measures (in real dollars) the net gain to the nation of a lower tariff. The area of these triangles ($T1$ and $T2$) is usually very small since it depends upon the square of a fraction (i.e., the change in the price due to the tariff change, this is almost always a small fraction). Of course, with the percent gain being small in absolute size, the gain as a fraction of output is even smaller.

The removal of resource-wasting trade barriers and liberalization of quantitative restrictions (if the quota rents were earned by foreigners prior to the liberalization) may be substantially larger. The

GRAPH 2

THE LACH OF ADVANTAGES IN STATIC TERMS

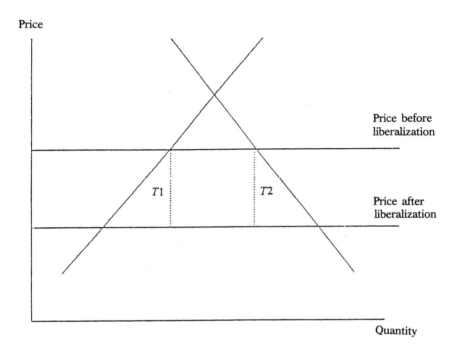

reason of course is because in both cases the gain as a percent of GDP is approximately equal to the percent change in the domestic price times the ratio of imports to GDP. Since imports may be a substantial fraction of a country's output, widespread liberalization of non-tariff barriers may have much larger effects. The policy changes implied by EEA are projected to reduce the costs of trade by 2.5% (Haaland and Norman [6]), and the EFTA countries' exports to the EEA countries account for about 20% of their GDP. Consequently, the static gains from the elimination of trade costs should be something like 0.5% of GDP. Imposing general equilibrium constraints on this type of gain generally lowers the estimates since the incipient output expansion is dampened as the price of scare resources are driven up.

Inclusion of scale effects and imperfect competition by Harris and Cox in the case of Canada, and the inclusion of scale effects and imperfect competition in the case of the EC by Tony Venables and Alasdair Smith (Smith and Venables [10]) leads to much larger estimates of the static effects. The sources of these gains are twofold. First removing artificial trade barriers will allow firms to operate at a more efficient scale. In the case of a highly fragmented market, firms may be chronically producing at too low of a level, so liberalization may have large cost-lowering effects. Second, the cost of market segmentation stems from the manner in which it restricts international competition among firms. When firms treat the various national markets as separate, in the sense that they feel that the quantity they sell in one market does not affect the price they receive in another market, the local firm tends to take a dominant position. This type of dominance typically leads to higher prices and therefore lower welfare. Another way of seeing this is to note that a market in which four firms have equal market shares tends to be more competitive (i.e., involves lower profit margins) than a market with four firms where one has the lion's share of the sales. By completing the internal market, it is hoped that the myriad of legal and informal arrangements that supports market segmentation will disappear leading to lower profits margins and more efficient pricing. This increased competition will also force further cost-lowering rationalization of industry structures. In the case of the EC, Gasiorek, Smith and Venables [5] have estimated these effects to be rather large.

## 4.1 *Dynamic Effects*

The addition of static gains stemming from consideration of scale effects and market segmentation have boosted the typical range of estimates of static gains from trade. Nevertheless the typical range of estimates is one-half to 1%. For instance, the *Cecchini Report* estimated gains of 2.5 to 6.5% of GDP. Many trade economists, however, are skeptical of the high end of this range. Despite this skepticism, the oral wisdom in trade economists asserts that trade liberalization is an important source of gains to nations. That is, most economists feel that bad trade policy can greatly hinder the welfare of a nation — certainly far more than a one-time fall in income by a few percentage points. Certainly most economists would agree that trade policies account for more than two percentage points of the per capita income difference between Korea and India. The adage that sums up this oral wisdom is that trade matters due to the dynamic gains from trade rather than the static gains from trade. Until recently it was often asserted that dynamic gains from trade were poorly understood and impossible to measure. Our understanding of growth effects began to blossom with the endogenous growth literature introduced by Paul Romer and refined by many including Robert Lucas. Starting with an article I wrote in 1989 (Baldwin [1]), we have begun to roughly estimate the impact of a number of dynamic gains from trade.

Of all the dynamic effects that have been examined in the theoretical advances, the 'best understood is that of endogenous capital formation. The reason for this is that in fact the techniques and empirical results developed since Solow's 1957 article can be directly applied. Other models and approaches are still in the experimental stage. The basic idea is that a change in trade policy large enough to have a noticeable economy-wide impact is likely to alter the marginal product of capital in the home market. Since the capital stock is endogenous, the change in trade policy will affect medium term growth by promoting or stifling investment. Suppose that manufacturing is intensive in its use of human and physical capital. The loss of sales and profits due to the decline in relative competitiveness discussed above will drive down the price of human and physical capital in EFTA, if they do not join the EC's single market. This is the well-known Stolper-Samuelson effect. In the long run this will result in a lower steady state capital labor ratio and a lower growth rate during the transition period. This point is extremely robust in the context of the neoclassical growth model. It holds up in models in which agents are completely rational and maximize everything they can get their hands on. It also holds up in the simplest Solow growth model.

The basic approach to measuring the growth effects of trade due to endogenous capital formation is straightforward. A change in trade policy large enough have a noticeable economy-wide impact is likely to alter the marginal product of capital in the home market. In the case of EFTA joining the EEA, Haaland and Norman [6] estimate the effects to be a little more than 1% (not one percentage point) increase in the return to capital. Since the capital stock is endogenous, this latter change will affect medium term growth by promoting investment. The key to gauging the importance of this effect in the long run is the following steady state condition:

$$MPK(K, Z) = \text{discount rate} + \text{depreciation rate}.$$

This states that in the long run, the capital stock in each country must be such that the real marginal product of capital just equals the discount rate plus the rate of depreciation of capital, assuming the usual diminishing marginal returns to capital and holding all other factors $Z$ constant. Given the changes in the return to EFTA and EC capital given by the Haaland-Norman estimates *(Table 1 and 2)*, the capital stock in EFTA and the EC should rise, if the EFTA countries join. If EFTA does not join, the capital stock in the EC will not rise by quite as much, and the EFTA capital stock should shrink. This of course would slow the rate of growth in EFTA countries until the new lower capital stock was reached.

In fact, if we are willing to assume a simple but standard functional form for the relationship, between capital, labor and GDP, then we can arrive at a back-of-the-envelope calculation directly. That is, assuming the relationship between capital, labor and GDP is such that GDP equals $AKL^h$, assuming that the initial capital stock is approximately in long run equilibrium, and assuming the labor force is approximately constant (as it has been in Western Europe for the past decade), we have:

$$(\% \text{ change in } K) = [1 - a]^{-1} (\% \text{ change in return to capital}).$$

The long run increase in output implied by the increase in the capital stock is:

$$(\% \text{ change in GDP}) = [1/a) - 1]^{-1} (\% \text{ change in return to capital}).$$

Of course full adjustment of the capital stock may take decades. As a result this dynamic effect will impact growth for a very long time.

The next step requires an estimate of $a$ which is just the capital output elasticity. This parameter is difficult to estimate correctly, but most estimates range from 0.25 and 0.5 . Using this range of estimates gives us the range of medium-run output effects between 33 and 100% larger than the static effects.

The last thing to note concerns the welfare implications of this induced capital formation effect. Baldwin [2] shows that the rise in output due to extra capital formation does not boost welfare to the same extent that static efficiency gains do. The point is that since capital formation requires foregoing consumption, the welfare gain from the extra output is offset substantially by the lower initial consumption.

TABLE 1

THE SAVINGS PRODUCED BY EEA FOR TRADE
(% variations - base year 1985)

| | EFTA | EC | USA | JAPAN |
|---|---|---|---|---|
| *EFTA does not join EEA* | | | | |
| Real income as % of GDP ............... | −0.10 | 0.48 | −0.00 | −0.00 |
| Return on capital ...... | −0.04 | 0.57 | −0.01 | −0.01 |
| Return on specialized labor ................. | −0.18 | 0.62 | −0.01 | −0.02 |
| *EFTA does join EEA* | | | | |
| Real income as % of GDP ............... | 0.69 | 0.50 | −0.00 | −0.00 |
| Return on capital ...... | 1.01 | 0.61 | −0.01 | −0.01 |
| Return on specialized labor ................. | 1.25 | 0.63 | −0.01 | −0.02 |
| *Gains from the union including losses avoided* | | | | |
| Real income as % of GDP ............... | 0.79 | | | |
| Return on capital ...... | 1.05 | | | |
| Return on specialized labor ................. | 1.43 | | | |

Source: HAALAND - NORMAN [6].

## 4.2 *Add-On Effects and Long Run Growth Effects*

The reasoning above pointed out that the return to human and physical capital in the EFTA nations would be unfavorable. The last section argued that the level of physical capital would, in the long run, be reduced to restore the steady state return to capital. Furthermore if physical and knowledge capital is internationally mobile yet human capital is not, the offshoring of production facilities could lower the return to human capital even more than it lowers the return to physical capital. The basic point here is that physical and human capital are complementary factors. The return to human capital in the EFTA countries depends positively on the stock of physical capital. The reduced level of physical capital in EFTA would therefore exacerbate the declining returns to human capital. To the extent that at least the most highly trained workers are able to migrate, this effect suggests that the EFTA countries would experience a brain drain.

In an endogenous growth model, the rate of growth depends upon the rate of accumulation of factors that do not experience diminishing returns. One well-known endogenous growth model by Robert Lucas supposes that the accumulation of the human capital does not run into diminishing returns from a societal point of view. That is, each generation is more and more highly educated, however the fraction of primary resources that must be devoted to getting them educated does not rise. This framework predicts that the depressed demand for human capital in the EFTA countries (if they do not join) will slow the rate of human capital formation permanently, and thereby permanently lower the growth rate in the EFTA countries.

A final effect, that plays an important role in the thinking of policy makers but has so far escaped quantification, stems from the recent economic geography literature associated with Paul Krugman and Tony Venables. The relevant aspect of this work is its emphasis on the importance of external economies of scale in production. For a wide variety of reasons, it appears that the competitiveness of a firm depends in part on the amount of economic activity that goes on in the surrounding area. This largely explains the fact that industries throughout the world tend to cluster geographically. In this light, the loss of industrial output if EFTA stays out of the EEA, and the gain if they join, will impact on the competitiveness of the remaining production. Thus the static effects discussed above will be amplified by external economies.

## 5. - Summary and Conclusions

This paper argues that there are very strong, well-documented economic reasons for the EFTA countries wanting to join the Single Market via the European Economic Area agreement (EEA). The economic rationale for going beyond this and actually joining as full EC members, however, is substantially weaker and to a large extent depends upon economic factors that have not been quantified and may be un-quantifiable. The political arguments for pushing beyond EEA to full membership, however, are rather compelling. EEA does not allow the EFTA countries a say in the formation of EC economic policies that may adversely affect their industries.

## BIBLIOGRAPHY

[1] BALDWIN R.: «Growth Effects of 1992», *Economic Policy*, n. 9, 1989.

[2] —— : «Measurable Dynamic Gains from Trade», *Journal of Political Economy*, 1992.

[3] COMMISSION OF THE EUROPEAN COMMUNITIES: «The Economics of 1992», *European Economy*, n. 35 (known as *Cecchini Report*), 1988.

[4] EFTA SECRETARIAT: «Effects of 1992 on the Manufacturing Industries of the Efta Countries», *Occasional Paper*, n. 38, 1992.

[5] GASIOREK M. - SMITH A. - VENABLES T.: «Competing the Internal Market in the EC: Factor Demands and Comparative Advantage», *European Integration: Trade and Industry*, Cambridge, Cambridge University Press, 1991.

[6] HAALAND J. - NORMAN V.: «Global Production Effects of European Integration» CEPR, *Discussion Paper*, 1992.

[7] KRUGMAN P.: «Efta and 1992», EFTA, *Occasional Paper*, n. 23, 1988.

[8] NERB G.: «The Completion of the Internal Market: A Survey of Europe's Perception of the Likely Effects», *Research on the Costs of Non-Europe*, Basic Findings, vol. 3, Commission of the European Community, 1988.

[9] PELKMAN J. - WALLACE H. - WINTERS A.: *The European Domestic Market*, London, Chatham House, 1988.

[10] VENABLES T. - SMITH A.: «Completing the Internal Market in the European Community: Some Industry Simulations», CEPR, *Discussion Paper*, n. 223, 1988.

# Growth and Specialization in an Enlarged Europe: Is a Virtuous Circle Possible?

**Carlo Andrea Bollino** - **Pier Carlo Padoan**
Eni, Roma                Università «La Sapienza»,
                         Roma

## 1. - Introduction

All processes of integration are complex and multifaceted, and as such cannot be analyzed from any single standpoint but must be approached using a variety of different instruments and points of view. What follows is a series of considerations concerning the problems involved in the integration of the economies of Eastern Europe with the European Community. In other words, in our discussion we consider crucial that integration has to be seen as a strategy to increase the sustainable growth rate of Eastern economies.

First, let us examine the issue from the viewpoint of the Eastern countries. The ultimate goal of the radical economic reforms they are undertaking is to enhance their capacity to grow in a framework of progressive opening to international trade. In other words, they want to maximize the growth rate consistent with current account equilibrium. Failing this condition, in fact, these countries would face an increasing foreign debt that would be unsustainable in the long run, eventually running into the severe problems faced by many developing countries in the recent past.

This issue can be framed in the following terms. In what way should the countries of Central and Eastern Europe modify their specialization pattern so as to raise growth rates without undermining the long-term current account equilibrium? This question immediately raises another one. Given that the relevant area for integration is the European Community, in what way should the Community's own specialization pattern be modified to "accommodate" the request for integration on the part of the former COMECON countries? And what are the institutional as well as the economic implications of such an enlargement of the Community?

In a few pages, it is clearly impossible to touch even superficially on all the complexities and facets of such an integration process. We shall try to sketch a general framework drawing on a recently completed research (Bollino-Padoan [2] (*)), to offer both theoretical and practical observations. We begin by considering the links between growth, specialization, and institutional arrangements. This is followed by a number of observations on the adjustment mechanisms most appropriate to achieving such a configuration.

## 2. - Growth and the Balance of Payments

A useful starting point is the relation of identity defining a growth rate consistent with on current account equilibrium, which for convenience we shall call the "equilibrium" growth rate (Fagerberg [9], Padoan [20]). It is as follows:

$$(1) \qquad g^* = q\,x - q\,m + (p - p\,w) + g\,w$$

Equation *(1)* establishes that the equilibrium growth rate of output $(g^*)$ is positively correlated to the change of the export share $(qx)$; negatively correlated to the change of the share of imports over GDP $(qm)$; positively correlated to the difference between the rate of increase of domestic prices $(p)$ and world prices $(pw)$, the term in brackets thus representing the rate of change in the country's terms of trade, assuming a fixed rate. Finally, $g^*$ is positively correlated to the rate of growth of world demand $(gw)$.

---

(*) *Advise:* the numbers in square brackets refer to the Bibliography in appendix.

The next step is determining what factors affect the changes in the foregoing variables.

The change in export and import shares depends, broadly, on competitiveness. For sake of simplicity, we can restrict our consideration to two determinants: price and technology (see Appendix 1 for a further development of this point). Without going into detail, it can be shown that as far as effects on the growth rate are concerned, these two factors present a twofold tradeoff. First, if domestic prices rise faster than world prices this has a positive effect on growth thanks to an improvement in the terms of trade but a negative one by undermining competitiveness. A country's technological capabilities may be improved either through domestic innovation or by diffusion, i.e. imports of technologies from the rest of the world (for a more extensive treatment of the influence of these effects on the equilibrium growth rate, see Padoan [20]).

In general, any country will have a number of alternatives at its disposal for raising the equilibrium growth rate. The relevant point here is that the alternatives themselves depend, to a large extent, on the country's pattern of international specialization. This is a complex topic indeed. For our purposes, however, we can consider it by turning directly to the case of integration of the East European economies in the European Community.

## 3. - Comparative Advantages in Europe

Table 1 summarizes the findings of a study by Guerrieri and Mastropasqua [11] (see also Appendix 2) on the economic specialization of the countries of Eastern Europe, comparing them with those of the major EC countries. The specialization patterns are analyzed by using an appropriately modified version of Pavitt's taxonomy [21], which is particularly well-suited to assess the links between technology, changes in relative prices and international competitiveness. Briefly (for a more extensive treatment, see Dosi, Pavitt and Soete, [8]), a number of sectors are identified, according to the source from which they draw gains in competitiveness. The relevant sectors are the following; the *science-based* industries, in which competitiveness

TABLE 1

REVEALED COMPARATIVE ADVANTAGES
EUROPEAN COUNTRIES

|  | Science based | Scale intensive | Specialized suppliers | Tradi-tional | Agricul-ture | Resource intensive | Energy |
|---|---|---|---|---|---|---|---|
| Germany . . . . | + | + | + | − | − | − | − |
| United Kingdom . . | + | + | + | − | − | − | + |
| France . . . . . . | + | + | + | − | + | − | − |
| Italy . . . . . . . . | − | − | + | + | + | − | − |
| Spain, Portu-gal, Greece . . | − | − | − | + | + | − | − |
| Czechoslovakia | − | + | − | + | − | + | − |
| Hungary . . . . | − | − | − | + | + | + | − |
| Poland . . . . . . | − | − | − | + | + | + | + |
| Former USSR | − | − | − | − | − | + | + |

*Source*: adapted from GUERRIERI - MASTROPASQUA [11].

derives from the ability to generate endogenous innovation; *scale-intensive* activites, which rely on market size and the consequent ability to exploit static and dynamic returns to scale so as to cut costs, where both technological and price competitiveness play an important role; *specialized suppliers*, which base competitiveness on price but also on technology, and are heavily dependent on innovations generated elsewhere; *traditional* sectors, where competitiveness depends chiefly if not exclusively on price. In other sectors of the economy, such as *agriculture, resource-intensive* industries that exploit their access to raw materials (such as petroleum and coal derivatives), and *energy-intensive* industries, improvement in the terms of trade plays a fundamental role.

Bearing the foregoing in mind, let us examine Table 1, which summarizes the distribution of comparative advantages in the former Soviet Union (now CIS), the countries of Central and Eastern Europe (EE), and the main EC member states according to Pavitt's classification (Guerrieri and Mastropasqua [11]). Singling out Eastern Europe, we find that Poland and Hungary present a comparative advantage in agricultural products and traditional manufactures and

Czechoslovakia also in scale-intensive industries. All three countries enjoy a comparative advantage in the resource-intensive and energy-intensive sectors, while the former Soviet Union presents comparative advantages only in the two latter sectors.

Combining these observations with those concerning the causal linkage between the determinants of competitiveness and the equilibrium growth rate gives rise to a number of indications.

In all the countries of Eastern Europe the relative importance of agriculture, energy, and resource-intensive sectors suggests that an improvement in the terms of trade would benefit growth. Accordingly, a real devaluation in an effort to make manufactures more competitive in world markets could have adverse effects on long-run growth. It would be more appropriate, rather, to seek to improve competitiveness in the manufacturing sector by increasing the pace of technological innovation, which can be achieved by technology imports. From this standpoint, a crucial role could be played by western foreign direct investment, an issue to which we shall return. In some cases, moreover — Czechoslovakia is an example — the possibility of an enlargement of markets will be important insofar as it allows exploiting the comparative advantage associated with economies of scale.

If we turn to the position of the EC economies a number of relevant elements appear. In the first place the comparative advantages of the three largest economies, Germany, United Kingdom and France are located in the sectors where the comparative disadvantages of EE lie, and viceversa. From this point of view these two groups of countries are in a highly favourable position as far as the process of integration is concerned. The comparative advantage that these three countries enjoy in the science-based sector suggest that these countries are in the position to produce and export the technology Eastern Europe needs to upgrade its competitive position, while they would become importers of the goods for which Eastern Europe enjoys a comparative advantage.

There are of course relevant exceptions to this optimistic scenario. France appears to have a comparative advantage in agriculture, while the UK in the energy sector. This could create problems to a "smooth" integration process in Europe.

Moreover, problems do exist if we turn to the position of Italy and of the group of southern members of the European Community, Greece, Portugal and Spain. Their comparative advantage lies in the traditional and agricultural sectors, and also in the specialized suppliers in the case of Italy.

In sum, this overall picture suggests that the integration of Eastern Europe into the European Community is far from being a painless task. Adjustments will have to be made from both "sides" of Europe. The problem is that as the situation stands today, the distribution of costs and benefits is far from symmetrical.

In the following paragraphs we will take a closer look at this issue.

## 4. - Integration as a Club Problem

In what follows we will use a simple model of club formation to consider the problem of the possible enlargement of the EC to include members from Eastern Europe (see De Benedictis and Padoan [2] for a more extensive treatment). The model we start from is a version of that introduced by Fratianni and Pattison [10] to explain the formation of international organizations.

The model assumes that costs and benefits are a function of the size of the club ($Q$) which can be thought of as the extension of the common "trade regime", i.e. the rules and institutions which govern trade relations of the club members among themselves.

As is usual in club theory we will assume rising marginal costs and declining marginal benefits with club size. Marginal costs are increasing with the extension of the club good provided because of congestion arising with an increasing number of members. In addition, as Fratianni and Pattison [10], stress, decision theory suggests that the addition of new members will raise the costs of finding agreements in a more than proportional manner. Costs will also rise more than proportionally for organizational reasons and because of political reasons each new member will have to be given equal opportunity, irrespective of its economic size, to express its viewpoint (Ward [24]). Institutional arrangements alter the behaviour of costs.

For example a shift from a unanimity rule to a majority rule in decision making within the club lowers marginal costs. Marginal benefits are decreasing because of rising congestion determined by the enlarged membership.

We start from the assumption that the actual situation, i.e. European Community with 12 ($EC12$) members is a club equilibrium. This means that $MC=MB$. It is easy to justify this assumption considering otherwise. If $MB<MC$ then the club is too large. In such a case there would be obviously no incentive for the EC to accept new membership. If $MB>MC$ then the club is too small and, therefore, new members would be seen as beneficial from the Community's point of view. The basic idea is that $EC12$ and $EC12$ plus $EE$ are two different clubs and that the latter is not just an extension of the former (Obviously, by $EC12$ we intend the actual configuration of developed, market economies; the same line of reasoning will still be valid, should the EC include one more Scandinavian country or Austria).

The incentives for $EC12$ and to launch the Single Market Program (on the incentives to promote the Single Market Programme see Cameron [4], and Moravcsik [17]) were rather different from those that are now being advanced to build a «Great Integrated Europe». To use the political scientists' jargon, "setting the agenda" for Europe '92 is quite a different matter from "setting the agenda" for the integration of the former CMEA members into the European Community.

To consider how we move from $EC12$ to $EC12$ plus $EE$ recall that the decision of the former members of CMEA to pursue a program of transition to a market system and integration with the West represents both a great opportunity and a great challenge for the industrialized countries. The opportunity lies in the additional market that $EE$ would represent for industrialized countries. The challenge lies in the large costs that $EE$ have to face in order to accomplish full market integration.

Both the opportunity and the costs can be represented graphically as follows (Graph 1). Point $A$ is the intersection of the $MB$ and $MC$ curves which defines the initial equilibrium point, $EC12$. A further enlargement would initially produce still decreasing $MB$ while marginal costs keep rising. Costs would increase because new member-

GRAPH 1

COSTS AND BENEFITS OF INTEGRATION

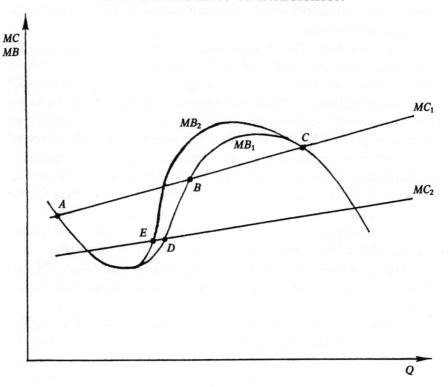

ship, even if at partial conditions such as forms of association (Mastropasqua and Rolli [15]), would increase the amount of negotiation required both with the new members and within the original twelve. At the beginning of the process, therefore, there are no obvious incentives for club enlargement as $MB < MC$. At higher levels of $Q$, however, as a consequence of enlarged membership and hence larger markets, marginal benefits for the club members start to rise and eventually become larger than marginal costs. Benefits would eventually increase — after what can be thought of as a transition phase — if we accept the previous assumption that the inclusion of $EE$ within the Community represents a great opportunity in terms of market exploitation and, more generally, because of the benefits of a larger integrated area for all participants.

*MB* and *MC* equalize at point *B* which, however, is not a stable equilibrium. To the right of point *B* increasing *MB* generate rising incentives to expand the club, i.e. to admit new members and to complete their market liberalization process. After a while congestion becomes important again, *MB* start to decrease until point *C* is reached and the new club "Greater Europe" is formed.

The crucial region is obviously the one included between *A* and *B*. In this region *MB* < *MC* and hence in this region there is no incentive to expand the club while there are incentives to return to point *A*. The region between points *A* and *B* represents the situation of initial adjustment and can be thought of as the present state of things; the economies of the Eastern European countries, much less that of the former Soviet Union, are such that their immediate *EC* membership is definitely out of question.

## 5. - Club Enlargement Problems for East and West

Graph 1 indicates that the adjustment problem requires that club size be pushed beyond point *B* in order for a virtuous process to start and lead to point *C*. A contribution to the start-off of the virtuous circle can come both from a change in cost and in benefit behaviour in the club.

The *MC* curve can be shifted downward (into *MC*2) by, e.g., a loosening of the voting rule (Fratianni and Pattison [10]), passing e.g. from a unanimity to a majority rule. This would move the unstable equilibrium point from *B* to *D* thus narrowing the dimension of the transition region. The *MB* curve can be shifted upwards (into *MB*2) by an acceleration and/or an improvement of the market liberalization process and of the access to the western market. The shift would further move the unstable equilibrium point to the right, into *E*.

This latter effect can be obtained essentially by two, mutually reinforcing, actions. From the "east side" effective transition programs will make the economies of *EE* more similar to the western ones. From the "west side" a decisive thrust towards greater liberalization would produce the same affect.

We shall deal with the second aspect in the next paragraph. Here let us consider a simple point about the first aspect. One of the most debated topics in the discussion about the characteristics of the stabilization and adjustment programs suitable for formerly planned economies is the controversy between shock therapy and gradualism. In this respect Daviddi and Manasse [6] suggest that the incentive for the (Eastern European) policy maker to implement a credible shock therapy program increases with the cost of reneging the program he announces. Such a cost, in turn, has both a fixed and a variable component. While the latter is dependent on the characteristics of the domestic economy, the former can be thought of as the cost of "international reputation". Much as in the case of the European Monetary System, "weak" or "undisciplined" economies can implement costly adjustment policies thanks to the discipline they import from the outside environment. It can be argued that future *EC* membership could play such a role in that Eastern Economies will not be granted full access to Western European markets unless their domestic stabilization programs are carried out. The higher are the expected gains of full *EC* membership the higher are the incentives of the Eastern European policy makers to complete the adjustment programs.

What is relevant from our point of view is that such a discipline effect increases the benefits of club membership for all the members, including the present ones, as far as it raises the speed at which eastern economies increase their capacity to absorb western exports.

A substantial obstacle to the enlargement, however, would probably come — as we have already mentioned — from the uneven distribution of costs and benefits for the present members of the European Community. This point is particularly relevant if one considers that the weaker members of the Community are presently facing two other "institutional shocks"; the completion of the single market program and the transition to a fully fixed exchange rate regime (whether in the form of Monetary Union or "hard EMS").

The effects of these three shocks would produce cumulative pressure on the "southern" members of the community. To see this in a very simple and impressionistic way consider Graph 2.

Assume two countries, both members of the EC: North ($N$) and South ($S$). Given the overall dimension of the EC market — the size of the box — the dotted vertical line separates national markets. In the presence of increasing returns if each country were to exploit only its domestic market for sheer reason of size, country $N$ would be able to produce at a lower cost with respect to $S$. The cost differential, $AB$, in the absence of barriers to factor mobility would make production location profitable in $N$ for firms operating at the European level. However a barrier of amount $T$ (Graph 2$a$) such as to offset the cost differential would maintain a location incentive in $S$. The Single Market can be thought of as the elimination of a barrier needed to offset such a cost differential (Krugman [13]).

Consider now $S$ credibly entering an exchange agreement (Graph 2$B$). As is well known (Branson [3], Krugman [12]), in such a case the currency of the "weak" country would experience a nominal and, subsequently, real appreciation. This would shift the $S$ cost curve upwards, to $S'$, as costs expressed in $N'S$ currency increase. The cost differential would rise to $BC$.

Let us now introduce the enlargement effect (Graph 2$C$) and assume that the increase in market size benefits only the North. This is not an unrealistic assumption — even though an extreme one — given the available empirical evidence (Collins and Rodrik [5], Guerrieri and Mastropasqua [11]). The dimension of the market increases and the $N$ cost curve shifts to $N'$ bringing the cost differential to $DC$.

Clearly the only way in which the South could resist such a combined pressure would be through a massive restructuring process (perhaps also through the support of some form of "horizontal industrial policy" aimed at improving locational advantages) such as to shift its curve cost down — as in Graph 2$D$ — thus narrowing the cost gap. Lacking this, one can easily see that the "Southern" members of the Community, assuming their loyal commitment to the Single Market program and to (some for of) monetary integration, would find good reasons for an opposition to a rapid accession of the Eastern European economies to the EC.

Up to now the policy of the European Community in favour of Eastern Europe has apparently followed quite a liberal approach (De Benedictis-Padoan [7], and Mastropasqua-Rolli [15] for a discussion).

GRAPH 2

## SINGLE MARKET AND INTEGRATION

*Domestic market*

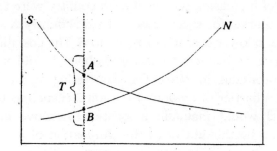

GRAPH 2*a*

*Fixed exchange rate*

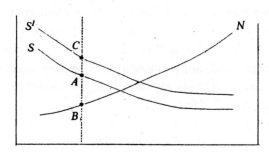

GRAPH 2*b*

*Enlargement*

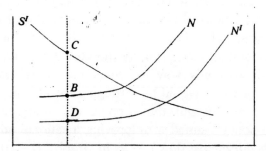

GRAPH 2*c*

*Restructuring*

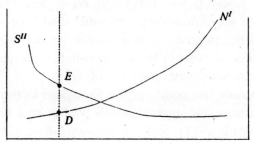

GRAPH 2*d*

An asymmetric opening-up policy in favour of Eastern Europe has been adopted and applied to all sectors, with the relevant exceptions, however, of agriculture, textiles, and, partially, steel; i.e. some of the sectors where Eastern Europe holds its comparative advantage.

From this point of view sectoral and national resistance within the Community still stands in the way of a full and smooth enlargement of the club.

### 6. - Policy Conditions for a Virtuous Circle

The previous discussion suggests that the elements of a strategy aimed at securing a successful process of integration of EE will have to include proper consideration for economic peculiarities and interests of at least four geographical areas: Northern regions in the EC which are clearly favourable to integration (given their relatively large capital and technological endowment conducive to specialization in scale-intesive activities), Southern regions in the EC which may resist the required domestic restructuring to compete in the enlarged market, labour-abundant and technology-starving regions in Eastern Europe which are unable to bear the adjustment costs in the short run, and resource-abundant regions in the East which are eager to trade their underground wealth for industrial diversification and economic development in the long run.

Clearly, a thorough assessment of all the implications for a detailed policy design would be beyond the scope of this paper. Here, we attempt to sketch some relevant elements of an integration strategy, drawing also from Bollino-Padoan [2]. Such a strategy should be based on three main building blocks:

*a)* in order to accelerate the "widening" process — i.e. the formation of a new "European club" — strengthening and deepening of the Community must be pursued. Given the asymmetrical distribution of costs and benefits between present EC members, the Community, directly or through some form of concerted action — a topic we cannot develop further — should secure that resources be devoted to sustain restructuring processes in those countries and regions of the Community which are likely to be hit most severely by the new competitive pressures. In this respect the role of "structural funds" should be both strenghtened and reconsidered within a framework of a Community industrial policy;

*b)* Eastern European countries should further strengthen their comparative advantages in the sectors (traditional, agricultural, resource intensive, energy intensive) where these lie. To this purpose they should first try to increase the acquisition of technology from the industrialized economies. As far as this point is concerned we support the view, often suggested in the literature, that diffusion of technology in Eastern Europe must be based on a robust flow of western foreign direct investment for which the appropriate incentives must be generated. Evidence already exists (Viesti [23]) that western direct investment flowing into Eastern Europe is concentrated in those sectors in which the host countries enjoy a comparative advantage.

To strengthen this trend by making investment location more profitable a crucial role will be played by domestic stabilization programs in Eastern Europe (Maugeri - Savarese [16]), the success of which, in turn, is not marginally influenced by the attitude that the European Community will assume towards enlargement;

*c)* in addition, Eastern European countries should stabilize their terms of trade with long-term structural policies, clearly much more far-sighted, and therefore wisely complementary, with respect to the existing exchange rate stabilization plans. We envisage that an active policy aimed at exploiting the comparative advantage in the energy sector in Eastern Europe should be started. The remaining section of the paper is devoted to developing this point in more detail.

Although we are aware of the risk of indulging in a pro-energy sector bias, we consider it crucial for the process of economic integration that natural resources, such as energy, and the related resource intensive activities, be developed through an active industrial policy intervention. Of course, an infant-industry argument may be invoked to justify, at least in the short-term, the nurturing of the revamping effort of the former Soviet oil and gas industry.

In any case, it seems worthwhile to pursue this line of reasoning, perhaps broadening the view to possible second best intervention, which we may call a trade diversion argument revisited. Therefore, let us consider the problem of policy intervention in favour of energy trade developments between the EC and Eastern Europe, notably the CIS.

Clearly, at the prevailing international market conditions, the equilibrium level of energy imported by the EC from the CIS reflects the diversification strategy of the EC, as a function of price, uncertainty and risk associated with the region, and future expectations of new developments. In turn, new capacity development in the CIS is a function, among others, of future expectations on price and demand potential of the EC.

A policy which can change such conditions may improve upon existing trade relations.

Consider a cooperation agreement, perhaps in the context of the new *European Energy Charter*, which is centered around the principle of long-term indexation of energy price exported from the CIS to the EC to the export price of manufactures of the EC to the CIS. It is obvious that the partial stabilisation of the relative price between energy and manufactures may contribute to halt the negative impact of deteriorating terms of trade on growth rate, as argued in the previous discussion concerning eq. *(1)*.

There will be four positive consequences. First, the reduction in uncertainty will spur foreign investment in the CIS, both for exploration and production of energy (oil and gas), and for new manufacturing activities.

This view is reflected in the contributions of the theoretical section of our research, dealing with the explanation of strategic motivation of the firm which undertakes foreign investment (Motta [18]): firms will not seek only to exploit existing cost advantages, but will attempt to actively modify their market power, through acquisitions, mergers and defensive investments to prevent new entrants. Therefore, a long-term commitment (such as the mechanism of real energy price stabilisation sketched above) may reinforce the firms' perception of new strategic opportunities, characterised by a reduction in uncertainty and risk. A follow-the-leader approach (in order to avoid exclusion from the new market), could probably result in a massive investment flow of western firms. The final result will undoubtely be an increase in productive capacity in the energy sector.

Second, there will be trade creation because stable energy export revenues will allow Eastern countries to increase their level of manufacture imports from the West.

Third, the diversification of EC energy imports will presumably increase the share of Eastern Europe as a stable and reliable supplier. This means that a new geographical diversification pattern of EC energy imports may result in significant changes in competition among energy suppliers. On the one hand, an increasing importance of Eastern Europe as an energy exporter could conflict with the Middle Eastern area, generating higher variability and instability. On the other hand, a more balanced market influence of these regions may result in higher competition and lower rental cost for the EC consumer. Most likely, the final outcome will depend on the relative degree of specialisation of each supplying area in different energy sources, as argued below.

Fourth, the relative mix of EC imports between oil and gas will probably shift in favour of the latter, given the availability of reserves in Eastern area and future trends in EC energy demand. It is in this sense that we envisage a virtuous scenario of stable market relationship, where EC additional gas requirements will be satisfied mostly by Eastern supplies, while oil requirements will continue to be predominantly satisfied by the Middle East. This scenario has two implications; first it will improve the environmental situation in Europe and, second it will also leave more oil available worldwide to satisfy the emerging needs of developing countries. In this scenario, a sustainable development of LDC's industrial base will become more and more feasible, because the fierce competition between LDC's and industrialised countries for a scarce resource, the existing oil, will be relaxed. Furthermore, it is rather superfluous to add that higher growth potential for LDC's may feed back into world trade and industrialised countries' output growth.

In this sense, the diverted development of gas resulting from a club-type agreement between EC and Eastern Europe may be beneficial for the world market as a whole.

## 7. - A Further Suggestion: Energy as the Fuel of Integration

We would like to end our policy consideration by touching upon the implications of a new integration pattern in Europe for the adequacy of financial supply in the short and medium term for Eastern Europe.

We recall that from a microeconomic viewpoint, using the terminology of the life cycle model of consumer behavior, there may be cases in which a country is faced with liquidity constraints, in the sense that the existence of capital market imperfections induce a higher saving rate with respect to situations without such imperfections, because life cycle consumption-smoothing is limited. Given the relationship of equality between the saving rate and the growth rate times the capital-output ratio which holds for a closed economy with liquidity constraint, at the beginning of the transition process, EE may suffer from a reduction in the saving rate.

This is so because EE, with the existing obsolete capital stock, may experience a consequent reduction in productivity generated by the incipient opening-up of trade.

Thus, the typical Eastern economy is caught in the trap of insufficient saving to maintain the previous high level of capital-output ratio, which may feed back into a lower growth rate, which generates even lower saving. Therefore, relaxing such liquidity constraint will allow a more efficient intertemporal resource allocation, i.e. larger possibilities to borrow against higher future income streams, providing a positive influence on growth.

Turning to a macroeconomic view point, the discussion of the relationship between liquidity constraint and savings highlights the difficulties of attracting foreign capital when low productivity and low growth potential tend to shift resources to finance import of consumption goods, therefore conflicting with the balance of payment constraint (for a discussion in terms of the balance of payments stages hypothesis see Manzocchi [14]). Once more, removal of capital market imperfections, within the country, may allow a better resource allocation internationally, paving the way for foreign direct investment.

A policy aimed at reducing market imperfections, such as excessive uncertainty associated with specific commodity export earnings and investment projects, is to reinforce the role of insurance played by international institutions.

There are two related examples, already widely used in the past at the international level: the first is a compensatory fund which can stabilize export earnings of natural resources such as energy resources (oil and gas); the second is a super-insurance fund which provides collateral guarantee for investment in sectors characterised by high risk and long-term profitability.

As far as the compensatory fund is concerned let us recall that the need for a special or complementary facility to assist developing countries with liquidity for shortfalls in their commodity export earnings has been under deliberation in UNCTAD literally since its first session in 1964 and was revamped in 1982, while the IMF also used such a scheme at the end of the 70s. The rationale was to alleviate the problem of export shortfall which may impair growth capability of LDC's. Among the justifications set forth in the past by international organisations such as UNCTAD and IMF, it suffices to indicate that under this scheme drawings from the facility were to be used to finance commodity related activities intended to stabilize the commodity sector and eradicate the root causes of instability, such as short-term income support in individual commodity sectors and structural adjustment in cases of chronic over-supply or under-supply. Access to the facility was seen as conditional on the elaboration of commodity development programmes in which the intended uses of the resources would be specified and mutually agreed upon between the applicant country and the facility.

Obviously, with such a volatile historical price record, oil is unlikely to be considered a commodity deserving a compensatory financing facility: funds of any amount would be dried up in a short period of time in case of crisis, without real benefits and possibly with the undesired consequence of rewarding speculative behavior.

A different approach, still aiming at stabilizing terms of trade between EC and Eastern Europe, could be based on the idea of long term indexation of the prices of energy exported from, say, CIS to EC to a basket of prices of manufactures exported from EC to CIS. Let us stress that according to this project, the players would not be simply an exporting country and a financial fund managed by an international institution (as in the IMF experience), but there shall come into play three actors; an oil exporting country, a manufactures exporting country and a financial fund, managed by an international institution.

In this case, it is obvious that in every commercial contract negotiated under this rule, whether we consider a gas supply, whose price is indexed to that of manufactures exported from EC to CIS or an industrial good supply, whose price is indexed to the gas price exported from CIS to EC, there is a built-in stabilizing mechanism in real terms.

The operational details are not important, here it suffices to establish the principle that even if only a fraction of CIS oil exports could be transacted under this scheme this would represent a sizeable amount. In fact, recall that the before-crisis Soviet oil export level was around 2 million b/d, and equivalent of 13 billion $ (at an approximate today's price of 18 $/b), while actual exports have declined by almost 30%, mainly as a consequence of declining productive capacity lacking adequate capital investment.

TABLE 2

FORMER SOVIET UNION OIL EXPORT AND REVENUES

|  | Annual flows |
|---|---|
| Oil, exports in million b/d (before crisis) ........ | 2.0 |
| Oil revenues valued at 18 $/b ................. | 13.0 billion $ |
| Long term contract indexation: (15% of total revenues)...................................... | 2.0 billion $ |
| memo: | |
| G-7 plus international institutions stabilization plan, per year ...................................... | 6.0 billion $ |

Thus, consider the possibility of restoring productive capacity to previous levels, arranging, say, 15% of total revenues under this long term indexation scheme: it shall generate approximately an annual flow of 2 billion $ in real terms, available for development of long-term trade relationships. This is not negligible if it is compared to the total of 6 billion $ envisaged each year by the plan of the *G7* and the international institution whose total amounts to 18 billion $ in 3 years (Table 2).

Notice that according to this scheme, the role of a compensatory fund managed by an international institution would be no different from that of an insurance fund, therefore requiring less financial resources than a trade financing facility. In principle, in the best of circumstances, there is no cost to the fund (or to the developed countries governments which would have to back it), if the indexation of trade flows is full. Otherwise, any financing requirement to cover the residual risks could be met with an escrow account (with the banking sector) or a government contingent fund (set aside in the government budget of financing countries).

As far as the super insurance fund is concerned, the previous discussion is equally valid in this case, if the fund is aimed at fostering investment in capital-intensive industries, say, the energy exploration and production, or refining and distribution. In fact, the amount of financial resources required to cover the burden of high risk and deferred profitability associated with such investment projects could be optimally drawn from a super-insurance fund backed by international institutions or by all governments of involved countries. Obviously, once the fraction of total risk associated with the intrinsic characteristics of energy market uncertainty is covered, financing of investment will flow from private enterprises and banking institutions according to prevailing international financial markets conditions.

In conclusion, we would like to stress that a strategic policy designed to foster market developments in Eastern Europe's energy sector could be beneficial for the whole process of integration, if it is able to stabilize East-West terms of trade. Starting from where there are comparative advantages makes sense: energy endowments in the CIS may very well represent the fuel for the whole integration process.

Backed by a stabilization or an insurance-type scheme, direct investment may start to flow to CIS energy sector. The result will be an optimal allocation of resources to the energy sector, higher productive capacity, higher energy exports revenues. These will, in turn, finance capital investment and, therefore, a positive contribution to the growth rate of the Eastern European economies' output shall be achieved via increased availability of foreign capital and technology for the Eastern countries.

## 1. - Growth, Competitiveness and Balance of Payments

In this appendix we develop the relationship between the rate of growth of output and the determinants of international competitiveness mentioned in the text. A more articulated discussion can be found in Padoan [20].

Starting from current account equilibrium

$$(A.1) \qquad Px\, X = Pm\, Z\, M$$

where: $Px$ is the price of exports, $X$ their quantity, $Pm$ the price of imports in foreign currency, $M$ the quantity of imports, $Z$ the exchange rate. Calling $W$ foreign demand, and $Y$ domestic output we can write

$$W\, Px\, X/W = Y\, Pm\, Z\, M/Y$$

and, calling $SX = X/W$ the export share and $SM = M/Y$ the import share we define the "equilibrium" level of output

$$(A.2) \qquad Y^* = W\, Px\, S\, X/Pm\, Z\, S\, M$$

taking logs (small letters)

$$(A.3) \qquad y^* = px + w + sx - pm - z - sm$$

Taking the time derivative of *(A.3)* we obtain *(1)* in the text, assuming a fixed exchange rate. To obtain the relationship between the equilibrium growth rate (i.e. the rate of growth consistent with balance of payments equilibrium) we first consider a model where each of the elements in *(A.3)* is expressed in terms of disequilibrium dynamic equations. We then compute the steady state values of output as a function of the determinants of both the terms of trade and of the trade shares. The equations of the model are as follows. $D$ is the derivative with respect to time.

(A.4)  $Dy = a_1 (y^* - y)$ output adjustment (policy reaction function)

(A.5)  $D sx = a_2 (sx^* - sx)$ export share

(A.6)  $sx^* = b_a + b_1 (pwz - px) + b_2 (t - tw)$

$D px = a_3 (px^* - px)$ export price

$px^* = b_b + b_3 pw + b_4 z + b_5 v$

(A.7)  $Dt = a_4 (t^* - t) + b_7 tw$ stock of "technology"

$t^* = b_c + b_6 f$

(A.8)  $D sm = a_5 (sm^* - sm)$ import share

$sm^* = b_d + b_8 (p - pw - z) - b_9 (t - tw)$

(A.9)  $Dz = a_6 (z^* - z)$ exchange rate
$z^* = b_e + b_{10} Dy + ...$

(A.10)  $Df = a_7 (f^* - f)$ investment in R&D
$f^* = b_f + b_{11} (px - v)$

Taking derivatives with respect to time of equation (A.3) we obtain (A.11), which is equivalent to equation (1) in the text, assuming that the exchange rate is fixed.

(A.11)          $r_1 = j_2 + (r_2 - j_1) + (r_2 - r_5)$

Substituting for the growth rates of the exogenous variables in equations (A.4) - (A.10) we obtain:

(A.12)  $r_1 = j_2 + [(b_5 j_3 - j_1)] + (b_1 + b_8) [(j_1 - b_5 j_3)] +$

$+ (b_2 + b_9) [b_6 b_{11} (b_5 j_3 - j_3) + (b_7 j_4/a_4 - j_4)]$

TABLE 3

## VARIABLES AND GROWTH RATES

*Endogenous variables*

| | |
|---|---|
| $y = y^* + r_1 \tau$ | output |
| $sx = sx^* + r_2 \tau$ | export share |
| $px = px^* + r_3 \tau$ | export price |
| $t = t^* + r_4 \tau$ | stock of technology |
| $sm = sm^* + r_5 \tau$ | import share |
| $z = z^* + r_6 \tau$ | exchange rate |
| $f = f^* + r_7 \tau$ | expenditure in R&D |

*Exogenous variables*

| | |
|---|---|
| $pw = pw^* + j_1 \tau$ | foreign price |
| $w = w^* + j_2 \tau$ | foreign demand |
| $v = v^* + j_3 \tau$ | nominal domestic wage |
| $tw = tw^* + j_4 \tau$ | stock of foreign technology |

\* indicates initial values, $\tau$ is time.

Equation *(A.12)* says that, given the rate of growth of foreign demand and the relevant elasticities, the equilibrium rate of growth increases with: an improvement in the terms of trade (first bracket), an improvement in price competitiveness (second bracket), an improvement in technological competitiveness (third bracket) itself determined by domestic innovative activity and/or by international diffusion. The amount of domestically produced "technology" depends on the amount of R&D expenditure out of profits and on the rate of success of the latter.

## 2. - Revealed comparative advantages. Eastern Europe (from Guerrieri-Mastropasqua [2]

The index considered is the contribution to the Trade Balance defined as follows.

$$CTB = \left[ \frac{(X_i - M_i)}{(X + M)/2} - \frac{(X - M)}{(X + M)/2} \times \frac{(X_i - M_i)}{(X + M)} \right] \times 100$$

$X_i$  = Exports of product $i$ for country $j$

$M_i$  = Imports of product $i$ for country $j$

$X$   = Total exports of country $j$

$M$   = Total imports of country $j$

The following charts exhibit the index for the period 1970-1989 for the former Soviet Union, Czechoslovakia, Hungary and Poland.

BIBLIOGRAPHY

[1] BOLLINO C.A. - MANCA S.: *Il settore energetico nella nuova Europa*, in BOLLINO - PADOAN [2].

[2] BOLLINO C.A. - PADOAN P.C.: *Il circolo virtuoso trilaterale. Commercio e flussi finanziari in un'Europa allargata*, forthcoming, Bologna, il Mulino, 1992.

[3] BRANSON W.: «Financial Market Integration, Macroeconomic Policy and the EMS», in BLISS C. - BRAGA DE MACEDO J. (eds.): *Unity with Diversity in the European Economy*, Cambridge, Cambridge University Press, 1990.

[4] CAMERON D.: «Sovereign States in the Single Market: Integration and Intergovernamentalism in the European Community», presented at the *Annual Meeting of the American Political Science Association*, San Francisco, August 1990.

[5] COLLINS S. - RODRICK D.: «Eastern Europe and the Soviet Union in the World Economy», Washington, Institute for International Economics, Policy Analyses, *Working Paper*, n. 32, May 1991.

[6] DAVIDDI R. - MANASSE P.: *Esiste una contrapposizione tra «big bang» e gradualismo? Lezioni dalle esperienze polacca e ungherese*, in BOLLINO - PADOAN [2].

[7] DE BENEDICTIS L. - PADOAN P.C.: *L'integrazione dei paesi dell'est nella Comunità europea. Un approccio in termini di teoria dei club e di gruppi di interesse*, in BOLLINO - PADOAN [2].

[8] DOSI G. - PAVITT K. - SOETE L.: *The Economics of Technical Change and International Trade*, New York University Press, New York, 1990.

[9] FAGERBERG J.: «International Competitiveness», *Economic Journal*, vol. 98, 1988, pp. 355-74.

[10] FRATIANNI M. - PATTISON J.: «The Economics of International Organizations», *Kyklos*, vol. 35, 1982.

[11] GUERRIERI P. - MASTROPASQUA C.: *Competitività, specializzazione e prospettive di integrazione commerciale dei paesi dell'est europeo*, in BOLLINO - PADOAN [2].

[12] KRUGMAN P.: «Macroeconomic Adjustment and Entry into the EC. A Note», in BLISS C. - BRAGA DE MACEDO J. (eds.): *Unity with Diversity in the European Economy*, Cambridge, Cambridge University Press, 1990.

[13] — —: *Integration Specialization and Regional Growth: Notes on 1992, Emu and Stabilization*, mimeo, 1992.

[14] MANZOCCHI S.: *Integrazione economica e fasi della bilancia dei pagamenti. Implicazioni per i paesi dell'est europeo*, in BOLLINO - PADOAN [2].

[15] MASTROPASQUA C. - ROLLI V.: *Il protezionismo dei paesi industrializzati verso l'Europa dell'est. Effetti dell'accordo di associazione della Cee sulle esportazioni di Polonia, Cecoslovacchia e Ungheria*, in BOLLINO - PADOAN [2].

[16] MAUGERI M. - SAVARESE E.: *Aspetti monetari e finanziari della transizione al mercato della Csi*, in BOLLINO - PADOAN [2].

[17] MORAVCSIK A.: «Negotiating the Single European Act: National Interests and Conventional Stratecraft in European Community», *International Organization*, vol. 45, Winter 1991.

[18] MOTTA M.: *Le motivazioni oligopolistiche e strategiche degli investimenti all'estero*, in BOLLINO - PADOAN [2].

[19] NUTI D.M.: «Lezioni dei programmi di stabilizzazione dei Paesi dell'Europa centrale e orientale, 1989-91», *Note economiche*, vol. XXI, n. 3, 1991.

[20] PADOAN P.C.: *Competitività, crescita e bilancia dei pagamenti. Considerazioni sull'equilibrio di lungo periodo*, in BOLLINO - PADOAN [2].

[21] PAVITT K.: «Sectoral Patterns of Technical Change. Towards a Taxonomy and a Theory», *Research Policy*, vol. 13, 1984, pp. 343-73.

[22] SCHIATTARELLA R.: *Impresa multinazionale e commercio intraziendale nella «Nuova teoria del commercio internazionale»*, in BOLLINO - PADOAN [2].

[23] VIESTI G.: *L'internazionalizzazione dell'industria e dei servizi*, in BOLLINO - PADOAN [2].

[24] WARD V.: «Understanding Cooperative Agreements: the Impact of Differing Objectives on Club Formation Behaviour», presented at the *Annual Meeting of the American Political Science Association*, Washington (DC), August 1991.

# IV - LESSONS FROM LATIN AMERICA

# Latin America's Economic Growth

**Vittorio Corbo** - **Patricio Rojas**
Catholic University
of Chile
Central Bank
of Chile

## 1. - Introduction

The decade of the 1980s has been considered a lost decade for many less developed countries and for Latin America as a region. The large external borrowing of the late 1970s and early 1980s proved to be unsustainable after the interest rate and terms of trade shocks of the early 1980s. The sudden cut off from international capital markets submerged Latin America into a deep recession. The severity of the crisis was such that simple solutions were not available. Indeed the whole development model of the previous three decades was called into question. As a result, one country after another embarked in economy-wide structural adjustment programs. The immediate objective of these programs was to restore the basic macroeconomic balances with the ultimate objective of creating the conditions to restore sustainable growth and make progress in the reduction of poverty. To acheve its objectives, structural adjustment programs include a macroeconomic component and a microeconomic component. The macroeconomic component includes measures to reduce public sector deficits and facilitate a real depreciation. The microeconomic component addresses the integration to the world economy, the reduction of distortions in domestic markets, the reforms and creation of institutions, and the restructuring of the public sector. The restructuring of the public sector has the twin objective of helping to reduce public sector deficits and strengthen the role of the market system in the allocation of resources.

Restoring macroeconomic balances and the reduction of distortions are supposed to help not only in getting a higher output out of existing resources but also should affect the level of the sustainable rate of growth. After the large efforts that have been made in many Latin American countries to restructure their economies, some countries are asking how to restore growth. In the traditional discussions about growth two schools usually appear, the ones that put all the weight on the need to increase investment rates and the ones that emphasize macroeconomic policies, human capital development, openness to trade, reduction of distortions in domestic markets, and the overall environment for private sector development.

The purpose of this paper is to study the factors accounting for the growth performance of Latin American countries in the last three decades. For this purpose we use a model based on the insights provided by the new growth theory developed by Romer [24] (*) and Lucas [19] and extended by Grossman and Helpman [14] and Romer [23]. As in Dervis and Petri [10] and Fischer [12] we introduce an explicit role for macroeconomic stability in accounting not only for differences in the level of output but also for the rate of sustainable growth.

The null hypothesis is that an unstable macroeconomic environment is detrimental to growth. In cases with high and variable inflation, relative prices become difficult to predict. Uncertain and fluctuating relative prices discourage long-term commitments. With this increase in uncertainty, the information content of relative prices is severely reduced. However, prices play a central role in providing incentives for restoring internal and external balance (through the information provided by real exchange rates and real interest rates) as well as in determining the efficiency in the allocation of resources. In accordance with the new growth theories not only the level of output will be affected but the rate of growth as well. An unstable macroeconomic environment also affects growth indirectly through the rate of investment.

The rest of the paper is divided into four sections. In the second section we present a brief overview of Latin American economic policies since the great depression. In the third section, we review the performance of Latin American countries in terms of economic and

---

(*) *Advise:* the numbers in square brackets refer to the Bibliography in appendix.

social indicators. In section 4, we use some insights provided by the endogenous growth literature to study the different factors that account for the growth performance of Latin America. Finally, in section 5 we present our main conclusions.


## 2. - Growth Policies

In the period up to the great depression, Latin American economic policies were quite liberal, trade barriers were low, and the role of the government was quite small. Macroeconomic adjustment was governed by the discipline of the gold standard to which Latin American countries had returned after World War I. Although some countries raised their tariff levels in the 1920s, they did so moderately and mainly for fiscal reasons. At this time, economic ideas were to be found in the writings or general essays of lawyers, historians and politicians (Hirshman [15]).

During this period, in general, trade policies were fairly neutral in the incentives to produce for local and foreign markets. International trade faced few restrictions; these were mainly in the form of low tariffs and exports taxes on primary products. At that time, trade taxes were the main source of revenues, but the size of the government was quite small. The discipline of the gold standard ensured a fairly stable macroeconomic situation. As a result, fiscal deficits were small and inflation was low. Capital inflows became important during the second half of the 1920s but fell substantially in 1929. Until then, balance of payment crises were rare. Growth resulted from factors accumulation in export-oriented economies.

Although most countries were very open to trade, some import substitution did develop — both naturally, as part of the normal development process following income growth and the increase in the size of the market, and artificially, when the flow of imports was interrupted during World War I.

The great depression had a major impact on economic activity and a long lasting effect on economic policies. Given the pessimistic view on foreign trade, most Latin American countries tried to isolate themselves from world economic conditions following countercyclical fiscal and monetary policies. They abandoned the gold standard, imposed exchange controls, and introduced a combination of quotas, tariffs, and multiple exchange rates, to restrict imports of consumer goods. World War II created a boom in the price of primary commodities and a suspension in the flow of imports from industrial countries. The twin effect of the sharp gain in terms of trade and the suspension of imports from industrial countries provided a strong boost to the development of the local industry.

After the war was over, political economy arguments took over, and the import substitution strategy started to take on a life of its own. New industrialist and labor groups in the emerging manufacturing sectors strongly lobbied for the enactment of tariff protection against the «unfair» competition of imports from industrial countries. Nationalist arguments were used to enlist protection for sectors that were ready to supply the local market when industrial countries were busy with their war efforts.

The early stage of import substitution was concentrated in light manufacturing where the cost disadvantage, *vis à vis* foreign competition, was small. As it became a common pattern in the early stages of import substitution, manufacturing initially achieved substantial growth; and it pulled the service related sectors. However, import substitution policies did not stop at light manufacturing and were soon extended to raw materials and capital goods. At this time, a debate started to emerge in Latin America on the appropriate long-term development strategy. Initially, the debate was restricted to local interests. Two groups participated in this debate. The first group was related to agriculture and mining, as well as to mainstream European educated economists. This group favored a return to the low protection policies of the pre-1930s period. The second group was composed of the new industrialists, who favored the intensification of protection to permit the continuous development of manufacturing. The latter group found a powerful ally in the United Nations Economic Commission for Latin America (ECLA) that was created in 1948. A 1950 article by Prebisch, the first secretary of ECLA, presented his views on the appropriate development strategy for Latin America. This article proved to be very influential on the future course of economic policies in the whole region. Prebisch recommended that the state promote industrialization through protection of import competing sectors and investment in the infrastructure required by the emerging industry. This article gave intellectual respect to the groups that were pressing for import substitution policies (Hirschman [15], Corbo [6]).

Import substitution policies were pursued the furthest in Chile (the home of ECLA), Uruguay, and Argentina. Mexico and Peru initially escaped the strong pro-import substitution bias of the trade regime that was typical of most Latin American countries. In the latter two countries import substitution became important in the 1960s.

As is a common pattern in the early stages of import substitution, manufacturing output growth was substantial and pulled the growth of the rest of the economy; but growth started to decline when the easy import substitution phase was well advanced. The slowdown in growth was faced with keynesian demand management policies that were making their arrival in Latin America (Prebisch [21], Pinto [20]). The expansionary demand policies led to a rapid use of foreign reserves accumulated during World War II, and the emerging balance of payments problems were faced with an intensification of import restrictions. Here a macroeconomic rationale for import restrictions was born. Given the pessimistic assessment of the potential for export growth, the emerging balance-of-payments problems had to be faced by economizing on imports. A further increase in protection was the answer. These policies not only failed to halt steady import growth; they also led to stagnation of exports, periodic balance-of-payments crises, an unstable macroeconomic situation and slow growth.

As a result, in the late 1950s and early 1960s, an important group of countries — Argentina, Chile, Colombia, Uruguay, Bolivia, and Brazil — were facing recurrent balance-of-payments problems and periodic outbursts of inflation. Macroeconomic problems were dominating the landscape of Latin America and the IMF started a series of programs with these countries. While the IMF was calling for a reduction of government deficits and money supply growth, ECLA was calling for the need to increase regional integration to save foreign exchange.

In the early 1960s some attempts were made to break away from the post World War II policies. The first country to do so was Brazil that started in 1964 a set of reforms designed to improve the functioning of its markets and the profitability of its export activities. The measures included *a)* a sharp devaluation and the introduction of a crawling peg mechanism to make the adjustment of the nominal exchange rate consistent with the underlying inflation; *b)* the introduction of a set of policies to reduce the anti-export bias of trade policies; *c)* a frontal attack on inflation by reducing the public sector deficit and the needs for its monetization; and *d)* the development of a capital market. Pulled by these reforms, the growth of Brazil in the post-1968 period was remarkable. GDP grew at an annual rate of 11% between 1968 and 1973, and 7.7% between 1973 and 1977. The value of exports rose at 23.1% a year on average between 1968 and 1977.

Colombia also adjusted its trade and exchange-rate policies to compensate for some of the bias against exports emerging from its import regime. The new policies had also some dramatic effects on export performance. The value of exports grew at an annual rate of 19.1% between 1968 and 1977, while they had only grown at an annual rate of 2.7% between 1961 and 1967. Mechanisms to compensate for the anti-export bias of the import regime were introduced also in Mexico, Argentina and Chile. In Mexico a free-trade regime was established for offshore assembly plants on the border with the US. Argentina, during the Ongania government of the late 1960s made progress in controlling inflation and in reducing some of the bias against manufacturing exports. In Chile, the Frei government during the second half of the 1960s initiated a very gradual process of tariff reductions, and introduced a crawling peg regime to make the rate of devaluation compatible with domestic inflation. The rationale for this policy was to have a stable and predictable real exchange rate.

Most of these experiments tried to control inflation, avoid the balance-of-payments crisis associated with unsustainable real appreciations, and reduce the pronounced anti-export bias of the import regime. However, instead of dismantling import restrictions they relied on the introduction of export subsidies. As the revenue capacity of governments was limited, a trade-off appeared between reducing fiscal deficits and reducing the anti-export bias of the trade regime. On the other hand, the large role of public enterprise in the production of private goods was not attacked, and the repression of the financial system continued.

A more radical reform attempt was initiated in Chile in 1975, in Mexico in 1983-1985, and in Bolivia in 1985. Both countries had entered into a deep economic crisis just before they started their reform efforts. The immediate causes of the crisis were the populist policies of the Allende regime in Chile, and the overexpansion of the public sector in Mexico during the Lopez-Portillo administration (1976-1982). However, the crisis in both countries was also the result of the policies of the previous 30 years. These policies had encouraged import substitution, had promoted the creation of public enterprises that dominated many key industries, had crowded out the private sector from the formal financial market, and had resulted in high and variable inflation. As the government was overextended, some basic public goods in the areas of education, health and nutrition did not receive adequate attention.

The Chilean and Mexican reforms had many objectives. First, to reduce the public sector deficit and to control inflation. Second, to restore macroeconomic equilibrium in a substantially open economy. Third, to increase the role of markets in the production and distribution of goods and services. Fourth, to liberalize the financial system to improve the efficiency in resource mobilization.

These reform efforts have been radical when compared with the historical experience of these countries. Therefore, both countries suffered some short-term cost while the whole economic system was being radically reformed. However, both countries are demonstrating today that they are on the road to sustainable growth. The economic record is impressive. By 1991 public sector deficits have been eliminated, inflation has been reduced to below 20% per year, export growth has become impressive, and growth appears to be sustainable. Furthermore, both countries have been very successful lately in attracting direct foreign investment.

Risking oversimplification, we conclude from this brief overview of economic policies, that from the great depression to the early 1930s, Latin America followed a state-driven import substitution development strategy where growth was oriented towards the internal economy. Import substitution manufacturing developed behind high tariff walls. A repressed financial system also facilitated the channeling of financial resources towards the protected sectors. As the expansion in the size of governments outpaced their capacity to collect revenues, public sector deficits financed at the Central Bank became the norm. The combination of domestic inflation and a fixed exchange rate resulted in large real appreciation and periodic balance-of-payments crises.

By the 1960s, some countries started to reform their policies. In particular they introduced an exchange rate system compatible with the outgoing inflation to protect the real exchange rate from large cyclical fluctuations. They tried to compensate the export sector for the anti-export bias of the import regime and introduced stabilization efforts. However, inflation contunued as a problem and not much progress was achieved in the reduction of import barriers. More recently Chile, starting in 1975, and Mexico, starting in 1983, carried out a radical transformation of the typical development model of the 1940s and 1950s. The new development model has as its central elements the use of the market as the main mechanism to allocate resources, the increase of integration with the world economy, the reduction in the size of the public sector, and the restoring of the basic macroeconomic balances. Furthermore, the model also includes the elimination of discrimination against direct foreign investment as a way to increase the flow of foreign resources and to encourage the transfer of technology. More recently, other countries of the region have initiated reform programs along the same lines. Two recent examples in this direction are Bolivia and Argentina.

## 3. - Latin American Growth Record

As Table 1 indicates, for the three decades ending in 1969, almost all countries in the region experienced a positive rate of growth of per capita GDP. By the end of this period import substitution was well advanced, and the anti export bias of trade policies quite pronounced. However, in the high income countries of Chile, Uruguay, and Venezuela, growth was already very low in the 1960s. Chile and Uruguay were paying the cost of a very protective trade regime that had isolated their small economies from the discipline of foreign competition. The star performer of this period was Brazil. Growth in

TABLE 1

## GDP PER CAPITA GROWTH
### (1941-1990)

| Country (*) | 1941-1949 | 1950-1959 | 1960-1969 | 1970-1979 | 1980-1989 | 1990 |
|---|---|---|---|---|---|---|
| Low income avrg | 2.7 | 0.9 | 2.1 | 1.4 | −2.4 | −2.5 |
| stdv | 3.6 | 1.5 | 1.5 | 1.9 | 1.0 | 3.0 |
| Haiti | 0.2 | 0.7 | −0.8 | 2.7 | −1.4 | −2.6 |
| Nicaragua | 4.2 | 2.4 | 3.6 | −2.5 | −3.8 | −2.8 |
| Guyana | n.d. | n.d. | n.d. | 0.7 | −2.9 | −6.1 |
| Bolivia | 0.6 | −1.7 | 3.2 | 1.9 | −3.0 | 0.2 |
| Honduras | 1.5 | −0.1 | 1.8 | 2.4 | −1.0 | −3.3 |
| El Salvador | 9.3 | 1.8 | 2.2 | 1.8 | −2.6 | 1.4 |
| Guatemala | 0.3 | 0.5 | 1.9 | 3.1 | −2.1 | 0.3 |
| Perù | 2.5 | 3.0 | 2.5 | 1.2 | −2.1 | −6.8 |
| Middle income avrg | 1.9 | 2.1 | 2.3 | 3.7 | 0.2 | −0.5 |
| stdv | 2.3 | 1.5 | 1.2 | 2.8 | 0.9 | 3.7 |
| Dominican Republic | 3.0 | 3.4 | 1.4 | 4.6 | 0.7 | −6.8 |
| Jamaica | n.d. | n.d. | n.d. | −2.0 | −0.5 | 2.6 |
| Paraguay | 0.6 | −0.7 | 1.1 | 5.0 | 0.9 | 0.2 |
| Ecuador | 4.1 | 2.4 | 1.8 | 7.0 | −0.1 | 0.0 |
| Colombia | 1.6 | 1.8 | 2.1 | 3.2 | 1.6 | 2.2 |
| Costa Rica | 4.7 | 2.8 | 2.2 | 3.3 | −0.8 | 0.6 |
| Panama | −2.2 | 1.8 | 4.8 | 1.9 | −0.6 | 3.1 |
| Brasil | 1.6 | 3.6 | 2.8 | 6.1 | 0.8 | −5.7 |
| High income avrg | 3.4 | 1.8 | 1.7 | 1.9 | −0.8 | 0.1 |
| stdv | 2.0 | 1.1 | 1.5 | 1.4 | 2.2 | 2.1 |
| Uruguay | 2.5 | 1.0 | 0.3 | 2.5 | 0.1 | 0.2 |
| Argentina | 2.3 | 0.8 | 2.8 | 1.3 | −2.3 | −1.4 |
| Mexico | 3.7 | 3.1 | 3.5 | 3.2 | −0.3 | 1.7 |
| Chile | 1.5 | 1.3 | 1.9 | 0.6 | 1.9 | 0.3 |
| Venezuela | 6.7 | 2.9 | 0.0 | −0.1 | −3.4 | 3.2 |
| Trinidad and Tobago | n.d. | n.d. | n.d. | 3.6 | −3.4 | −0.3 |
| Barbados | n.d. | n.d. | n.d. | 2.1 | 1.5 | −3.3 |
| Latin America | n.d. | n.d. | n.d. | 3.1 | −0.4 | −1.7 |

(*) Countries are classified by their 1990 GDP per capita at constant 1980 dollars. Low income countries are those with a GDP per capita lower than US$ 1000. Middle income countries are those with a GDP per capita higher than US$ 1000 and lower than US$ 2000. High income countries are those with a GDP per capita higher than US$ 2000.
*Source*: ECLA data files.

Brazil initially originated from the integration of the local economy and starting in 1964 from the economic reforms introduced (Carvalho and Haddad [5]). Mexico's growth is also quite impressive, but this growth was pulled by an incredible expansion in the public sector that later proved to be unsustainable (Corden [7]). Performance on the inflation front was also favorable (Table 2). In the 1960s only Brazil and Uruguay achieved inflation levels above 30% per year. Inflation in Brazil was not a major hindrance on growth as mechanisms were introduced to protect the profitability of the tradable sector from stable inflation in the range of 30% per year (Table 2).

In the 1970s, economic performance improved, on average, for the middle income and the high income groups. The star performers of this decade were Brazil, Colombia, Ecuador, The Dominican Republic, Trinidad and Tobago, Paraguay, and Mexico. Among the large countries, Brazil was getting the fruits of the reforms implemented during the second half of the 1960s. Ecuador's growth was associated to a major expansion in government expenditures facilitated by the oil boom. Colombia continued its fiscal discipline, and thanks to a coffee boom, was collecting the dividends of a stable real exchange rate policy. Paraguay was in the middle of a construction boom pulled by the construction of the Itaipu dam. Mexico achieved its growth through a large and unsustainable expansion in the public sector funded by the oil boom and the access to foreign borrowing. On the inflation front (Table 2), Chile and Argentina achieved an average, for the decade, of over 100% per year. These results were the manifestation of severe macroeconomic crisis that both countries suffered as a result of populist policies in the first half of the 1970s (Larraín y Meller [16]; Sturzenegger [26]).

The growth and inflation performance of the 1980s was very poor. This period has been called the "lost decade" of Latin America. In this decade, 16 out of the 23 countries listed in Table 1 achieved negative growth in GDP per capita. The improvement in growth performance of the 1970s soon proved to be unsustainable. The increase in international interest rates and the drop in terms of trade of the early 1980s triggered the debt crisis of the early 1980s. As a result of the shocks and the reduced access to foreign borrowing, most middle-income and high-income countries entered into a deep

TABLE 2

## INFLATION RATE
### (1951-1990)

| Country (*) | 1951-1959 | 1960-1969 | 1970-1979 | 1980-1989 | 1990 |
|---|---|---|---|---|---|
| Low income avrg | 13.5 | 3.3 | 14.0 | 687.0 | 3,044.0 |
| stdv | 26.2 | 3.2 | 6.7 | 1,229.3 | 5,011.3 |
| Haiti | 1.1 | 2.2 | 10.2 | 7.5 | 26.1 |
| Nicaragua | n.d. | n.d. | 19.4 | 3,787.5 | 13,490.9 |
| Guyana | 1.6 | 2.0 | 9.9 | 20.4 | n.d. |
| Bolivia | 77.3 | 6.3 | 19.0 | 1,113.7 | 18.0 |
| Honduras | 1.2 | 1.7 | 7.4 | 6.9 | 36.4 |
| El Salvador | 4.2 | 0.4 | 9.9 | 19.2 | 19.3 |
| Guatemala | 1.2 | 0.5 | 8.9 | 13.3 | 59.6 |
| Perú | 7.9 | 9.8 | 27.5 | 527.7 | 7,657.8 |
| Middle income avrg | 8.3 | 9.1 | 14.8 | 70.6 | 233.8 |
| stdv | 11.0 | 14.2 | 7.8 | 131.5 | 511.5 |
| Dominican Republic | 1.2 | 1.3 | 10.3 | 22.4 | 100.7 |
| Jamaica | 2.2 | 3.5 | 17.7 | 15.7 | 29.7 |
| Paraguay | 32.6 | 4.3 | 12.5 | 19.7 | 44.1 |
| Ecuador | 0.8 | 4.0 | 11.4 | 35.8 | 49.5 |
| Colombia | 7.4 | 11.2 | 18.5 | 23.5 | 32.0 |
| Costa Rica | 2.0 | 2.0 | 10.5 | 27.1 | 27.5 |
| Panama | 0.3 | 1.0 | 5.1 | 2.8 | 1.5 |
| Brasil | 19.8 | 45.8 | 32.7 | 417.6 | 1,585.2 |
| High income avrg | 16.6 | 15.8 | 57.7 | 135.3 | 225.6 |
| stdv | 14.7 | 16.8 | 60.9 | 252.1 | 458.2 |
| Uruguay | 15.6 | 50.1 | 58.5 | 64.8 | 129.0 |
| Argentina | 30.2 | 22.9 | 126.7 | 750.3 | 1,343.9 |
| Mexico | 8.1 | 2.7 | 14.1 | 69.7 | 29.9 |
| Chile | 41.3 | 25.1 | 170.7 | 20.7 | 27.3 |
| Venezuela | 1.8 | 1.1 | 7.5 | 23.8 | 36.5 |
| Trinidad and Tobago | 2.5 | 3.0 | 11.9 | 11.5 | 9.5 |
| Barbados | n.d. | 5.5 | 14.5 | 6.5 | 3.4 |

(*) For country classification see Table 1.
*Source:* ECLA data files.

recession. In the low-income countries, the political conflicts in Nicaragua and El Salvador, and the associated collapse of the Central American common market, submerged this region into a deep recession too. The best performance in the region was achieved by Chile, a country that, in the middle of the previous decade, initiated a profound transformation of its institutions and policies. On the other hand, Colombia continued its steady growth under very stable macroeconomic policies. The other countries were struggling to survive a deep macroeconomic crisis (Brazil, Argentina, Uruguay, and the Central American countries) or initiating a profound structural transformation (Bolivia and Mexico).

This was also the decade in which high inflation became more of a regional problem. In the middle of severe balance-of-payments crises, most countries went through large devaluations that in many cases triggered a devaluation-prices-wages spiral. The worst performers were Nicaragua, Bolivia, Argentina, and Peru. However, the increase in inflation was a manifestation of a region-wide macroeconomic crisis. Inflation, on average, accelerated in all the country groups. At the country level, inflation accelerated in 16 out of 23 countries. On the positive side, Bolivia was successful in controlling its hyperinflation, moving to an inflation at a rate between 10 and 20% per year. Chilean inflation was also sustained in the 30% range.

Now we will examine the evolution of some indicators of human capital. For this purpose we examine the evolution of life expectancy and infant mortality data. Life expectancy is perhaps the most comprehensive indicator of the population's health status. It is the result of a large number of inputs that affect longevity in a complex and, as yet, not well understood way. Many of these inputs (for example adult literacy and access to clean water) are, by their nature, quite resilient to the economic cycle.

Life expectancy indicators show a marked improvement through time in all the countries of the region (Table 3). The improvement continued during the crisis years of the 1980s. The infant mortality figures (Table 4) also show a marked improvement through time in all the countries. The speed of the improvement is most marked in the case of Chile that went from the fourth highest among the 15

TABLE 3

## LIFE EXPECTANCY (YEARS)
### (1950-1990)

| Country (*) | 1950-1955 | 1955-1960 | 1960-1965 | 1965-1970 | 1970-1975 | 1975-1980 | 1980-1985 | 1985-1990 |
|---|---|---|---|---|---|---|---|---|
| Low income avrg | 43.6 | 46.4 | 49.1 | 51.7 | 54.5 | 56.3 | 58.5 | 61.2 |
| stdv | 5.2 | 5.6 | 5.7 | 5.5 | 5.5 | 5.3 | 5.4 | 5.2 |
| Haiti | 37.6 | 40.7 | 43.6 | 46.3 | 48.5 | 50.7 | 52.7 | 54.7 |
| Nicaragua | 42.3 | 45.4 | 28.5 | 51.6 | 54.7 | 56.3 | 59.8 | 62.3 |
| Guyana | 55.2 | 58.7 | 61.2 | 62.5 | 64.1 | 66.5 | 68.2 | 69.7 |
| Bolivia | 40.4 | 41.9 | 43.5 | 45.1 | 46.7 | 48.6 | 50.7 | 63.1 |
| Honduras | 42.3 | 45.0 | 47.9 | 50.9 | 54.0 | 57.7 | 61.9 | 64.0 |
| El Salvador | 45.3 | 48.6 | 52.3 | 55.9 | 58.8 | 57.4 | 57.2 | 62.2 |
| Guatemala | 42.1 | 44.2 | 47.0 | 50.1 | 54.0 | 56.4 | 50.0 | 62.0 |
| Perú | 43.9 | 46.3 | 49.1 | 51.5 | 55.5 | 56.9 | 58.6 | 61.4 |
| Middle income avrg | 53.6 | 56.7 | 59.5 | 61.7 | 63.5 | 65.3 | 67.9 | 69.3 |
| stdv | 5.5 | 4.9 | 4.5 | 4.1 | 3.3 | 3.3 | 4.2 | 3.9 |
| Dominican Republic | 46.0 | 50.9 | 53.6 | 57.0 | 60.0 | 62.1 | 64.1 | 65.9 |
| Jamaica | 57.2 | 61.2 | 64.3 | 66.3 | 67.8 | 69.0 | 73.4 | 74.0 |
| Paraguay | 62.6 | 63.2 | 64.4 | 65.0 | 65.6 | 66.0 | 66.4 | 66.9 |
| Ecuador | 48.4 | 51.4 | 54.7 | 56.8 | 58.9 | 61.4 | 64.3 | 65.4 |
| Colombia | 50.6 | 55.1 | 57.9 | 60.4 | 61.6 | 64.0 | 67.2 | 68.2 |
| Costa Rica | 57.3 | 60.2 | 63.0 | 65.6 | 68.1 | 70.8 | 73.5 | 74.7 |
| Panamá | 55.3 | 59.3 | 62.0 | 64.3 | 66.3 | 69.2 | 71.0 | 72.1 |
| Brasil | 51.0 | 53.4 | 55.9 | 57.9 | 59.3 | 61.8 | 63.4 | 64.9 |
| High income avrg | 57.7 | 60.9 | 63.2 | 64.7 | 66.3 | 68.2 | 69.9 | 71.0 |
| stdv | 5.3 | 4.5 | 4.0 | 3.2 | 2.5 | 1.9 | 1.8 | 1.7 |
| Uruguay | 66.3 | 67.2 | 68.4 | 68.6 | 68.8 | 69.7 | 70.9 | 72.0 |
| Argentina | 62.7 | 64.7 | 65.5 | 66.0 | 67.3 | 68.7 | 69.7 | 70.6 |
| Mexico | 50.8 | 55.4 | 58.6 | 60.3 | 62.6 | 65.4 | 67.4 | 68.9 |
| Chile | 53.8 | 56.2 | 58.0 | 60.6 | 63.6 | 67.2 | 71.0 | 71.5 |
| Venezuela | 55.2 | 58.1 | 61.0 | 63.8 | 66.2 | 67.7 | 69.0 | 69.7 |
| Trinidad and Tobago | 57.9 | 62.4 | 64.8 | 65.7 | 66.5 | 67.5 | 68.7 | 70.2 |
| Barbados | 57.2 | 62.6 | 65.9 | 67.6 | 69.4 | 71.3 | 72.0 | 73.9 |

(*) For country classification see Table 1.
*Source: Statistical Yearbook for Latin America and the Carribean;* ECLA 1989.

TABLE 4

## INFANT MORTALITY (**)
### (1950-1990)

| Country (*) | 1950-1955 | 1955-1960 | 1960-1965 | 1965-1970 | 1970-1975 | 1975-1980 | 1980-1985 | 1985-1990 |
|---|---|---|---|---|---|---|---|---|
| Low income avrg | 162.7 | 147.0 | 131.4 | 118.3 | 105.9 | 95.7 | 83.7 | 71.4 |
| stdv | 37.3 | 35.3 | 33.9 | 31.0 | 28.4 | 26.7 | 26.9 | 25.6 |
| Haiti | 219.6 | 193.5 | 170.5 | 150.3 | 134.9 | 120.9 | 108.2 | 96.6 |
| Nicaragua | 167.4 | 148.3 | 130.9 | 114.8 | 100.0 | 92.9 | 76.4 | 61.7 |
| Guyana | 93.0 | 76.0 | 61.0 | 56.0 | 56.0 | 49.0 | 36.0 | 30.0 |
| Bolivia | 175.7 | 169.7 | 163.6 | 157.5 | 151.3 | 138.2 | 124.4 | 109.9 |
| Honduras | 195.7 | 172.0 | 147.2 | 123.7 | 100.6 | 89.3 | 78.4 | 68.4 |
| El Salvador | 151.1 | 137.0 | 122.7 | 110.3 | 99.0 | 87.3 | 77.0 | 57.4 |
| Guatemala | 140.6 | 131.1 | 119.0 | 107.6 | 95.1 | 82.4 | 70.4 | 58.7 |
| Perú | 158.6 | 148.2 | 136.1 | 126.3 | 110.3 | 104.9 | 98.6 | 88.2 |
| Middle income avrg | 104.0 | 91.6 | 79.6 | 69.9 | 61.0 | 51.3 | 44.1 | 39.4 |
| stdv | 24.8 | 23.6 | 23.9 | 22.8 | 21.6 | 21.2 | 20.3 | 19.0 |
| Dominican Republic | 89.0 | 76.0 | 63.0 | 55.0 | 49.0 | 44.0 | 36.0 | 31.0 |
| Jamaica | 85.0 | 71.0 | 54.0 | 45.0 | 36.0 | 25.0 | 21.0 | 18.0 |
| Paraguay | 73.4 | 69.7 | 62.3 | 58.6 | 54.8 | 52.5 | 53.0 | 48.9 |
| Ecuador | 139.5 | 129.4 | 119.2 | 107.1 | 95.0 | 82.4 | 69.6 | 63.4 |
| Colombia | 123.3 | 102.2 | 84.5 | 74.2 | 66.9 | 59.4 | 53.3 | 48.6 |
| Costa Rica | 93.8 | 87.7 | 81.3 | 67.7 | 52.6 | 36.5 | 23.3 | 19.4 |
| Panama | 93.0 | 74.9 | 62.7 | 51.6 | 42.8 | 31.6 | 25.7 | 22.7 |
| Brasil | 134.7 | 121.9 | 109.4 | 100.1 | 90.5 | 78.8 | 70.7 | 63.2 |
| High income avrg | 107.3 | 87.4 | 77.0 | 67.2 | 57.9 | 41.1 | 38.8 | 34.1 |
| stdv | 34.1 | 30.8 | 28.5 | 25.2 | 21.7 | 21.2 | 20.0 | 17.4 |
| Uruguay | 57.4 | 53.0 | 47.9 | 47.1 | 46.3 | 41.7 | 37.6 | 34.0 |
| Argentina | 65.9 | 60.4 | 59.7 | 57.4 | 49.0 | 40.5 | 36.0 | 32.2 |
| Mexico | 113.9 | 97.7 | 86.3 | 78.5 | 70.9 | 59.0 | 49.9 | 42.6 |
| Chile | 126.2 | 118.3 | 109.4 | 90.1 | 69.9 | 46.6 | 23.7 | 18.1 |
| Venezuela | 106.4 | 89.0 | 72.8 | 59.5 | 48.6 | 43.3 | 38.7 | 35.9 |
| Trinidad and Tobago | 149.4 | 132.2 | 117.0 | 105.0 | 93.5 | 84.3 | 74.5 | 65.0 |
| Barbados | 132.0 | 61.0 | 46.0 | 33.0 | 27.0 | 14.0 | 11.0 | 11.0 |

(*) For country classification see Table 1.
(**) Annual number of deaths before the age of 12 months per 1000 live births.
*Source: Statistical Yearbook for Latin American and the Carribean;* ECLA, 1989.

middle-income and high-income countries in the 1965-1970 period, to the third lowest of the group by the period 1985-1990. This shows that even during recessions the improvement in health indicators can continue with well targeted programs aimed at the lowest income groups in the population (Castañeda, 1991). For other countries, the steady progress in immunization and oral rehydration is the most likely reason for the continuing progress in the reduction of infant mortality. The life expectancy and child mortality data shows that the increased availability of affordable, low technology, life saving procedures permits increased progress even in hard times.

We now investigate the evolution of the illiteracy rates (Table 5), one of the measures of the level of human capital used in the next section. There are wide variations in the illiteracy rate across Latin American countries. Through time, most countries show a continuous improvement. Some deterioration appears in 1985. However, the data for this year is from a different source. Progress in school enrollment (not shown here) also continued through time. It could be argued that the recession may have the most immediate impact on the quality of education rather than on school enrollment. We do not have quality adjusted measures to test this hypothesis.

We also have a larger data base which we use for our econometric analysis of the next section. The larger data base is taken from the Summer and Heston *International Price Comparisons (IPC)* project and is taken from Summer and Heston [27]. This data base includes indicators of macroeconomic performance and policies as well as indicators of human capital development. The regional indicators are presented in Table 6. When compared with Asia and the OECD averages, the average growth performance of Latin America appears very poor. The difference in performance is more pronounced for the 1980s. The Latin American average performance is also poor for inflation and for the investment rate.

Social indicators, presented in Table 7, show a marked improvement in all regions. However, the improvement in primary enrollment and infant mortality is more pronounced in Latin America than in Asia.

*Vittorio Corbo - Patricio Rojas*

TABLE 5

## ILLITERACY (**)
### (1950-1990)

| Country (*) | 1960 | 1970 | 1980 | 1985 (***) |
|---|---|---|---|---|
| Low income avrg | 52.1 | 41.7 | 29.8 | 29.2 |
| stdv | 20.8 | 20.2 | 13.3 | 19.2 |
| Haiti | 85.5 | 78.7 | — | 62.4 |
| Nicaragua | 50.4 | 42.5 | — | 13.0 |
| Guyana | 12.9 | 8.4 | — | 4.1 |
| Bolivia | 61.2 | 36.8 | 18.9 | 25.8 |
| Honduras | 55.0 | 43.1 | — | 40.5 |
| El Salvador | 51.0 | 42.9 | 38.0 | 27.9 |
| Guatemala | 62.2 | 54.0 | 44.2 | 45.0 |
| Perù | 38.9 | 27.5 | 18.1 | 15.2 |
| Middle income avrg | 27.2 | 20.7 | 16.9 | 15.8 |
| stdv | 8.4 | 10.1 | 8.5 | 6.0 |
| Dominican Republic | 35.5 | 33.0 | 31.4 | 22.7 |
| Jamaica | 18.1 | 3.9 | — | — |
| Paraguay | 25.5 | 19.9 | 12.3 | 11.8 |
| Ecuador | 32.5 | 25.8 | 16.5 | 17.6 |
| Colombia | 27.1 | 19.2 | 12.2 | 17.7 |
| Costa Rica | 15.6 | 11.6 | 7.4 | 6.4 |
| Panama | 23.2 | 18.7 | 12.9 | 11.8 |
| Brasil | 39.7 | 33.8 | 25.5 | 22.3 |
| High income avrg | 16.4 | 11.8 | 8.7 | 6.9 |
| stdv | 14.0 | 9.4 | 6.1 | 3.7 |
| Uruguay | 9.5 | 6.1 | — | 4.6 |
| Argentina | 8.6 | 7.4 | 6.1 | 4.5 |
| Mexico | 34.5 | 25.8 | 16.0 | 9.7 |
| Chile | 16.4 | 11.0 | 8.9 | 5.6 |
| Venezuela | 37.3 | 23.5 | 15.3 | 13.1 |
| Trinidad and Tobago | 6.6 | 7.8 | 5.1 | 3.9 |
| Barbados | 1.8 | 0.7 | 0.5 | — |

(*) For country classification see Table 1.
(**) As a percentage of population 15 years and over.
(***) Source: UNESCO.
*Source: Statistical Yearbook for Latin American and the Carribean;* ECLA, 1989.

TABLE 6

## BASIC INDICATORS

| | Africa | | | | Asia | | | |
|---|---|---|---|---|---|---|---|---|
| | 1960-1969 | 1970-1979 | 1980-1984 | 1985-1988 | 1960-1969 | 1970-1979 | 1980-1984 | 1985-1988 |
| Per capita GDP growth (%) (1) (*) | 1.66 | 2.34 | -1.51 | -0.62 | 4.15 | 4.30 | 2.89 | 2.98 |
| Population growth (%) (*) | 2.47 | 2.65 | 2.96 | 3.05 | 2.65 | 2.41 | 2.08 | 1.94 |
| Inflation rate (**) average (%) | 4.50 | 12.58 | 20.28 | 19.32 | 12.30 | 11.90 | 23.86 | 14.27 |
| St. deviation | 3.99 | 6.45 | 8.03 | 8.68 | 8.52 | 6.81 | 12.70 | 12.29 |
| Rate of growth (**) of export to GDP ratio (%) | 2.20 | 2.95 | 0.44 | 0.63 | 3.45 | 5.13 | 0.55 | 2.24 |
| Trade balance to GDP (2) (**) ratio (%) | 2.98 | 6.65 | 10.09 | 5.77 | 3.68 | 3.21 | 4.77 | -0.03 |
| Total trade to GDP (3) (**) ratio (%) | 49.09 | 56.69 | 59.63 | 54.41 | 47.81 | 59.95 | 69.28 | 70.19 |
| Investment to GDP (4) ratio (*) (%) | 10.06 | 12.65 | 11.92 | 10.48 | 18.75 | 23.13 | 23.55 | 20.69 |
| Government expenditure (4) (*) to GDP ratio (in %) | 20.50 | 23.79 | 23.07 | 22.01 | 16.84 | 17.06 | 17.41 | 18.55 |
| Direct investment to (5) (**) GDP ratio (%) | 1.05 | 0.63 | 0.55 | 0.40 | 0.26 | 0.52 | 0.55 | 0.44 |

(1) Real GDP per capita in constant dollars adjusted for changes in the terms of trade (1985 international prices).
(2) Defined as (import − export)/GDP.
(3) Defined as (import + export)/GDP.
(4) Real investment and real government share of GDP % in constant dollars (1985 international prices).
(5) Net direct investment = credits or net increase in liabilities - Debits or net increase in assets. First period is 1966-1969.
(*) Source: SUMMERS-HESTON [28].
(**) Source: WORLD BANK Data Base.

TABLE 6 *continued*

## BASIC INDICATORS

| | Latin America | | | | OECD | | | |
|---|---|---|---|---|---|---|---|---|
| | 1960-1969 | 1970-1979 | 1980-1984 | 1985-1988 | 1960-1969 | 1970-1979 | 1980-1984 | 1985-1988 |
| Per capita GDP growth (%) (1) (*) | 2.48 | 3.14 | −2.28 | −0.33 | 4.28 | 2.80 | 0.86 | 2.96 |
| Population growth (%) (*) | 2.60 | 2.28 | 2.12 | −0.43 | 1.05 | 0.81 | 0.58 | 0.51 |
| Inflation rate (**) average (%) | 10.26 | 29.73 | 58.52 | 216.10 | 4.01 | 10.89 | 13.84 | 7.81 |
| St. deviation | 4.92 | 17.87 | 44.09 | 293.13 | 1.46 | 3.58 | 4.38 | 2.21 |
| Rate of growth of export to GDP ratio (**) (%) | 0.63 | 3.28 | 1.78 | 2.35 | 1.60 | 2.29 | 4.13 | −1.91 |
| Trade balance to GDP (2) (**) ratio (%) | 0.97 | 2.29 | 2.63 | 1.19 | 0.89 | 1.32 | 1.18 | −0.47 |
| Total trade to GDP (3) (**) ratio (%) | 43.87 | 49.85 | 50.19 | 51.78 | 50.69 | 59.15 | 68.73 | 68.18 |
| Investment to GDP (4) (*) ratio (%) | 15.80 | 17.21 | 15.57 | 13.49 | 26.19 | 26.85 | 23.90 | 23.98 |
| Government expenditure (4) (*) to GDP ratio (%) | 14.15 | 15.71 | 16.87 | 16.53 | 13.72 | 13.91 | 15.02 | 14.71 |
| Direct investment to (5) (**) GDP ratio (%) | 1.74 | 1.06 | 0.72 | 0.69 | 0.36 | 0.23 | −0.00 | −0.32 |

(1) Real GDP per capita in constant dollars adjusted for changes in the terms of trade (1985 international prices).
(2) Defined as (import − export)/GDP.
(3) Defined as (import + export)/GDP.
(4) Real investment and real government share of GDP % in constant dollars (1985 international prices).
(5) Net direct investment = credits or net increase in liabilities - Debits or net increase in assets. First period is 1966-1969.
(*) *Source:* SUMMERS-HESTON [28].
(**) *Source:* WORLD BANK Data Base.

TABLE 7
## SOCIAL INDICATORS

|  | Africa | Asia | Latin America | OECD |
|---|---|---|---|---|
| Enrollment ratio for primary education (*) | | | | |
| 1960 ................... | 42.57 | 82.31 | 84.85 | 109.58 |
| 1970 ................... | 58.14 | 93.76 | 91.55 | 106.46 |
| 1985 ................... | 75.07 | 98.15 | 102.55 | 102.13 |
| Enrollment ratio for secondary education (*) | | | | |
| 1960 ................... | 4.38 | 25.96 | 18.20 | 50.38 |
| 1970 ................... | 9.79 | 38.78 | 29.00 | 70.63 |
| 1985 ................... | 23.52 | 60.08 | 48.10 | 85.92 |
| Infant mortality rate (ages 0-1) | | | | |
| 1965 ................... | 15.23 | 7.62 | 9.30 | 2.95 |
| 1985 ................... | 11.11 | 4.40 | 5.51 | 1.29 |
| Mortality rate for ages 0 through 4 ................... | — | — | — | — |
| Average of 1965 and 1985 .... | 15.53 | 6.67 | 8.27 | 2.30 |

(*) Constructed as ratio of total students enrolled in primary (secondary) education to estimated number of individuals in the age bracket 6-11 (12-17) years.
*Source*: ROBERT BARRO and HOLFER C. WOLF, [2].

## 4. - Accounting for Growth: Econometric Results

### 4.1 *Growth Accounting*

The neoclassical framework has provided the starting point for a number of studies to investigate the different sources of growth. The typical methodology of these studies (Levine and Renelt [17]; De Gregorio [8]; Fischer [12]; Barro [1]) is to start with a neoclassical production function of the type

$$(1) \qquad Y_t = e^{\mu t} F(K_t, L_t)$$

where $K$ is capital, $L$ is labor input and $\mu$ is a constant rate of productivity growth. Putting this function in growth terms yields:

$$(2) \qquad Y_t = \beta_L l_t + \beta_K k_t + \mu$$

where small letters denote rates of growth. With constant returns to scale and perfect competition the $\beta$'s represent factor shares in output. Then, the first two terms on the right hand side of the last equation represent the contribution of labor and capital to growth while the last term represents the contribution of technical progress. The standard approach to growth accounting is to obtain input shares directly from the data. Solow [25] used the observed factor shares and growth rates of capital and labor to decompose the contributions of both factors to output growth. The part of growth that cannot be explained by input growth, represents the growth in total factor productivity which is assumed to come from exogenous technical change.

Since capital stock data is generally not available, adding the assumption of a constant capital output ratio, one can write the rate of growth of the capital stock in terms of the investment rate. Then, the equation usually estimated by many empirical studies both for time-series data for a single country as for cross-sectional country studies is:

$$(2) \qquad\qquad y_t = a_0 + a_1\,l_t + a_2\,i_t$$

where $i$ is the investment rate, and given the assumption that capital-output ratios and technology are the same in all countries, $a_1$ and $a_2$ should represent the marginal product of capital and labor share respectively.

Basically, most cross-sectional studies begin with this basic model and then include other regressors. Levine and Renelt [17] present a list of forty one cross-sectional growth studies published since 1980. Each study regresses the output growth rate over a given period against a set of variables that includes variables relating to trade policy, fiscal policy, exchange rate policy, political and social stability, human capital, and macroeconomic policy and outcomes.

For a sample of 101 countries, Levine and Renelt [18] analyze the effects of including new variables besides the standard ones of initial GDP per-capita, investment rate, rate of population growth, and the rate of secondary school enrollment. The main finding of Levine and Renelt is that several measures of economic policy are related to long-run growth and that, except for the investment ratio, the relationship between growth and every particular macroeconomic indicator is fragile.

On the other hand, Fischer [12], using a cross-sectional regression for average growth in a sample of 73 countries and a pooled cross-sectional time-series regression for annual growth in the same sample of countries, finds a significant relation between macroeconomic-policy related variables and growth, supporting the view that the quality of macroeconomic management matters for growth. In this paper we use the same type of models.

## 4.2 *Overview of the Data*

With the exception of the data used to generate the trade openness variables, the inflation rate variable and the direct foreign investment variable, which are taken from the World Bank Data Base, our source of all annual data is Summers and Heston [27]. They have compiled internationally comparable annual figures on output and its composition, prices, and exchange rates for 134 market economies from 1950 to 1988. The data for the time invariant variables is taken from the data base of Barro and Wolf [2].

Given the characteristics of the data, we can choose its organization, ranging from averaging each country's experience into one data point and estimating a single cross-sectional equation to pooling cross-sectional and time-series data and estimating a panel equation.

The single cross-sectional equation has been the alternative most used in the empirical growth literature. However, averaging over the entire sample period eliminates the information contained in the sample about the effect of changing conditions of growth in individual countries and allows only cross-country variation to inform the estimates. Therefore, trying to obtain as much as possible from the data, a panel estimation using sub-periods averages was considered for the period between 1960 and 1988. However, and since we are interested in secular growth patterns, some amount of averaging was required to net out irregular fluctuations in the annual data. For this purpose, the data was pooled using five-year averages and one four-year average.

The periods are: 1960-1964; 1965-1969; 1970-1974; 1975-1979; 1980-1984; and 1985-1988. Further averaging was discarded because it could destroy the information contained in the sample.

Given several differences among countries, it is important to test the validity of pooling all the data into a single equation. Then, in our estimations we test for the appropriateness of pooling a wide variety of countries into a single sample. Specifically, we divide the sample into the Latin American countries (LA) and the rest of the world (ROW). With 6 periods of data both on the 17 LA countries and on the 69 ROW countries, we obtained 516 total observations for analysis (1).

## 4.3 *Econometric Results*

In this part of the section we present different specification estimates of growth equations. As we use time invariont variables in our panel data, the estimates are obtained using Random effects. We start obtaining estimates for the Latin American countries of the net return to investment as well as of the contribution of other variables usually used in the literature like initial per-capita GDP, current and lagged investment to GDP ratio, current government expenditure to GDP ratio, and proxies for the stock of initial human capital (2).

Table 8 summarizes the regression results. Two key findings emerge from these results. First, the investment rate has a positive and statistical significant effect on growth explaining around 37% of the variation of the per-capita GDP growth. Second, the contribution of additional variables allows to increase the explanatory power of the regression only by six percentage points.

As control for world economic conditions we include in the regression four time-period dummy variables. For our purposes, the equation that includes the dummies will be taken as our basic model.

---

(1) The appropriateness of pooling a wide variety of countries into a single sample is tested respect to two samples, one that includes the African countries and another one that excludes the African countries.

(2) We consider as human capital proxies the primary and the secondary-school enrollment rate of 1960, these variables, based on information from the United Nations, measure number of students enrolled in the designated grade levels relative to the total population of the corresponding age group. Because of this definition it is possible for the values to exceed 1.0.

TABLE 8

POOLED REGRESSIONS ON FIVE-YEARS
AVERAGED DATA, 1960-1988: LA COUNTRIES
(*t*-statistics in parentheses)

| Variable | (1) | (2) |
|---|---|---|
| Constant......................... | 0.0014 (0.309) | 0.0036 (0.541) |
| Investment in (*t*) ................. | 0.0077 (5.984) | 0.0070 (5.714) |
| Investment in (*t* − 1) ............. | −0.0069 (−5.531) | −0.0062 (−5.236) |
| Initial per-capita GDP ............. | — | −0.0038 (−1.583) |
| Government spending in (*t*) ........ | — | −0.0010 (−3.577) |
| School primary rate ............. | — | 0.0259 (2.203) |
| $R^2$ ............................ | 0.3874 | 0.4549 |
| $R^2$ ............................ | 0.3748 | 0.4259 |
| Sample size ..................... | 100 | 100 |

We test for the existence of separate regimes in the data using specifications tests which take a single regime model as the null hypothesis. We do this by mechanically splitting the data into sub-groups based upon two different regions and examining whether model parameters are equal across regions. Thereafter, we include additional control variables and test if their inclusion led to accept the hypothesis that LA and ROW countries have the same slope coefficients.

### 4.3.1 Basic Model Estimation

Table 9 presents the least squares estimates of the basic model for the LA countries, for the whole sample, and for the whole sample excluding the African countries (3). A comparison of the three regressions reveals the following major differences:

---

(3) Since we are working with grouped data, we report robust "White standard error" that are consistent under the possibility of heterokedasticity.

TABLE 9

POOLED REGRESSIONS ON FIVE-YEARS AVERAGED DATA, 1960-1988:
BASIC MODEL
(*t*-statistics in parenthesis)

| Variable | Latin America | Whole sample | Whole sample excluding Africa |
|---|---|---|---|
| Constant............. | −0.0089 (−0.5054) | −0.0061 (−0.7808) | 0.0020 (0.1955) |
| Investment in (*t*) ...... | 0.0054 (4.6836) | 0.0038 (7.9125) | 0.0038 (6.7948) |
| Investment in (*t* − 1) .. | −0.0048 (−4.3317) | −0.0032 (−6.8051) | −0.0031 (−6.0601) |
| Initial per-capita GDP .. | −0.0039 (−1.6126) | −0.0028 (−2.6248) | −0.0027 (−2.1070) |
| Government spending .. | −0.0010 (−3.8423) | −0.0002 (−0.8352) | −0.0003 (−0.8401) |
| School primary rate.... | 0.0266 (2.2155) | 0.0259 (3.5269) | 0.0201 (1.6518) |
| *Dummy* for 1965-1969 | 0.0094 (1.2331( | 0.0103 (2.6503) | 0.0089 (2.0337) |
| *Dummy* for 1970-1974 | 0.0269 (3.0675) | 0.0164 (3.8237) | 0.0144 (2.8545) |
| *Dummy* for 1975-1979 | 0.0062 (0.7262) | 0.0058 (1.3204) | 0.0048 (1.0361) |
| *Dummy* for 1980-1984 | −0.0191 (−2.0647) | −0.0149 (−3.6534) | −0.0142 (−2.8319) |
| $R^2$ ................. | 0.5307 | 0.3673 | 0.3540 |
| Sample size ......... | 100 | 430 | 305 |

Specification test of regional split: LA countries respect to ROW countries

| | | | |
|---|---|---|---|
| *F*-statistic ........... | — | 2.3798 | 3.2722 |
| Significance level ...... | — | 0.0095 | 0.0005 |

1) in the LA sample, initial per-capita GDP has a negative and non significant coefficient, while for the whole sample, including and excluding the African countries, the coefficient is negative and significant confirming the convergence hypothesis for two large samples;

2) the coefficient of the current government expenditures to GDP ratio is not statistically significant in the two large samples, but is negative and significant in the LA countries;

3) the coefficient of the primary school enrollment variable is positive and significant in the three samples (4);

4) both the current and the lagged investment to GDP ratio are significant, having a positive total effect on growth in the three samples. Finally, the LA regression explains around 53% of the variation in the dependent variable, while the other two regressions explain only around 36%.

The adjustment degree of the regression, before controlling for policy variables, is significantly higher than that obtained for other pooling estimates for LA countries. For example, Grier and Tullock [13], controlling by initial GDP per-capita, the share of government expenditures in GDP, population growth, variation of GDP growth, and inflation measures, obtained a $R^2$ statistics of 0.29; Cardoso and Fishlow [4] controlling only for investment share of GDP and growth rate of labor force explain around 23%, while De Gregorio [8] after controlling by initial GDP per-capita, investment share of GDP, human capital variable, foreign investment, and variance of inflation, explains around 52%.

Even though the results for the whole sample are relatively satisfactory, we find substantial evidence that the laws of motion for growth within LA and the ROW countries are different. Including Africa in the sample, the *F*-statistic testing the appropriateness of combining the data is 2.38, which is significant at the 0.010 level and strongly rejects pooling the two groups of countries in a single sample. In the case where we exclude the African countries, the *F*-statistic is 3.27 with a significance level of 0.0005, supporting the view that in both cases the data are generated at least by two regimes.

### 4.3.2 Additional Control Variables

One explanation of the last results is that the set of control variables is not enough to account for the relevant differences in

---

(4) The basic model was also estimated considering other proxies of human capital: adult literacy in 1960, enrollment ratio for secondary education in 1960 and the difference of this ratio between 1970 and 1960. In all the cases, the coefficients of these variables were positive and significant, and the behavior of the rest of the variables in

growth performance across regions. Then, the evidence of different regimes can be explained by an omitted variable problem, so the inclusion of additional variables that belong to the basic model but have been left out would correct the specification error and eliminate the statistical significance of the sample splits. In this case, the different growth performance between the LA countries and the ROW countries could not be explained by different specifications but possibly by differences on policy implementation across regions.

Before testing the hypothesis of pooling the two groups of countries into a single sample, we estimate a set of growth equations for LA countries that consider, in addition to the variables of the basic model, variables to control for economic instability — inflation rate, trade balance deficit, and foreign direct investment —, for degree of external trade openness, and for constitutional changes and political and labor stability.

The econometric results of the growth equations for LA countries are presented in Table 10. The first model, in addition to the variables of the basic model, controls the trade openness effect on growth (5). The estimates indicate that the coefficient of the openness variable is negative and not significant. On the other hand, the coefficients of investment variables, the human capital proxy variable, and government spending continue to be significant and have the same expected signs as before. The initial per-capita GDP coefficient is negative, indicating the existence of convergence, however, it is still not significant.

Controlling for economic instability, model 2 and model 3 consider the inclusion of two inflation measures: mean inflation rate and the standard deviation of inflation. In both models the inflation coefficient is negative and significant. For developing countries, the negative effect on growth can be explained because inflation is often caused by political crisis or economic instability that additionally

---

the basic model was the same as that showed in Table 9 for enrollment ratio for primary education in 1960.

(5) We consider import plus export over GDP as a proxy of the decree of openness of the economy. Export as share of GDP and import as share of GDP were also considered. Since the result in those cases does not change respect to those obtained by considering import plus export as share of GDP, they are not reported.

depress growth. Also, in economies with 'cash-in-advance' constraints, anticipated inflation reduces capital accumulation and growth, implying a negative coefficient (6). The other variables in model 2 and model 3 present the same behavior as that shown in model 1, except that the coefficient of government spending has lost its significance.

Model 4 considers another variable to control for economic instability: the trade deficit share of GDP. The inclusion of this variable has a negative and significant effect on growth for LA countries. In particular, it causes the adjustment degree of the regression equation (measured by the corrected $R2$) to increase from around 53% to 61.5%. Controlling for the trade deficit, we obtain a negative and significant coefficient of initial per-capita GDP, confirming the convergence hypothesis for LA countries. Finally, it allows a reduction of the standard errors of inflation and school primary rate coefficients, causing an increase in their significance.

The last model in Table 10 considers the inclusion of foreign investment to GDP ratio as a variable to control for the adaptation and production of technology (Romer [24]). Even though the coefficient of foreign investment is positive, it is not significant, marginally increasing the degree of adjustment of the regression equation to 62.2%. The other coefficients have the same behavior as that obtained in model 4.

In the five models presented in Table 10, the significance of the time-period dummy variables indicates that holding other factors constant would leave some evidence of a rising average growth, at least, during the period of the early seventies. However, this effect was reverted during the early eighties as it is indicated by the negative and significant coefficient of the 1980-84 period dummy.

Finally, in Table 11 we present the last model that considers the inclusion of variables to control for constitutional changes and political stability (7). The coefficients of these variables were significant and negative, but were not enough to substantially increase the

---

(6) See STOCKMAN, 1981.

(7) We report only the result for the variable number of assassinations per million population per year (1960-1985). Others variables were also considered but the results do not change significantly respect to those reported in table 11. These variables were: index of civil liberties, index of political rights, and number of strikes per year.

TABLE 10

POOLED REGRESSIONS ON FIVE-YEARS AVERAGED DATA FOR
LATIN AMERICAN COUNTRIES, 1960-1988:
(*t*-statistics in parenthesis)

| Variable | model 1 | model 2 | model 3 | model 4 | model 5 |
|---|---|---|---|---|---|
| Constant.......... | −0.0078 (−0.464) | −0.0031 (−0.176) | −0.0032 (−0.183) | −0.0006 (−0.032) | −0.0022 (−0.119) |
| Investment in (*t*) ............. | 0.0056 (4.675) | 0.0056 (4.699) | 0.0057 (4.730) | 0.0064 (5.525) | 0.0062 (5.045) |
| Investment in (*t*−1) ........... | −0.0048 (−4.321) | −0.0048 (−4.260) | −0.0048 (−4.304) | −0.0060 (−5.316) | −0.0058 (−4.878) |
| Initial per-capita GDP ........... | −0.0035 (−1.490) | −0.0033 (−1.440) | −0.0033 (−1.451) | −0.0101 (−5.157) | −0.0100 (−5.299) |
| Government spending in (*t*) ........ | −0.0008 (−2.015) | −0.0007 (−1.607) | −0.0006 (−1.594) | −0.0004 (−1.325) | −0.0001 (−0.417) |
| School primary rate ............. | 0.0234 (2.052) | 0.0208 (1.855) | 0.0201 (1.795) | 0.0292 (3.926) | 0.0299 (4.164) |
| Dummy for 1965-1969 ........ | 0.0090 (1.216) | 0.0070 (0.939) | 0.0072 (0.979) | 0.0061 (0.858) | 0.0044 (0.604) |
| Dummy for 1970-1974 ........ | 0.0264 (3.073) | 0.0245 (2.856) | 0.0247 (2.865) | 0.0250 (2.987) | 0.0243 (2.824) |
| Dummy for 1975-1979 ........ | 0.0056 (0.663) | 0.0039 (0.453) | 0.0039 (0.450) | 0.0059 (0.734) | 0.0065 (0.801) |
| Dummy for 1980-1984 ........ | −0.0195 (−2.157) | −0.0211 (−2.284) | −0.0211 (−2.294) | −0.0156 (−1.758) | −0.0160 (−1.757) |
| Additional variable Trade openness  .. | −0.0065 (−0.676) | −0.0104 (−1.057) | −0.0010 (−1.033) | −0.0027 (−0.352) | −0.0050 (−0.570) |
| Inflation rate...... | — — | −0.91E-5 (−2.399) | — — | −0.13E-4 (−4.006) | −0.13E-4 (−4.254) |
| Variance of inflation .......... | — — | — — | −0.57E-5 (−2.860) | — — | — — |
| Trade deficit ...... | — — | — — | — — | −0.3221 (−4.138) | −0.3192 (−4.260) |
| Foreign investment........ | — — | — — | — — | — — | 0.2066 (1.545) |
| $R^2$ .............. | 0.5275 | 0.5287 | 0.5293 | 0.6150 | 0.6221 |
| Sample size  ...... | 100 | 100 | 100 | 100 | 100 |

TABLE 11

POOLED REGRESSIONS ON FIVE-YEARS AVERAGED DATA, 1960-1988:
FINAL MODEL
(*t*-statistics in parenthesis)

| Variable | Latin America | Whole sample | Whole sample excluding Africa |
|---|---|---|---|
| Constant .............. | 0.0020 (0.105) | −0.0080 (−0.896) | 0.0056 (0.466) |
| Investment in (*t*) ...... | 0.0061 (5.101) | 0.0044 (8.317) | 0.0043 (7.373) |
| Investment in (*t* − 1) .. | −0.0059 (−5.191) | −0.0038 (−7.495) | −0.0037 (−6.543) |
| Initial per-capita GDP .. | −0.0105 (−5.463) | −0.0030 ( 2.699) | −0.0034 (−2.747) |
| Government spending .. | −0.0005 (−1.483) | −0.194E-4 (−0.068) | 0.90E-4 (−0.256) |
| School primary rate.... | 0.021 (3.876) | 0.0230 (2.831) | 0.0101 (0.840) |
| Dummy for 1965-1969 | 0.0070 (0.968) | 0.0107 (2.668) | 0.0107 (2.348) |
| Dummy for 1970-1974 | 0.0261 (3.118) | 0.0163 (3.829) | 0.0159 (3.204) |
| Dummy for 1980-1984 | −0.0149 (−1.694) | −0.0127 (−3.021) | −0.0113 (−2.241) |
| Additional variables Trade openness ........ | 0.0046 (0.603) | 0.0094 (2.054) | 0.0107 (2.290) |
| Inflation rate .......... | −0.13E-4 (−4.332) | −0.15E-4 (5.655) | −0.15E-4 (−5.814) |
| Trade deficit .......... | −0.3374 (−4.523) | −0.0626 (−1.472) | −0.1100 (−2.285) |
| Assassinations ........ | −0.0025 (−1.890) | −0.0016 (−0.779) | −0.0029 (−1.243) |
| $R^2$ ................. | 0.6711 | 0.4122 | 0.4295 |
| $L^2$................... | 0.6213 | 0.3929 | 0.4035 |
| Sample size ......... | 100 | 403 | 299 |

Specification test of regional split: LA countries respect to ROW countries

| | | | |
|---|---|---|---|
| *F*-statistic ............ | — | 1.9060 | 1.9114 |
| Significance level ...... | — | 0.0245 | 0.0253 |

explanatory power of this regression equation with respect to the adjusted $R2$ obtained in model 4. The other variables in model 4 present the same behavior as before. However, the effect of a change in the investment rate on the growth rate decreased by two percentage points.

Table 11 also presents the estimates of this model for the whole sample of countries including and excluding the African countries. The main differences among these three samples are:

1) the coefficient of the primary school enrollment rate is positive and significant in the LA sample and in the whole sample, but it is insignificant when we exclude the African countries;

2) the trade openness coefficients are positive but are only statistically significant for the whole sample, including and excluding the African countries;

3) the coefficient of the trade deficit is not significant in the whole sample when the African countries are included; however, for LA sample and the whole sample excluding the African countries, they are significant and negative;

4) the number-of-assassinations variable is significant only for the LA sample;

5) the significance of the time-period dummy variables indicates that there is some evidence of a rising average growth, at least during the period from the second half of the sixties to the end of the seventies for the sample of all countries, while for the LA sample this rising average growth was present only during the first half of the seventies. However, for the three samples, this effect was reversed during the first half of the eighties.

Table 11 also presents the specification test for the significance of the sample split. Considering the African countries, the $F$-statistic to test the null hypothesis (that the slope coefficients are constant across regions) is 1.90 while, excluding the African countries, the statistic is 1.91. Both statistics are significant at the 0.025 level, rejecting pooling the two groups of countries into a single sample in favor of the separate regressions for LA and ROW countries. Thus, the evidence of multiple regimes seems robust with the addition of these variables, although the significance was a little reduced compared with the basic model presented in Table 9.

The results presented in this section tend to support not only the hypothesis that we do not have a single empirical model of secular growth that applies around the world but also that the inclusion of some specific additional control variables is not enough to reduce the significance of the regional split.

Additionally, these results tend to support the view that the differences in growth performance between LA countries and ROW countries could be explained not only by differences in the values of the explanatory variables but also by the way in which they affect growth. The latter effect is reflected in the differences between the coefficients of the LA and ROW regressions. To decompose the difference in growth rate between a difference in coefficient and a difference in the variables component we use a decomposition that has been used in labor economics. The source of this decomposition is Blinder [3]. The decomposition analysis presented in Table 12 indicates that for all periods but the last, a substantial part of the difference in average growth between the ROW and the LA countries can be accounted for by the difference in the coefficients. For example, the first line of Table 12 indicates that from a difference in rate of growth of 2.47 percentage points, 2.38 percentage points are accounted for by the differences in the coefficients of the two equations, while only 0.09 percentage points are accounted for by a more favorable set of explanatory variables. In the last period, the difference in the coefficients accounts for 1.5 percentage points of

TABLE 12

DECOMPOSITION OF THE DIFFERENCES
IN GROWTH BETWEEN ROW AND LA COUNTRIES

| Period | Differences in weight | Differences in determinants |
|--------|----------------------|----------------------------|
| 1965-1969 ................. | 0.023839 | 0.000906 |
| 1970-1974 ................. | 0.006614 | 0.005927 |
| 1975-1979 ................. | 0.017567 | −0.005640 |
| 1980-1984 ................. | 0.028419 | 0.014988 |
| 1985-1988 ................. | −0.015450 | 0.045807 |
| 1985-1988 ................. | (0.02088) (*) | (0.02264) (*) |

(*) Excludes the African Countries from the ROW regression.

lower growth for the ROW sample in comparison with the LA countries. However, a full 4.6 percentage points are due to more favorable explanatory variables for the LA countries than for ROW countries. When we exclude the African countries from the ROW regression, both factors account for similar amounts.


## 5. - Conclusions

Latin America's growth performance up to the late 1960s did not provide any warning for the crisis that was about to unravel. However, problems were building up with the deterioration of the overall macroeconomic balances and the increasing cost of market interventions that had accumulated since the previous 30 years. The first oil shock shacked some of the countries of the region. But when the second oil shock came, easy access to foreign borrowing prolonged the use of the existing development model. The external shocks of the early 1980s were the factors that detonated a crisis that was in the making during the previous thirty years.

Sooner or later, the countries in the region recognized the need to carry out a profound transformation of their economic system to adjust to the crisis and to start a process of sustained growth while creating the conditions for a permanent reduction in poverty.

As a consequence of the external shocks and the policies and institutions developed in the previous 30 years, Latin America had in the 1980s its worst decade of the century. Only 6 out of the 23 countries in the region experienced a positive rate of growth in per capita GDP. The deterioration in inflation was jus as dramatic. In 16 out of 23 countries the inflation accelerated and in 5 of the 16 it reached over 3-digit annual level for the decade as whole.

Chile, Bolivia and Mexico are the three countries that have progressed the most in the structural transformation of their economies. Among them, Chile is on a path to sustainable growth while Mexico and Bolivia are initiating a growth process after many years of much needed and painful adjustment. These three countries are benefitting today from below 20% annual inflation and positive growth in per capita income. However, growth is still low in Mexico and Bolivia and there is increasing demand in both countries to accelerate growth.

For quite a while, development economists had been advocating the need to restore the basic macroeconomic balances and to reduce distortions to get output close to its potential and to accelerate growth. However, only with the new insights of the "new growth theory", a respectable theoretical base has been developed to understand the channels through which better policies and factor accumulation affect not only the level of output but also its rate of growth.

In explaining Latin America's growth using only the investment ratio, that is, using a Harrod-Domar type of model, one does not explain more than 37% of the variation in the per capita growth rate. However, this is the single most important variable accounting for growth. But still there is a 63% of the variation in per capita growth to be accounted for.

Following the insights of the new growth theory, we add to the model the initial level of per capita GDP, the current government expenditures to GDP ratio, human capital variables, and two measures of macroeconomic instability (the inflation rate, and the trade deficit). When we include these variables, the explanatory power of the model increases to 62% of the variation in the rate of per capita GDP growth. On top of the investment rate, among the variables that we considered, the most significant ones were the two indicators of macroeconomic stability (i.e. the inflation rate and the trade deficit to GDP ratio), and the proxy for human capital. However, current government expenditures to GDP and the indicator of openness were not significant. These results compare very favorably with the ones obtained by previous studies (Cardoso and Fishlow [4]; Grier and Tullock [13]) and are also comparable to those of De Gregorio [8].

Our results for the LA countries indicate convergence of per capita GDP growth in the region. That is, holding everything else constant, the countries with the lowest level of per capita income grew at a higher rate than countries with a higher level of per capita income. The single most important variable accounting for a negative coefficient in the initial level of income per capita is the trade deficit to

GDP ratio. The later is one of the measures that we use for the stability of macroeconomic policies.

We also estimated the full model for a large sample of countries that include Latin America, OECD countries, Asian countries and African countries. In this "whole sample", the results with respect to significance of the coefficients were similar except that the trade openness variable was significant. However, when we tested for the equality of the growth equation of Latin American countries and ROW countries (the "whole sample" excluding the Latin American countries), we found that the null hypothesis of both groups of countries belonging to the same sample was rejected.

Since the growth equation for the Latin American countries is different than the one for the rest of the world, we carried out a decomposition analysis of the difference in the explained rate of per capita income growth in both groups of countries. From this decomposition analysis, we found that in all periods but the last one, the difference in the coefficients of the two equatins in the most important factor accounting for the higher rate of growth of the ROW countries.

BIBLIOGRAPHY

[1] BARRO R.J.: «Economic Growth in a Cross-Section of Countries», *Quarterly Journal of Economics*, May 1991.

[2] BARRO R.J. - WOLF H.C.: *Data Appendix for Economic Growth in a Cross-Section of Countries*, mimeo, Harvard University, 1989.

[3] BLINDER A.: «Wage Discrimination: Reduced Form and Structural Estimates», *Journal of Human Resources*, vol. 8, n. 4, 1973.

[4] CARDOSO E. - FISHLOW A.: «Latin American Economic Development: 1950-1980», NBER, *Working Paper Series*, n. 3161, November 1989.

[5] CARVALHO J.L. - HADDAD C.: «Foreign Trade Strategies and Employment in Brazil», in KRUEGER A.O. *et AL.* (eds.): *Trade and Employment in Developing Countries. Individual Series*, vol. 1, Chicago, University of Chicago Press for the NBER, 1981.

[6] CORDO V.: «Problems, Development Theory, and Strategies of Latin America», in RANIS G. - SCHULTZ T.P. (eds.): *The State of Development Economics: Progress and Perspectives*, London, Basil Blackwell, 1988.

[7] CORDEN M.: «Macroeconomic Policy and Growth», *Proceedings of the World Bank Annual Conference on Development Economics*, 1991.

[8] DE GREGORIO J.: *Economic Growth in Latin America*, mimeo, IMF, May 1991.

[9] DE LONG B. - SUMMERS L.: «Equipment Investment and Economic Growth», *Quarterly Journal of Economics*, n. 104, May 1991.

[10] DERVIS K. - PETRI P.: «The Macroeconomics of Successful Development: What are the lessons?», NBER, *Macroeconomics Annual*, 1987.

[11] DURLAUF S.N.: *Local Versus Global Convergence Across National Economies*, mimeo, Department of Economics, University of Oregon, 1991.

[12] FISCHER S.: «Growth, Macroeconomics, and Development», NBER, *Macroeconomics Annual*, Cambridge, MIT Press, 1991.

[13] GRIER K.B. - TULLOCK G.: «An Empirical Analysis of Cross-National Economic Growth, 1951-80», *Journal of Monetary Economics*, n. 24, 1989.

[14] GROSSMAN G. - HELPMAN E.: *Innovation and Growth in the Global Economy*, Cambridge (Mass.), MIT Press, 1992.

[15] HIRSCHMAN A.O.: «Ideologies of Economic Development in Latin America», in HIRSCHMAN A.O. (eds.): *Latin American Issues: Essays and Comments*, New York, Twentieth Century Fund, 1961.

[16] LARRAÍN F. - MELLER P.: «The Socialist-Populist Chilean Experience: 1970-1973», in DORNBUSCH R. - EDWARDS S. (eds.): *The Macroeconomics of Populism in Latin America*, Chicago, The University of Chicago Press, 1991.

[17] LEVINE R. - RENELT D.: «Cross-Country Studies of Growth and Policies: Methodological, Conceptual, and Statistical Problems», World Bank, *PRE Working Paper Series*, n. 608, 1991.

[18] — —: «A sensitive Analysis of Cross-Country Growth Regressions», World Bank, *PRE Working Paper Series*, n. 609, 1991.

[19] LUCAS R.E. Jr.: «On the Mechanocs of Economic Development», *Journal of Monetary Economics*, n. 22, 1988.

[20] PINTO A.: *Ni Estabilidad ni Desarrollo: la Política del Fondo Monetario Internacional*, Santiago, Editorial Universitaria, 1960.

[21] PREBISCH R.: *Introduccion a Keynes*, Buenos Aires, Fondo Cultura Económica, 1947.

[22] RENELT D.: «Economic Growth: A Review of the Theoretical and Empirical Literature, World Bank, *PRE Working Paper Series*, n. 678, 1991.

[23] ROMER P.: «Two Strategies for Economic Development: Using Ideas vs. Producing Ideas», paper presented at the *World Bank Annual Conference on Development Economics*, 1992.

[24] ——: «Increasing Returns and Long-Run Growth», *Quarterly Journal of Economics*, May 1986.

[25] SOLOW R.M.: A Contribution to the Theory of Economic Growth», *Quarterly Journal of Economics*, n. 70, 1956.

[26] STURZENEGGER F.A.: «Description of a Populist Experience: Argentine, 1973-1976, in DORNBUSCH R. - EDWARDS S. (eds.): *The Macroeconomics of Populism in Latin America*, Chicago, The University of Chicago Press, 1991.

[27] SUMMERS R. - HESTON A.: «The Penn World Table (Mark 5): An Expanded Set of International Comparison, 1950-1988», *Quarterly Journal of Economics*, May 1991.

# Inflation Fall, Financial Recovery and Endogenous Growth in Latin American Countries

**Michele Bagella - Martino Lo Cascio** (*)
Università «Tor Vergata», Roma

## Introduction

Monetary stabilization, free trade policies and the removal of exchange controls in the main Latin American countries appear to be succesful in terms of decline of the inflation rates. Foreign debt growth subsided to an halt in Argentina, Mexico and Venezuela owing to conditional restructuring, namely debt reductions agreed with IMF on the basis of the achievement of monetary targets (performance criteria and policy understandings) (Sachs [37]). Finally, privatization policy seems to provide a substantial contribution to stock exchange uprise and to the repatriation of capital flight (IMF [18]).

Although these facts mark the novelty of an important recovery as far as monetary tendencies and financial investment control are concerned, the expected positive reactions on the real side are still far from being in act (this is particularly the case for Argentina). Finding the growth path abandoned a decade ago is supposed to be a complex task requiring time. Confidence in the national economy is needed on behalf of foreign and internal investors, confidence that affects the time necessary to overcome this phase that would be seen as a phase from "stabilisation to growth" (Selowski [38]; Dornbush [11]). How

(*) The authors would like to thank Dr. Leonardo Becchetti, Dr. Carlo De Nicola and Dr. Luciano Mauro for the ir help in preparing the database and estimates.

*Advise*: the numbers in square brackets refer to the Bibliography in the appendix.

long will this phase last? An *a priori* answer to this question is hard to be found, even because every country has its own past records. In Italy, for instance, the monetary stabilization achieved in 1948 by L. Einaudi forerunned by at least three years the beginning of the recovery in the fifties (Bagella [1]). German recovery in the aftermath of first world war arrived still later. After the end of the hyperinflation of the twenties, recovery started only in the mid-thirties (Bresciani Turroni [6]).

The history of countries is very rich with many other cases of recovery lags (Kindleberger [20]), so it is no wonder then that every Latin American country has its own. But, just taking into account this reality, what suggests the theory, what reaction mechanism does it provide in order to push the economy to a new recovery phase, after a long period of hyperinflation?

In order to represent the two realities of the present Latin American cycle we analyze the inflation fall and real long-term growth factors effect in two different sections of this paper.

In the first section, the fall from hyperinflation is considered in relation to the consequences on the saving-investment mechanism provided by the theory and on the different recoveries of financial and credit markets. Are these mechanisms automatic and sufficient in quantitative terms to change the long run tendencies? These theoretical reaction mechanisms are then compared with the empirical evidence of inflationary trends of the eighties of their relationship with net capital inflows, internal investments and per capita foreign debt. The analysis is carried out for three countries: Argentina, Brazil, and Chile.

In the second section, long run real trends for the same countries are considered with regard to the growth-development relationship, to the mechanisms of endogenous growth and finally to the technical progress issue. The aim of the second part of the paper is to provide a reference framework which is necessary to evaluate, in perspective, the harmonization of international financial institution policies.

In the end, we discuss those policy prescription that fitting the previously outlined macroeconomic framework may drive Latin American economies from stabilization to recovery and sustainable growth.

## 1. - Inflation Fall, Real Interest Rates and Financial Conditions for the Recovery of Real Economy: Six Macroeconomic and Cycle Theory Propositions

1.1 *A Few Notes on Macroeconomics*
*and the Theory of Economic Fluctuations*

1.1.1 The slowdown of economic activity as a consequence of antinflationary policies has been widely considered by both keynesian and neoclassic macroeconomic theories.

While the former highlighted the recessive effects of these policies and warned not to "burn down the house to roast the pig", the latter emphasized, on the contrary, the positive consequences stemming from progressive money value recovery.

So while "keynesian-oriented" theories suggest an active economic policy in favor of aggregate demand investments, even if internationally supported (Dornbush [11]), the "neoclassical-oriented" theory prescribes *laissez-faire* policies, persuaded that the market may provide sufficient incentives for growth recovery.

Six theoretical propositions may be distinguished, highlighting how the incentives work.

*The first theoretical proposition* is the "quantitative" one. When the inflation rate falls, an increase in real money balances is determined. If this increase is offset by a rise in money demand, or, in other terms, by a reduction of money velocity of circulation, the new equilibrium is achieved without real effects (Fischer [12]). If, conversely, a real money balance expansion outruns the desired level, it may affect aggregate demand growth, giving rise to an increase in production and employment provided that aggregate supply is highly elastic (Patinkin, [34]). More formally, if we consider the traditional quantitative equation, with $M$ for the given money stock, $P$ for the price level, $Q$ for real income and $K$ for the propensity to hold money balances, a fall of $P$ may determine the following results. Given that:

$$(1) \qquad M = KPQ, \text{ if } - \Delta P = \Delta K$$

monetary equilibrium is achieved without effects on $Q$. If on the contrary $- \Delta P > \Delta K$, this will affect $Q$ given that $\Delta Q/Q/\Delta M/P/M/P > 0$. As this condition is linked to the hypothesis of an incomplete utilization of productive resources, it is verified for countries recovering from hyperinflation. More generally it must be remembered that this mechanism, the real balance effect, is weak (Leijonhufwud [22]) and seldom empirically tested (Mayer [30]).

*The second theoretical proposition* is related to the first one and is based on the positive effect of the inflation rate fall on propensity to save. Inflation decline causes an increase in the real interest rate leading savers to switch from consumption to saving. Given that:

(2)   $S = f(i_r)$, given that $i_r = i_n - \pi$, when $\pi = 0$ then $i_r = i_n$

but when inflation rate is greater than zero, the saving function is obviously influenced by price behaviour and then it must be rewritten as $S = f(in, \pi)$, and its linear specification may then be expressed as $S = \alpha + \beta i - \gamma \pi$.

Then with a negative $\Delta \pi$ an increase of $S$ will follow due to the shifting of the saving function. If the reaction will be more than proportional the new equilibrium on the real market will be attained at a lower real interest rate with a positive effect on production and employment (Wicksell [43]).

*The third proposition* the positive effect on money balance and on saving to a change of expectation. If inflation fall is not perceived as permanent the above mentioned positive effects will not occur as economic agents will anticipate and discount a future inflation recovery. If, on the contrary, they assume that the antinflationary policy stance will be consistently maintained through time they will then change their saving and investments preferences. This theory associates positive effect on aggregate supply to the re-attainment of monetary stability introducing expected prices as a key variable in the reaction mechanism (Lucas [28]).

Assuming $Y_t^s$ as the aggregate supply at time $t$ and $p_t$ and $p_t^*$ respectively as the price level at time $t$ and the expected price level always at time $t$:

(3)                          $Y_t^s = Y_o + d(P_t - P_t^*)$

if we consider an expected price fall of $-P_t^*$ according to *(3)* there will be a positive effect on aggregate supply $Y_t^s$ given that $Y_o$ is full employment income.

The *(3)* establishes then an inverse relationship among expected prices and aggregate supply that can be expressed dynamically as:

$$(4) \qquad\qquad d\,Y_t^s = -\,a\,d\,P_t^*$$

As a consequence, if an inflation fall is expected, according to this theory, a positive effect on aggregate supply will follow.

*The fourth proposition* analyses the inflation fall effect on the real interest rate. Considering an intertemporal resource allocation model (Lucas - Rapping [29]; Barro - King [5]), labor supply is positively correlated with real interest rates, as workers will be induced to work more in order to save more. Put in other terms, an increase in real interest rates corresponds to an increase in the price for leisure and if the substitution effect prevails there will be a positive effect on the hours worked with a reduction of leisure and consumption. Given that $N_{st}$ is labor supply at time $t$, $i_r$ the real interest rate and $w/p$ the real wage:

$$(5) \qquad\qquad N_{st} = \alpha\,i_r + \beta\,w/p \text{ with } d\,N_{st} = z\,d\,i_r$$

This means the labor supply positively reacts to a decline of $P$ and to a rise in $w/p$ even for increasing $i_r$.

The so-called "intertemporal substitution effect" is then another channel through which an inflation fall may positively affect growth. This theory, like the real balance one, has not been succesfully tested and in recent empirical papers the increase in real interest rate seems to affect more career choice than the number of hours worked (Phelps [35]; Blanchard-Fischer [4]).

*The fifth proposition* analyses the effect of inflation fall on financial investments when no restrictions to capital mobility among countries are allowed. According to Fischer's theory (Fischer [12]) with free capital circulation real interest rates tend to equalize among countries. In equilibrium, if we indicate with $i_{dr}$ the domestic interest rate and with $i_{inr}$ the international interest rate, we will have:

$$(6) \qquad\qquad\qquad i_{dr} = i_{inr3}$$

If, however, we depart from certainty and assume that, due to the presence of risk in the domestic economy, capital mobility may be hindered by country risk or by policy stances that determine conditions for domestic currency devaluation, we have to admit that investors do not accept equality between the real domestic rate and the international one (as in the hypothesis of perfect mobility and no uncertainty). A premium has then to be added necessarily to compensate investors for the country risk they are running (Frankel [14]). The condition for investing in a market at risk will then be:

$$(7) \qquad\qquad i_{rs} \geqslant i_{inr}; \text{ where } i_{dr} + \sigma = i_{rs}$$

is the real subjective interest rate, required by the single investor according to $\sigma$. Equation *(7)* may be regarded also as a "non capital flight condition", a condition which must be satisfied in order to induce foreign capital to be directed toward domestic economy. $i_{rs}$ obviously changes from individual to individual, but it is also obvious that this rate will push upward market rates, the higher the evaluation of country risk by domestic and foreign investors will be. Condition *(7)* has not occurred in past records of high inflation when Latin American countries experienced capital flight. Their condition may be expressed as:

$$(8) \qquad\qquad\qquad i_{drs} > i_{dr}$$

This means that if the real subjective interest rate is higher than the corresponding market rate, (this latter one in most cases negative), foreign capitals are invested abroad. Everytime the inflation rate falls, and everytime this fall is considered permanent by the market, $i_{rs}$ declines as the price needed to face risk from inflation is reduced.

The capital flow may then be inverted provided that inflation fall determines:

(9)                                $i_{drs} \geq i_{dr} \geq i_{inr}$

*The sixth proposition* is linked to the fifth one and is based on the effect of a risk premium fall on investments. A risk premium fall causes a decline of the subjective discount rate used by investors to evaluate the shadow price of capital (Blanchard - Fisher [4]). Assuming $p_{ks}$ as the shadow price of capital, $RN^*_t$ as net revenues from investment for the period $t$ and $i_{rs}$ the subjective discount rate (as shown in (7)), $p_{sk}$ will be determined by the following equation:

(10)
$$p_{sk} = \sum_{t=1}^{T} \frac{RN^*_t}{(1 + i_{rs})^t}$$

The condition for the investment to be realized is:

(11)                                $p_{sk} > p_k$

If, on the contrary, the market price of capital is higher than the shadow price the investment will not be enacted. The effect of a risk premium fall ensuing an inflation fall in equation *(10)* is to reduce $i_{sr}$ increasing $p_{sk}$. If *(11)* is verified due to this fall condition, investments are bound to increase.

1.1.2 The above described theoretical propositions focus on the positive impact of an inflation rate fall on monetary or real sector. Each of the six propositions highlights an automatic reaction mechanism in the two sectors which are not connected to one another. Due to this dichotomy, the links between the real and the financial sector, neither obvious nor irrelevant, are neglected.

If we consider that the productive capital is placed in the saving market through the issue of shares, share price is determined by the market and is subject to the condition that subjective price is higher or equal to the market price (Minsky, [31]). For the market price to be in turn an incentive to a new share issue the Tobin condition must hold, namely, market price must be higher than the substitution price of capital (Tobin [41]). If we consider with $p_{ks}$ the subjective capital demand price, with $p_{km}$ the market price and with $p_{ksos}$ the substitution price of capital, the "share purchase" condition for the investor is:

*(12)* $$p_{ks} > p_{km}$$

The inequality in *(12)* is a fundamental condition for stock market speculative behaviour. We can link it with another inequality:

*(13)* $$p_{km} > p_{ksos}$$

indicating a "share issue" condition for firms. This new issue, according to Tobin, would allow for firms new investment financing, drawing funds directly from the market.

It seems then that an inflation fall would reduce risk premium, reducing also subjective real interest rates, and increasing demand price for capital. This increase should in turn elevate capital market price and if the latter is higher than the substitution price of capital, firms would react positively expanding their share supply to the market, directly financing, in this way, their new investments. Financial market should then be the channel through which the economy could foster its recovery.

*This seventh recovery mechanism*, though, doesnot take into account an asymmetry of the financial market that has to be evidenced dealing with the issue of antinflationary recovery.

We refer to the relationship between the stock market and the banking system. In the above described virtuous cycle, banks are not taken into consideration. Bank intermediation constitues for all non stock owned firms the traditional financing channel. Even though in the stock market there will be an index upturn due to *(12)*, nothing similar occurs in the banking system. Interest rates remain high for two reasons: 1) they are not an immediate incentive for depositors, not accustomed to this saving option after a long period of high inflation; 2) the same banks have higher operating costs due to the previous lack of human capital and machinery investment. While the real subjective interest rate falls due to the risk premia fall (exchange risk and country risk), real interest rates on bank loans are high due to the credit rationing ensuing deposit growth lag. Generally speaking a firm will not finance its investments through bank lending if the following condition is not verified:

$$(14) \qquad\qquad i_{rcrb} \leq i_{rs}$$

Namely, if real subjective interest rate $i_{rs}$ is not higher or equal to loan interest rate $i_{rcrb}$. Until a real interest rate decline occurs, there will be a slackening of bank financed investments, even in presence of a stock exchange boom.

The inflation fall determines a process where financial recovery is a necessary but not sufficient condition for productive recovery. For the beginning of the latter, bank intermediation recovery is to occur.

1.1.3 In present conditions, almost all Latin American countries need to consolidate the inflation fall, and there seems to be no room for public investments given that foreign debt drains a large part of national resources, included public ones. On such premises, deficit spending policies bound to reinvigorate inflation are simply not viable, while foreign government aids, albeit coming in a large measure, cannot satisfy the demand for investments of the whole continent.

We need to explore other theoretical views for Latin American recovery and with this respect, the mechanisms prescribed by neo-classic theory in order to reinvigorate investments seem better to adapt to the present situation of these countries.

Monetary stability is considered by these theories as the fundamental prerequisite for creating favorable conditions for consumers and firm choices. Monetary and real reactions are in fact associated to the inflation fall according to them.

The inflation fall has the effect of increasing real interest rates, given that nominal rate reduction is lower than inflation one. In this case the propensity of holding money as a financial asset will increase as a result of its growing value, provided that expectations will rationally discount the effects of antinflationary policy (Lucas [28], Fischer [13]).

If we consider a small open economy this process (if pursued systematically and then credibly) should lead to the equalization of real internal rates with average foreign rates. Opting for capital movement deregulation and for freedom in converting activities in the desired currency, domestic exchange rate should reflect in its change the tendency of interest rates (Fischer [12]). In this framework exchange-risk and country-risk should be reduced, if for the second we keep in consideration the risk from expectation of i.e. barriers to capital outflows or fiscal and administrative restraints to them (Frankel [14]).

As a result of a credible monetary policy, domestic and international investors and savers will then happen to decide for their investment levels discounting all positive effects stemming from a fall in price growth, included those ones deriving from the reactivation of banking and financing formal mechanisms, all the more if they can realize gains from the exchange of the inflationed currency.

Yet, the fall of risk premia has another important consequence as far as firm investment decisions are concerned. It should lead to a fall in the subjective discount rate with which, according to an application of Ramsey model to open economies (Blanchard - Fisher [4]), investors evaluate the shadow price of capital. Discounting expected profits with a lower subjective rate will make them grow and will be induced to select on the aggregate a higher level of investment.

Neoclassical-oriented theories add real reactions to monetary reactions because of a real interest rise effect on labor supply. This effect should be positive according to the intertemporal substitution model, which includes the saving argument among the determinants of labor supply. If an increase in the real interest rate positively affects savings, it will consequently have a positive effect even on the propensity to work, reducing consumption and leisure. (Barro - King [5]; Lucas - Rapping [29]). With these assumptions and a multiplicative production function there would be a better use of capital services and an increase in the marginal productivity of capital together with a reduction of consumption and of the marginal productivity of labor).

## 1.2 *Inflation and Foreign Debt Reduction:*
*the Effects on Internal and Foreign Credibility*

This paragraph will take into consideration the statistical relationship between the rate of inflation and some national accounting variables for Argentina, Brazil and Chile. The aim is to verify consistence of stylized facts with the above-mentioned theoretical arguments.

1.2.1 The first phenomenon analyzed in the tables is the relationship between per capita debt and per capita GDP (Graph 1). A first remark is that of an inverse correlation among the two variables. This correlation is clear-cut for Argentina from 1989, for Brazil from 1985 and for Chile from 1986.

This seems to confirm the Bagella-Lo Cascio empirical analysis (Bagella-Lo Cascio [2]) testing the negative incidence of foreign debt on the long run rate of growth and on internal savings for Argentina and Brazil.

This evidence may also be confirmed if we plot annual foreign per capita debt growth rate against an estimated annual growth rate of foreign per capita debt based on the difference between total debt service and net exports (Graph 2), where it can be observed that an increase in the debt service and/or a decrease in net exports has a positive effect on foreign debt (Blanchard - Fischer [4]). More formally if we indicate with $db/dt$ the variation of per capita foreign debt and with $ib$ the service $i$ paid on the debt $b$ and with $nx$ net per capita exports, we may write:

$$(15) \qquad \frac{db}{dt} = ib - nx$$

We can verify the above-mentioned relationship in Graph 2: for Argentina foreign per capita debt grew according to the increase in total per capita debt service and to the decrease of net exports. The trend is inverted in 1989 when there was a substantial increase in net exports and a nonincreasing profile for debt service. Brazil's data show a less evident correlation among estimated and effective debt

GRAPH 1

PER CAPITA GDP AND PER CAPITA EXTERNAL DEBT

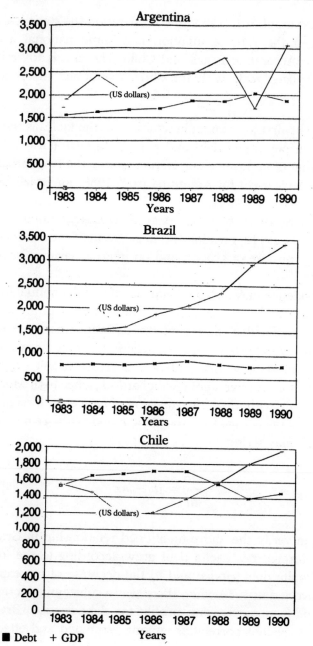

■ Debt    + GDP          Years

## PER CAPITA DEBT GROWTH INDICATORS

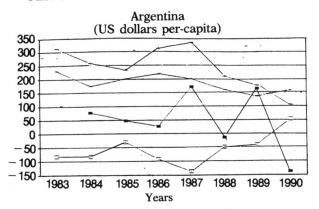

Argentina
(US dollars per-capita)

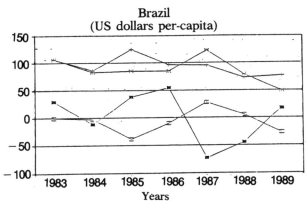

Brazil
(US dollars per-capita)

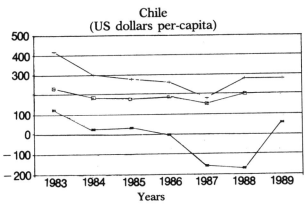

Chile
(US dollars per-capita)

■ eff. growth      + est. growth
Debt service      Net exports

growth, while it is evident the inverse relationship between effective debt growth and net export behaviour from 1988. With regard to Chile we find a decline of effective and estimated debt growth until 1988, while for 1989-1990 the effective rate of growth increases and the estimated rate of growth is constant due to the almost absent variation both in debt service and in net exports.

1.2.2 If we compare foreign debt with the inflation rate, we may note a strong positive relationship for the three countries considered. The negative effect of inflation is also confirmed by the inverse link emerging between consumer price growth and fixed investments (Graph 3). There is an almost perfect symmetry for Argentina: between 1983 and 1985 we assist to the negative trend of an outsurge in inflation and a decline of investments, while between 1985 and 1987 the trend is reversed. The evidence is clear-cut for Chile where we assist at a decline of inflation and an increase of investments for the period 1985-1988. Similar considerations apply to Brazil which exhibits a soaring rate of inflation from 1986 and a temperate fall of investments.

This statistical scenario seems to confirm that inflation has a negative impact on credibility and future profitability prospects for investments. What previously asserted about the somewhat surprising nonnegative reponse of investors to the increase of real interest rates as a consequence of antinflationary policies seems to be confirmed by the data. Investments seem to react positively — even though with moderate positive elasticity — to the reduction of inflation and of risk premia. The effect of the increase in real interest rate seems thus more than balanced by a shift in investors' expectations which discount at a lower rate future net expected profits.

1.2.3 Nonetheless, as Phelps observed, there is no persuasive empirical evidence of a direct link between high real rates and expansion, or low real interest rates and recession (Phelps [35]), nor in his opinion, does the contribution of Greenwood, Hercowitz and Huffman (Greenwood - Hercowitz-Huffman [15]) seem decisive for the explanation of the business cycle. These authors start from the assumption of a marginal efficiency shock on the new installed capital

## INFLATION AND INVESTMENT

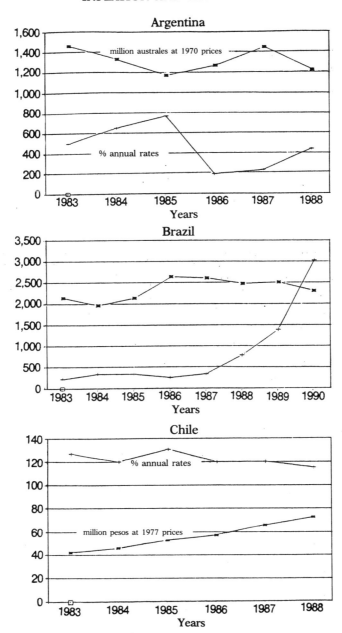

■ Gross fixed inv.   + Inflation

GRAPH 4

## INFLATION AND NET RESOURCE FLOWS

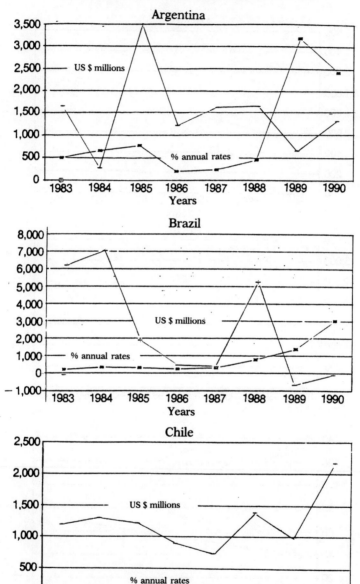

■ Inflation   + Net Resource Flows

and derive from it the consequence of a quick depreciation of the old capital together with the increase of labor marginal productivity. It should be inferred that this process determines a positive effect on real interest rates even for the assumed increase in the demand of new capital goods.

This does not seem until now to be the case for Latin America, where the increase in real interest rates is not matched by an increase in the hours worked and in employment (CEPAL [8]), even though there are some symptoms of recovery in some countries (Mexico, Chile and Colombia) and positive, even though still weak, signals of response of private investments to the inflation rate fall come from Brazil and Argentina. This trend, if reinforced, would appear to be consistent with simulations carried out in a past paper (Bagella - Lo Cascio [2]) which established for Brazil and Argentina a link between marginal propensity to save and the increase in the long run growth rate of income.

What are still to be awaited are now the conditions for a shock in the marginal efficency of capital. Without this shock it is hard to imagine the inception of a growth "virtuous cycle" of the "creative destruction" ones modelled by Greenwood, Hercowitz and Huffman and thoroughly analyzed by Grossman and Helpman (Grossman - Helpmann [16]). Creative destruction occurs when investments in new capital goods spreads to sectors with dated technology. The consequence in these sectors will be the one of a strong tendency to the substitution of the old capital and to the production of higher quality one due to the induced technological spillovers. Even human capital should benefit from the process owing to learning-by-doing on the new technology and to an increase in the hours worked for the business cycle effect.

What we wonder now is if Latin America is ready to receive the desired technological shock. The answer to this question lies in three important events concerning Latin American countries: *a*) privatization; *b*) GATT agreements; *c*) the MARCOSUR process of regional integration.

The privatization process is taking big leaps forward in Argentina, Chile, Brazil, Mexico and Venezuela. There are involved in the process firms operating in telecommunications, transportation and primary good sectors. In all sectors, especially in the tertiary one, technological innovation is one of the most important factors of competitiveness for the state enterprise buyers, which are represented by big European and American firms. In these sectors endogenous growth theories should happen to be succesfully tested.

On the contrary, agreements for the reduction of tariff and non-tariff barriers do not seem to have progressed so much. The potential consequences from positive agreements are still not clear cut but it is certain that for agricultural and manufacturing exports the removal of trade barriers could foster an increase of investments, and the expansionary effect of it could be enhanced if small and medium scale firms with higher propensity to innovate should take part in the process.

MARCOSUR regional integration may also result to be beneficial for investment expected profitability. Past records say that cross border exchanges of the involved countries have always gained from a trade liberalization. They may boost the renewal of equipment and their technological advancement.

Contrary to what happened in the eighties, there seem to exist in the nineties the prerequisites for avoiding another "lost decade" and to sustain growth. In the last decade protectionism, statalism and deficit spending caused widespread iperinflation and recession. In this decade monetary policies together with trade and exchange liberalization policies seem to realize the economic and the institutional framework for a favorable economic perspective (CEPAL [8]).

The reduction of inflation seems to have beneficial effects not only on internal investments but also on foreign resource flows for the three countries considered. A strong inverse relationship is in fact evident for the 1988-1990 period (Graph 4). When inflation increased net resource flow has experienced a decline. In Chile where inflation rate is constant and moderate from 1983, net resource flows are always positive, while this is not the case of Brazil which experienced for the period 1989-1990 net resource outflows with growing inflation.

1.2.4 We may be tempted from the analysis to discuss the credibility of the policies adopted by these countries. Without running the risk of inferring too much from the overall picture presented we

GRAPH 5

RATE OF CHANGE OF EXTERNAL DEBT PRICE
IN SECONDARY MARKETS

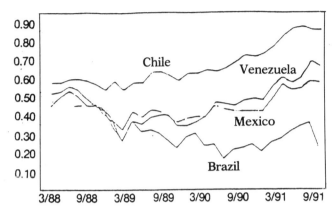

may argue that it seems to stress the salience of the credibility issue. With this respect it could be interesting to examine some financial market data (FMI [18]).

Financial markets seem in fact to provide the most significant indications for our analysis. If we analyze secondary market price of foreign debt for Chile, Venezuela, Mexico and Brazil, we note from the reported World Bank table (World Bank [44]), Graph 5, that debt price has significant growng since 1990, the starting year of antinflationary policies. On the contrary, the price of Brazilian debt is

TABLE 1

PERCENT INCREASE OF THE US DOLLAR INDEX
OF MAJOR LATIN AMERICAN STOCK EXCHANGES
AND NEW YORK STOCK EXCHANGE INDEX
(1.1.1991-30.11.1991)

| | |
|---|---|
| Argentina | 295.6 |
| Brazil | 73.6 |
| Mexico | 90.5 |
| Chile | 90.2 |
| Venezuela | 20.2 |
| New York | 18.5 |

*Source*: IFC.

GRAPH 6

## TRADE VOLUME AND PERCENT COMPOSITION
## OF LATIN AMERICAN EXTERNAL DEBT
(US $ billions)

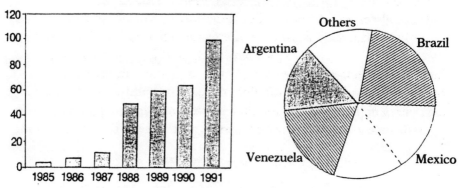

declining even for the last months of 1991. Another remarkable feature of the market in these last years is the sustained stock exchange growth starting from 1988, with a more significant increase in 1991 (see Table 1, Graphs 6 and 7).

GRAPH 7

## MONTHLY VARIATION
## OF BUENOS AIRES STOCK EXCHANGE INDEX

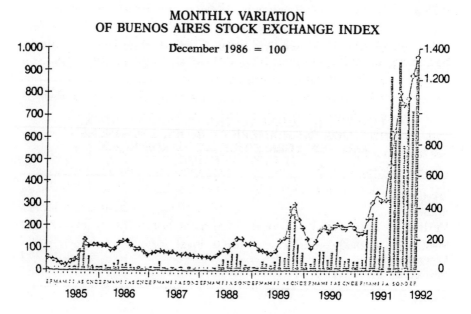

## 1.3 *First Conclusions on Monetary Trends*

If we consider stock exchange trends as indicators of the change in expectations we many observe that from 1991 the rise in the stock exchange index in Latin American countries has been far more significant than the one registered by New York stock exchange. The repatriation of capital fled abroad has been at the origin of this boom (FMI [18]; World Bank [44]).

With regard to Argentina, the above — mentioned repatriation has not yet yelded the expected results in terms of real investment recovery. It should seem that capital inflow still follows the "waiting option" with substantially speculative determinants. The waiting option, as Dornbush emphasized (Dornbush [11]), is the one followed in the eighties by capital flight in the main countries (Lessard - Williamson [23]). Capital preferred the "outside option" not only because internal remuneration was lower than foreign one, but also because internal remuneration did not offset investment illiquidity risk with a consistent premium (Bagella - Lo Cascio [3]). Investors preferred to maintain capital liquidity, i.e. depositing it in a Miami bank.

In present conditions capital is coming back and fostering sustained stock exchange flows - in May 1992 there has been registered 120 milion $ a day for the third week - (Instituto Argentino de Mercado de Capitales [19]). A large part of them is certainly represented by sellings of ex-state owned firms participations.

We must now see when capital owners will terminate their "wait and see" period, with respect to the already repatriated capital and will open a new phase turning to the market to finance new real investments.

Something similar seems about to happen in "more credible" countries. In Chile and Mexico the relationship between real interest rates and employment (CEPAL [7]) seems to confirm the passage for the capital from the "financial" to the "productive" phase.

In graph 8*a* and 8*b* it may also be observed that industrial employment increased in the period 1980-1990 together with an increase in real rates. The joint effect is stronger in Chile and less

GRAPH 8*a*

## EMPLOYMENT AND REAL INTEREST RATES

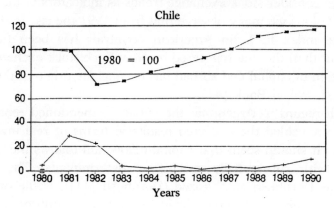

GRAPH 8*b*

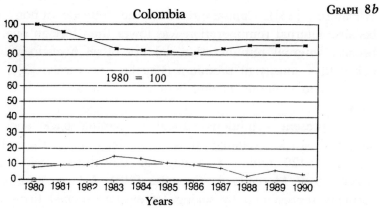

GRAPH 8*c*

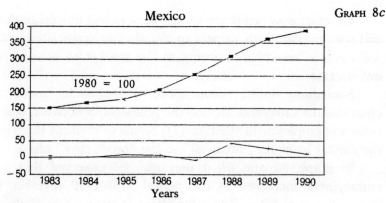

■ Employment   + Real interest rate

evident for Colombia. This could lead us to think that antinflationary policy has been so credible in Chile as to induce the industrial system to increase production and employment. This fact, without inferring too much, seems to be consistent with the previously mentioned theoretical arguments.

Finally we can remark that for the countries considered, an important impulse for industrial recovery must be given by the recovery of banking systems. As in a few occasions asserted by Stiglitz [39] and [40], the banking constraints link growth in the real sector to the financial sector, given that the extent of the risk of bankruptcy for firms and banks poses a serious hindrance on productive investment recovery. If the banking and financial systems are not efficient it is difficult to reduce credit rationing and the risk of bankruptcy is present.

In the end it may be inferred according to what is often observed and affirmed that a more efficient monetary circulation — which may be achieved by guaranteeing self-determination to central banks with regard to public deficit covering decisions and linking central bank action to national money value restoring — has several positive effects. In addition to what has been already revealed by data on investments, external debt and saving, it is necessary not to neglect the positive consequence concerning the banking and financial inter-mediation system. While hyperinflation destroys it, price stability restores it to its natural role, which is the one of contributing to optimal resource allocation, reducing risks and uncertainties affecting financial wealth.

As Graphs 9 and 10 show, the relationship between inflation variability and deposit growth is negative. The curves verify this tendency for 9 Latin American countries in the period 1983-1990 for time deposits and demand deposits in real terms. The inflation variability as monetary policy indicator underlines the need for a systematic inflation fall to realize a change in the liquidity preference functions in favor of deposits. As stressed above, if this does not happen, the intermediation system will not be able to support the recovery of investment activities with enlarged credit lines and with moderately falling real interest rates.

GRAPH 9

### INFLATION VARIABILITY AND REAL DEMAND DEPOSITS
### IN LATIN AMERICAN COUNTRIES
### (1983-1990 normalized data)

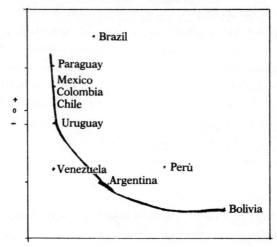

GRAPH 10

### REAL TIME DEPOSITS AND INFLATION VARIABILITY
### IN LATIN AMERICAN COUNTRIES
### (1983-1990 normalized data)

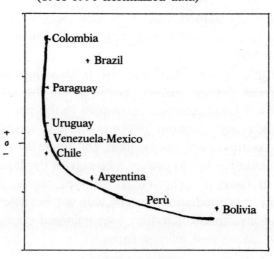

## 2. - The Econometric Analysis of Long-Term Endogenous Growth and Technical Progress.

The above-mentioned facts and issues leave a few questions unanswered. Statistical estimates can help us find our way in this theoretical jungle; however, the analysis of statistical relations based on a model has, in general, the characteristic of possessing "a mother" (i.e. the data available to the researcher) but potentially more than one father, meaning that a number of theories can produce the same specification or model structure (the reduced form of the model). At most one can reach the probabilistic conclusion that one (or more) of the theories considered is not consistent with the data, but not vice-versa.

This is the reason why the econometric analyses carried out for this second section of the paper do not imply, strictly speaking, precise theoretical references to a specific short-run approach: in other words, they are consistent with a broad spectrum of theoretical approaches. The relevant point, however, is the attempt to capture the long-run structural mechanisms.

This analysis of Latin American economies, is aimed to give a general evaluation of the following issues: 1) the relationship between economic growth and development; 2) the mechanism of growth financing, with specific reference to Argentina and Brazil as "representative" cases for the entire South American continent; 3) the role played in this mechanism by the internal economic progress of production factors, which constitutes the most promising aspect of a physiological interaction between North and South.

### 2.1 *The Relationship Between Economic and Development*

This issue involves, in turn, two distinct problems in economic measurement: $a$) the measurement and the determinants of economic growth and, within this subject, the utility of a discussion on the issue of balanced growth; $b$) the relationship — or even the close link — existing between economic growth and development; $c$) the crucial importance given to the internal economic progress of primary factors and to the external economic progress which, combined, «explain» at least 50% of global factor productivity.

Regarding the first item in the first problem (the second item will be discussed in paragraph 2.2), the criticism against adopting *per-capita* GNP or *per-capita* consumption and their growth rates as a measure of consumption is well known.

In particular, a number of recent studies have pointed out the opportunity to introduce socio-economic components in the analysis of the welfare level and degree of development attained by different countries.

For this purpose multivariate analysis methods, with a large number of socio-economic variables considered as representative of the degree of development reached, have been used in this study: these methods allow the researcher to draw a synthetic picture of these phenomena through a limited number of complex variables.

The ensuing relationship between growth and socio-economic factors in each country's responsiveness to development makes it possible to discern the outline of an actual long-term evolutionary path along which the various countries can be placed.

In this particular study the information used consists of elementary data on 18 socio-economic variables for a set of 55 countries, at different levels of economic development, including all Latin American countries considered in this analysis. The details are given in prospect 1.

The principal component analysis gives the possibility to describe the original data through a smaller number of "explanatory latent variables" and, therefore, to examine each country-observation in a composite dimension that identifies whole groups of variables. The resulting "new variables", represented in principal component terms, depend on the original data structure and translate into regression/correlation coefficients between each synthetic indicator and each elementary variable.

The first component, which "explains" nearly half of the total variability of the indicators used, is characterized by variables which can be seen as proxies of each country's welfare, quality of life and/or availability of *per-capita* social overhead capital, and therefore can be identified with that dimension which identifies the "non-GNP" components of development.

### PRINCIPAL COMPONENT ANALYSIS
(the elementary indicators used for this principal component analysis
are hereafter listed and classified into three major groups)

| Group | Variables |
|---|---|
| Socio-demographic | Life expectancy, primary and secondary education, urban population share, *per-capita* energy consumption (\*). share of cities with large population (\*\*). |
| Infrastructural | Highway and railway mileage (*per-capita*), number of commercial vehicles, private vehicles, telephones, hospital beds (\*\*). number of doctors per person (\*). |
| Economic structure | Share of agriculture, mining and manufacturing industries, services and investment over GNP (\*). |

55 countries were considered: among them are nearly all OECD countries some North-African, Mediterranean and Middle-Eastern countries and 5 Latin American countries.

From the analysis, 4 principal components, accounting for about 74% of total variance, were isolated.

The first component (which explains 50% of total variance) could be named "quality of life", as the variables which characterize it belong, in particular, to the first and second group.

For the details concerning the other components see LO CASCIO [25].

(\*) *Source*: UNCTAD, 1990.
(\*\*) *Source*: *Calendario Atlante De Agostini*, 1991.

In the second quadrant (upper left section of Graph 11) large increments in quality of life can be found in association with limited increments in *per-capita* GNP; in the first quadrant (upper right section of Graph 11), with the exception of a few extreme cases, to identical increments in quality of life correspond more than proportional increments in *per-capita* GNP. For the highest values of the scores obtained on the first factor and on *per-capita* GNP, each country's relative placement does not configure unequivocal developments; the curve depicted in this diagram gives a reasonable graphic interpolation.

The interpretation of Graph 11 is not absolutely univocal: while

GRAPH 11

RELATION BETWEEN *PER-CAPITA* GNP
AND "QUALITY OF LIFE" DIMENSION

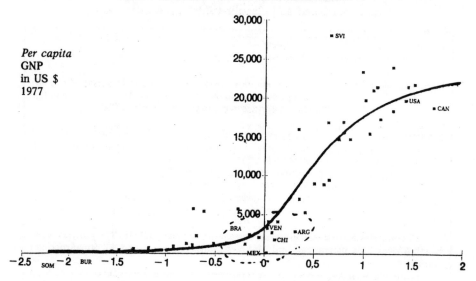

the components of quality of life affect economic productivity (as represented by *per-capita* GNP aggregate indicators), the inverse relationship is also true, that is, larger economic resources correspond to a higher welfare level. Actually the important point is that the two dimensions are interdependent but not linearly related.

Along this curve the countries located in the second quadrant (that is, below the average score for quality of life and social overhead capital) are still far away from the point where increments in infrastructure endowment and private and public consumption correspond to large increases in the system's productivity. Other countries, however, are placed, in this "ideal" growth path, at a point where, for every increase in the amount available of social overhead capital, the growth of *per-capita* GNP is more than proportional.

Regarding the countries considered in this study, their relative placement along the curve in this diagram, which represents the situation at the year 1987, suggests a few comments:

*a*) as an area, the most important Latin American countries (Argentina, Brazil, Chile, Mexico and Venezuela) are located in the exponential portion of the long-term growth curve: this gives some evidence of a high growth potential for these countries;

*b*) Brazil has the lowest value of the "quality of life" factor in this group but has a higher *per-capita* income than Mexico: this result is due in part to Mexico's demographic pressure and to the soft prices prevailing in the energy markets in 1987;

*c*) Argentina has the highest score in the group with respect to the factor "quality of life" but is unable to reach her potential per capita income level: the reason for the first fact can be traced back to the high income levels of the 1950s and '60s which allowed the satisfaction of most welfare needs and high investments in social overhead capital. The second fact is mostly due to the compression of growth and to the strain put on the entire economic structure by various negative factors, both internal (economic policy and the connected phenomena of capital flight) and international (high interest rates in the financial markets).

*d*) Chile and Venezuela are closely placed with respect to the factor "quality of life", but Venezuela fares substantially better in terms of per capita income levels, nothwithstanding the low oil prices in the international market. Apparently, in the latter country the size of the oil revenues and the income produced by the industrial structure built around the oil business, compared to a relatively small population is sufficient to keep up per-capita income.

## 2.2 *The Mechanism of Growth Financing and of Real Savings Formation*

The mechanism of capital formation (saving) and investment is described in its essential parts in the model by Bagella and Lo Cascio [2], to which we refer the reader, and an extension of the model is contained in Lo Cascio [24].

In short, the model presented here has the following characteristics:

1) it is derived from the statistical treatment of time series which assumes *ex ante* disequilibrium while allowing, in the model itself, a simulation of steady growth as a special case;

2) it uses, therefore, the resulting estimates for the analysis of the internal structure of the economies under scrutiny while a forecasting-type of analysis is left, if needed, to the time-series model without introducing steady growth hypotheses;

3) it specifies and estimates a model, although an extremely simplified one, which has been tested, with satisfactory results, with reference to developing areas/countries which are part of different sectorial (national or international) contexts (Sabattini and Lo Cascio [27]).

For instance, for a given equilibrium growth rate, the marginal propensities to save and to invest (both in real terms) derived from the econometric estimates, turn out to be costant both *ex ante* and *ex post*. If, however, in using the model the steady growth hypothesis is omitted, the parameters allow the simulation of trajectories which account for short-run adjustment dynamics.

The in-depth, although outdated, analyses done by Kuznets on US historical data, from which it emerges that the acceleration of the long-run growth rate is responsible for a reduction in the propensity to consume (and, hence, an increase in the propensity to save) while the latter is stable for a given income growth (rate), are in accordance with the more recent empirical findings by Hendry and others and are not inconsistent with Pasinetti's critique [33] and of proportional growth models (Lo Cascio [25]).

While for the estimation procedures the reader is referred to prospect 2, we would like to present and briefly comment on Graphs 12, 13, 14, 15 and 16.

Each one of them represents the pattern of long-term average propensities to save and to invest which correspond to the different values of the long-run steady growth rate of GDP.

From Graph 12, referred to Argentina, it is apparent that, in absence of financial flows from outside, the investment requirements are constantly larger than the endogenous financing capabilities and it is, therefore, impossible to indicate a sustainable growth path for the country's economy. As long as structural policies (especially the wage policy) in that country remain unchanged equilibrium seems unattainable.

Quite different is the case of Brazil (Graph 13), for which, in a

## ESTIMATION OF THE MODEL OF CAPITAL
## FORMATION AND INVESTMENT IN EQUILIBRIUM

The specification of the consumption function is the following:

*(1)*     $\log C_t - \log C_{t-1} = a + d_1 (\log Y_t - \log Y_{t-1}) + d_2 (\log Y_{t-1} - \log C_{t-1})$ (*)

The propensity to consume, in a steady growth case ($d \log Y_t = k$, $dY/Y$ = constant) can be computed:

$$MPC = \exp \left[ \frac{a - (1 - d1) \dfrac{dY}{Y}}{d_2} \right]$$

It follows that the average propensity to save is:

$$MPS = 1 - MPC = 1 - \exp \left[ \frac{a - (1 - d1) \dfrac{dY}{Y}}{d_2} \right]$$

For the basic specification of the investment function the following form was used:

*(2)*     $I_t = \lambda m Y_t - (1 - \gamma)(\lambda m Y_{t-1}) + (1 - \lambda) I_{t-1}$

where:

— $m$ represents the long-run accelerator;
— $\lambda$  represents the speed of adjustment of capital levels;
— $\gamma$  represents the rate of depreciation.

The investment function, simultaneously with equation *(1)* was:

$$I_t = a Y_t - b Y_{t-1} + c d Q_t + d I_{t-1}$$

where $d Q_t$ represents the yearly change in the share of net import over GNP. The latter variable is introduced in order to shift the estimate of equation *(2)* due o the production *surplus* or *deficit* over resource use.

So the propensity to save in a steady growth hypothesis is:

*(3)*     $$MPI = \gamma m + m \frac{dY}{Y}$$

*The estimates* (*)

The model formed by equations *(1)* and *(2)* has been estimated simultaneously, using the following accounting identity as a closure:

$$Y - CT + I + X - M$$

PROSPECT 2 *continued*

### The results obtained for Brazil:

$$ln\, C_t = \exp\left[ln\, C_{t-1} + d_0 + d_1 (\log Y_t - \log Y_{t-1}) + d_2 (\log Y_{t-1} - \log C_{t-1})\right]$$

| parameter $d_0$ | parameter $d_1$ | parameter $d_2$ | | statistical indicators | |
|---|---|---|---|---|---|
| value $\quad$ t | value $\quad$ t | value $\quad$ t | | $R^2$ | DW |
| −0.076 $\quad$ 2.2 | 0.93 $\quad$ 13.32 | 0.345 $\quad$ 2.31 | | 0.999 | 1.76 |
| (0.04) | (0.00) | (0.03) | | | |

$$I_t = a\, Y_t - b\, Y_{t-1} + c\, d\, Q_t + d\, I_{t-1}$$

| parameter $a$ | parameter $b$ | parameter $c$ | parameter $d$ | statistical indicators | |
|---|---|---|---|---|---|
| value $\quad$ t | value $\quad$ t | value $\quad$ t | value $\quad$ t | $R^2$ | DW |
| 0.419 $\quad$ 7.94 | −0.418 $\quad$ 732 | 3146 $\quad$ 3.23 | 0.938 $\quad$ 12.82 | 0.988 | 1.989 |
| (0.00) | (0.00) | (0.00) | (0.00) | | |

### The results obtained for Argentina:

$$ln C_t = \exp\left[ln C_{t-1} + d_0\, dQ_t + d_1 (\log Y_t - \log Y_{t-1}) + d_2 (\log Y_{t-1} - \log C_{t-1})\right]$$

| parameter $d_0$ | parameter $d_1$ | parameter $d_2$ | | statistical indicators | |
|---|---|---|---|---|---|
| value $\quad$ t | value $\quad$ t | value $\quad$ t | | $R^2$ | DW |
| 1.211 $\quad$ 60.7 | 0.717 $\quad$ 8.92 | 0.0395 $\quad$ 2.57 | | 0.979 | 1.892 |
| (0.00) | (0.00) | (0.02) | | | |

$$I_t = a\, Y_t - b\, Y_{t-1} + d\, I_{t-1} + e\,(Dummy)$$

| parameter $a$ | parameter $b$ | parameter $d$ | parameter $e$ | statistical indicators | |
|---|---|---|---|---|---|
| value $\quad$ t | value $\quad$ t | value $\quad$ t | value $\quad$ t | $R^2$ | DW |
| 0.394 $\quad$ 5.98 | −0.395 $\quad$ 5.97 | 0.970 $\quad$ 68.86 | −18.49 $\quad$ −1.48 | 0.874 | 2.001 |
| (0.00) | (0.00) | (0.00) | (0.15) | | |

---

(*) where $d_1$ represents the short run income elasticity of consumption, $d_2$ the adjustment speed of real income elasticity with respect to expected income and $(\log Y_{t-1} - \log C_{t-1})$ is the correction factor which brings the short-run consumption growth path back to its equilibrium trajectory.

GRAPH 12

ARGENTINA:
REAL PROPENSITY TO SAVE (MPS) AND PROPENSITY
TO INVEST (MPI) FOR DIFFERENT STEADY GROWTH RATES

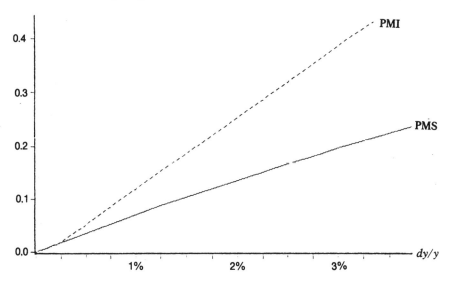

situation of external accounts balance and of internal growth financed with domestic savings, a long-run endogenous growth rate around 3% could be achieved. This rate is, however, far from the "natural" or "potential" growth rate that Brazil could attain in a sitituation of full employment of all resources. A compression of growth below this limit could balance this country's external accounts but in the long run would not be justified even assuming the economic system behaves exactly as in the last twenty years. Given the slope of MPS and MPI an impulse to development financed by transfers from abroad is capable to set in motion endogenous growth mechanisms so as to ensure the repayment of long-term loans while leaving unchanged the ratio foreign-debt/GNP, on condition that the real interest rate does not exceed 5% per year.

In the case of Brazil, the relevant issue is a more complete integration in the international trade and a growth of world demand for Brazilian products. To simulate this situation the consumption function has been adjusted with the inclusion of a term representing

GRAPH 13

BRAZIL:
REAL PROPENSITY TO SAVE (MPS) AND PROPENSITY
TO INVEST (MPI) FOR DIFFERENT STEADY GROWTH RATES

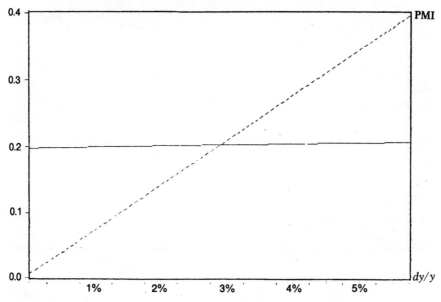

the balance of trade flows (export less import of goods and services), in constant terms. If the situation corresponding to the most favourable period for Brazilian exports (in years of vigourous expansion of the international trade) is simulated, the characteristic parabola of the marginal propensity to invest crosses the line of the marginal propensity to save at two different income growth rates, i.e. at about 3.5 and at 6.5%.

For Argentina as well the effectiveness of continuing restrictive policies is doubtful.

Three alternative scenarios have been explored for this country.

In the first case the idea for the simulation originates from the "break" found in the historical data for savings and investments before and after the year 1982. The structural change found in the data was captured in the model by a "dummy variable" which represented the effect of low interest rates on capital loans before 1982. If the value taken by the "dummy" variable before 1982 is used throughout the model, it turns out that Argentina could reach the equilibrium between saving and investment at income growth rates of 0.5% (Graph 14).

The second and more interesting case is suggested by the importance taken by the degree of openness to international trade in the function used to compute the long-run MPS (see prospect 2).

A 0.5% acceleration of the growth rate of exports would be capable to generate an endogenous, equilibrium growth rate above 2% (Graph 15).

A combination of the hypotheses made in the two previous scenarios would bring endogenous growth slightly below 3% (Graph 16).

Given the slope of MPS and MPI, an inflow of financial resources from abroad could be even more effective than for the case of Brazil. In fact, these results are perfectly consistent with those emerged in paragraph 2.1 and with the ones that will be discussed in paragraph 2.3 in connection to the potential of human capital in these two countries.

GRAPH 14

ARGENTINA: SCENARIO I

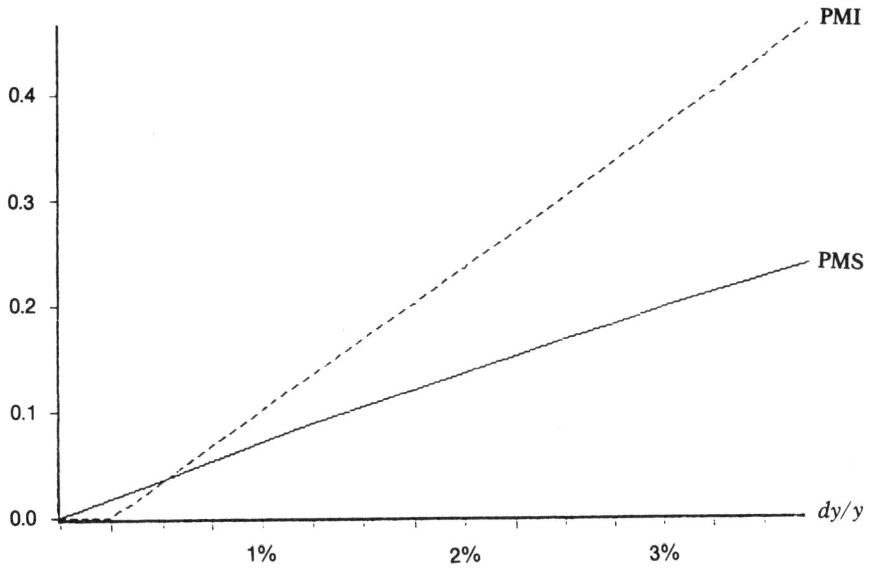

GRAPH 15

ARGENTINA: SCENARIO II

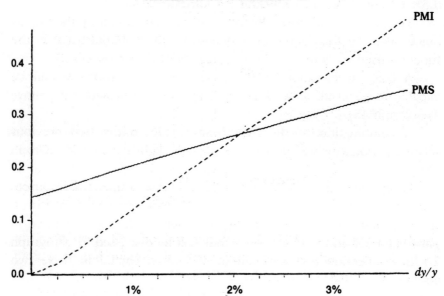

GRAPH 16

ARGENTINA: SCENARIO III

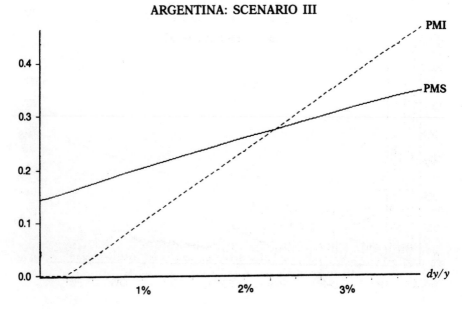

## 2.3 *The Role of Technical Progress*

For this subject it will be only necessary to remind the reader of the long and many-faceted journey of the economic thought. It will suffice to highlight the following facts:

1) the impact of technology on global productivity growth in the most developed economic systems of the western world;

2) the extent, for the newly industrialized countries, of the adjustment costs in the use of technologies employed in more developed countries, as well as the resistance of the latter — in terms of market, institutions, economic policy — to make technology transfers easier.

The failure of policies aimed to restore a balance between weak and strong areas of the international system can be imputed to the two aforementioned factors, together with the difficulties stemming from the international capital market.

Triffin [42] has stressed the peculiarity, in the last decade, of a mechanism of formation and investment of world real savings for which the *surplus* from Japan and the FDR has not been able to offset the US *deficit*, so it turns out that the whole of external areas is presently financing OECD's growth rather than the reverse, which could be expected given the differences in consumption and welfare levels.

In this overview, however, one positive aspect, in connection to economic and financial relations among areas, should be stressed. The reference is, in particular, to the favourable impact of the labor input on net productivity (i.e. of the labor augmenting technical progress).

The remarks proposed in paragraph 2.2 with reference to Argentina, largely depend upon the local responsiveness to foreign investment and to the progressive transition to a true market economy.

This responsiveness is, in turn, subject on one hand to the characteristics of primary inputs, particularly to the improvement in their quality (factor augmenting progress) and, on the other hand, on the evolutionary potential of the productive mix and of the competitive position on the international markets.

The first of these aspects has been evaluated, for Argentina and Brazil, through translog specifications of the cost and factor demand

## ESTIMATION OF FACTOR AUGMENTING TECHNICAL PROGRESS

In this model the translog (transcendental logarithmic) form was adopted for the cost function ($TC$), considering only two factor inputs: labor ($L$) and capital ($K$):

$$\log CT = a_0 \log Y + b_0 \log X + \sum_{i=L,K} \alpha_i (\log P_i - \gamma_{it}T) +$$

$$+ \frac{1}{2} \sum_{i,j=L,K} \beta_{ij} (\log P_i - \gamma_{it}T)(\log P_j - \gamma_{jt}T)$$

$$\sum_{i=L,K} \delta_i (\log P_i - \gamma_{it}T) \log X$$

where:

$a_0$ : is the scale economies parameter. If $a0 = 1$ economies to scale are constant; if $a0 < 1$ economies to scale are increasing, if $a0 > 1$ economies to scale are decreasing;

$\alpha i$ : are parameters of income distribution to primary factors;

$\beta_{ij}$ : are substitution parameters;

$\gamma_{it}$ : are parameters representing technical progress;

$P_i$ : $i = L, K$ represents factor $i$ price;

$x$ : indicates exports as a "state" variable representative of the degree of integration in international markets.

In order to obtain homogeneity in prices and symmetry properties it is necessary to impose a few contraints on the equation parameters:

$$\sum_i \alpha_i = 1 \qquad \beta_{ij} = \beta_{ji}$$

$$\sum_i \beta_{ij} = \sum_j \beta_{ij} = 0$$

$$\sum_i \delta_i = 0$$

The estimation procedure has been carried out simultaneously with the equations of factor share over total cost:

$$q_i \frac{d \log CT}{d \log P_i} = \alpha_i + \sum_j \beta_{ij} (\log P_j - \gamma_{jt}T) + \delta_i \log X$$

Actually, the model would require introducing higher order terms, which, however, have been neglected to avoid having too large a number of parameters to estimate. Furthermore we have assumed constant returns to scale ($a = 1$) while the parameter that should represent capital augmenting technical progress has not taken a value significantly different from zero.

PROSPECT 3 *continued*

Therefore the estimated model has taken the following form:

$$\log CT = \log Y + \alpha_L \, (\log P_L - \gamma_{Lt}T) +$$

$$+ (1 - \alpha_L) \log P_K + \frac{1}{2} \beta \, (\log P_L -$$

$$- \gamma_{Lt}T)^2 + \frac{1}{2} \beta \, (\log P_K)^2 -$$

$$- \beta \, (\log P_L - \gamma_{Lt}T) \log P_K + \delta \, (\log P_L - \gamma_{Lt}T) \log X +$$
$$b_0 \log X - \delta \log P_K \log X$$

$$q_L = \alpha_L + \beta \, (\log P_L - \gamma_{Lt}T) - \beta \log P_K + \delta \log X$$

$$q_K = 1 - q_L = (1 - \alpha_K) + \beta \log P_K - \beta \, (\log P_L - \gamma_{Lt}T) - \delta \log X$$

*For Brazil the following estimates have been obtained*

| parameter $\alpha_L$ | | parameter $\beta$ | | parametero $\beta_{Lt}$ | | parameter $b0$ | | parameter $\delta$ | |
|---|---|---|---|---|---|---|---|---|---|
| value | $t$ | value | $t$ | value | $t$ | value | $t$ | value | $t$ |
| 0.745 | 6.96 | 0.263 | 8.02 | 0.014 | 4.385 | 0.244 | 17.34 | 0.033 | 2.56 |
| | (0.00) | | (0.00) | | (0.00) | | (0.02) | | |
| statistics | | $R^2$ | | | | 0.999 | | | |
| | | $DW$ | | | | 0.546 | | | |

*For Argentina the results obtained were:*

| parameter $\alpha_L$ | | parameter $\beta$ | | parameter $\gamma_{Lt}$ | | parameter $b0$ | | parameter $\delta$ | |
|---|---|---|---|---|---|---|---|---|---|
| value | $t$ | value | $t$ | value | $t$ | value | $t$ | value | $t$ |
| 0.796 | 133 | 0.231 | 44.7 | 0.030 | 21.8 | | | | |
| | (0.00) | | (0.00) | | (0.00) | (*) | | (*) | |
| statistics | | $R^2$ | | | | 0.988 | | | |
| | | $DW$ | | | | 1.4 | | | |

(*) The parameter was not significantly different from zero thus has been constrained to a zero value in the equation.

functions. This approach allows the identification of some characteristics of a productive structure without necessarily involving a particular production function.

In the model specification, as usual, time has been introduced, in multiplicative form, as a proxy for factor augmenting technical progress.

The procedural details and statistical results are reported in prospect 3.

From the empirical results a clear-cut differentiation between the labor and the capital factor emerges. The former shows a growth rate of the factor augmenting scale (evolution of the intrinsic productivity or factor quality) which can be estimated close to 1.4% for Brazil and to 3% for Argentina. As for the capital input, the estimated growth rate is close to zero and the statistical significance of the parameter does not allow a rejection of the null hypothesis: this is why the estimate has been constrained to zero.

The results are consistent with other assessments of the evolution of human capital, for the educational and training related aspects, in Argentina as well as in other developing countries (Corbo [9]).

Similar estimates have been obtained for other countries in the early stages of development, such as Egypt: the same functional specification however gives, for this country, a growth rate of the labor augmenting technical progress around 2.2%.

## 3. - Conclusions

The corrective measures prescribed by the World Bank and by the IMF show some sort of squint: on one hand very rigorous short term monetary and fiscal policies are urged, which would be capable of a substantial reduction of the external debt nothwithstanding the high (in real terms) interest rates; on the other hand, structural convergence measures, implying an improvement of the overall efficiency of each country's economic system, are required. Rigorous monetary and fiscal policies and structural policies can be combined: it is, however, necessary to evaluate the different timing during which the desired effects can be produced.

Regarding Latin American countries, it is of paramount importance to avoid stopping the enormous progress obtained from the human capital. The negative ripercussions could be unbearable by those countries and extremely serious for the US and the world economy.

In a historical perpective encompassing several decades, international constraints and deferred effects of "institutional changes" within individual countries bear a considerable weight.

It is not by chance, in this regard, that the major countries in Latin America held their ground better than other extra-OECD countries: in recent times aid given in form of grants, as well as arrangements to convert short-term debt into long-term debt, have partly offset the burden of debt servicing. On the other hand, in a long-term perspective, it becomes clear that a stronger trade integration is called for, as well as careful monitoring of the accumulation, in multiplicative form, of the effects of balancing policies simultaneously adopted by the majority of world countries.

If expectations regarding the levels of demand are poor and the user cost of capital (in real terms) is too high, a reinvestment of additional real savings (assuming they can be generated) in activities aimed at widening the productive base becomes difficult to envisage.

Of course, in different countries the effectiveness of restrictive monetary and fiscal policies in modifying the behaviour of economic agents can be stronger or weaker. In general, the constraints, deriving from such policies, to the exploitation of technical progress and the divergence between its rate of growth and the growth rate of demand, configure a situation of deficiency in effective demand coupled with structural, inflationary pressures, which would cast serious doubts on the possibility of achieving the goals set on long-term debt reduction.

Restoring sustained growth paths in Latin American countries is then a difficult and not readily attainable task. Foreign and domestic policies are called for to shorten the transition from stagnation to recovery, mainly through: *a*) the restoration of domestic currency values avoiding public deficit monetization; *b*) measures to increase the efficiency of the banking and financial systems; *c*) the adoption of institutional and structural policies aimed to increase the openness of the industrial sector to international competition (privatization and removal of both tariff and non-tariff barriers).

Moreover, referring to the condition of small open economies, as Latin American countries may generally be considered, it is necessary: 1) a higher degree of openness of G7 markets to Latin American exports; 2) the achievement of an integrated regional market in Latin America; 3) a strengthened Nord-South economic cooperation aimed at mitigating the social costs of stabilization policies (infrastructural, educational and health investments).

On the extent to which these objectives will be attained depends a positive change in domestic and foreign agents expectations with respect to: *a*) money re-evaluation and the credibility of economic policies in Latin American countries (with particular regard to monetary policy); *b*) an increase in expected profits from productive investments; *c*) an increase of savings no longer distorted by inflationary expectations; *d*) the debt servicing capability.

If human capital is still nowadays a fundamental resource of Latin America with respect to other non-OECD countries, no short-cuts are allowed along the way to prevent its waste. A way that must be carefully followed as it bridges the gap between stagnation and the long-sought recovery.

## BIBLIOGRAPHY

[1] BAGELLA M.: *Gli istituti di credito speciale ed il mercato finanziario (1947-1962)*, Milano, F. Angeli, 1987.

[2] BAGELLA M. - LO CASCIO M.: «External Debt and Savings in Latin American Countries», *Rivista di politica economica*, October 1990.

[3] —— - —— : «Ragioni di scambio, debito esterno e crescita dei paesi dell'America Latina: considerazioni in tema di politiche di aggiustamento», *Quaderni dell'osservatorio sull'economia internazionale*, n. 1, 1990.

[4] BLANCARD O.J. - FISCHER S.: *Lectures on Macroeconomics*, Cambridge (Mass.), MIT Press, 1989.

[5] BARRO R.J. - KING R.G.: «Time-Separable Preferences and Intertemporal Substitution Models of the Business Cycle, *The Quarterly Journal of Economics*, vol. 66, n. 6, 1984.

[6] BRESCIANI TURRONI C.: *The Economics of Inflation, a Study of Currency Depreciation in Postwar Germany*, London, Sir Halley Stewart Publications, 1937.

[7] CEPAL: «El Comercio de Manifacturas de America Latina: Evolucion y Estrutura 1962-1989», *Doc. LC/R*, n. 1506, 1991.

[8] —— : «Estabilization y Equidad en America Latina en los Ochenta», *Doc. 1944, Division de Desarrollo Economico*, n. 91-12, 1992.

[9] CORBO V.: «Debt, Adjustment and Growth», *Quaderni dell'osservatorio sull'economia internazionale*, 1990.

[10] CORDEN W.M.: «Macroeconomic Policy and Growth: Some Lessons of Experience», Proceedings of the *World Bank Annual Conference on Development Economics*, Washington (DC), 1990.

[11] DORNBUSH R.: «Policies to Move from Stabilization to Growth», Proceedings of the *World Bank Annual Conference on Development Economics*, Washington (DC), 1990.

[12] FISHER J.: *The Theory of Interest Rate*, New York, MacMillan, 1930.

[13] FISCHER S.: *Rational Expectations and Economic Policies*, Chicago (Ill.), University of Chicago Press, 1980.

[14] FRANKEL J.A.: «Quantifying International Capital Mobility in the 1980's», in BERNHEIM E.D. - SHOVEN B.J.: *National Saving and Economic Performance*, NBER, n. 2856, Chicago (Ill.), The University of Chicago Press, 1989.

[15] GREENWOOD J. - HERCOWITZ Z. - HUFFMAN G.W.: «Investment, Capacity Utilization and the Real Business Cycle», *American Economic Review*, vol. 78, n. 3, 1988.

[16] GROSSMAN G.M. - HELPMAN E.: *Innovation and Growth in the Global Economy*, Cambridge (Mass.), MIT Press, 1991.

[17] HENDRY D.F. - WALLIS K.F. (eds.): *Econometric and Quantitative Economics*, Oxford, Blackwell, 1984.

[18] IMF: *Private Market Financing for Developing Countries*, Washington (DC), World Economic and Financial Survey, 1991.

[19] INSTITUTO ARGENTINO DE MERCADO DE CAPITALES: *Informe Mensual*, Buenos Aires, March 1992.

[20] KINDLEBERGER C.: «A Historical Perspective», in LESSARD D.L. - WILLIAMSON J. (eds.): *Capital Flight and Third World Debt*, Washington (DC), Institute for International Economics, 1987.

[21] KIDLAND F. - PRESCOTT E.C.: «Rules rather than Discretion: the Inconsistency of Optimal Plans», *Journal of Political Economy*, vol. 85, 1977.

[22] LEJIONHUFWUD A.: *On keynesian Economics and the Economics of Keynes*, Londra, Oxford University Press, 1968.

[23] LASSARD D.L. - WILLIAMSON J.: *Capital Flight and Third World Debt*, Washington (DC), Institute for International Economics, 1987.

[24] LO CASCIO M.: «La crescita del risparmio reale nell'Europa occidentale: analisi delle tendenze», *Rivista di politica economica*, May 1991.

[25] —— : «Methodes Quantitatives Pour l'Analise du Dévelopment Economique: Background Théorique et Etude des cas d'Especes», Class-notes, Geneva, 1992.

[26] —— : «La dimensione dello sviluppo, il sistema degli scambi ed il finanziamento della crescita», paper presented at the International Conference *Culture and Development of the Southern Shore of the Mediterranean*, Anacapri, 20 June 1992.

[27] LO CASCIO M. - SABATTINI G.: «L'economia sarda nei rapporti economici internazionali», *Rapporto Ecoter/IPRE*, Milano, F. Angeli, 1992.

[28] LUCAS R.E.: *Studies in Business Cycle Theory*, Cambridge (Mass.), MIT Press, 1981.

[29] LUCAS R.E. - RAPPING L.A.: «Real Wages, Employment and Inflation», *The Journal of Political Economy*, vol. 77, n. 5, 1969.

[30] MAYER T.: «The Empirical Significance of the Real Balance Effect», *Quarterly Journal of Economics*, 1959, vol. LXXIII.

[31] MINSKY H.: «L'instabilità finanziaria: l'attuale dilemma e la struttura del sistema bancario e finanziario», in CESARINI F. - ONADO M. (eds.): *Struttura finanziaria e stabilità del sistema finanziario*, Bologna, il Mulino, 1979.

[32] MUNDELL R.: «Trade Balance Patterns as Global General Equilibrium: the Seventeenth Approach to the Balance of Payments», *Rivista di politica economica*, June 1989.

[33] PASINETTI L.: *Structural Change and Economic Growth: a Theoretical Essay on the Dynamics of the Wealth of Nations*, Cambridge, Cambridge University Press, 1981.

[34] PATINKIN D.: *Money, Interest, and Prices*, New York, Harper and Row, 1965.

[35] PHELPS E.S.: *Seven Schools of Macroeconomic Thought*, Oxford, Oxford Economic Press, 1990.

[36] RODRIGUEZ C.A.: «Managing Argentina's External Debt: the Contributions of Debt Swaps», Centro de Estudios Macroeconomicos de Argentina, Documentos de Trabajo, n. 68, 1990.

[37] SACHS J.D.: «Conditionality, Debt Relief and the Developing Countries Debt Crisis», in SACHS J.D. (eds.): *Developing Country Debt and the World Economy*, NBER, Chicago, University of Chicago Press, 1989.

[38] SELOWSKY M.: «Preconditions for Recovery of Latin America's Growth», *Finance and Development*, vol. 27, n. 2, 1990.

[39] STIGLITZ J.E.: «Credit Rationing in Markets with Imperfect Information», *American Economic Review*, vol. 73, n. 5, 1981.

[40] —— : «Capital Markets and Economic Fluctuations in Capitalist Economies», Papers and Proceedings, *European Economic Review*, 1992, vol. 36 - n. 2/3.

[41] TOBIN J.: «A General Equilibrium Approach to Monetary Theory», *Journal of Money Credit and Banking*, n. 1, 1969.

[42] TRIFFIN R.: «IMS: International Monetary System... or Scandal?», *Rivista di politica economica*, May 1991.

[43] WIKSELL K.: *Lectures on Political Economy*, vol. II, Londra, Routledge e Kegan Paul, 1935, reprint 1962.

[44] WORLD BANK: *World Debt Tables*, Washington, World Bank, 1992.

# V - LESSONS FROM JAPAN

# Engine of the Rising Sun:
# Productivity Growth in Postwar Japan

**Koichi Hamada - Tetsushi Honda** (*)
Yale University

## 1. - Introduction

When World War II ended in August 1945, the Japanese economy was really devastated. One could see only weeds and debris in the center of Tokyo. Nobody would have imagined that Japan would recover from the damage of the war within several years, much less that in the following decades she would achieve such a rapid growth, later called "the miracle of the rising sun".

In a longer perspective, Japan maintained a reasonably high rate of growth after she started her "modern economic growth" around the mid 1880s (Ohkawa and Rosovsky [33]) as illustrated by graph 1 (adapted from Ito [16]). At the same time, the graph and table 1 (adapted from Summers and Heston [37]) show that Japan enjoyed economic growth at a remarkably high speed from 1960 through 1973, a rate that has rarely been observed in economic history. This paper is designed to explore the enigmas of this fast growth in postwar Japan.

Growth accounting literature provides us alternative, often quite different, estimates of the contributions of factors of growth. They do not give, however, the story that explains the qualitative nature of the development process. Now the new growth theory focusses its attention to the qualitative process of invention, technological diffusion,

(*) We thank Munehisa Kasuya for useful discussions and Carolyn Beaudin for her editorial advice.

*Advise*: the numbers in square brackets refer to the Bibliography in the appendix.

GRAPH 1

### JAPAN'S GNP (*)

(*) (Logarithm of GNP. Billion yen, 1980 price). Adapted from ITO [16].

TABLE 1

### GROWTH RATES FOR 1960-1973, 1973-1980, 1980-1988
### GDP AND GDP PER CAPITA (*)

|              | 1960-1973 | | 1973-1980 | | 1980-1988 | |
|--------------|-----|---------|-----|---------|-----|---------|
|              | GDP | GDP/pop | GDP | GDP/pop | GDP | GDP/pop |
| Japan .............. | 9.8 | 8.7 | 3.9 | 2.7 | 3.6 | 3.0 |
| France.............. | 5.7 | 4.6 | 2.6 | 2.1 | 1.6 | 1.1 |
| Germany .......... | 4.4 | 3.5 | 2.1 | 2.2 | 1.6 | 1.7 |
| Italy............... | 5.1 | 4.4 | 4.2 | 3.8 | 2.3 | 2.0 |
| U.K. ............. | 3.2 | 2.7 | 1.1 | 1.1 | 2.9 | 2.7 |
| U.S.A. ............ | 4.0 | 2.7 | 2.1 | 1.1 | 3.3 | 2.3 |

(*) Adapted from SUMMERS - HESTON [37].

externalities, learning by doing, and increasing returns. The empirical assessment of various possible reasons of endogenous growth is still at its incipient stage. This paper is an attempt to evaluate empirically, taking Japan as an example, which factors were important for motivating the rapid growth process.

In section 2 we will give a concise history of the postwar Japanese economy in order to give the background for our empirical analysis. In section 3, after reviewing growth accounting studies, we will give heuristic explanations of possible factors that drove Japan's rapid growth. In section 4, we will ask by the Granger causality analysis how investment in general, or that in machinery and equipment, affected productivity increase and growth. In section 5, we will analyze the role of borrowed or imported technology, and point out the importance of the environment in which people assimilated, and adjusted themselves to, the borrowed technology. In section 6, we will give an overview of the pattern in the mobility of factors, in particular, of labor. In the last section we will summarize our results and comment on the impact of government policies on Japan's rapid growth.

## 2. - The Trajectory of Japan's Postwar Growth

Let us start from a short history of Japan's postwar growth in order to give the reader a concrete image of the process we will discuss in this paper. Emphasis will be placed on the role of the postwar reforms under the US occupation, because, in our opinion, the reforms substantially changed the incentive structure and laid the foundation for Japan's postwar development.

Before commencing the discussion of the role of occupational reforms, we may mention the legacy of wartime goods-mobilization and price-control policies that substantially affected the economic policies of the immediate postwar period. According to Nakamura ([28], Chapter 1) the spread of life-time employment and seniority wage was facilitated by the wage and price freeze during the war. The price and production control of rice started with the food administration system established in 1941. The authority of the Ministry of

International Trade and Industry (MITI) stems from the power of the Commerce and Industry Ministry under the wartime emergency (Nakamura [28], pp. 14-9). Thus, even though there are views that emphasize economic rationales rather than wartime control as the causes of the emergence of seniority wages and lifetime employment (See, for example, Taira, [38], chapter 5), we cannot neglect the institutional effect of wartime policies.

At least, the *Material Mobilization Plan* dated in 1937 seemed to have triggered the idea of the *Priority Production System*. This system, which was adopted at an earlier stage of the postwar recovery and based on an idea similar to Leontief's input-output analysis, was purported to channel products reciprocally among the more important sectors first: surplus steel to coal and resulting production of coal to steel. Only when the targets for the most important products were fulfilled, would the surplus would be put into the next priority sectors.

In order to finance the loops of the priority production system, the Reconstruction Finance Bank wa established in January 1947. Savings are directly channelled to investment projects. In March 1949, the Reconstruction Finance Bank owned about one third of the total nationwide loans to industries. This point is important with reference to the interesting thesis by Zysman [43] that the industrial policy of Japan has been implemented through the allocation of financial resources by the *Fiscal Investment Loan Program* (*FILP*).

So much for the effects of war-time policies. When World War II ended, Japan was under the occupation of the Supreme Commander of Allied Powers (SCAP) or the General Head Quarters (GHQ). (Even though SCAP represented thirteen countries, including the United Kingdom and the Soviet Union, the occupation policies actually adopted were mostly planned and executed by the United States). First, the occupation's objective was to demilitarize and democratize Japan, and not necessarily to promote the economic recovery of Japan. Due to the deepening of the cold war in Asia, the American occupation policy changed around 1947 to help economic reconstruction in Japan and to build an industrial power in the Pacific.

Three important economic reforms implemented by the occupation were land reform, the dissolution of the *zaibatsu*, and labor reform. We will add the educational reform to the list because it helped Japan mold the excellence in human capital that was an essential ingredient of the postwar growth.

## 2.1 *Land Reform*

A radical land reform was implemented in October 1946. The maximal amount of land held by non-cultivating residents was normally limited to 1 cho ($=2.45$ acres or a little than 1 hectare); that of landed tenants was 3 cho. The land in excess of the limit held by the land owners was sold to their tenant farmers at nominal prices, which was tantamount to confiscation in many cases (Cohen [4]). Thus the ownership of about 81% of all the tenant land was transferred to the former tenants (Uchino [40]; Kosai [24]). The fragmented land ownership, which has not been changed up to the present, is a constraint against developing a large, more productive, farm. At the time of implementation, however, the positive impact of the reform was obvious. New farmers with land were more motivated to work, to improve land and to modernize agricultural technology, all of which led to a remarkable increase in agricultural productivity.

## 2.2 *Dissolution of* Zaibatsu

The *Zaibatsu*, the family-based, large industrial and financial combine, was regarded by GHQ as an important source of Japan's military power and an obstacle to democratic business practices (Hadley [10]). Stock-holding companies were liquidated or deprived of their stock-holdings. Two typical trading companies, Mtsui Bussan and Mitsubishi Shoji were dissolved. In 1947 *Antitrust Law* was enacted and the Fair Trade Commission was established. The breakup of a large concentration of business power gave industries more flexible structures where new enterprises were able to compete freely regardless of whether they belonged to a *zaibatsu* group. At the same time, GHQ purged business leaders who were thought to have cooperated with the military government. Younger people were promoted as the leaders of many companies so that new management conducted business activities with youthful vigor and flexibility.

After the *San Francisco Peace Treaty* in 1952, *Antitrust Law* was revised in the direction of relaxation of restricting monopoly power. In the meantime, *zaibatsu* firms and others were reorganized as keiretsu, financial linkages. The effect of *zaibatsu* resolution, however, should not be undervalued, because it helped the creation of a competitive, kin-free business atmosphere. Business relations in keiretsu are much less hierarchical, more democratic and more functional than those in *zaibatsu* used to be (Hadley [10]).

## 2.3 *Labor Reform*

Three statutes were enacted to establish the basic rights of workers: 1) *Trade Union Law* (1945) for the right of workers to unionize; 2) *Labor Standards Law* (1947) for the minimum requirements for working conditions, which had sometimes been inhumanly harsh particularly for women and minors; and 3) *Labor Relations Adjustment Law* (1947) for the settlement of labor disputes through strikes, negotiations and agreements. Encouraged by the legislation, the number of unions increased at a tremendous speed. Compared to about five hundred unions that existed in 1945, the number of unions exceeded twenty three thousand in 1947 and thirty three tousand in 1948. In 1947 more than half of the workers were unionized (Kosai [24]). Disputes and strikes took place quite frequently, and productive processes were disrupted seriously in many firms.

A general strike was planned on February 1st in 1947. To the disappointment of Japanese labor leaders, GHQ ordered the strike stopped; reflecting the fact that the occupation policy had become less liberal due to emergence of the cold war. In any case, though Americans probably had in mind to develop the American-style craft or industry-wide trade unions, Japanese unions turned out to be enterprise-based unions. At first those unions were quite militant, and Japanese industrial relations traced a thorny path. It was not until the resolution of the Miike coal mine strike in 1960 that Japanese labor relations attained some calmness. Somehow, with skillful tactics, carrots and sticks, the management in private sectors succeeded in taming trade unions after many serious strikes (Gordon [8]).

## 2.4 *Social and Educational Reforms*

The new constitution based on an idealized form of pacifism and democracy was drafted by the GHQ and "imposed" on the Japanese in 1947. Educational reforms, which were introduced by *American New-Dealers* who viewed Japan as experimental ground, brought the core curriculum, and a single educational channel of 6 (elementary), 3 (junior high), 3 (senior high), 4 (college) system in place of the multi-channel system that screened students into *elites*, technicians, and non-*elites* in their young age. After the occupation period, reactionary changes moved Japan's education back towards more traditional directions. Even the left-wing teachers union ironically transformed the education based on pragmatism into a style of extremely un-individualistic uniformity.

On the whole, however, the educational reform secured homogeneous workers that possessed high verbal and quantitative skill, and embedded competitive meritocracy that turned Japan into a highly mobile society with respect to social status. Moreover, pacifism enabled the Japanese economy to dispense with large military expenditures. Although there was an element of luck in the course of political events in the Pacific, one could say that the economic success of postwar Japan was partly a dividend of her pacifism.

At the end of the war, there was a wide gap between the limited availability of goods and the massive level of accumulated nominal wealth, a gap that naturally triggered inflation. The war destroyed about one-quarter of the nation's wealth. On the other hand, an enormous amount of liquid assets including government debt was in the hands of the public. Prices were controlled, even after the war, by the government at lower levels so that purchasing power based on accumulated nominal wealth created intense excess demand in almost all sectors. Thus the postwar Japanese economy faced a typical case of monetary overhang. Black-market prices soared. It is fascinating to describe the process of monetary stabilization and recovery (Hamada and Kasuya [12]), but here we will briefly summarize the course of the events.

As an attempt to cure inflation, the emergency monetary measures were announced in February 1946 by GHQ. All the deposits in financial institutions were frozen, all the old yen currency was to be exchanged for the new yen, and wages could be paid up to 500 yen monthly in new yen, but the remainder was to be paid into the frozen accounts.

The effects of these drastic measures, however, turned out to be only temporary for the following reasons: first, there were hidden subsidies for carrying out the priority production plan as well as for keeping multiple exchange» rates. Those subsidies created budget deficits, which were financed by the Bank of Japan credit, that is, by printing money. Secondly, there were several loopholes in these measures. For example, while the payment of taxes using the blocked deposit was possible, government expenditures to private sectors were made by issuing new notes or unblocking deposits. Also companies were allowed to withdraw new yen by checks to pay for operating expenditures. Naturally, attempts to contain inflation by a scheme, without coherent measures for restraining the government budget and for linking the current account deficit to the reduction of money supply, had only a limited impact on the stabilization of the economy.

One of the crucial questions of the postwar Japanese economy is how to evaluate the effectiveness of the priority production system. In a budget speech of July 1946, citing explicitly *The General Theory*, Fiscal Minister Ishibashi told the Diet, in defense of the priority production system, «In order to achieve the goal of resuming production there is no harm if government deficits occur. Since both capital stock and labor force were clearly underemployed, the problem was simply that bottleneck factors such as the lack of raw materials from overseas stood in the way» (Kosai [24], p. 43).

We must give some credit to the priority production system and the macroeconomic policy that supported it. Production level recovered steadily by 8.6% in fiscal year (FY: April to March next year) 1947 and by 12.6% in FY 1948. Industrial production showed a more vigorous upward trend that was close to 50% in (calendar year) 1948 (1).

However, in terms of the modern disequilibrium analysis, the Japanese economy was not under the Keynesian unemployment

---

(1) For a positive assessment of the priority production system, see UCHINO [40]).

where excess supply exists in both the goods and the labor market. It was a typical case of classical unemployment in which excess supply exists in labor market but excess *demand* exists in goods market. «To cure Keynesian unemployment, one would lower prices or raise wages. To cure classical unemployment one should do precisely the reverse» (Malinvaud [27]). From this standpoint, Ishibashi mistook the classical unemployment for the Keynesian one.

To start a sustained growth, price stability was essential for recovering business confidence, and for motivating people to work harder as well as to save more. In order to prepare her remarkable growth trajectory, Japan needed to pass through a painful period of recession. In 1948 the US government sent Joseph Dodge, a Detroit banker, who helped stabilize the postwar economy of West Germany, to advise on the Japanese economy.

As a strong believer of market economy, Dodge advised the Japanese government to achieve a genuine balance in the general budget. A fixed exchange rate for the yen, 360 yen per US dollar, was established in April 1949, and was to continue until 1971. In the international environment in which the rest of the world was under price stability, a return to a fixed exchange rate meant a commitment to price stability through the price-specie-flow mechanism: we may reverse the logic of Milton Friedman and say that a fixed exchange rate is good when one *cannot* trust one's own monetary authority.

As a result of the *Dodge Plan*, the volume of Bank of Japan notes declined; black market prices fell steeply; the abolition of commodity and price controls gradually progressed; and increases in savings rates occurred. On the other hand, this cold-turkey policy had a substantial cooling impact on economic activities. Mining and manufacturing production faltered. The future of exports under the fixed exchange rate was threatened by the devaluation of the pound sterling in October. Inventories piled up due to the financial stringency and the sluggishness of demand.

Coincidentally, on June 25, 1950, the Korean War broke out, involving the US military as well. As orders for special procurement accumulated, exports grew rapidly along with the increasing world-wide demand. Markets boomed, inventory backlogs were wiped out, and mining and manufacturing production also started to increase at a fast tempo which eventually reached an increase of about 50% during the year. The balance of payments improved, sources of funds became ample, and profits rose as well.

The decade of 1950s can be regarded as the period of preparation and transition to the golden era of high speed growth after 1960. The drastic stabilization policy of the *Dodge Plan* and the Korean War procurement boom that followed enabled the Japanese economy to complete its reconstruction stage. The GNP exceeded the prewar level in 1953. The 1956 *Economic White Paper* of the Economic Stabilization Board stated: «We are no longer in the postwar reconstruction period».

Macroeconomic management in these years traced a path of "stop and go" policy in order to maintain the fixed exchange parity. Excessive expansion of the domestic economy generated a balance of payments deficit, which necessitated monetary contraction. Thus followed the succession of booms and recessionary balance-of-payments adjustment periods (Nakamura, [28], pp. 51-4). In 1955 Japan enjoyed a growth rate above 10% with price stability and balance-of-payments surplus, this was called "boom in volume" (instead of price). The prosperity was interrupted in 1956 by a balance of payments deficit, but soon after the next prosperity started. The *Economic White Paper* named the successive booms by referring to Japan's mythology in reverse order: the Jimmu Boom (1956-1957, the best since Emperor Jimmu who was assumed to be the first emperor in Japan), and the Iwato Boom (1959-1961, the best since Iwato, the stone cave behind which the Sun Goddess hid herself out of rage).

In the meantime, the prerequisites for the forthcoming high growth period were steadily established. The Japanese labor force incorporated highly educated and disciplined human capital. During the 1950s there was an abundant, if not unlimited, supply of labor from rural areas. In 1955 a new system of wage bargaining *shunto* (Spring Offensives) started, in which management and trade unions bargained once a year in the spring. In the negotiation of *shunto*, relevant economic data such as productivity increases, and producer as well as consumer price indices were taken into consideration for calculating the rates of wage increases. One may interpret this as the Japanese form of incomes policy. Serious labor confrontations in large companies in the private sector ended with the Miike coal mine strike in 1960, though unions in public or semi-public sectors such as those of public school teachers and of National Railway workers remained quite militant for many years.

The savings rate and the investment rate remained low during the 1940s, but started to increase in the 1950s. Both the household savings rate and the rate of private plant and equipment investment exceeded 10% in this decade, though still short of the high rates of more than 20% during the next decade. Technological improvement in both agriculture and manufacturing industry was also proceeding, resources were transferred from less productive to more productive sectors, and the pace of progress quickened through import of foreign technology (Goto [9]).

In 1960, the question of whether or not to renew the *US-Japan Security Treaty* that had been initially signed with the *Peace Treaty*, sharply divided the Japanese into two groups, those who advocated the continuation of military alliance and those who did not. Prime minister Kishi, who had once been a Commerce minister of the wartime cabinet and was a conservative, had to cancel the visit of President Eisenhower and subsequently resigned due to strong protests and demonstrations. Tokyo looked as if it were on the eve of revolution. Labor relations were also heated by the Miike coal mine strike.

Prime Minister Ikeda, who succeeded Kishi, took a more modest political attitude and tried to direct people's attention to economic growth. The famous *Income Doubling Plan* by Ikeda, — that was nothing more than an indicative plan without any enforceability in a market economy like Japan — opened the way to the era of high-speed growth during the 1960s (Kosai [24]). Ikeda forecasted that the real GNP would be doubled in the following ten years. People hardly believed that the plan would be realized; nominal income might be doubled, they thought, but inflation would wipe out the nominal gain. To the surprise of the public, real income more than doubled in the next decade, and per capita real income even tripled between 1960 and 1973. The 1960s was the most remarkable decade of the Japanese economy as far as the real growth rate is concerned. The unemployment rate was low, around 1.1-1.3%, except for 1960 when it was 1.6%.

The Tokyo Olympics in 1964 were instrumental in modernizing the road network; in 1970, nearly one third of the non-agriculture households (and more of the agriculture households) owned a car. By the end of the decade, "the three Cs" (car, cooler and color televisions) became popular belongings of many households.

Along with this rapid development, environmental problems that had already started in the late 1950s became more and more serious. Water and air were polluted by industrial waste and automobile emissions. In some extreme circumstances, students fainted in a schoolyard photochemical smog; policemen used masks to control traffic in Tokyo. Serious cases were brought to courts and the government was compelled to legislate the *Anti-pollution Act* in 1967.

Because of the seriousness of air pollution, the emission standard was set at a level that was much stricter than abroad. This motivated automobile companies to invent more efficient engines with less energy consumption. Fortunately for Japanese automobile makers, these technical progresses enabled them to export many cars with excellent mileage.

Until around 1967, the world price level in the commodity market was rather stable. Hence, under the fixed exchange rate, Japan could keep fairly stable wholesale price levels because the wholesale price index (WPI) was linked to the price level of traded goods abroad. However, starting in 1968, price levels abroad started rising so that the policy of maintaining a stable price level in Japan began to imply a substantial surplus on the current account.

Japan could have appreciated the yen in order to keep its domestic price stability. However, the monetary authorities had been accustomed to the fixed parity for such a long time, and in fact with such a pride for keeping it, that they hardly considered as a feasible alternative appreciating the yen, much less floating it. In order to maintain the exchange rate, the choice was either to accumulate current-account surpluses while keeping domestic price stability, or to inflate the economy with world inflation. The first alternative was taken until the announcement of President Nixon's *New Economic Policy* in August 1971, which opened the overture of the tumultuous 1970s, a decade we might call the decade of *Sturm und Drang* in the Japanese economy.

The *New Economic Policy* cut off the already weakened link between the dollar and gold, and impose a 10% surcharge on US imports. After a reckless attempt to keep the exchange rate by opening the exchange market when other markets were closed — the attempt imposed eventually a large burden on Japanese taxpayers — Japan finally allowed the yen to float.

After a short interlude of the Smithsonian system of fixed exchange rates with a widened band, the yen was again floated. This time, however, the Japanese government turned to the second alternative mentioned above, that is, to adopting an inflationary policy to prevent the yen from appreciating further. In the meantime, prime minister Tanaka launched an ambitious plan of regional remodeling: the *Japan Archipelago Plan*. The oil crisis hit at the worst time when the Japanese economy had already been inflamed by excess liquidity.

The cartel activities of the Organization of Petroleum Exporting Countries (OPEC) worsened Japan's terms of trade by 25% between 1973 and 1974. The Japanese economy was brought to the brink of catastrophe. In 1974 the WPI rose by 31%, the CPI by 24%, and nominal wages in the manufacturing sector by 26%, people called these "frenzied prices". Housewives rushed to grocery stores to buy toilet rolls because of the rumor that paper products would disappear due to the oil shortage. A science fiction novel by a MITI official called *Yudan (inadvertence)* — literally translated as "oil cut" — became a best-seller. The Bank of Japan suddenly contracted the money supply; real GNP declined in 1974 for the first time since World War II. The Japanese economy suffered a long adjustment period of stagflation. The unemployment rate jumped to 1.89% in 1975 — an unusually high level for the Japanese unemployment statistic since 1960 — and kept increasing until 1978.

From these bitter experience, people learned a great deal. The monetary authorities learned the danger of sacrificing the objective of price stability for other objectives such as the stable parity of the yen; the labor union leaders learned the costly impact of a large wage increase on employment.

The Japanese economy responded to the second oil crisis much more smoothly than to the first one. (Ito [16], pp. 71-3). In the 1980s Japan's real growth rates reached a plateau, but still continued to be higher than most developed economies. Price levels of flow of goods and services remained relatively stable. Trade surplus including the surplus vis-a-vis the United States soared in the middle of the decade. After the *Plaza Accord* of the G-5 Finance Ministers in 1985, joint interventions by monetary authorities of advanced economies succeeded in correcting the overvaluation of the dollar. The yen started to appreciate dramatically, but the trade surplus remained high. In 1986, the current account surplus reached 4% of the GNP.

In order to reduce the large current account surplus that triggered trade conflicts with the United States, the Japanese government agreed to implement voluntary export restraints (VERs) in several manufacturing sectors. Moreover, it appealed to an expansionary fiscal policy that amounted to six trillion yen as well as a monetary policy of reducing the discount rate to 2.5% for more than two years (1987-1989). The domestic price level of flow of goods did not rise much because of the appreciating yen, but stock-market prices as well as land prices were strongly stimulated.

Accordingly, in the later years of the 1980s, there was a strong surge in the stock price and in the land price. For example, the total land value of Japan was valued four times as much as the total land value of the United States. In the high growth era, the Japanese economy had been characterized by "the flow economy" where the level of national wealth lagged behind the flow of GNP. The Japanese used to say that they lacked the treasure of the British Museum or Roman remains. In contrast, in the late 1980s the news media coined the phrase "the stock economy", which meant that (seemingly) overvalued asset prices became driving forces to activate domestic and international investments through inflated loans.

Now we are in the last decade of the twentieth century, for which we have yet little to say. The real rate of growth stayed at a substantial level (5.2% for 1990 and 4.5% for 1991) for the first two years of the century, but now turned into negative. From the first month of the decade, January 1990, the Tokyo stock market started tumbling down. In two and a half years, it lost more than a half of its value. The recent losing trend was accelerated by the fall in the value of financial stocks, in particular, in banking. The Japanese financial market boasted of its enormous scale because of the funds supplied by Japan's high savings. But rules in the financial market are not clear enough; informal guidance by the Ministry of Finance (MOF) often discourages financial innovations. This seems to indicate that Japan's financial service sectors have still a long way to go in order to prove its quality in the world as manufacturing sectors did so marvellously in the past.

## 3. - Growth Accounting
## and Structural Changes

There are many attempts to evaluate the contribution of various factors to the fast postwar growth of Japan by the method of growth accounting pioneered by Solow. Ohkawa and Rosovsky [31] was probably the first work that applied growth accounting to the Japanese economy. Among subsequent studies are Watanabe and Egaitsu 1967, Sato [35], Ohkawa and Rosovsky [32], Kanamori [19], Yoshihara and Ratcliffe [42], Denison and Chung [6], Okawa and Rosovsky [33], Shinohara [36], Kuroda *et* Al. [25].

These studies all point to the importance of technological progress. However, the estimates of its relative contribution range from 27% (Yoshihara and Ratcliffe [42], to 70% (Watanabe and Egaitsu, 1967). These studies also agree that the contribution of labor input was much smaller than that of capital input. Kuroda *et* Al. [25] estimate that capital input grew at an annual rate of 8.2 percent and labor input at 2.6% between 1960 and 1979; the contribution by capital, labor, and technological progress were 4%, 1.3% and 2.4%, respectively.

In one of the most recent studies, Kuroda *et.* Al. [25] compared the growth performance of Japan with that of the United States. According to them, the Japanese growth rate was 2.5 times higher than the US growth rate, and the absolute contribution of technological progress in Japan was 6 times higher than in the United States.

Growth accounting gives us useful aggregate indicators. Behind these aggregate figures, however, are hidden many structural, that is, sectoral and qualitative changes in the Japanese economy. One of the main messages of this paper is that we can attain a better understand-

ing of the growth process by studying structural changes in each
component carefully rather than by containing those structural
changes into the term of aggregate technological progress. In order to
illustrate those structural changes, let us describe more or less
intuitively what we think drove the engines of Japan's rapid postwar
growth.

We can count at least the following qualitative factors that drove
the engines of the rapid postwar growth: *(i)* the high rate of investment that was supported by the high national savings rate; *(ii)*
abundance of well educated and diligent labor, *(iii)* the high degree of
mobility of labor from rural to urban and from less efficient to more
efficient sectors; *(vi)* opportunity of borrowing and adapting foreign
technology, and; *(v)* organizational and institutional set-up that enabled to combine those factors efficiently and flexibly.

We will briefly discuss in the final section whether government
policies, both macroeconomic and microeconomic, positively helped
the successful performance of the Japanese economy.


## 3.1 *High Investment Rates*

As is often pointed out, the high rate of investment is one of the
most important sources of Japan's high growth. Japanese entrepreneurs had generally optimistic views in the future at least until the
first oil crisis. Thus investment was an important driving force of the
growth. Since the Japanese saved much for reasons that are not yet
completely clear (e.g. Horioka [14]), the high rate of investment was
supported by domestic savings without substantial reliance on foreign
capital. Even though studies of growth accounting do not regard
investment as the most dominant component, they generally find that
the contribution of capital investment is much more important in
Japan than in the United States.

The recent literature on endogenous growth emphasizes the role
of machinery/equipment investment on technological progress (De
Long and Summers [5]). We will study in Section 4 by time series
analysis how investment, productivity growth and economic growth
were interrelated to each other in Japan.

## 3.2 *Abundant and Well-Educated Labor*

Growth accounting studies do not attribute much to education as a factor of promoting Japan's economic growth: they conclude that the contribution of labor quality and, in particular, that of education were small and even smaller than in the United States and in European countries. Indeed schooling years did not increase much during the high growth era. Therefore it may be difficult to detect a strong relationship between technological progress and the quantitative indexes for education. But did the level and quality of Japan's education not contribute to the high growth? Did the discipline of Japanese workers help the productivity increase?

The quality of labor is closely related to the role of growth factors to be discussed below. Reallocation of labor from rural to urban sector, from less efficient to more efficient sectors, and in particular from less needed to more needed jobs in a firm could be possible only when workers had a sufficient capability for learning new skills and adjusting to a different environment. The Japanese type of management was effective only when people were well disciplined for group activities. In particular, borrowing and improving foreign technology enhanced productivity only because people had proficient technical skills to absorb new technology and to improve on it. We will study this role of education in our empirical study in section 5.

## 3.3 *Mobility of Labor*

Ohkawa [30], and Ohkawa and Rosovsky [32] pointed out the dual structure of the Japanese economy as well as the important role played by the sectoral adjustment from low-productivity agriculture to high-productivity manufacturing sectors (or traditional sectors to modern sectors). This is also part of the common sense view. Denison and Chung [6] estimate that the (absolute) contribution of improved resource allocation between 1953 and 1971 was 0.95% (out of 8.81%) in Japan and 0.30% (out of 4.00%) in the United States. In section 6 we will study the degree of mobility of factors in the postwar Japanese economy, and show that the mobility was a major factor for growth until the mid 1960s and not so thereafter.

## 3.4 *Borrowing and Adapting Foreign Technology*

The rapid technological progress in Japan can certainly be attributed much to the opportunity of borrowing technologies from more developed countries, especially from the United States. Abundant human capital made it possible to adopt, to adapt borrowed technologies into more palatable form to the Japanese environment and even to improve on them. Growth accounting attempts to contain these qualitative elements into a single term of technological progress, which often happens to be a residual term, and thus fails to capture the role of structural changes.

Nelson and Phelps [29] emphasize the role of capacity of absorbing knowledge and utilizing it effectively into the production process. «In a technologically progressive or dynamic economy, production management is a function requiring adaptation to change: the more educated a manager is, the quicker will he be to introduce new techniques of production». In section 5 we will study the effect of managerial resources on the catching up process of Japanese industries by borrowing technology abroad.

## 3.5 *Organizational Skills of Japanese Firms*

In his careful comparison between Japanese and western firms, Koike ([20], [22]) shows that the on-the-job skill formation in Japan has interesting features. In particular, job rotations are more frequent so that workers are not confined into a specific skill category. Communication among Japanese workers seems to generate technical improvement more easily in a group like in Quality Control (QC) circles. Aoki [1] convincingly argues that an important characteristic of the J-firm (an ideal type of Japanese firms) is its horizontal information structure as compared with that of the A-firm (an ideal type of American firms). The empirical assessment of these organizational aspects will be a challenging research subject.

Finally, let us consider the claim that Japan, as West Germany and Italy, grew faster because of the defeat. Modernization of equipment is certainly helped by the wartime damage. But we do not believe that possibility of faster modernization was a crucial factor in the Japanese growth. If the defeat had helped the growth at all, it would have done through changes in incentive structures by the postwar reforms such as production incentives of farmers, more democratic and rejuvenated business leaders, less hierarchical business practices and meritocratic education.

## 4. - The Effect of Machinery and Equipment Investment on Productivity

### 4.1 *Real and Nominal Equipment Investment Shares of GDP*

De Long and Summers [5] find that international comparison data shows a clear relationship between the share of equipment investment in GDP and the growth rate of GDP per worker, and that investment in electrical and non-electrical machinery has much stronger influence on the GDP growth than investment in structures. They confirm, by cross-section data, Patrick and Rosovsky's [34] view that Japan's rapid growth can be attributed to her high rates of investment in equipment. Let us start, using the time-series data, by asking what was the importnace of equipment investment in economic growth.

Graph 2 compares real GDP growth rate and the share of private machinery/equipment investment in GDP both in nominal and real terms (2). Surprisingly, this share of real investment in real GDP did not decline but increased from 14.6% in 1960-1969 to 16.2% in 1970-1979 to 17.6 in 1980-1988. This fact may be surprising because of the slowdown in GDP growth since 1973 and because one tends to presume a close association between GDP growth and the volume of equipment investment. In nominal terms, on the other hand, the equipment investment share of GDP declined. The difference in the behavior of the real and nominal series was caused by the decline in

---

(2) Data was taken from the *Report on the National Accounts*. Although this investment is called (by the government of Japan) «private machinery/equipment investment», it includes structure investment and other components of investment. It may be more appropriate to call its firms' investment in tangible assets.

GRAPH 2

### INVESTMENT/GDP AND GDP GROWTH RATE

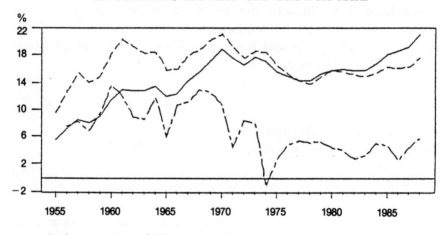

_____ Real investment/real GDP (1980 price)
- - - - Nominal investment/nominal GDP
· - - — Real GDP growth rate

the price of investment goods relative to other goods. The price change was probably the result of fast productivity growth in the investment goods sector relative to that in other sectors.

The effectiveness of real investment in raising real GDP apparently declined around 1970. Exploring the reason for this change may offer a clue to understand the qualitative nature of rapid economic growth. The argument that may guide us is that of borrowed technology. If, as this argument goes, the growth is primarily driven by the introduction of foreign technologies, then technological catch-up will make further technological progress more difficult, thereby reducing the effectiveness of investment.

### 4.2 *Investment and GDP Growth*

Let us first confirm the importance of equipment investment in the GDP growth by means of the Granger tests. We consider a system consisting of the growth rate of real GDP and real private machinery/

equipment investment, denoted respectively by $Y$ and $I$. These data series are not seasonally adjusted and are transformed to growth rates from the same quarter of the previous year. This transformation is approximately equivalent to transforming to logs and then taking seasonal differences. The sample period is 1956.1 - 1989.1.

The two-variable VAR considered is:

$$(1) \qquad Y_t = \alpha_1 + \sum_{k=1}^{p} \beta_{1k} Y_{t-k} + \sum_{k=1}^{p} \gamma_{1k} I_{t-k} + u_{It}$$

$$(2) \qquad I_t = \alpha_2 + \sum_{k=1}^{p} \beta_{2k} Y_{t-k} + \sum_{k=1}^{p} \gamma_{2k} I_{t-k}$$

To select the lag length $p$, we employed the Akaike Information Criterion (AIC) and the Schwarz Baysian Information Criterion (SBIC). The former picked $p = 10$ while the latter picked $p = 3$. Since similar results were obtained for $p$ between 3 and 10, we report the regression outputs for $p = 4$ (table 2).

With four lags, observations used in regressions starts at 1957.1 and ends at 1989.1, and they are 129 in number.

The Durbin-Watson statistic and Ljung-Box $Q$-statistic in table 2 suggest the absence of serial correlation in residuals. Coefficient $\gamma_{12}$ of lagged $I$ is significantly different from zero in the first equation, suggesting causality of $Y$ by $I$. Two coefficients of lagged $Y$ are, on the other hand, significantly different from zero in the second equation, suggesting causality of $I$ by $Y$. The latter causality may be viewed as induced investments instead of those investments which are planned based on forward-looking calculation by firms.

The Granger test yields $F$-statistics:

$F = 4.490$ for the restriction that $\gamma_{1k} = 0$ for all $k$

$F = 4.983$ for the restriction that $\beta_{2k} = 0$ for all $k$.

The corresponding marginal significance levels are 0.002 and 0.0009. Thus, we may conclude that in the period 1957.1-1989.1,

TABLE 2

ESTIMATES OF EQUATIONS *(1)* AND *(2)*:
1957.1-1989.1 (*)

Equation *(1)*
dependent variablie: $Y_t$ (GDP growth rate)

$\alpha_1$  = 0.010          (2.617)     $\beta_{11}$ = 0.715  (7.409)    $\gamma_{11}$ = 0.133  (3.867)
                                         $\beta_{12}$ = 0.354  (3.040)    $\gamma_{12}$ = 0.177  (–3.817)
                                         $\beta_{13}$ = –0.337  (–2.852)  $\gamma_{13}$ = 0.069  (1.480)
                                         $\beta_{14}$ = 0.097  (0.999)    $\gamma_{14}$ = –0.004  (–0.117)

$\bar{R}^2$  = 0.785.  *D.W.* = 2.047
$Q(33)$ = 29.9964 (significance level = 0.617)

Equation *(2)*
dependent variable: $I_t$ (investment growth rate)

$\alpha_2$  = 0.006          (0.563)     $\beta_{21}$ = 0.060  (0.231)    $\gamma_{21}$ = 0.954 (10.216)
                                         $\beta_{22}$ = 0.987  (3.125)    $\gamma_{22}$ = –0.049 (–0.392)
                                         $\beta_{23}$ = –0.676  (–2.100)  $\gamma_{23}$ = 0.035  (0.274)
                                         $\beta_{24}$ = 0.055  (0.207)    $\gamma_{24}$ = –0.253 (–2.830)

$\bar{R}^2$  = 0.861.  *D.W.* = 1.874
$Q(33)$ = 29.9964 (significance level = 0.617)

(*) *t*-statistics in parentheses.

there is a bilateral causation between the growth rate of real GDP and that of real private machinery/equipment investment.

A consensus view on Japanese macroeconomic time series is that there was a break in 1973 due to the first oil shock. We split the sample at 1973 and reiterated the Granger test. The lag length $p$ was set at 4 for the earlier period, and $p = 5$ for the later period. For the period 1957.1-1973.4,

$F = 5.101$ for the restriction that $\gamma_{1k} = 0$ for all $k$

$F = 3.665$ for the restriction that $\beta_{2k} = 0$ for all $k$

and the corresponding significance levels are 0.0015 and 0.010. For the period 1976.2-1989.1, on the other hand,

$F = 1.667$ for the restriction that $\gamma_{1k} = 0$ for all $k$

$F = 0.708$ for the restriction that $\beta_{2k} = 0$ for all $k$,

and the corresponding significance levels are 0.164 and 0.621.

    In summary: 1) investment growth causes GDP growth in Granger's sense in both periods, 2) the influence of investment growth on GDP growth is, however, weak in the period after the first oil shock; 3) GDP growth causes investment growth in the first period, but not in the second period. This contrast between the two periods probably reflects that the Japanese economy became open in the latter period: with capital inflow and outflow, the increase in savings resulting from a high rate of growth no longer implied an increase in domestic investment.

    So far we have considered the relationship of the growth rate of GDP and that of investment. We turn now to the relationship of the growth rate of GDP and the logarithm of investment level. Since the logarithm of investment level may have a unit root, we conducted the following Dickey-Fuller test as a preliminary analysis. We estimated the equation:

(3)                 $$\Delta I_t = \mu + \delta t + \pi I_{t-1} + \sum_{j=1}^{4} \Delta I_{t-j} + v_t$$

where $\Delta I_t = I_t - I_{t-1}$. For the period before the oil shock, the lag length was set at four because additional lags were not significantly different from zero. The estimate of $\pi$ was $-0.230$ and the $t$-statistic for testing $\pi = 0$ was $-4.238$. The unit-root hypothesis was thus rejected at the 1% level of significance. For the entire sample period and the period after the oil shock, however, the Dickey-Fuller test could not reject the unit-root hypothesis. We therefore studied the relationship between the level of investment and the growth in GDP only for the first period.

    For this period, both the AIC and the SBIC selected $p = 5$.
    The result of the Granger test was as follows:

$F = 3.372$ for the restriction that $\gamma_{1k} = 0$ for all $k$,

$F = 3.176$ for the restriction that $\beta_{2k} = 0$ for all $k$.

Both null hypotheses were rejected (the significance levels were 0.0099 and 0.136). That is, the level of investment causes the growth in GDP, and vice versa in the period before the oil shock.

## 4.3 *Investment and Labor Productivity Growth*

Since we have confirmed the importance of investment in GDP growth, we now proceed to the question of what induces investment. We study the relationship between investment and labor productivity growth and that between labor productivity growth and GDP growth. A consistent timeseries of labor productivity is available from 1959. This is defined as the ratio of the mining and manufacturing output to the total number of persons engaged in production in these sectors. Since this index increases with labor hours for a given level of employment, it may be more appropriate to incorporate labor hours into regression. But, because of the limited sample size, we use this index without modification. The system we consider consists of real GDP, real private machinery/equipment investment, and labor productivity index, denoted respectively by $Y$, $I$, and $LP$.

We executed Granger tests to see: *a)* whether investment affects labor productivity growth; *b)* whether labor productivity growth affects investment; and *c)* whether labor productivity growth affects GDP growth.

Presumably, *a)* past investments would have positive effects on labor productivity growth; *b)* labor productivity growth would, in turn, have positive effects on investment in the future for various reasons. For example, labor productivity growth may be caused by increases in or qualitative improvement in the input that is a complement of equipment, such as skills of workers who operate equipment, technological knowledge, and organizational arrangements. In these cases, labor productivity growth would cause equipment investment in Granger's sense; *c)* certainly, GDP growth is closely related to the growth in labor productivity of the economy. This relationship is, however, contemporaneous and hence may not be detected by the Granger test. Moreover, recall that our labor productivity index covers only the mining and manufacturing sectors. If there are substantial inflow or outflow of labor, the relationship between GDP growth and labor productivity growth will not be direct. Let us begin with the period before the oil shock: 1960-1973 (3). We attempt two specifications: the first specification uses the growth rate of investment from the same quarter of the previous year and the second the logarithm of the investment level. In each model, real GDP and labor productivity were both transformed to growth rates. Using the AIC and the SBIC, we chose a lag length of four for the first model and three for the second model. The two panels of table 3 report the resulting *F*-statistics for the null hypothesis that a variable on the right-hand side does not Granger cause a variable on the left-hand side. In panel 1 (i.e., the model using the logarithm of investment), for instance, *Y* does not affect *LP* ($F = 0.527$) but exerts a strong influence on *I* ($F = 5.216$), and *Y* is not affected by *LP* ($F = 0.508$) but by *I* ($F = 2.229$).

The two panels look similar. Although *Y* is affected by *LP* and *LP* is affected by *I* in panel 2, the causal relationship is still weak. From these panels, we observe that, during the period 1960-1973: *a)* investment had at best weak influence on labor productivity growth; *b)* labor productivity growth had strong effects on investment; *c)* labor productivity growth had at best weak influence on GDP growth. This seems to indicate that the productivity gain was the exogenous source that drove the era of high growth of Japan.

One might think that *a)* would be a result of not taking a sufficient number of lags to allow adjustment. So, we took $p = 8$ and 10 and tested against the hypothesis that the logarithm of investment does not Granger cause labor productivity growth. The *F*-statistic was 0.4848 for $p = 8$ and 0.7979 for $p = 10$. The corresponding marginal significance levels were about 0.85 and 0.80, respectively. Thus the lack (or weakness) of influence of investment on labor productivity growth cannot be attributed to the short lag length.

In order to ascertain the weakness of causation from investment to labor productivity growth in this earlier period, we also computed the relative contributions to the variance of the 24-step forecast error

---

(3) A consistent time-series data for productivity is available from 1959.1. Since we work on the rate growth from the same quarter of the previous year, our sample period starts from 1960.

for the vector autoregressive model with log of investment. Since there is substantial correlation among innovations in variables as shown at the bottom of table 3, the decomposition of variance depends strongly on the order of factorization. We attempted all possible orders (with three variables, there are 6 combinations). The innovations in investment experience at most 38% of the variance of labor productivity growth for one case, and, for other orders of factorization, the relative contribution was less than 10%. Although

TABLE 3

GRANGER CAUSALITY TESTS: 1960.1-1973.4
*F*-statistics (*)

| Effect | Cause | | |
|---|---|---|---|
| | GDP growth $Y$ | Labor productivity growth $LP$ | Log of investment level $I$ |
| GDP growth .......... $Y$ ................. | 8.688 (0.000) | 0.508 (0.730) | 2.229 (0.084) |
| Labor productivity growth .............. $LP$ ............... | 0.527 (0.717) | 23.57 (0.000) | 0.837 (0.510) |
| Log of investment Level ............... $I$ ................. | 5.216 (0.002) | 3.691 (0.010) | 940.04 (0.000) |

Lag length: $p = 4$
Correlations of residuals: $r_{Y,LP} = 0.430$, $r_{Y,I} = 0.425$, $r_{LP,I} = 0.426$

| Effect | Cause | | |
|---|---|---|---|
| | GDP growth $Y$ | Labor productivity growth $LP$ | Investment growth $I$ |
| GDP growth .......... $Y$ ................. | 8.575 (0.000) | 1.715 (0.178) | 1.520 (0.223) |
| Labor productivity growth .............. $LP$ ............... | 0.575 (0.635) | 34.65 (0.000) | 1.882 (0.147) |
| Investment growth .............. $I$ ................. | 5.571 (0.002) | 3.093 (0.004) | 15.79 (0.000) |

Lag length: $p = 3$
Correlation of residuals: $r_{Y,LP} = 0.421$, $r_{Y,I} = 0.489$, $r_{LP,I} = 0.375$

(*) Marginal significance levels in parentheses.

this does not imply the absence of causation from investment to labor productivity growth, it confirms that investment was not a decisive factor in the determination of productivity growth in the period before the oil shock.

*a)* and *c)* are somewhat counter-intuitive and accordingly curious. Before discussing their interpretation, however, let us review for comparison the result for the period after the oil shock. Since the hypothesis of a unit-root for the logarithm of investment could not be

TABLE 4

GRANGER CAUSALITY TESTS:
AFTER THE FIRST OIL-SHOCK *F*-statistics (*)

| Effect | Cause | | |
|---|---|---|---|
| | GDP growth $Y$ | Labor productivity growth $LP$ | Investment growth $I$ |
| GDP growth .......... $Y$ ................. | 1.753 (0.158) | 2.013 (0.111) | 2.192 (0.087) |
| Labor productivity growth ............. $LP$ .............. | 1.990 (0.115) | 31.22 (0.000) | 1.839 (0.140) |
| Investment growth ............. $I$ ................. | 0.133 (0.969) | 0.641 (0.637) | 45.17 (0.000) |

1976.1-1989.4: Lag length: $p = 4$
Correlations of residuals: $r_{Y,LP} = 0.220$, $r_{Y,I} = 0.340$, $r_{LP,I} = 0.348$

| Effect | Cause | | |
|---|---|---|---|
| | GDP growth $Y$ | Labor productivity growth $LP$ | Investment level $I$ |
| GDP growth .......... $Y$ ................. | 2.381 (0.070) | 3.974 (0.009) | 2.309 (0.077) |
| Labor productivity growth ............. $LP$ .............. | 3.254 (0.022) | 34.67 (0.000) | 2.665 (0.048) |
| Investment growth ............. $I$ ................. | 0.609 (0.659) | 1.866 (0.138) | 27.13 (0.000) |

1976.1-1989.4: Lag length: $p = 4$
Correlations of residuals: $r_{Y,LP} = 0.192$, $r_{Y,I} = 0.392$, $r_{LP,I} = 0.285$

---

(*) Marginal significance levels in parentheses.

rejected by the Dickey-Fuller test for this later period, only the growth rate of investment was used for the test. Panel 1 of table 4 reports the result for the period 1976.1-1989.1. In contrast to the result in table 3, GDP growth now affects labor productivity growth while the causation of *I* by *Y* and the causation of *I* by *LP* disappear in this latter period. The contrast from the table 3 becomes more conspicuous if a shorter sample period is used as shown in panel 2. In this period, investment has a strong influence on labor productivity growth. In summary, after the first oil shock, *a)* investment caused labor productivity growth; *b)* labor productivity growth had at best weak influence on investment; and *c)* labor productivity growth caused GDP growth.

To summarize, we detected the following causality chains:

*(i)* GDP growth and investment: in both periods investment caused GDP growth. On the other hand, GDP growth causes investment in the first period but did not in the second. This change probably reflects that the Japanese economy became open in the second period;

*(ii)* labor productivity growth and investment: in the first period, labor productivity growth caused investment but not vice versa. In the second period, investment caused labor productivity growth and labor productivity growth had at most a weak influence on investment. This reversal can be explained, in our opinion, by declining opportunities for borrowing foreign technologies;

*(iii)* labor productivity growth and GDP growth: in the first period, we could not find any causal relationship between the two. Labor productivity growth, if it influenced GDP growth, did affect GDP growth through the effect of investment. In the second period, there were mutual causal chains between them. In fact, investment affected both labor productivity and GDP growth.

The fact that during the first half labor productivity growth influenced economic growth indirectly through investment presents us with a puzzle that cannot easily be answered by conventional growth theory. If technological progress is neutral like a mana from heaven, it should have directly influenced GDP growth. If, on the other hand, technological progress is embodied in capital, the investment should lead productivity growth. This suggests that there were some hidden factors behind the process.

Our tentative hypothesis on the process of the rapid growth period may go as follows: technical growth was brought by importing technology, but to assimilate it for increased productivity, there was need to invest jointly in human capital as well as in machinery and equipment. As we will see in the next section, new investment created firm-speccific skills that could be handed down by the on-the-job training. The combination of borrowed technology and the firm-specific skill formation to adapt to new technology was the key of the rapid growth era.

## 5. - Borrowed Technology and Internal Labor Market

Thus the process of improving productivity by borrowing technology has a somewhat different nature from what the conventional growth theory tends to postulate. Available technologies do not lend themselves to be utilized by simply importing them, but must be adapted and reorganized by firm-specific skills. For the theoretical implication of this view of technological progress, see Honda [13].

Two aspects of Japanese technological progress in the high growth era have been emphasized. First, borrowing technologies was its important driving force. Second, the skills of managers and workers in doing so was mainly cultivated by on-the-job training (Koike [20], 1981). Although intuitively appealing, these arguments were mostly supported by case studies and not subjected to econometric tests. Here, we will use cross-section data and attempt a primitive test for these propositions.

When foreign technologies are rapidly introduced, firms in the same industry are likely to have different sets of techology and equipment. As Baranson [2] documented, it then appears as if firms had firm-specific technologies although, in fact, they are adapting a set of universal technologies that are developed in foreign countries. In these circumstances, skill formation would naturally take the form of on-the-job training.

On the other hand, for such skill formation to be effective, the long-term employment is a prerequisite. A firm cannot recover training costs if turn-overs of workers and managers are frequent. Employees will have no incentive to learn firm-specific skills if long-term employment is not secured. Other incentive schemes such as the wage and the promotion schedule must be designed accordingly. The wage profile should be upward-sloping to prevent quitting and to the provide incentive to learn, and an internal promotion system will be adopted. Thus the internal labor market is an indispensable complement to on-the-job skill formation.

One may expect that the opening-up of the opportunity of borrowing technologies will induce the establishment of internal labor market. Indeed, in the Japanese machinery industry, the internal promotion system became common during the high growth period (Koike [20]). However, such changes in institutional arrangements like this can be slow. If we look at various industries by cross-section, the degree of the penetration of the internal labor market will depend on historical events and industries' technological characteristics. For example, the internal labor market is more common to process industries such as chemical and steel industries than those industries which make less intensive use of huge equipment and require less collaboration. (Koike [20]).

Our hypothesis is that the speed of technological progress in the manufacturing sector is determined by the opportunity of borrowing foreign technologies and by the degree of the prevalence of internal labor market in that industry. For Japan's high growth period, the technological gap between the United States and Japan may serve as a measure of this opportunity. We use as data the estimates of the levels of total factor productivity provided by Jorgenson and Kuroda [18], for twenty manufacturing subsectors and nine other sectors in Japan and the United States.

The first column of table 5 shows the Jorgenson-Kuroda estimates of the US-Japan technology gap as of 1960 for twenty manufacturing industries, and the second and third columns show the average annual rates of technological progress between 1960-1970. Except for the petroleum refining industry, every Japanese manufacturing industry was behind the US counterpart in 1960 and recorded faster technological progress in the subsequent decade. These nineteen industries constitute our sample set.

Our regression equation is basically the same as the model of

TABLE 5

## TECHNOLOGY DIFFUSION
## AND INTERNAL LABOR MARKET:
### (1960-1970)

| Industry | US Japan productivity gap 1960 | Average annual rates of productivity growth | | Wage gap 1966 (*) (Thousand Yen) |
|---|---|---|---|---|
| | | Japan | US | |
| Foods ............... | 21.625 | 1.030 | 0.609 | 10.307 |
| Textile mill porducts .... | 15.657 | 1.619 | 1.393 | 4.541 |
| Apparels ............. | 52.543 | 2.712 | 0.991 | 0.717 |
| Lumber ............. | 29.293 | 1.773 | 1.236 | 4.562 |
| Furniture & fixtures .... | 20.675 | 1.145 | 0.544 | 1.565 |
| Paper ............... | 7.598 | 1.788 | 1.018 | 14.630 |
| Printing & publishing .. | 61.847 | 1.260 | − 0.254 | 16.820 |
| Chemical............. | 16.312 | 3.274 | 1.523 | 13.770 |
| Petroleum refinery...... | − 4.724 | − 1.840 | 1.625 | 24.696 |
| Rubber ............. | 66.106 | 2.637 | 1.851 | 3.759 |
| Leather ............. | 24.487 | 0.753 | 0.483 | 6.921 |
| Stone, clay, & glass .... | 29.719 | 1.945 | 0.761 | 12.589 |
| Primary metal ........ | 10.759 | 0.642 | 0.269 | 15.128 |
| Fablicated metal ...... | 48.592 | 2.491 | 0.689 | 6.442 |
| Machinery ........... | 13.970 | 1.851 | 0.982 | 7.087 |
| Electric machinery .... | 23.664 | 3.331 | 1.686 | 7.452 |
| Motor vehicles & equip. | 27.117 | 2.974 | 0.538 | 15.842 |
| Transportation equip. (**) | 81.014 | 4.393 | 1.231 | |
| Precision instruments .. | 31.873 | 2.110 | 1.215 | 7.389 |
| Miscellaneous manufac. | 33.986 | 2.610 | 0.623 | 6.724 |

(*) Difference in total compensation per month between establishments with more than 30 regular employees and those with 5-29 regular employees.

(**) Except motor vehicles and equipment.

*Source* for productivity: JORGENSON - KURODA [18]; for compensation: MINISTRY OF LABOR: *Monthly Labor Survey.*

technological diffusion considered by Nelson and Phelps [29]. It is written:

$$(4) \qquad \dot{A}(t) = \pi [T(t) - A(T)]$$

where $T(t)$ is the theoretical level of technology as of time $t$ and $A(t)$ the actual level. If we treated $\pi$ as a parameter, equation *(4)* would express the first half of our hypothesis: the rate of technological diffusion depends on the opportunity of borrowing technology that is approximated by the gap $(T - A)$. We take $A$ as the technological level of the Japanese industry and $T$ as that of the US industry.

The second half is that $\pi$ is not a parameter but an explanatory variable representing the prevalence of internal labor market, which makes the on-the-job training more effective and hence facilitates the abosorption of new technologies.

Nelson and Phelps [29], assumed that $\pi$ is a function of average educational level. Since average educational level is common for all industries, this assumption would, if taken literally, imply that $\pi$ is a constant. But it should be clear that we share the same view as Nelson and Phelps: the capacity to absorb knowledge and make effective use of it plays an important role in the determination of the rate of technological progress.

Our proxy of the degree of penetration of internal labor market in an industry is the wage gap between large firms and small firms in that industry. If skills are accumulated on the on-the-job basis, each firm will form its own wage profile and hence there will coexist different wage profiles in the same industry. Because of the limited availability of data, we could not use other measures of variation in wage profiles within an industry. Wage gaps between small firms and large firms in manufacturing industries in 1966 are shown in the fourth column of table 5. While Jorgenson and Kuroda [18], divide the transportation equipment industry into two parts, the corresponding data of wage gap is not available.

To take account of technological characteristics, we incorporate the rate of technological progress of the US industry into our regression equation. Let $g^J_i$ and $g^{US}_i$ denote the technological growth rates of the $i$-th industry in Japan and the United States. Let $WG$ be the wage gap in the $i$-th industry in Japan. Since we do not have a separate data for the wage gap for the motor vehicle industry and the other transportation equipment industry, we worked on two sample sets: one assumes that the two industries have the same $WG$, and the other excludes these industries from the sample set. In the first case, the number $N$ of observation is 19, and in the second case, $N = 17$. The regression outputs are as follows:

$N = 19$

$$g_i^J = \begin{array}{cccc} 0.051 \ WG_i + & 0.0020 \ [T_i - A_i] + & 1.117 \ g_i^{US} \\ (2.360) & (3.098) & (5.132) \end{array}$$
$$\bar{R}^2 = 0.592$$

$N = 17$

$$g_i^J = \begin{array}{cccc} 0.034 \ WG_i + & 0.018 \ [T_i - A_i] + & 1.213 \ g_i^{US} \\ (1.634) & (2.763) & (6.034) \end{array}$$
$$\bar{R}^2 = 0.529$$

where $t$-statistics are shown in the parentheses. In each case, the coefficients are, as expected, all positive and highly significant. Thus our hypothesis of the interaction of borrowed technologies and internal labor market has passed this simple test.

According to Jorgenson and Kuroda [18], the US-Japan technological gap tended to contract in the period 1970-1985, but the gap widened in some manufacturing subsectors. This suggests that the real relationship between the rate of technological diffusion and the technology gap may be nonlinear so that the response of $\dot{A}$ to $(T - A)$ becomes negligible as $(T - A)$ tends to zero. As far as Jorgenson and Kuroda's estimates show, the Japanese manufacturing industries seem to have approached the nonlinear part of the equation as early as the mid 1970s. This is consistent with our earlier result that the effect of labor productivity growth on investment becomes negligible after the oil shock.

## 6. - Labor Mobility and Productivity Growth

In this brief section we will overview labor mobility during the
process of the postwar Japanese growth. A related, interesting, study
by Barro and Sala-I-Martin [3] indicates that one can detect the
convergence of growth rates among 50 prefectures in Japan, but here
we are concerned with labor mobility among sectors.

Graph 3 shows changes in the composition of the total labor force
in the postwar period. The share of the agriculture sector steadily
came down during all the period, but quickly reduced around 1966-
1967. The released labor from the agriculture sector was absorbed
roughly in equal proportion into the manufacturing sector and into
the tertiary sector.

Graph 4 shows changes in the composition of the male labor
force in a similar but shorter period, the difference in the observation
period merely reflects the availability of data. A comparison of graph 3
and 4 tells us that the outflow of rural male labor force proceeded
earlier, and then female labor force followed. Moreover, the manufac-

GRAPH 3

COMPOSITION OF TOTAL LABOR FORCE

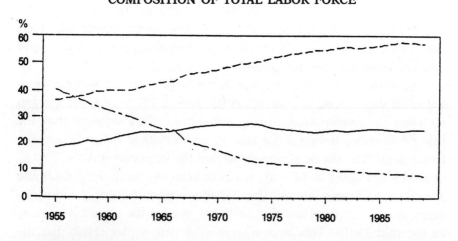

_____ Manufacturing sector
- - - - Tertial sector
- — - Primary sector

GRAPH 4

### COMPOSITION OF MALE LABOR FORCE

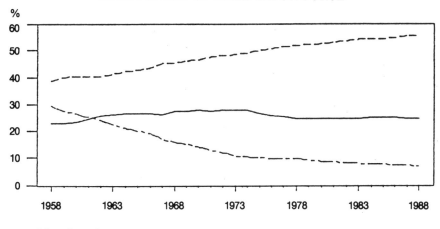

_____ Manufacturing sector
- - - - Tertial sector
- — - Primary sector

turing sector did not add much male labor force during the second half of the rapid growth era.

To what extent did the structural shift of labor force contribute to the overall productivity growth? Graph 5 depicts the ratio of nominal GDP per eployee in each sector to the average nominal GDP per employee for the total economy. Obviously, it tells that any shift from the agricultural sector not only to the manufacturing but to the tertiary sector implied a substantial productivity increase in the Japanese economy.

Incidentally, a similar diagram depicting the ratio of "real" — that is, the index deflated by its own product price index — GDP per employee in each sector to the average "real" — deflated by GDP price deflator — GDP per employee for the total economy is interesting (graph 6). It shows that "real" productivity measured by its own product increased a great deal in the manufacturing sector, but that "real" productivity declined in the tertiary sector even though its level is still much higher than that in the agriculture sector.

All the figures indicate that the shift of labor resource between

GRAPH 5

## NOMINAL GDP PER EMPLOYEE (*)

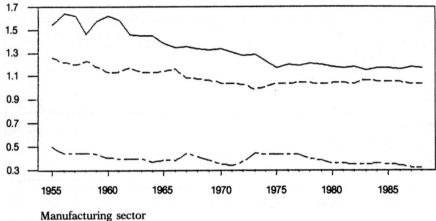

_____  Manufacturing sector
- - - -  Tertial sector
- — -  Primary sector

(*) Ratio of nominal value added per employee in each sector to nominal GDP per employee in the total economy.

GRAPH 6

## REAL GDP PER EMPLOYEE (*)

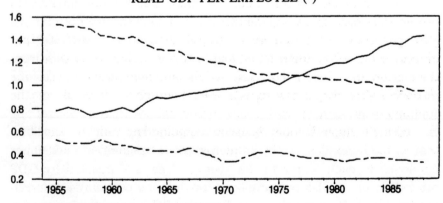

_____  Manufacturing sector
- - - -  Tertial sector
- — -  Primary sector

(*) Ratio of real value added per employee in each sector to real GDP per employee in the total economy (1980 price).

sectors are an important source of national productivity gain. In order to improve Japan's overall productivity, productivity increase in the primary industry seems to be needed.

## 7. - Concluding Remarks

We have traced the trajectory of Japan's rapid postwar growth. We emphasized the importance of postwar reforms to the incentive structure, and argued that structural and qualitative factors are behind the conventional growth accounting. We can summarize our empirical findings in the latter sections as follows.

(*i*) By the Granger test, we can detect the causal chain from the investment growth rate to GDP and vice versa during the period before the first oil crisis. In the period after the first oil crisis the investment growth rate affected the GDP growth rate but not vice versa. This contrast between the two periods probably reflects that the Japanese economy became open in the latter period: the increase in savings resulting from a high rate of growth no longer implied an increase in domestic investment.

(*ii*) In a test that incorporates three variables the investment growth rate, productivity increase and the GDP growth rate, we detect strong causal link from productivity increase to both investment and GDP growth, but not strong links from these two variables to productivity in the former period. In the latter period, investment growth affected productivity growth and productivity growth affected GDP growth.

(*iii*) The productivity gain in the high growth era can be explained by the combination of the two hypotheses: that of borrowed technology and that of the capacity to absorb. A large gap between the US and Japan was an inducement of technical progress in Japan, but the capacity to assimilate knowledge that was measured by the degree of internalization of labor market seemed to have decided the capacity to absorb and to take advantage of the technological availability.

(*iv*) Throughout the development process, and in particular during the years before the first oil crisis, the movement of labor from the agricultural sector to both the manufacturing and the tertiary sector contributed to the productivity gain at the national economy level. The tertiary sector does not increase its productivity level so fast, but the shift from the inefficient agricultural sector would mean a productivity gain at the national level.

An intriguing question on the postwar Japanese growth is to what extent the government contributed to the rapid economic growth. Many empirical issues remain unanswered concerning this question, and another paper will be needed to deal with them. Here we will indicate briefly where the critical issues are:

1) macroeconomic policies: the policy mix of Japan's macroeconomic policy was often characterized by a combination of tight budget and easy money. According to the old view of the "neoclassical synthesis", this combination would have encouraged private investment, which in turn would have led a higher rate of growth along the mechanism we analyzed in this paper. Even according to the neo-Ricardian view, a small government should have worked as encouragement for the private capital formation.

Stable monetary policy was another contributing factor in Japan's macroeconomic environment. The commitment to a fixed exchange parity with the dollar helped monetary stability as long as the international price was relatively stable until the mid 1960s, but caused the inflationary pressure later on. Even under the flexible regime, expansionary monetary policy to prevent the yen's appreciation created excess liquidity before the first oil crisis in 1973, and expansionary monetary policy to curb trade surplus triggered the "bubble economy" in the late 1980s;

2) industrial policy: much was written about the industrial policy — the term is used for a set of microeconomic policies affecting industries and conducted mainly by the MITI — in particular by foreigners who regarded this as the secret of success of the Japanese industrial development (e.g. Johnson [17]). In Japan conventional economists at first did not have a high appraisal of the industrial policy. According to them, price mechanism with private incentives would achieve desirable industrial development. Thus except for the cases in which the infant industry argument applies, Japanese industries would have achieved a similar success without government interventions. With the advent of new trade theory and information

economics, economists are now ready to invent many situations that would make government interventions useful. Empirical and quantitative evidence for the effectiveness of the industrial policy is still very sparse.

We have to divide the postwar period into two, the period before and the period after 1965. In the first period, MITI has instruments that could affect industries such as licensing imports of important materials and imports of foreign technology. Thus certainly had the industrial policy some effects. But in which direction, for better or worse we do not know. MITI helped many industries such as mining, coal, marine industries that did not succeed much in the fast growth process. It tried unsuccessfully to reorganize the automobile industry into oligarchic groups headed by Toyota and Nissan. It did not encourage much the newcomers such as Sony and Honda that were unaffiliated to industrial groups. Dore [7] mentions interesting cases where the administrative guidance by MITI helped declining industries in the short run.

Horiuchi and Ohtaki [15] studied the effectiveness of the industrial policy through government financing. The channeling of savings from postal saving association through the government was considered by Zysman [43] as a major tool of Japan's industrial policy. Horiuchi and Ohtaki show that funds through Japan Development Bank went to many inefficient, and unsuccessful sectors such as agriculture and forestry, mining, coal and marine. Using the causality analysis they show that the inducement effect of the public sector lending on the private sector lending is limited to certain, mostly inefficient, industrues. They show also that the effects of government related finance on private investment as well as on productivity growth are not so strong. Their work seems to indicate that the importance of the industrial policy through government finance should not be overstated. In the latter period, MITI lost many instruments. It started engaging in drawing blueprints — called "visions" in Japanese — and coordinating research activities. Some are successful: the determination of a strict emission standard for automobiles by the joint effort of the Environment Agency and the MITI paved the way for expansion of automobile export. The joint research project on the Very Large Scale Integrated Circuits (VSLI) acclaimed success. Some other projects might have been just a little more than devices for self-justification of the role of MITI officials. In one of the rare attempts to quantify the effect of industrial policy, Wakasugi [41] notes that although the number of patents by the VSLI project is very large the R and D cost per patent was rather large in the project.

Except for these few interesting studies, quantitative research lags far behind many anecdotes that are told about the effectiveness or ineffectiveness of the industrial policy. More research will be needed for us in order to have scientific evaluations of the effectiveness of the industrial policy. Identification of the role of learning in the technical progress from that of externalities among firms as well as among industrial or regional levels would be required.

## BIBLIOGRAPHY

[1] AOKI M.: *Information, Incentives and Barganing in the Japanese Economy*, Cambridge (Mass.), Cambridge University Press, 1988.

[2] BARANSON J.: *Technology and the Multinationals Corporate Strategies in a Changing World Economy*, Lexington (Mass.), Lexington Books, 1978.

[3] BARRO R.J. - SALA-I-MARTIN X.: «Regional Growth and Migration: a Japan-US Comarison», Yale University, Economic Growth Center, *Discussion Paper*, n. 650, 1991.

[4] COHEN J.B.: *Japan's Economy in War and Reconstruction*, Minneapolis, University of Minnesota Press, 1949.

[5] DE LONG J.B. - SUMMERS L.H.: «Equipment Investment and Economic Growth», *Quarterly Journal of Economics*, vol. CVI, 1991, pp. 327-68.

[6] DENISON E.F. - CHUNG W.K.: *Economic Growth and its Sources*, in PATRICK K. - ROSOVSKY H. [34].

[7] DORE R.P.: *Flexible Rigidities: Industrial Policy and Structural Adjustment in Japan 1970-1980*, Athdone Press, 1986.

[8] GORDON A.: *The Evolution of Labor Relations in Japan: Heavy Industry 1853-1955*, Cambridge (Mass.), Council on East Asian Studies, Harvard University, 1985.

[9] GOTO A.: *Technology Importation: Japan's Postwar Experience*, London, Yale University, Department of Economics, 1991.

[10] HADLEY E.M.: *Antitrust in Japan*, Princeton (NJ), Princeton University Press, 1970.

[11] HAMADA K.: «Lessons from the Macroeconomic Performance of the Japanese Economy», in ARGY V.E. - NEVILLE J.W. (eds.): *Inflation and Unemployment*, Londra, Allen & Unwin, 1985.

[12] HAMADA K. - KASUYA M.: *The Postwar Economy*, in DORNBUSCH R. (eds.), MIT Press, forthcoming, 1992.

[13] HONDA T.: *Managerial Resource Accumulation and International Trade*, Ph. D. Dissertation, London, Yale University, 1992.

[14] HORIOKA C.Y.: «Savings in Japan», 1991, in HEERTJI A. (eds.): *World Saving*, Oxford, Basil Blackwell, Forthcoming, 1991.

[15] HORIUCHI A. - OHTAKI M.: «Seifu Kainyu to Ginko Kashidashi no Juosei (The Importance of Government Intervention and Bank Credit)», in HAMADA K. - KURODA M. - HORIUCHI A. (eds.): *Macroeconomics Analysis of the Japanese Economy*, Tokyo, University of Tokyo Press, 1987.

[16] ITO T.: *The Japanese Economy*, London, MIT Press, 1992.

[17] JOHNSON C.: *MITI and the Japanese Miracle*, Standford, Standford University Press, 1980.

[18] JORGENSON D.W. - KURODA M.: «Productivity and International Competitiveness in Japan and the United States, 1960-1985», Harvard Institute of Economic Research, *Discussion Paper* n. 1510, 1990.

[19] KANAMORI H.: «What Accounts for Japan's High Rate of Growth?», *Review of Income and Wealth*, vol. 18, June 1972, pp. 155-71.

[20] KOIKE K.: *Shokuba no Rodo Kumiai to Sanka* (Japanese), Toyo Keizai Shimposha, 1977.

[21] — —: «Skill Formation System in the US and Japan: A Comparative Study», in AOKI M. (ed.): *The Economic Analysis of the Japanese Firm*, Chapter 2, Amsterdam, North Holland, 1984.

[22] KOIKE K.: «Human Resource Development and Labor Management Relations», in YAMAMURA K. - YASABA Y. (eds.): *The Political Economy of Japan, The Domestic Transformation*, vol. I, Standford, 1987.

[23] KOMIYA R. - OKUNO M. - SUZUMURA K. (eds.): *Nihon no Sangyo Seisaku (The Industrial Policy of Japan)*, Tokyo, University of Tokyo Press, 1986.

[24] KOSAI Y.: *The Era of High-Speed Growth*, Tokyo, University of Tokyo Press, 1986.

[25] KURODA M. - YOSHIOKA K. - SHIANIZA M.: «Economic Growth: Decomposition of Factors and Interindustry Repercussions», in HAMADA K. - KURODA M. - HORIUCHI A. (eds.): *Macroeconomics Analysis of the Japanese Economy*, University of Tokyo Press, 1987.

[26] LEONTIEF W.: *The Structure of the American Economy*, 1941.

[27] MALINVAUD E.: *The Theory of Unemployment Reconsidered*, New York, John Wiley & Sons, 1977.

[28] NAKAMURA T.: *The Postwar Japanese Economy*, Tokyo, University of Tokyo Press, 1981.

[29] NELSON R.R. - PHELPS E.S.: «Investment in Humans, Technological Diffusion and Economic Growth», *American Economic Review*, n. 56, 1966, pp. 69-75.

[30] OKAWA K.: «Effects of Structural Chane on Productivity Growth: A Longer-term Measurement», in KOSOBUD R.F. - MINAMI R. (eds.): *Econometric Studies of the Contemporary Economy of Japan*, Chicago, 1972.

[31] OKAWA K. - ROSOVSKI H.: «A Century of Japanese Economic Growth», in LOCKWOOD W.W. (eds.): *The State of Economic Enterprises in Japan*, Princeton (NJ), Princeton University Press, 1965.

[32] — — · — —: *Nihon no Keizai Seicho-Nijuseiki no okeru Susei Kasoku (The Economic Growth in Japan: Trend Acceleration in the Twentieth Century)* (Japanese), Toyo Keizai Shiposha, 1972.

[33] — — · — —: *The Economic Growth of Japan*, Stanford University Press, 1973.

[34] PATRICK H. - ROSOVSKY H. (eds.): *Asia's New Giant*, Brookings Institute, 1976.

[35] SATO K.: «Nihon no Hiichiji Keizai no Seichi to to Gijutsu Shimpo 1930-1967 (The Growth of the Japanese non-primary sectors and Technological Progress 1930-1967», *Economic Studies Quarterly*, vol. 22, 1971, pp. 38-54.

[36] SHINOHARA M.: *Nihon Keizai Kougi (Lectures on the Japanese Economy)* (Japanese), Toyo Keizai Shiposha, 1986.

[37] SUMMERS R. - HESTON A.: «The Penn World Table (Mark 5): An Expanded Set of International Comparison, 1950-1980», *Quarterly Journal of Economics*, vol. CVI, 1991, pp. 327-68.

[38] TAIRA K.: *Economic Development and Labor Market in Japan*, New York, Institute of East Asian Studies, Columbia University Press, 1970.

[39] TAKEMAE E.: *GHO, Iwanami Syoten* (Japanese), 1983.

[40] UCHINO T.: *Japan's Postwar Economy*, Tokyo, Kadanshasha International, 1978.

[41] WAKASUGI R.: *Gi jutsu Kakushin to Kenkyu Kaihatsu no Keizai Bunseki — Nihon no Kigyo Kodo Sangyo Seosaku (The Economic Analysis of Technological Innovation and the Industrial Policy)* (Japanese), Toyo Keizai Shiposha, 1986.

[42] YOSHIHARA K. - RATCLIFFE T.: «Productivity Change in the Japanese Economy, 1905-1965», *Economic Studies Quarterly*, vol. 22, May 1972, pp. 56-74.

[43] ZYSMAN J.: *Governments, Markets, and Growth*, Ithaca, Cornell University Press, 1983.

# VI - THE MECHANISMS OF ECONOMIC GROWTH

# Growth: the Role
# of Macroeconomic Factors

**Stanley Fischer** (1)

MIT, Cambridge (Mass.)

It is now widely accepted that a stable macroeconomic framework is necessary though not sufficient for sustainable economic growth (2). Three major World Bank studies of adjustment lending (3) — balance of payments support loans made to help finance policy reforms in developing countries — affirm this basic conclusion, as does the World Bank [29], *The Challenge of Development.*

This view is supported by much striking evidence. For instance, in Latin America, the recovery of economic growth in Chile and Mexico was preceded by the restoration of budget discipline and the reduction of inflation. By contrast, the current or very recent economic crises in Brazil and Argentina coincide with high inflation puctuated by stabilization attempts and continued macroeconomic instability. The fast growing countries of East Asia have generally maintained single or low double-digit inflation, have for the most part avoided balance of payments crises, and when they have had them — as for instance in Korea in 1980 — moved swiftly to deal with them. The lessons of the case study evidence amassed in the major World Bank research project headed by Little *et* Al. [19], summarized in Corden [4], support the conventional view. The notion that macroeconomic stability is not sufficient for growth appears to be supported

(1) I am grateful to Ruth Judson and Michael Lee for research assistance, and the National Science Foundation for financial support.

*Advise*: the numbers in square brackets refer to the Bibliography in appendix.

(2) The word "sustainable" is meant here in its literal and not environmental sense.

(3) See WORLD BANK [27], [28], [30].

by evidence from Africa, where most of the countries of the franc zone — whose exchange rate has been rigidly fixed to the French franc for nearly fifty years and which have therefore maintained low inflation — have grown slowly since 1980, and from India, which grew steadily but slowly while pursuing conservative macroeconomic policies from 1947 to the end of the 1980s.

In this paper (4) I first discuss the notion of a stable macroeconomic framework and then summarize theoretical considerations linking growth to macroeconomic policies. In Sections 2 and 3 I present evidence supporting the view that macroeconomic stability is conducive to growth. In Section 4 I introduce some apparent anomalies, countries where high growth took place despite high inflation and/or high deficits, and conclude that the statement that macroeconomic stability is necessary for sustainable growth is too strong, but that the statement that macroeconomic stability is conducive to sustained growth remains accurate.

## 1. - Definitions and Theoretical Considerations

There is no single, simple, quantitative definition of good macroeconomic policies or a stable macroeconomic framework. Conceptually, the macroeconomic framework can be described as stable: 1) when inflation is low and predictable; 2) real interest rates are appropriate; 3) fiscal policy is stable and sustainable; 4) the real exchange rate is competitive and predictable; and 5) the balance of payments situation is perceived as viable (5).

Of the five criteria specified in this definition, only low and stable inflation is readily quantifiable (6). None of the specified variables in

---

(4) I draw extensively on results in my paper FISCHER [12].

(5) This definition is based on WORLD BANK ([28], p. 4).

(6) With regard to quantification of the other four variables: measures of the fiscal deficit provide some information about fiscal policy; however it is difficult to characterize fiscal policy by a single variable (MACKENZIE [21]), and international fiscal data are poor. Estimates of sustainable deficits could in principle be calculated along the lines of HAMILTON and FLAVIN [16], but that level of detail is difficult to attain in a large cross-sectional study. In addition, the stochastic processes for deficits required by the Hamilton-Flavin approach may be especially difficult to estimate for developing coun-

directly controllable by policy, and each should optimally vary in response to shocks. There is no simple way of determining the appropriate levels of the real interest or exchange rate in each period, or for that matter the inflation rate, from which to judge deviations that would indicate an unstable macroeconomic environment.

A country's macroeconomic indicators may be unstable either because policy is unstable or because the exogenous variables that affect the country are unstable. In either case, we expect growth to be adversely affected. If there were sufficient instrumental variables available, it would be possible to separate out those elements of instability of the policy variables that arise from responses to exogenous shocks, and then to test whether reactions to the two elements of instability differ (7).

I shall use the inflation rate as the best single indicator of the stability of the macroeconomic environment (8), and the budget deficit as the second basic indicator. There is no major industrialized economy in which inflation has exceeded 20% for any sustained period in the last 40 years. There is no economy in which the authorities do not have the avowed aim of eventually reducing inflation to a low level, and there is therefore no economy in which high inflation can be regarded as a stable situation. While there are economies in which inflation remains at moderate levels for prolonged periods (Dornbusch and Fischer [8]), economic agents in a high inflation economy have to expect an attack — typically many attacks — on inflation at some point. Governments that have succeeded in creating a stable low inflation environment, such as those of Japan or Germany, can be expected to continue with their macroeconomic policies.

---

tries, where both stationarity and data availability are problematic. The competitiveness of the real exchange rate could in principle be estimated by its implications for current and future levels of the current account, while the appropriateness of the real interest rate is difficult to specify.

(7) AIZENMAN and MARION [1] attempt to quantify the random element in policy by estimating autoregressive processes for policy variables and using the standard deviations of policy surprises as a measure of uncertainty. This is promising approach, which however does not distinguish contemporaneous variability caused by responses to exogenous shocks from purely random variability.

(8) The potential links between inflation and growth are discussed and developed in FISHER [11] and by implication in FISCHER and MODIGLIANI [13].

In essence, the argument is that the inflation rate serves as an indicator of the overall ability of the government to manage the economy. Since there are no good arguments for very high rates of inflation, a government that is producing high inflation is a government that has lost control. Economic growth is likely to be low in such an economy.

Along with the level of the inflation rate, the variability of inflation is an indicator of the stability of the macroeconomic environment and macroeconomic policies. It is well known that the inflation rate and the variance of the inflation rate across time for an individual country are highly correlated in the cross-section, with an $R^2$ that generally exceeds 0.9. Thus effects attributed to the level of the inflation rate may instead be attributable to uncertainty about inflation, but at the level of aggregation of this paper, those effects cannot be distinguished.

Countries may for a long time succeed in maintaining low and stable inflation through policies that are not ultimately sustainable. Such countries, for instance those in the franc zone, may face fiscal or balance of payments crises that could necessitate sharp changes in macroeconomic policy and that certainly increase macroeconomic uncertainty. The fiscal deficit is a good, though imperfect, indicator of such an unsustainable situation. I will also use changes in the real exchange rate, in the black market exchange premium, and changes in the terms of trade, as subsidiary or alternate indicators of the stability of the macroeconomic framework.

The emphasis on the stability of the macroeconomic framework suggests that the main reason macroeconomic factors matter for growth is through uncertainty. The literature has concentrated on two channels here. First, policy-induced macroeconomic uncertainty reduces the efficiency of the price mechanism, as in the classic Lucas [20] contribution. This uncertainty, associated with high inflation or instability of the budget or current account, can be expected to reduce the level of productivity, and, in contexts where the reallocation of factors is part of the growth process, also the *rate of increase* of productivity. Second, temporary uncertainty about the macroeconomy tends to reduce the rate of investment, as potential investors wait for the resolution of the uncertainty before committing themselves (Pindyck [24]). This channel suggests that investment would be lower at times when uncertainty is high, and its presence should therefore be more noticeable in the time series than cross-sectional data (9). Capital flight, which is likely to increase with domestic instability, provides another mechanism through which macroeconomic uncertainty reduces investment in the domestic economy.

The early growth theory literature on inflation and growth emphasized the positive impact of inflation on capital accumulation that occurs as a result of the portfolio shift away from money when the rate of return on money drops, the Mundell-Tobin effect (10). Subsequent contributions, noting various complementarities between real balances and capital — whether through the production function or because of a cash-in-advance constraint — predicted that higher inflation would reduce capital accumulation (11). Similarly, all the costs of inflation detailed in Fischer and Modigliani [13] — including the impact of inflation on the taxation of capital — would imply a negative association between the level of income and inflation, and through the new growth theory mechanisms, between inflation and growth.

Turning to the other macroeconomic indicators: the budget surplus should be positively associated with capital accumulation. There are again two reasons. The first is crowding out, which occurs in many models. The second is that, like the inflation rate, the deficit serves as an indicator of a government that is losing control of its actions.

Improvements in the terms of trade are likely to make investment more attractive at home. An increase in the black market exchange premium is an indicator of expectations of depreciation of the exchange rate and foreign exchange rationing. This suggests that capital accumulation and the black market premium are likely to be negatively related. One influence in the opposite direction arises from the fact that when foreign exchange access is controlled, there is frequently preferential treatment for the import of investment goods. Devalu-

---

(9) SOLIMANO [26] presents time series evidence supporting this relationship.

(10) The mechanisms producing the Mundell and Tobin effects actually differ, though both imply that an increase in expected inflation increases capital accumulation.

(11) For references to the literature through 1983, see FISCHER [11].

ation of the exchange rate is likely to make investment more attractive.

In the short run, neither the inflation rate nor the budget deficit are unaffected by the growth rate. A supply shock will both reduce the growth rate and raise the inflation rate; and given government spending a reduction in growth will increase the deficit. Two types of regressions are reported in this paper. In the cross-sectional regressions, the period average (usually 1961-1987) growth rate or other dependent variable for each country is regressed on period average values of such right-hand side variables as inflation and the budget deficit. In the panel regressions, similar regressions are run using both the time series variation within each country and the cross-sectional variation. The problem of reverse causation is more likely to arise in the panel regressions. In principle, the use of instrumental variables can deal with the endogeneity problem, but in practice appropriate instruments are difficult to find. The endogeneity problem is less severe in the cross-sectional regressions, where the length of period is more than 25 years. The government can certainly set the inflation rate and the deficit independently of the growth rate over such a long period.

## 2. - Existing Empirical Evidence

The simple statistical evidence supports the basic proposition that macroeconomic stability is conducive to growth. Inflation in fast-growing Asia is well below the rates of price increase in slower-growing Africa and Latin America (table 1), and across the three periods shown in table 1, inflation in each area has moved inversely with growth (12). Levine and Renelt [18] show that high growth countries are also lower inflation countries, have smaller governments, and

---

(12) A similar table is presented in FISCHER [12]. The inflation rate for Asia in that table (for which the first period is 1960-1973) is shown as increasing from period to period, with an average of only 2% for 1960-1973. Both tables are taken from the same source, and I am unable to account for the different patterns of Asian inflation, though they must arise from changes in country coverage and data revisions.

lower black market exchange rate premia, the latter reflecting dise-
quilibria in the official foreign exchange markets.

In the last few years a large volume of empirical work has been
carried out, inspired by the new growth theory. This work consists
largely of cross-country regressions, typically using the Summers-Heston, 1988, ICP data (13). The results of these studies have been
reviewed and their robustness examined in an extremely useful paper
by Levine and Renelt [18], who list forty cross-sectional growth
studies published since 1980 (14).

TABLE 1

INFLATION AND ECONOMIC GROWTH
(% per annum)

| | Africa | | | Asia | | | Latin America | | |
|---|---|---|---|---|---|---|---|---|---|
| | 1965-1973 | 1973-1980 | 1980-1990 | 1965-1973 | 1973-1980 | 1980-1990 | 1965-1973 | 1973-1980 | 1980-1990 |
| GDP growth  .. | 3.7 | 3.4 | 2.1 | 5.8 | 5.8 | 6.9 | 6.0 | 5.0 | 1.1 |
| GDP per cap. growth . . . . . . | 1.1 | 0.4 | − 1.0 | 3.2 | 3.7 | 4.9 | 3.3 | 2.5 | − 0.9 |
| Inflation  . . . . . . | 5.2 | 15.8 | 18.9 | 14.8 | 8.9 | 6.9 | 22.0 | 53.0 | 249.0 |

*Source*: WORLD BANK.

Each study regresses the growth rate over a given period against
a variety of variables; well over 50 regressors have been used in these
studies. Among the regressors are variables relating to trade and trade
policy, and exchange rates; fiscal policy; political and social stability
and rights; human capital; and macroeconomic policy and outcomes.
Early studies tended to focus on trade policy and investment; studies

---

(13) For examples, see BARRO [2] and the many studies listed in LEVINE and RENELT
[18].
(14) Their list is necessarily incomplete; in particular, it does not include the
comparative cross-country analysis by MORRIS and ADELMAN [23], which is based on
work dating back to the 1960s. Several other earlier cross-country studies are listed by
Chenery, (Chapter 2 in CHENERY, ROBINSON and SYRQUIN ([3], p. 27). REYNOLDS, 1986,
p. 101, also presents a cross-sectional growth regression, despite his general preference
for time-series studies.

associated with the new growth theory typically include initial real income and some measure of human capital as well as investment.

For a sample of 101 countries, over the period 1960-1989, Levine and Renelt present a basic regression:

*(1)*             $GYP = -0.83 \quad -0.35 \quad RGDP60 -$
                  $(-0.98) \, (-2,50)$

$$-0.38 \quad GN + \quad 3.17 \quad SEC + \quad 17.5 \quad INV$$
$$(-1.73) \qquad\quad (2.46) \qquad\qquad (6.53)$$

$$R_2 = 0.46 \qquad \text{$t$-statistics in parentheses}$$

where *GYP* is the growth rate of real per capita income (from the World Bank data base), *RGDP*60 is (Summers - Heston) real income in 1960, *GN* is the rate of population growth, *SEC* in the 1960 rate of secondary school enrollment, and *INV* is the share of investment in GDP. Applying Leamer's extreme bounds analysis to equation *(1)*, the robust relationships are shown to be those between growth and initial income, and between growth and investment (15).

They then extend the analysis to include a variety of other variables. Their two broad findings are, first, that several measures of economic policy are related to long-run growth; and second, that the relationship between growth and almost every particular macroeconomic indicator other than the investment ratio is fragile. The strongest results are that investment in physical capital, and either the level or the rate of change of human capital, increase the rate of growth.

In Fischer [12], I extended the basic equation *(1)* to include macroeconomic indicators. Regressing per capita real (Summers - Heston) growth over the period 1970-1985 (16) against the standard

---

(15) DE LONG and SUMMERS [7] present evidence that growth is linked primarily to the share of equipment investment in GNP.

(16) The period was chosen in a tradeoff between the length of period and number of macroeconomic variables that could be included in the regression.

new growth theory variables, plus indicators of macroeconomic performance, yields:

$$(2) \qquad GY = \quad 1.38 \quad - 0.52 \quad RGDP70 + \\ \qquad\qquad\qquad (1.75) \, (-5.90)$$

$$+ 2.51 \; PRIM70 + \quad 11.16 \; INV - 4.75 \; INF + \\ (2.69) \qquad\qquad (3.91) \qquad (-2.70)$$

$$+ 0.17 \; SUR - 0.33 \; DEBT80 \; - 2.02 \; SSA \; - 1.98 \; LAC \\ (4.34) \qquad (-0.79) \qquad\quad (-3.71) \qquad\quad (-3.76)$$

$$R_2 = 0.60 \qquad N = 73 \qquad \text{$t$-statistics in parentheses}$$

where $PRIM70$ is the enrollment rate for primary school, $INF$ is the average inflation rate over the period 1970-1985, $SUR$ is the ratio of the budget surplus to GNP over the period 1970-1985 (17); $DEBT$ is the foreign debt to GNP ratio in 1980; and $SSA$ and $LAC$ are sub-Saharan Africa, and Latin America and the Caribbean dummies, respectively. The sample includes all countries for which data were available (18).

The rates of investment and inflation, and the budget surplus enter regression (2) significantly. The signs of all variables are as expected. When the continent dummies are excluded (19), the coefficent on inflation and the debt rise (20). Recalling that several of the

---

(17) The period is chosen to increase the number of countries included in the sample. I have also run similar regressions for the period 1974-1989, using LEVINE and RENELT's [18] data, provided by Ross Levine. No major differences in conclusions emerge using the Levine-Renelt data.

(18) It can be argued that the developing countries are sufficiently and systematically different from the industrialized countries that the latter should be excluded from the regressions. While it is easy to agree with this view at the extremes, it is hard to know where to draw the line, and I therefore worked mostly with all countries for which there were data. For some regressions (not reported here), I excluded all countries that in 1970 had an income level above Italy's; if anything, this gave stronger results with respect to macroeconomic variables, particularly the debt.

(19) Continent dummies enter most growth equations significantly. Lance Taylor has suggested that the negative coefficients for Africa and Latin America may reflect their particularly adverse terms of trade shocks in the 1980s.

(20) There was relatively little experimentation in arriving at equation (2). In some versions, the variance of inflation was entered along with the rate of inflation; it was not significant and was excluded because it is highly correlated with the rate of inflation ($R = 0.94$). The $SEC70$ variable was initially included but was dropped since its

mechanisms relating inflation to growth that were discussed in section 1 operate by affecting investment, it should be noted that the coefficients on both inflation and investment in equation *(2)* are statistically significant. This implies that inflation has effects other than those that operate through investment. For instance, inflation could affect the efficiency of operation of the given factor inputs. Regression *(2)* strengthens the arguments that macroeconomic indicators are correlated with growth, at least over the period 1970-1985.

As discussed in section 1, the macroeconomic indicators included in *(2)* cannot be regarded as truly exogenous. In this respect their status is no different than that of investment. Instruments are difficult to find; for instance, such candidates as measures of political instability not only cause but also are caused by inflation. Instrumental variable estimation of equation *(2)* using as instruments initial GDP and primary enrollment, the frequency of crises and riots, military spending, foreign aid, and the debt in 1980, resulted in a regression in which no coefficient was significantly different from zero. Instrumental variable regression using the above instruments plus the variance of inflation, the frequency of constitutional changes, and government consumption spending, produced results very similar to *(2)*, except that primary education lost its statistical significance.

The instrumental variables regression, which does not include the continent dummies, is:

$$
\begin{aligned}
(3) \qquad GY = \;\; &0.55 \;\; - 0.33 \; RGDP70 \; + \\
&(0.28) \; (-4.33)
\end{aligned}
$$

$$
\begin{aligned}
&+ 2.32 \; PRIM70 \; + \;\; 12.79 \; INV \; - \; 7.10 \; INF \\
&\;\;\;(1.32) \qquad\qquad\;\; (3.51) \qquad\quad (-4.45)
\end{aligned}
$$

$$
\begin{aligned}
&\;\;\; 0.28 \; SUR \; - \; 0.03 \; DEBT80 \\
&\;\;\; (3.06) \qquad (-0.04)
\end{aligned}
$$

$R_2 = 0.41 \qquad N = 54 \qquad$ *t*-statistics (with White, 1980, correction) in parentheses

exclusion made little difference and since *PRIM70* was generally more significant. The budget surplus variable is available for the period 1975-1985 for a smaller sample of (56) countries; the *t*-statistic on the budget surplus is smaller in that sample, but the coefficient is still significant at the 5% level. However in those regressions the significance level on the inflation rate drops below 5%, while that on the debt rises. The inclusion of the black market foreign exchange premium is discussed below.

Given both the similarity between equations *(2)* and *(3)*, and the difficulties of choosing instruments, I will not pursue instrumental variables regressions in the remainder of this paper.

Relatively little of the cross-sectional variance in growth rates is accounted for by the macroeconomic variables alone. When only the inflation rate, debt, and the deficit are included, the (corrected) squared correlation coefficient is only 0.16. When the continent dummies are 'added, 32% of the variance is accounted for.

The external debt to GNP ratio serves in *(2)* as an indicator of the exchange rate overvaluations of the late 1970s. The average black market foreign exchange premium could serve as another such (partial) indicator. Examination of simple correlations between the black market premium and other variables suggests it might be strongly related to growth. The simple correlation between the average growth rate over the period 1970-1985 and the average black market premium for the same period, for a group of forty countries for which the data are available, is − 0.24. The simple correlation between the premium and investment is − 0.36, and between the premium and the budget surplus − 0.34 (21). However, the coefficient on the average black market premium is never significant in any regression that includes the other macroeconomic variables, and this applies also to various non-linear transformations of the premium. Its major impact seems to be to reduce the coefficient on the external debt, but because its inclusion also changes the sample size, not much can be deduced from any such effect.

The negative relationship between inflation and economic growth in equations *(2)* and *(3)* has been found also in other papers, for instance in Fischer [11], De Gregorio [5] and Gylfason [14]. Easterly and Rebelo [9] find a consistent negative relationship between growth and budget deficits.

---

(21) The premium is available for 67 countries for the period 1970-1985, but there are only forty countries for which the variables in equation *(2)* plus the premium are all available. The weakness of the simple correlation between growth and the black market premium may be a result of the wide range of the premium, from zero to an average of 717% (for Nicaragua). The premium is high for African countries, excluding those in the CFA zone, and for Latin America. Nicaragua aside, the highest premia, frequently exceeding 100%, are found in North and Sub-Saharan Africa.

The evidence reviewed in this section supports the view that a stable macroeconomic framework is conducive of growth.

## 3. - Interpreting the Evidence

The approach taken in equations *(2)* and *(3)*, adding macroeconomic variables to the standard equation (1), is a natural outgrowth of the convergence literature. The key empirical result in this literature is that of conditional convergence, that conditional on the rate of saving (represented by the investment ratio), growth is negatively related to initial income.

However, adding macroeconomic variables to regressions that already include the rate of investment makes interpretation of the resultant regression difficult (22).

In this section I use a simple production function-based approach, pioneered by Victor Elias [10], essentially a regression analogue of growth accounting, which helps identify the channels through which macroeconomic variables affect economic growth. As a matter of accounting, growth can be attributed to increases in supplies of factors, and to a residual productivity category, reflecting changes in the efficiency with which factors are used. The approach is to examine the relationships between growth and macroeconomic variables, and then between the macroeconomic variables and changes in both the supplies of factors, and the residual, or productivity.

Consider the production function:

$$(4) \qquad\qquad Y_t = F(K_t, L_t, H_t, A_t)$$

---

(22) One diagnosis would be that we lack an adequate theoretical framework in which to interpret the empirical results. Certainly we lack a tightly specified model in which the relationship between macroeconomic policies and growth can be analyzed. That situation will continue for some time, even though suggestive models that isolate particular relationships between growth and macroeconomic factors are being developed. (For instance DELLAS [6], presents a model in which macroeconomic instability tends to increase long run growth by encouraging investment in human capital, which is assumed to be less vulnerable to economic downturns). The approach outlined here presents a clear analogy here with the literature on the costs of inflation, where general theoretical and institutional considerations were able to guide the discussion well before fully articulated — but still incomplete — models of the costs of inflation were available.

where $K$, $L$ and $H$ are physical capital, raw labor, and human capital respectively, and $A_t$ is an overall efficiency factor, including not only the level of technology, but also for example representing the quality of government management of the economy, or institutional factors. Differentiating *(4)*, we obtain the conventional growth accounting equation:

*(5)*     $\dot{Y}/Y = \eta_1\,(\dot{K}/K) + \eta_2\,(\dot{L}/L) + \eta_3\,(\dot{H}/H) + \eta_4\,(\dot{A}/A)$

where $\eta_i$ is elasticity with respect to argument $i$ in equation *(4)*. The variable $(\dot{A}/A)$ will be referred to as the productivity residual.

Macroeconomic factors can in principle affect economic growth through all four factors on the right-hand side of the growth accounting equation *(5)*. The standard procedure of adding macroeconomic variables to a growth regression that already includes some of the right-hand side variables, such as the rate of investment (closely related to the rate of growth of the capital stock), thus implicitly assumes that that policy variable does not affect the other included variables, and affects growth only through its impact on the right-hand side variables in *(5)* not explicitly included in the regression, typically the productivity residual.

## 3.1 *Productivity Residuals*

Productivity residuals have been calculated in this paper in three ways. Bhalla residuals start from an estimated regression equation like *(5)*, with the three factor inputs included explicitly. The data are those provided by Surjit Bhalla of the World Bank, through the Bank's 1991 *World Development Report* (WDR) database. Two different types of Bhalla regression were estimated: 1) a cross-sectional regression with only 68 observations; and 2) a panel regression, with 1826 observations per variable (23). In each case there is little evidence of

---

(23) Ten observations are missing from the Bhalla dataset (68 countries for 27 years implies 1,836 observations).

increasing returns to scale; in both regressions the coefficients on capital and labor growth are each close to one half, and the coefficient on the average education level is small. It is negative in the panel regressions, and typically very small and positive in cross-sectional regressions, but not significantly different from zero in either case.

The Bhalla production function estimated on the full panel by *GLS* is:

(6)  $ZGDP = 0.487\ ZKAP + 0.560\ ZLAB - 0.022\ ZED + RD_i$
          (18.03)            (4.31)            $(-0.40\ )$

$N = 1826;$     *t*-statistics in parentheses.

*ZGDP* is the growth rate of real GDP (in 1980 prices); *ZKAP* is the growth rate of capital; *ZLAB* is the growth rate of the labor force; and *ZED* is the growth rate of the educational stock in the labor force (24). Regional dummies $(RD_i)$ are included for the five World Bank regions as of 1991 (25); none of the coefficients on the regional dummies exceeds 1% in absolute value, and none is significantly different from zero.

The Bhalla panel regression implies productivity residuals for each country for each year; the mean productivity residual for each country, plus the dummy for its region, is an estimate of the average rate of productivity increase for that country, on the (maintained) assumption that the production function for each country is the same up to the productivity variable.

Because of the difficulties with the coefficient on the human capital variable in the Bhalla regression *(6)*, two other sets of

---

(24) The underlying variable, *ED*, is calculated as the product of the average years of education of the adunt population and the labor force. Its rate of change is thus to a first approximation equal to the sum of the 'growth rate of the labor force and the growth rate of average yearts of education. The results thus suggest that changes in average years of education do not much affect the growth rate of output.

(25) EMENA (Europe, Middle East and North Africa), with a coefficient of 0.0045; LACAR (Latin America and Caribbean), with a coefficient of − 0.0089; AFRIC, with a coefficient of − 0.0084; EASIA, with a coefficient of 0.0049; and SASIA, with a coefficient of − 0.0040.

residuals were calculated for each country. Solow residuals are calculated as:

(7)
$$RES_{it} = ZGDP_{it} - 0.4\ ZKAP_{it} - 0.6\ ZLAB_{it}$$
$$i = 1,\ldots,\ 1968 \qquad t = 1961\ \text{to}\ 1987$$

Mankiw-Romer-Weil residuals are calculated as:

(8) $REMRW_{it} = ZGDP_{it} - 0.333\ ZKAP_{it} - 0.333\ ZLAB_{it} - 0.333\ ZED_{it}$
$$i = 1,\ldots,\ 1968; \qquad t = 1961\ \text{to}\ 1987$$

Calculation of the Solow residuals imposes a common Cobb-Douglas production function in which the share of capital is somewhat higher than in the industrialized countries, as it generally estimated to be in developing countries (perhaps because agriculture is not properly accounted for). The Mankiw-Romer-Weil residuals are calculated imposing coefficients used in their 1992 paper.

The productivity residuals constructed by these three methods are, not surprisingly, very highly correlated in the time series for each country, and we therefore use the Solow residuals in the remainder of the paper. Table 2 presents the minima and maxima of the mean rates

TABLE 2

ESTIMATED PRODUCTIVITY GROWTH, 1961-1987
(% per annum)

| Region | Number of countries | Regional mean | Maximum | | Minimum | |
|---|---|---|---|---|---|---|
| | | | Country | Rate | Country | Rate |
| EMENA .. | 12 | 0.94 | Malta .. | 2.37 | Marocco | − 0.52 |
| LACAR .. | 15 | − 0.56 | Brazil .. | 1.06 | Haiti .... | − 2.36 |
| AFRICA .. | 27 | − 0.56 | Congo .. | 1.80 | Nigeria .. | − 2.84 |
| SASIA .... | 4 | 0.08 | Pakistan | 1.20 | Bangladesh | − 0.94 |
| EASIA .... | 10 | 1.17 | Hong Kong | 2.75 | Philippines | − 0.32 |

*Legend*: EMENA = Europe, Middle East and North Africa; LACAR = Latin America and Carribean; SASIA = Southern Asia; EASIA = Eastern Asia.
*Source*: calculations of Solow's residuals (equation *(7)*) based on the World Development data-base.

of Solow productivity growth calculated for each of the five World
Bank regions (26).

The range of rates of productivity growth for the 27-year period is
large, from Hong Kong's 2.75% *per annum*, to Nigeria's minus 2.84%
(27). At these rates of productivity increase, Hong Kong's income
would have risen by a factor of 4.3 relative to that of Nigeria over the
27-year period, had the two countries had the same rates of capital
and labor force growth. Even the range across regions — 1.73% — is
large.

## 4. - Results in the Growth Accounting Framework

Cross-sectional regressions for the largest possible number of
countries on single macroeconomic indicator variables are presented
in table 3. These are regressions in which there are no regional
dummies, and only a constant in addition to the variable indicated.
However, the coefficients change very little when regional dummies
are added. The only variables that are individually significantly
correlated with the growth rate are the inflation rate and the budget
surplus.

When the variables are entered in combination, none of them is
individually significant, though this may be due in part to the reduction in the number of observations, there is a maximum of 36
observations in any regression in which the fiscal variable is included.

In using only period averages, the cross-sectional regressions
discard the information in the time series for individual countries. The
results of similar panel regressions are presented in table 4 (28).

The panel regressions confirm the relationships between inflation
and growth, and the budget surplus and growth, seen in table 3. In

---

(26) EMENA = Europe, Middle East and North Africa; SSA = Sub Saharan
Africa; LAC = Latin America and Caribbean.

(27) Calculations of Nigerian growth rates are exceptionally sensitive to the base
year, and it is quite likely that the 1980 base, in which oil has a large share, exaggerates
the decline in Nigerian output in the 1980s, relative to the implications of a base year in
which oil is less important.

(28) The standard deviation of inflation is not included because I have not yet
created a time series for this variable for each country.

TABLE 3

## CROSS-SECTIONAL GROWTH REGRESSIONS (*)

| Equation | *INFLAT* | *SURRAT* | *ZTOT1* | *EXCHPREM* | *ZREER* | *SINFLAT* | n. of obs. |
|---|---|---|---|---|---|---|---|
| *(9)* .... | −0.041 (−2.95) | | | | | | 62 |
| *(10)* .... | | 0.158 (1.99) | | | | | 36 |
| *(11)* .... | | | 0.089 (0.78) | | | | 65 |
| *(12)* .... | | | | −0.00114 (−1.45) | | | 79 |
| *(13)* .... | | | | | −0.136 (−1.23) | | 61 |
| *(14)* .... | | | | | | 0.019 (−1.83) | 86 |

(*) *t*-statistics are in parentheses. Dependent variable is *ZGDP*, growth rate of real GDP. Other variable definitions are: *INFLAT* = inflation rate; *SURRAT* = ratio of budget surplus to GDP; *ZTOT1* = change in terms of trade; *EXCHPREM* = black market exchange premium; *ZREER* = change in real exchange rate (increase = deviation); *SINFLAT* = standard deviation of inflation rate (over entire 27-year period).

addition, in the context of the panel regression, changes in the terms of trade are now significantly and positively associated with growth. The numerical values of the coefficients on inflation and the deficits are both very similar to those in table 3. They imply that a country that has an inflation rate 100 percentage points higher than another (e.g. 110% *per annum* rather than 10% *per annum*) will have a growth rate that is 3.9% lower; and that a country with a budget surplus that is higher by 1% of GDP, will have a growth rate that is 0.14% larger. Similar regressions that include regional dummies give almost identical coefficients on the macroeconomic variables.

In panel regressions that include all or most subsets of the right-hand side variables in table 4, the coefficients on all the variables except the inflation rate lose their individual significance. The coefficients retain their signs, except for the black market premium, but are reduced in absolute value and their standard errors rise. However, because these regressions had to be run on a much smaller sample, it is not clear to what extent the changes arise from a change in the

TABLE  4

PANEL GROWTH REGRESSIONS (*)

| Equation | INFLAT | SURRAT | ZTOT1 | EXCHPREM | ZREER | n. of obs. |
|---|---|---|---|---|---|---|
| *(15)* ........ | −0.039<br>(−8.31) | | | | | 1,490 |
| *(16)* ........ | | 0.141<br>(3.70) | | | | 633 |
| *(17)* ........ | | | 0.032<br>(3.62) | | | 1,381 |
| *(18)* ........ | | | | −0.0014<br>(−1.48) | | 1,703 |
| *(19)* ........ | | | | | −0.005<br>(−0.55) | 1,350 |

(*) *t*-statistics in parentheses. Variables are as defined in table 3. Regressions are run using *GLS* (seemingly unrelated regressions).

sample size and composition rather than as a result of the inclusion of multiple right-hand side variables (29).

The issue of endogeneity is clearly present in tables 3 and 4. Of the right-hand side variables in table 4, the terms of trade are probably closest to being exogenous. A regression that includes both the inflation rate and the change in the terms of trade shows coefficients that are almost identical to those in table 4 (30):

$$(20) \quad ZGDP = \quad 0.046 \quad - 0.039 \ INFLAT + \quad 0.030 \ ZTOT1$$
$$\quad\quad\quad\quad (17.44) \quad (-6.84) \quad\quad\quad\quad (3.27)$$

$$N = 1098$$

Equation *(20)* shows at least that the partial relationship between inflation and growth — conditional on changes in the terms of trade

---

(29) The problem of changing sample size when the number of observations changes because of the unavailability of some variable — typically the fiscal deficit — is very common in this literature.

(30) In regressions that include all three of the inflation rate, budget surplus, and change in the terms of trade on the right-hand side, only the inflation rate retains its statistical significance. This statement applies for all the dependent variables in this paper.

— is the same as the total relationship. Further, since many theories predict a positive rather than negative relationship between inflation and growth within the cycle, the negative coefficient on inflation found throughout this paper is not obviously a sign of reverse causation.

These basic regressions reinforce the evidence in favor of the view that macroeconomic stability, as measured for instance by the inflation rate or the budget surplus, is on average good for growth. We turn now to the mechanisms through which the macroeconomic variables affect growth.

## 4.1 Capital Accumulation

Pursuing the approach described in section 3, we start with equations in which the rate of capital accumulation is regressed on the same macroeconomic variables as in tables 3 and 4. The results presented in table 5 are all for panel regressions estimated by *GLS*. (Results for the corresponding cross-section regressions will be discussed below). Variable definitions are as in table 3. Regressions are estimated by *GLS*.

TABLE 5

PANEL REGRESSIONS, CAPITAL ACCUMULATION (*)

| Equation | *INFLAT* | *SURRAT* | *ZTOT1* | *EXCHPREM* | *ZREER* | n. of obs. |
|---|---|---|---|---|---|---|
| *(21)* ........ | − 0.046 (− 11.75) | | | | | 1,478 |
| *(22)* ........ | | 0.108 (3.05) | | | | 600 |
| *(23)* ........ | | | 0.016 (2.40) | | | 1,281 |
| *(24)* ........ | | | | − 0.00031 (− 4.21) | | 1,540 |
| *(25)* ........ | | | | | − 0.022 (− 3.10) | 1,300 |
| *(26)* ........ | − 0.038 (− 9.25) | | 0.013 (2.09) | | | 1,098 |

(*) Dependent variable is *ZAP*, the growth rate of the real capital stock.

All coefficients in table 5 are of the expected sign, and all are statistically significant at the 5% level. When more than one variable is entered in a panel regression, the coefficient on the inflation rate is always significant, while the others are generally not statistically significant (except in equation *(26)*).

The coefficient on inflation implies that an increase in the inflation rate by 100 percentage points (e.g. from 10 to 110% *per annum*) reduces the growth rate of the capital stock by 4.6 percentage points. This is a large effect: if the investment rate is about 20% of GDP, and the capital output ratio is 2.5, then the growth rate of capital is 8%. According to the regression, capital in such a country would stop growing when the inflation rate reaches about 175% *per annum*. An increase in the budget deficit of 1% of GDP would reduce the growth rate of capital by 0.14 percentage points.

In simple cross-sectional regressions corresponding to those in table 5, the coefficients on the first three variables (inflation, the budget surplus, and the terms of trade) retain their significance but are generally larger than in table 5. The other variables are not significant in the cross-sectional regressions.

These results suggest that capital accumulation is an important channel through which inflation and the deficit affect economic growth. The numerical values of the coefficients are plausible, even though these cannot be thought of as structural regressions.

## 4.2 *Productivity Growth*

The impacts of the macroeconomic variables on productivity growth estimated by the Solow residual are presented in table 6. The inflation rate is significantly negatively correlated with the rate of productivity growth, with a coefficient implying that an increase in the inflation rate by 100% is associated with a decline in the rate of productivity growth of 2.2% *per annum*. Increases in the budget surplus, and improvements in the terms of trade, are associated with improvements in productivity growth. The effect of inflation is robust to the inclusion of the change in the terms of trade. The black market exchange rate premium is not significantly associated with the rate of

TABLE 6

## PANEL REGRESSIONS, PRODUCTIVITY GROWTH (*)

| Equation | *INFLAT* | *SURRAT* | *ZTOT1* | *EXCHPREM* | *ZREER* | n. of obs. |
|---|---|---|---|---|---|---|
| *(27)* ........ | − 0.022<br>(− 4.64) | | | | | 1,478 |
| *(28)* ........ | | 0.098<br>(3.05) | | | | 600 |
| *(29)* ........ | | | 0.025<br>(3.03) | | | 1,281 |
| *(30)* ........ | | | | − 0.000<br>(− 0.66) | | 1,450 |
| *(31)* ........ | | | | | − 0.012<br>(− 1.42) | 1,300 |
| *(32)* ........ | − 0.023<br>(− 4.48) | | 0.025<br>(2.86) | | | 1,098 |

(*) Dependent variable is *RES*, the Solow residual, calculated as in equation *(7)*. Other variable definitions are as in table 3. Regressions are estimated by *GLS*.

productivity growth, a result which is surprising if the black market premium is interpreted as an indicator of the degree of distortion in the exchange markets.

When more than one of the macroeconomic indicator variables is included in a regression for productivity growth, usually the inflation

TABLE 7

## GROSS-SECTIONAL PRODUCTIVITY REGRESSIONS (*)

| Equation | *INFLAT* | *SURRAT* | *ZTOT1* | *EXCHPREM* | *ZREER* | n. of obs. |
|---|---|---|---|---|---|---|
| *(33)* ........ | − 0.015<br>(− 1.36) | | | | | 61 |
| *(34)* ........ | | 0.079<br>(1.39) | | | | 34 |
| *(35)* ........ | | | − 0.054<br>(− 0.61) | | | 60 |
| *(36)* ........ | | | | − 0.00100<br>(− 1.39) | | 66 |
| *(37)* ........ | | | | | − 0.113<br>(− 1.39) | 59 |
| *(38)* ........ | − 0.020<br>(− 1.54) | | − 0.074<br>(− 0.84) | | | 54 |

(*) *t*-statistics are in parentheses. Equations are estimated by *OLS*.

rate retains its statistical significance while the other variables lose their significance (except in equation *(32)*).

In the cross-sectional regressions, (table 7), none of the macroeconomic variables are significantly related to productivity growth (except the black market premium), but the results for inflation are consistent with those of the panel regressions.

Theories in which inflation distorts signals suggest that uncertainty about inflation should have an impact on productivity. Given the high correlation between the inflation rate and its variance, within countries, it is difficult to disentangle the uncertainty impacts of inflation from its other channels of influence. The strong regression results in table 6 may reflect inflation uncertainty as much as the rate of inflation.

### 4.3 *Labor Force Growth*

For the sake of completeness, table 8 presents estimates of the panel equations for labor force growth. These show inflation increasing the rate of growth of the labor force, and a budget surplus reducing it, while none of the other variables is statistically significant. However, the size of the statistically significant effects is so small as to

TABLE 8

PANEL REGRESSIONS, LABOR FORCE GROWTH (*)

| Equation | INFLAT | SURRAT | ZTOT1 | EXCHPREM | ZREER | n. of obs. |
|---|---|---|---|---|---|---|
| *(39)* ........ | 0.001 (1.96) | | | | | 1,998 |
| *(40)* ........ | | 0.0016 (−2.66) | | | | 679 |
| *(41)* ........ | | | 0.0008 (−0.79) | | | 1,689 |
| *(42)* ........ | | | | 6E-7 (0.07) | | 2,126 |
| *(43)* ........ | | | | | 6E-5 (0.08) | 1,685 |

(*) Dependent variable is ZLAB, the growth rate of the labor force. Regressions are estimated by GLS.

render them economically meaningless. It would have been surprising if the macroeconomic variables had large effects on the growth of the labor force, given that these labor force variables are almost certainly at best crude estimates.

## 5. - Some Reservations

The results so far are supportive of the view that macroeconomic instability, as reflected in the inflation rate and the budget deficit, is associated with lower growth. While the endogeneity problem has not been disposed of, the evidence from the regressions and from case studies is consistent with the view that the causation is not fully from low growth to high inflation, and therefore that countries that are able to reduce the inflation rate in a sustainable can on average expect higher growth to follow. There is nothing in the results to contradict the view that inflation is merely a symptom of a government out of control, but there is nothing in that argument that contradicts the view that controlling inflation will help restore growth.

While the regressions provide suggestive evidence, it is also useful to look at the exceptions. Table 9 shows that some countries have experienced rapid growth at high inflation rates. During the period 1960-1988, at least fifteen countries experienced an annual inflation rate greater than 50% in at least one year (31). Growth in some of these countries exceeded 5% during a year or more of 50% or more inflation. Table 9 lists those cases, as well as information about growth and inflation during the entire period of high inflation of which the high growth period is a part.

Similarly, treating the budget deficit as a macroeconomic indicator, 17 countries have experienced deficits in excess of 10 percent of GDP during the period covered by the WDR data (32). Some of

---

(31) There are 15 such countries in an 89-country sample, from *International Financial Statistics*, for the period 1961-1989.

(32) The seventeen are: Brazil (3 years); Cote d'Ivoire (1 year); Ethiopia (1 year); Greece (3 years); Israel (11 years); Malaysia (5 years); Malawi (1 year); Mauritius (5 years); Morocco (5 years); Nicaragua (6 years); Pakistan (1 year); Sri Lanka (7 years); Syria (1 year); Tanzania (1 year); Togo (2 years); Zambia (13 years); Zimbabwe (6 years).

TABLE 9

## HIGH INFLATION AND ECONOMIC GROWTH
(% per annum)

| Country | High growth period | | | Entire spell (*) | | |
|---|---|---|---|---|---|---|
| | Period | Inflation | GNP growth | Period | Inflation | GNP growth |
| Argentina | 1977 | 101.5 | 6.2 | 1975-1989 | 117 | 0.5 |
| | 1979 | 95.4 | 6.8 | | | |
| | 1986 | 64.5 | 5.3 | | | |
| Brazil .... | 1980 | 60.3 | 8.7 | 1980-1987 | 90 | 3.5 |
| | 1984-1986 | 105.3 | 7.1 | | | |
| Chile .... | 1977 | 65.2 | 9.4 | 1972-1977 | 115 | − 1.2 |
| Ghana .... | 1978 | 54.9 | 9.4 | 1977-1978 | 66 | 5.6 |
| Israel .... | 1979-1980 | 70.3 | 6.0 | 1979-1985 | 95 | 3.8 |
| Peru...... | 1979 | 51.1 | 5.6 | 1979 | 51 | 5.6 |
| | 1986-1987 | 59.8 | 7.9 | 1983-1987 | 73 | 2.4 |
| Uganda .. | 1981 | 73.6 | 8.0 | 1981 | 74 | 8.0 |
| | 1988 | 104.3 | 6.3 | 1985-1988 | 102 | 0.1 |

(*) A spell is a period in which the annual inflation rate exceeds 50 percent each year.
*Source*: International Financial Statistics.

them, including Brazil and Israel, are also listed in table 9. Others, listed in table 10, include rapid growers such as Mauritius and Malaysia; and some high growing countries, such as Turkey, that are not on the list, have had large deficits and inflation during their periods of high growth (33).

The data presented in tables 9 and 10 raise the question of the circumstances under which countries can continue to grow fast when such standard indicators of the macroeconomic situation as the deficit and inflation are exceptionally high. Every country that appears in table 9 ran into severe trouble at some later stage. Thus table 9 seems to show only that rapid growth is possible for a time even with high inflation. In some cases, such as Peru, the period of rapid growth is associated with a rapidly accelerating inflation and a situation that is heading rapidly for disaster.

---

(33) Industrialized countries such as Italy are not included in the database from which table 10 is drawn.

TABLE 10

### LARGE DEFICITS, INFLATION AND GROWTH

| Country | Period | Deficit/GDP | Growth rate | Inflation |
|---|---|---|---|---|
| Brazil ........... | 1985-1987 | 12.1 | 6.2 | 109 |
| Israel ........... | 1974-1984 | 19.4 | 3.6 | 64 |
| Malaysia ......... | 1980-1983 | 15.9 | 6.5 | 6 |
| Mauritius......... | 1978-1982 | 11.6 | 2.2 | 16 |
| Morocco ......... | 1976-1978 | 14.5 | 6.8 | 10 |
| Nicaragua ....... | 1981-1986 | 20.8 | − 0.4 | 70 |
| Sri Lanka ....... | 1978-1983 | 13.3 | 5.7 | 14 |
| Zambia (*) ....... | 1975-1978 | 15.8 | − 0.1 | 15 |
| Zimbabwe (**) .... | 1978-1980 | 10.6 | 3.6 | 10 |

(*) Between 1971 and 1987, Zambia's deficit exceeded 10% of GNP in 13 years. The longest continuous spell is 1975-1978.

(**) Zimbabwe's deficit exceeded 10% of GNP in six of the years 1978-1987; 1978-1980 is the longest continuous spell.

*Source*: WDR: Database.

By drawing the line in table 9 at 50% inflation, I omit those countries that have succeeded in growing over sustained periods with inflation that persisted in the moderate range of 15-30%, typically with the assistance of extensive indexation (34). Such situations are sustainable, provided the government takes action to prevent inflation rising above the 30% range. The explosive situations appear to be those in which governments believe the inflation rate is of no major consequence, and permit it to continue rising even after it leaves the moderate range.

The data in table 10 provide a less clear lesson. Som of the countries are growing fast and are able to sustain high deficits with the assistance of a high saving rate (35). Others are clearly countries in trouble, such as Zambia and Zimbabwe. Notice though that even the countries in trouble may have low inflation rates. Obviously, supplementary studies of the budgetary situation are needed to determine

---

(34) See DORNBUSCH and FISCHER [8].

(35) There is a serious data problem in table 10, in that the deficit is that of the central government. Apparently, in the case of Malaysia, the deficit was financed almost entirely by the social security system, so that the consolidated deficit would have been small.

whether a large deficit is sustainable — and therefore consistent with macroeconomic stability — or unsustainable, and therefore a harbinger of macroeconomic instability.

## 6. - Concluding Comments

The evidence in this paper supports the conventional view that a stable macroeconomic environment, as reflected in a low rate of inflation and a respectably small budget deficit, is conducive to sustained economic growth. The growth accounting framework makes it possible to identify the main channels through which inflation reduces growth. As a great deal of prior theory predicts, the results presented here imply that inflation reduces growth by reducing investment, and by reducing the rate of productivity growth.

The cross-sectional regression methodology that is associated with the new growth theory has been extended in this paper to include panel regressions, whose results typically reinforce those of the simple cross-sections. The endogeneity issue is difficult to deal with formally, but several reasons are given to believe that the relationship between inflation and growth is not purely a result of low growth producing high inflation.

The examples presented in tables 9 and 10 show that low inflation and small deficits are not necessary for high growth, over even quite long periods. They do suggest that very high inflation is not consistent with sustained growth. The results also suggest that the sustainability of the budget deficit has to be investigated in more detail than is possible in the aggregative approach that has been taken in this paper.

While the results presented here are sensible, they also reveal the limits of the methodology. Not only are the results at best reduced forms, but they are almost certainly also subject to the Levine-Renelt finding that inclusion of other variables associated with growth — for instance, measures of the extent of financial intermediation, or openness to trade — would affect the estimated coefficients and their standard errors. This phenomenon is the combined result of the collinearity of the typical right-hand side variables in these regressions and the low explanatory power of most of the regressions (36).

To make further progress in defining a stable and sustainable macroeconomic framework, and in clarifying the channels through which macroeconomic variables affect growth, it will be necessary to undertake more detailed case studies of individual countries, based on more structural models. A good start on this approach has already been made in some of the contributions in Little *et* Al. [19] and it is ecouraging that those results agree with those in this paper.

---

(36) I am grateful to Robert Pindyck for discussion of this issue.

BIBLIOGRAPHY

[1] AIZENMAN JOSHUA - MARION NANCY: *Macroeconomic Uncertainty, Persistence and Growth*, Darthmouth College, mimeo, 1991.

[2] BARRO ROBERT J.: «Economic Growth in a Cross Section of Countries», *Quarterly Journal of Economics*, vol. 106, n. 2, May 1991, pp. 407-44.

[3] CHERNEY HOLLIS B. - ROBINSON SHERMAN - SYRQUIN MOSHE: *Industrialization and Growth*, New York, Oxford University Press, 1986.

[4] CORDEN MAX: «Macroeconomic Policy and Growth: Some Lessons of Experience», *Proceedings fo the World Bank Annual Conference on Development Economics*, 1990, pp. 59-84.

[5] DE GREGORIO JOSE: *The Effects of Inflation on Economic Growth: Lessons from Latin America*, IMF, mimeo, October 1991.

[6] DELLAS HARRIS: *Stabilization Policy and Long Term Growth: Are They Related? A Darwinian Perspective*, University of Maryland, mimeo 1990.

[7] DE LONG J. BRADFORD - SUMMERS LAWRENCE H.: «Equipment Investment and Economic Growth», *Quarterly Journal of Economics*, vol. 106, n. 2, May 1991, pp. 369-406.

[8] DORNBUSCH RUDIGER - FISCHER STANLEY: «Moderate Inflation», NBER, *Working Paper*, n. 3896, November 1991.

[9] EASTERLY WILLIAM - REBELO SERGIO: *Fiscal Policy and Growth: An Empirical Investigation*, World Bank, mimeo, 1992.

[10] ELIAS VICTOR J.: *Sources of Growth*, San Francisco, ICS Press, 1992.

[11] FISCHER STANLEY: «Inflacion y Crecimiento», «Inflation and Growth», *Cuadernos de Economia*, n. 20, December 1983, pp. 267-78, English version, «Sidrausky Memorial Lecture», NBER, *Working Paper*, n. 1253, 1983.

[12] — —: «Macroeconomics, Development, and Growth», NBER, *Macroeconomics Annual*, 1991, pp. 329-64.

[13] FISCHER STANLEY - MODIGLIANI FRANCO: «Towards an Understanding of the Real Effects and Costs of Inflation», *Weltwirtschaftliches Archiv*, pp. 810-32, 1978, reprinted in FISCHER S.: *Indexing, Inflation, and Economic Growth*, London, MIT Press, 1986.

[14] GYLFASOR THORVALDUR: «Inflation, Growth, and External Debt: A View of the Landscape», *The World Economy*, vol. 14, n. 3, September 1991, pp. 279-98.

[15] GRIER KEVIN B. - TULLOCK GORDON: «An Empirical Analysis of Cross-National Economic Growth, 1951-1980», *Journal of Monetary Economics*, vol. 24, n. 2, September 1989, pp. 256-76.

[16] HAMILTON JAMES D. - FLAVIN MARJORIE A.: «On the Limitations of Government Borrowing: A Framework for Empirical Testing», *American Economic Review*, vol. 76, n. 4, September 1986, pp. 809-19.

[17] KORMENDI ROGER C. - MEGUIRE PHILIP G.: «Macroeconomic Determinants of Growth: Cross-Country Evidence», *Journal of Monetary Economics*, vol. 16, n. 2, September 1985, pp. 141-64.

[18] LEVINE ROSS - RENELT DAVID: *A Sensitivity Analysis of Cross-Country Growth Regression*, World Bank, mimeo, 1990.

[19] LITTLE IAN - COOPER RICHARD - CORDEN MAX - RAJAPATIRANA SARATH: *Boom, Crisis and Adjustment: The Macroeconomic Experience of Developing Countries*, mimeo, 1992.

[20] LUCAS ROBERT E.: «Some International Evidence on Output-Inflation Tradeoffs», *American Economic Review*, n. 63, June 1973, pp. 326 34.

[21] MACKENZIE G.A.: «Are All Summary Indicators of the Stance of Fiscal Policy Misleading?», IMF, *Staff Papers*, vol. 36, n. 4, December 1989, pp. 743-70.

[22] MANKIW N. GREGORY - ROMER DAVID - WEIL DAVID N.: «A Contribution to the Empirics of Economic Growth», *Quarterly Journal of Economics*, vol. 107, n. 2, May 1992, pp. 407-38.

[23] MORRIS CYNTHIA T. - ADELMAN IRMA: *Comparative Patterns of Economic Development 1850-1914*, Baltimore, Johns Hopkins Press, 1988.

[24] PINDYCK ROBERT: «Irreversible Investment, Capacity Choice, and the Value of the Firm», *American Economic Review*, vol. 78, n. 5, December 1988, pp. 969-85.

[25] ROMER PAUL M.: «Human Capital and Growth: Theory and Evidence», NBER, *Working Paper*, n. 3173, 1989.

[26] SOLIMANO ANDRES: «How Private Investment Reacts to Changing Macroeconomic Conditions: The Case of Chile in the Eighties», World Bank, *Working Paper WPS*, n. 212, 1989.

[27] WORLD BANK: «Adjustment Lending: An Evaluation of Ten Years of Experience», *Policy and Research Series Paper*, n. 14, 1989.

[28] ——: «Adjustment Lending Policies for Sustainable Growth», *Policy and Research Series Paper*, n. 14, 1989.

[29] ——: *World Development Report*, 1991.

[30] ——: *The Third Report on Adjustment Lending: Private and Public Resource for Growth*, 1992.

# Concluding Remarks

## Edmund S. Phelps
### Columbia University

Two questions have hovered over our explorations: what explains why some countries have grown much faster than others in the postwar period and in longer periods? And what can a country do to improve its growth performance? Of particular interest to some of the authors is the role that globalization of certain markets may have played in the convergence of productivity levels over much of the world in recent decades. Another issue of particular interest is the role that membership of countries in an economic area may have played in their economic growth.

Why, we may begin by asking ourselves, are so many laymen and economists worried over their countries' growth performance? I would agree that rational observers are cheered when their country finds itself the recipient of a free lunch, especially if a decent share of the repast goes to those whose hard work is poorly rewarded. No surprises there. The same observers are unlikely to lose sleep over what they cannot control, however. What people in a country worry about, I suggest, is whether it is performing efficiently and hence, in particular, making efficient use of its opportunities for growth. A country's growth performance is inefficient if it would be possible through better resource allocation to increase the future consumption consistent with a given level, to get more consumption growth for given sacrifice in terms of saving and work. Also, the growth performance inefficient if it would be possible to improve the terms at which additional saving can be converted into additional future consumption.

I would go further in suggesting that what drives the newfound anxiety over growth is the specter that if factor returns fall in the home country relatively to factor returns in some reference-countries in the rest of the world with which the home country is normally compared, there could be a departure of capital and an accompanying brain drain on a large scale, thus threatening the future of the country's culture. People want to believe that their country's heritage of customs and art will continue to be robust, not weakened by economic competition. That is why people are more concerned with their country's own performance than with, say, the rate of world technological advance. (I have been struck by how little interest there is in world aggregates even in the economics profession).

There is a renewal of curiosity among economists these days in these questions. The predominant reason, I suspect, is that growth economics has become econometric, thanks to the accumulation of lengthy time series for tens of countries and to the availability of low-cost high-speed computers. It is now possible to test the statistical validity of certain propositions and models in the "growth theory" of the 1950s and 1960s: *a)* the property known as the natural rate of growth (which is invariant to the fraction of income saved); *b)* rival views about the role of education in the growth process; *c)* the notion that technical progress is produced according to a production function, etc. This is nice to see, and fun to do. Another reason for renewed interest is the arrival of a new hypothesis that has intrigued the younger theorists and econometricians: the hypothesis of increasing returns to scale in the economy as a whole, despite constant returns to scale at the individual firm, because certain investments at a firm — in skills, in markets, in fixed capital, and so forth — generate spillover effects on productivity at other firms. The pursuit of this new wrinkle has inevitably stimulated a resumption of the growth theory begun in the 1960s. The role of research and of education in the process of growth are being picked up again. It could be, ironically, that there is little validity to the new idea, yet it can serve as a stimulus to better understanding of the way technology and education operate in the growth process.

The basic econometric apparatus of growth economics, which derives from the 1950s work of Robert Solow, is the familiar growth rate equation. It treats the growth rate of labor productivity as a linear combination of several contributive factors: the growth rate of the stock of fixed capital or else the volume of fixed investment; the capacity of the population (proxied by the average educational attainment of the labor force) to acquire and to assimilate technologies; the rate of investment in research and development; some other factors relating to the efficiency of the growth process as proxied by measures of the financial system, international exchange, and government policy.

In the stylized account of the thrust of this volume I am trying to present here I will emphasize those papers that seek to explain national growth rates in these terms. As it happeans, most of the papers adhere pretty closely to that attractive and useful formulation, and most of those not using it explicitly still have some bearing on the growth rate equation.

The papers using that formulation in the way just described tend to confirm that fixed investment does matter for the growth rate. The DeLong-Summers paper infers that investment in *equipment* matters but not investment in plant, in commercial structures. How can it be that business investment in structures yields no positive return measured in output? As I commented in the discussion, I think an important part of the explanation for this result is that, to a considerable extent, industrial structures in which workers and machines operate can be viewed as an amenity of the workers for which they are willing to pay through reduced wages, not as capital to make the work go faster or better. Go to the luxurious and frequently elegant law offices in lower Manhattan to see how remote business structures can be from production. At work in many cases, of course, is a tax motive as well as a nonpecuniary consumption motive.

A lively discussion followed the thesis of Robert Mundell in his paper that much of the convergence of productivity levels in a *subset* of the national economies witnessed in the postwar era is to be attributed to the heightened international mobility of financial capital believed to have occurred during that period. It is true that the world capital market apparently curtailed America's share of the world supply of saving in the early 1970s, perhaps earlier; by the early 1980s Western Europe could be said largely to have "converged" with

America. When the American government stimulated investment and otherwise drove up real interest rates in the 1980s, the investment slowdown spread to Western Europe; during this decade Japan and the tigers of East Asia recorded extraordinary gains in capital stock and productivity relatively to Europe and America. Unfortunately, though, the countries experiencing the capital outflow also seem to suffer non-classical slumps, and the world growth rate perhaps slows on balance. In the two decades as a whole the United States did not serve as a net exporter of capital, ˙nor did Africa and Latin America manage to import much capital. Capital flows relative to income did not set historical records. It is a mixed pattern in which government policies play significant roles (1).

More than one of the papers showed an interest in whether various kinds of public infrastructure also matter for the growth rate. David Canning in his paper hypothesizes that it helps not only the level of productivity to have a telephone system; it also facilitates the growth of productivity. In his econometric estimations, Canning finds some positive evidence in favour of this hypothesis, but evidently the data are not rich enough to detect the separate influences of different kinds of infrastructure.

Understandably, I was delighted to see that the Nelson-Phelps thesis of 1966 on the role of education received some striking econometric support. Prior to that, it may be recalled, there was available only the conventional view, which is due to Schulz, which held that human capital is like fixed capital. So human capital is to be entered into production functions rather like fixed capital. The Nelson-Phelps thesis held that the education level of the population largely determines its capacity to comprehend and introduce new technologies (embodied or not in new gadetry) made possible by the theoretical and applied work of scientists and engineers overseas and at home. In the Benhabib-Spiegel paper it was found that the growth rate of productivity is a function not at all of the growth of human

---

(1) Japan exported considerable capital for more than a decade, much of it absorbed by American capital imports that were driven by American fiscal stimulus and immigration, not exactly by low wages. (Japan now exports primarily to neighboring countries). The former West Germany, also a large net exporter of capital, is now exporting less, primarily to the former East Germany and parts of Eastern Europe, which is another pattern driven by governmental policy.

capital, as measured by average educational attainment, but rather by the level of educational attainment, precisely as predicted by the Nelson-Phelps thesis.

What other explanatory factors find their way into the growth rate equation? No one at this conference took up the theme of Edwin Mansfield and a few contemporaries in the 1960s, the theme that the rate of technical progress in a country is a function of the scientific input of that country. Perhaps this idea is increasingly a victim of globalization. Small and medium-size countries like Uruguay and Belgium produce little of the technology they use. The rate of technological progress is best thought of as a function of the world aggregate of scientific and engineering input.

If for all or most countries the preponderant part of technological advances regularly originates overseas rather than in the home country, the degree of contact with foreign suppliers and foreign customers must be an important determinant of the rate of transmission of foreign technologies. Although Keynes in a notorious paper asserted that nations should exchange ideas but not trade goods, today we would say that many ideas, perhaps most are transmitted in the course of buying or selling goods. In the paper by Paganetto and Scandizzo, it is hypothesized accordingly that the rate of technical improvements introduced into a country is a function of the size of that country's export volume. There is no econometric test of the significance of this variable, though.

Both education and scientific activity are closely dependent on public policy, of course, much of it being purchased by the public sector. How do other activites of the public sector contribute to the growth rate? David Canning found that aggregate public expenditure enters negatively in his reduced-form version of the growth rate equation. It could be that this negative effect is solely a reflection of the crowding out of productive investment expenditures (in the private sector or for that matter in the public sector) by big-government spending in the welfare/entitlements state. But it could be that the effect of most public spending is antagonistic to growth through another mechanism: large government transfers and correspondingly high tax rates may have the consequence of discouraging risk-taking in the population, hence dampening the rate of innovation, and thus slowing economic growth. Some interesting distinctions among the kinds of government spending and among the types of taxation could be investigated if the effort were put forward to disaggregate the data.

The effects of macroeconomic policy on the growth rate have also been overdue for attention. Fischer in his paper showed that if a country suffers an increase of its inflation rate, an effect is to slow the rate of increase of the domestic capital stock, and also to dampen a bit the rate of technical improvement enjoyed in the country. Here it would be good to distinguish between an involuntary increasey of the domestic inflation rate resulting from an adverse exogenous development and a voluntary increase of the inflation rate springing from a newfound desire to have the near-term benefits of the transient elevation of output and employment generated by the acceleration of the price level.

Rather little turned up in this volume in the way of a test of the "endogenous growth theory" of the 1980s. The agreed-upon meaning or meanings of this theory were not clear to very many of us in this volume. To some the centerpiece is the learning-by-doing phenomenon, which goes back to Arrow and the RAND Corporation in the early 1960s. To a few a central strand is the role of education in keeping abreast of the technology, as in Nelson and Phelps. Others point to the postulate of increasing returns to scale, which originates with the 1931 paper of Allyn Young. These themes were sometimes drawn upon in this volume, especially in the more applied papers. But there was rather little explicit testing of them. Of course, the mechanical notion of a production function exhibiting increasing returns to scale in fixed and human capital perishes if the Schulzian conception of human capital is empirically rejected. But there could still be some sort of increasing returns to being a large country if doubling capital, land, and labor — with an accompanying doubling of the number of educated persons in the working age population — causes a narrowing of the gap between that country's actual-practice technology and the best-practice level. (The average delay in introducing a new technology may be a function of the delay in the earliest introduction, and the latter may be shorter the larger the population of potential innovators on the lookout for a new technology or a new gadget worth introducing).

Yet these themes show signs of having moved with the times. Today economists recognize that the growth performance of a country — the efficiency with which it grows — is to an important degree a matter of the incentives created by the financial system and the system of corporate governance that interconnects with the financial system. The financial system is, so to speak, the brain of the economy, privatization merely the bone and muscle waiting for the brain's direction. There are, after all, many firms in an economy in which investment may be made. Which ones are to obtain debt or equity finance?

Modern economic theory suggests that the nature of the institutions that receive and process information on the firms and allocate capital to them can go seriously awry. So a well-functioning financial system seems to be rather important, if not crucial, to the efficiency of the growth process. On the other hand, casual observation suggests that virtually every country's financial system has elements that leave something to be desired. In most countries banks are guilty of short-termism, a focus on collateralizable loans, and failure to supply venture capital to start-up firms.

The paper by Joseph Stiglitz modeled some ways in which the design of the financial system may make an important contribution to the efficiency of the growth process. Yet, persuasive as these arguments are, we are not yet at the point where we can characterize financial systems in terms of one or two variables and demonstrate how these variables affect the growth rate of productivity. In the near future we hope to be able to find that the profession has reached that point.

# VII - ROUND TABLE: ECONOMIC POLICY «RECOMMENDATIONS»

## Stanley Fischer
MIT, Cambridge (Mass.)

I wish to attempt to make some concluding remarks on the papers in this volume.

The question springs to mind whether we can offer governments different policies based on the new theories of economic growth that have been developed.

However, it would appear that no new indications have actually emerged. Most of the policies proposed by the new theories of growth can, in fact, be found in existing literature on growth economics and have been coherently substantiated for some considerable time now.

One of the most interesting things to emerge is, however, the proof that some tenets that were considered obvious are in fact not so. The most interesting of these are the arguments concerning human capital or, more precisely, its importance and how it influences the growth rate by encouraging the adoption of improved technologies, a thesis that is upheld by many of this volume's authors, which characteristics of the educational system are important and how to measure the quality of education.

We have, therefore, a new theory of growth which has not furnished any new responses, but has instead provided a large number of brilliant scholars, who were previously engaged in researching other topics, with a stimulus to resume their study of these issues. It is therefore very probable that in the coming five years we will have much more accurate responses which will derive not from this methodology, but rather from studies of the return rates of education in different countries that are much more detailed than the very general analyses that have been carried out to date.

I would therefore maintain that the theory furnishes a good

reason for more detailed study in this field and a fresh close examination of the basic issues. It is not at all clear why some people ask: «why
are we interested in growth?». The reply is obvious. Unlike most of
our fellow citizens of the world, we all have comfortable living
conditions, and hence our interest in growth is legitimate. If you go to
India, you will no longer ask why we are interested in growth. Growth
is, for economics, the main issue, no other issue has a similar
importance, and so economics should basically concern itself with
how to increase mankind's well-being. Perhaps economists are repu-
ted to be "hard" and hence unauthorised to speak about the welfare of
others; perhaps this is why someone, fearing being thought "soft", did
not give the correct reply, namely that we economists are in fact very
interested in people's well-being.

What else can we say about growth, in addition to the attention
that has been paid to human capital?

Investment analysis is unarguably an important topic, and has
been perfected by De Long and Summers, who emphasised a particular type of physical investment. I do not know up to what point we
can support their thesis. Basically, sooner or later one needs a factory
in which to put all this sophisticated machinery and houses in which
to live, and so forth. Moreover, it is not easy to accurately measure
the production of structures, especially in the non-productive sectors,
and this leads to houses being attributed with only a marginal value.

It has maintaioned that this volume does not teach much about
the determinant factors of productivity growth and it is hoped that
microeconomic analysis can provide new results.

If I had to choose one topic for these concluding remarks, I
believe that one of the most positive aspects is that we are beginning
to concentrate our attention on those aspects which are important for
economic policy. This concerns both the fiscal variables (since neither
the deficit, nor the level of consumption nor public investments are by
themselves significant), and also the different types of public spending
or public investment. Moreover, I will also ask how government
contributes to growth, and also how it does not contribute or, worse,
"brakes" growth. Similarly, with regard to the financial system, we
are turning our attention only to the fact that we need a "good
financial system». This argument would not appear to be verv convin-

cing as it is those countries with the best financial systems which have experienced slower growth (the United States and United Kingdom), while those with very bad financial systems have experienced very strong growth. In fact, when Japan improved its financial system, its growth rate decreased. Hence it is not the simple correlations which are not persuasive, but rather the specific aspects and these will examined below.

Furthermore, as has already been pointed-out, the problem of the nature of the trade regime is also important.

Hence all these issues, which are crucial for growth, are once again on the "agenda" of all macroeconomists, and this is a positive fact.

What is the key issue at the moment? The key issue is to understand to what extent the simple things that we have learned (free market, property rights, legislative system, etc.) are all that is necessary to ensure growth. It is obvious that they are important, in a certain sense essential, but something else is taking place which can be observed very clearly in the experience of Eastern Asia.

It is assumed, as has been emphasised by some, that we still have much to learn from future studies on the differences between the economies of Eastern Asia which are very dependent on the market, and are not controlled by the state in the "traditional" manner, and those in which the state often plays, in one form or another, a strong guiding role. But to what extent can these experiences be imported, and to what extent do we need a diligent and committed public sector? In some countries the politicians affirm, "I have been to South Korea, and we also badly need that type of industrial policy». Even though this might be true, it has to be seen whether this is feasible, or even, given the country's structure, whether it is better to have no industrial policy at all. There are in fact considerable differences from country to country. Hence all these issues should be studied in greater detail.

Finally, as regards economists' influence on growth, I fear that the conclusions reached are correct. It is held that the quality and number of economists in a country are inversely correlated to that country's growth rate. Twenty years ago the United States and the United Kingdom had the best economists, the European continent had very weak economists and Japan practically none at all. When Koichi Hamada arrived in the United States, it was believed Japan's growth would slow, but instead it was growth in the United States that slowed! The emergence of an active school of Italian economists should therefore give rise to serious concern for Italy's future growth!

**Romano Prodi**
Università di Bologna

After Prof. Yotopoulos' speech we can conclude this meeting with some very interesting conclusions. I don't want to repeat of course what has already been said but I would just like to make some personal observations.

First of all we have to reflect, (and we will have to do it more and more) whether to 1) consider new areas of development in which all the different countries show different behaviours, or 2) keep on analysing areas which are already very well known, such as the Western world. I should like to underline that today the analysis of the most recent changes in Asia is fondamental.

The first observation is that the performance of all Asian countries is increasing and improving although each country behaves in its own way. It is hard in fact to find a trait d'union among the good and varied performances of the area. All the seven Tigers are growing up tremendously, each of them in a different way.

This Asian region needs to be studied carefully because of the huge potentials that has been demonstrated by its most recent economic successes.

China and India, it is true, are separate cases, but also in this area extraordinary changes are taking place. Actually, China and India, are now the most interesting areas in the world. In these two regions the process towards development is inevitably different from the one going on elsewhere. The development is extraordinarily rapid in terms of infrastructures; let's remember that China is growing at an average rate of 10% a year and India is trying to implement a strategy of development completely different from all the previous forms of centralized planning so far implemented. Both China and India are growing through the introduction of a more flexible industrial structure and through the reduction of the huge bureaucracy that has strangled their systems.

The second observation is that, after the fall of the Berlin wall much attention has been paid, obviously, to Eastern Europe; nevertheless no strategic plans of intervention have been put forward. It is true that changes in Eastern Europe have been enormous both from the institutional and the socio-political point of view, and all that is of great interest. Nevertheless it is very negative that we have not fully realized what is going on and that the evolution of events could lead to a total change in economic and trade relations with Western Europe.

A policy of financial support and technical assistance has been put forward (although in practice it has been very little implemented). Tensions existing among European countries and the decision to protect some important sectors of production (starting from agriculture and steel) have made dramatic the already heavy decline of production that Eastern Europe is facing. From this point of view the example of the US experience is completely different from that of EEC countries.

The realization of a free trade area between Canada, Mexico and United States is the example that should be imitated and implemented in Europe too. In cases, such as the above-mentioned, of regional integration, the alternative to goods mobility is human mobility.

What I call continental competition, as for example that between Mexico, USA, Canada, and Latin America on one side; between Western and Eastern Europe on the other side and to summarise between Japan and the Asian countries, is extremely important in opening up the market to global competition.

We have to reflect very carefully on the consequences of the continental competition which is growing between the United States and Mexico.

This competition is the example of an interesting plan of economic cooperation that the European Community has not yet been able to realize with Eastern Europe. The evolution of the agreement between Mexico and United States heralds a big change and shows particularly the new trend towards wider borders, towards the elimination of that economic protectionism that for years has characterized a large stream of thought within the US. It is a very positive phenomenon that is also taking place in many other areas.

Continental competition makes it possible to develop price policies more easily and to improve firms' performances. A free trade area is obviously convenient in terms of negotiating power towards third countries. Unfortunately similar areas have not been created everywhere and Europe embodies the lack of this goal. As a matter of fact, despite all the institutional changes between countries, which are typical of Europe and should create synergies, no competitive conditions have been set yet. Eastern Europe does not seem to have competitive and challenging conditions for development. It is significant that the price system does not work, productivity is low and environmental problems enormous; until any consistent plan of intervention from the EC is implemented and a free trade area created, Eastern countries will continue being isolated countries with very little negotiating and contracting power and with different and inefficient industrial policies.

Coming back to a reflection on multiple systems, we have to underline that successful and long term growth, apart from international cooperation, also depends on 1) a correct macroeconomic politicy and stability of the economic environment; 2) a clear and correct institutional framework as well as a working and dynamic financial system. We have already discussed the importance of a correct economic policy. It would be useful now to adress a few words to the importance of *clearness* within an institutional framework.

This problem in fact focuses criticisms, conflicts and in my opinion, mistakes which will bring enormous consequences. The fall of Eastern regimes at the end of the 80s and the fact that each process of change has always had the United States as a referee, has brought about a conviction that the only model of capitalism (therefore the only one exportable to the East), is the American one.

There is no need to remember the deep institutional differences existing between the United States, Europe and Japan. It is well known what are the differencies in the role of shareholders and managers, in the relations between companies and the Community, in financial market trends, in trade unions, in shareholders, rights and therefore in the criteria of optimization of the main firms' functions.

Setting aside this kind of analysis (which has been made during recent months), I should like to recall that an uncritical adhesion to the dominant model of capitalism (the American one) has created other difficulties in the process of the transformation of economies in Eastern Europe that have been forced to look at models fundamentally different and absolutely far distant in terms of experience and mentality. In other words, among the majority of the management in Eastern countries, there is the conviction that only one model of development is worth following and would be the only effective one. This conviction is a mistake that has already produced and will continue to produce huge negative consequences, and it is exacerbating the already difficult and complex step towards a market economy.

The market economy certainly has some aspects (such as basic rights and limits to property) which are common to all countries and have therefore to become common property in Eastern as well as in EEC Europe. Nevertheless, so far as many aspects of the economy are concerned, it is diversity rather than conformity which characterises the organization of different countries. From this point of view, the error of Western countries cannot be underestimated. The energy addressed to the analysis of the system, and to the research of new models responding to needs and traditions, has been generally negligible.

This lack of energy is even more relevant from the Italian side, because of our particular historical experience which could offer a model much more adaptable to countries that are entering the market for the first time.

A deep analysis of the adaptability of our public enterprises and industrial districts would certainly have helped to develop a specific experiment which would have been useful to our country as well as to many realities of Eastern Europe.

In practice no such thing happened and we missed the opportunity to enrich a difficult passage of their industrial development with possible alternatives.

In any case it is understandable why all this did not happen: the possibility of exporting different intellectual models depends not only on their quality but also on the awareness of who develops them. And such an awareness is far from abundant in Italy.

**Clark W. Reynolds**

Stanford University

The following are some of the main conclusions and policy recommendations, based on the papers of this volume. Some of the comments go beyond those in the volume proceedings.

1. - The papers show that international differences in economic growth cannot be explained by conventional neo-classical growth theories, which abstract from country and region-specific social, institutional, and structural characteristics. Structure and institutions matter to such critically important elements in the growth process as macroeconomic stability, productive investment and entrepreneurship, the effectiveness of capital markets, the diffusion of technology and productivity, education and human-capital formation, and research and development. These papers demonstrated that recent endogenous growth theories and the new institutional economics are reviving the importance of institutional aspects of economic structure and growth that had been the focus of attention twenty years ago.

The papers illustrate that privatization and liberalization of markets are not enough. Government and private enterprise must work together to achieve the potential gains from liberalization, the removal of barriers to exchange, and international economic integration, if the result is to be consistent with social stability and widespread sharing in the benefits from growth.

*Policies:* Ensure the establishment of a stable policy regime with fiscal balance (on current account), consistent with increasing international integration of real and financial markets. This involves the implementation of laws, institutions, and regulatory mechanisms that are transparent, nondiscrimatory, and enduring, to reduce risk and uncertainty. Fiscal deficits can be reduced, consistent with growth and social equity, by working on both the expenditure and tax side. Expenditure reduction can be achieved through *a)* the lowering of entitlement expenditures for upper income groups; *b)* the lowering of subsidies and shifting of incidence of public services, including health, welfare, housing programs, and education, from upper to lower income groups; *c)* privatization of public enterprise, with full-cost-pricing, taking advantage of competitive markets insofar as possible to increase the availability of "public goods" and "services", targeting groups and regions for support on the basis of need; *d)* encouraging the channeling of investment and technical assistance to micro, small, and medium-scale enterprise to diffuse the social and regional gains from growth.

Deficit reduction on the tax side involves increasing non-distorting revenue flows through *a)* increased enforcement of existing tax laws (often revenues can be increased by lowering tax rates but increasing enforcement); *b)* elimination of double taxation of profits and disincentivation of private savings and investment, shifting toward the taxation of sumptuary consumption, land and dwellings, and non-distorting participation in the rents from natural resources; *c)* where possible increasing the transparency and simplicity of tax implementation ("single tax" and VAT tax approaches merit attention); *d)* elimination of largely regressive and distorting tax shelters; *e)* encouragement of regional and international fiscal harmonization to improve the efficiency of investment and resource allocations as markets integrate.

Reduce interregional fiscal transfers that work against efficiency and equity, substituting them with policies and institutions that incentivate productive investment, provide infrastructure, and promote human capital formation, so as to release the potential for growth of backward regions while broadening social participation. Italy provides an excellent example in this regard. The so-called "Third Italy" experience (focused on the Northeastern provinces) is characterized by the rapid growth of trade and investment of small and medium-scale enterpise, assisted by the cooperation of local and provincial governments and regional financial institutions. These provinces have shown the immense potential of local private producers to compete in upscale niche markets with goods of high quality, design, and reliability at rising levels of wages, profits, and value added.

This experience contrasts with the more conventional stereotype of Italian "North-South" fiscal transfers, involving credit subsidies and other outlays, to support enterprises and public sector employment in the South and Southwest, often with mixed results in terms of growth and efficiency. The Third Italy "model" of local and regional cooperation between the public and private sectors, focusing on small and medium-scale enterprise, including links with larger firms at home and abroad, and now with increasing EC and national government support, offers a pattern for developing countries as well as for diffusion within the European "South" and "East". (Reynolds - Pessoa [1] [2]).

2. - Growth is related to the type of investment (e.g. machinery and equipment, economic and social infrastructure), especially for so-called "follower" economies, in order to take advantage of actual and potential factor endowments and prior innovations. Such economies illustrate the importance of the removal of market barriers, plus the implementation of positive incentive schemes that favor the generation and channeling of savings into productive investment (e.g. machinery and equipment; economic and social infratructure). The appropriate mix of public policy and private sector initiative permits followers to catch up during periods of accelerated growth.

*Policies:* favor the financing of investment in machinery and equipment as well as in economic and social infrastructure, with less emphasis on easily collateralized "structures" per se. Deal with the collateralization problem (that stresses the use of land and "structures" for collateral) that biases credit flows away from machinery and equipment and infrastructure (including education) that are difficult to collateralize and which tends to favor those individuals and institutions which have already-existing property by which to secure future credit. The direction of financial flows, in terms of real investmens, appears to matter importantly to growth (and distribution). The goal of financial market completion may well require attention to the spread between lending and borrowing rates, for particular types of financial intermediation, in order to reduce the distortions in incomplete or imperfect credit markets, so as to establish a more "neutral" financial regime when the market introduces distortions.

Examples of the above include the provision of credit to those borrowers who show promise for productive investment but who are less-able to provide collateral (e.g. startups, small enterprise, and venture capital requiring operations, as well as cooperatives for marketing, product development, business management, and other forms of technical assistance). This also applies to small enterprise clustered in areas of common types of production (e.g. specific crops, or products, such as shoes or ceramics) where there is high multicollinearity of cash flow among the borrowers, which when added to moral hazard and adverse selection problems and diseconomies of small-scale credit provision tend to marginalize such enterprises in capital markets. Here again the role of financial policy, in the form of technical assistance, partial loan guarantees, encouragement of borrower cooperatives, and the provision of bridges between the broader capital market and these sectors, regions, and small-scale enterprise can facilitate market-completion, the diffusion of investment, productivity, and income, and growth.

3. - Growth rates do not appear to be related to initial levels of income and productivity, and there is no overwhelming evidence of convergenze among regions, sectors, and income groups whether positive or negative, as a general phenomenon, although in important instances low income economies have grown past their initially more prosperous peers while in other cases the gap has widened. Since the diffusion of growth is needed for social justice, positive expectations, and regime stability which depends on the above, improved social capability and institutions are needed to facilitate the diffusion of growth in productivity and income.

*Policies:* liberalization, privatization, reduction of public sector deficits, removal of barriers to exchange, and fiscal harmonization offer necessary but not sufficient conditions for the social and regional diffusion of the gains from economic integration. However economic integration provides gains that can be used to support the diffusion of further growth. This calls for policies that incentivate private savings and investment for the diffusion of growth to less-developed regions, sectors, and social groups. Nondistorting fiscal transfers, incentives, and regulatory policies can also play a role, to the extent that they complete markets which would otherwise be imperfect.

Where private markets for such diffusion processes are incomplete, the state can cooperate with private enterprise to further the channeling of voluntary savings into more diffused patterns of investment (e.g. small enterprises, economic and social infrastructure, and support for the productive growth of backward areas). In Mexico this is the objective of the government-supported Solidarity program (Pronasol), which provides both public revenue and private contributions to expenditures at the local and regional level for projects that are prioritized by committees comprised of both private and public sector representatives including representatives of local government. As mentioned above, Italy through local and regional government initiatives has established programs of cooperation with private entrepreneurs to further the growth of exports of small and medium-scale enterprises, enhancing the operation of market forces. The EC and Japan have also exhibited important aspects of public-private sector cooperation for successful international market-penetration. The main issue is to ensure that such efforts are non-distorting of efficiency and equity either within or between countries.

4. - Increased incentives are needed to increase private capital flows from more to less-developed sectors, regions, and countries. The flow of capital in the 1980s was largely from "south" to "north". This flow was associated less with maximization of global growth potential than with different degrees of political and economic risk (related to ineffective monitoring of previous borrowing and the debt crisis). Policies to develop the capacity to effectively monitor borrowing institutions are important to ensure that domestic and international capital flows maximize sustainable growth potential by reducing risk premia, removing barriers to trade and investment, and eliminating unproductive rentseeking.

*Policies:* The removal of obstacles to international financial and equity capital flows between "North" and "South" is crucial. The recovery of credit markets between Latin America and the OECD countries is beginning to take place in response to stabilization and structural adjustment policies in the Americas and the integration of regional markets. The "open regionalism" approach which focuses on region-wide reduction in transaction cost and other barriers to exchange, along with external opening, offers the greatest incentives for the restoration of attractive credit markets in the region. Already "flight capital" is beginning to return, as reflected in a shift in the goods and non-financial services balance of selected Latin American countries, representing a net inflow of capital. Mexico is an example of the combination of stabilization, opening, and structural adjustment, plus pro-integration policies in the North American region, which have attracted capital inflows. In addition the fall in real interest rates in OECD countries, as a stimulus to recovery from recession, have made the higher real interest rates in Latin America more attractive to savers, especially where there has been a reduction in exchange risk and political uncertainty. However there is still a need for venture capital for enterprises in Latin America that are pursuing gains from innovation and international market penetration.

Italy has much to offer in terms of experience in the integration of trade and financial markets within the EC, as well as between regional and national financial institutions. As a country which has been integrating its own less-developed regions, and which has successfully grown through trade and investment in an increasingly competitive world market, it is in a position to provide assistance to Latin America and other developing countries on growth-promoting capital market policies and institutions, especially in terms of public-private sector cooperation to increase credit flows to small and medium-scale enterprise on a non-distorting basis.

## BIBLIOGRAPHY

[1] REYNOLDS C. - PESSOA A.P.: «The Promotion of Micro and Small Enterprise Development in Mexico: a Preliminary Report», *Americas Program*, Stanford, Stanford University, Working Papers, October. 1991, pp. 91-2.

[2] ——: «Small and Medium Scale Enterprise in the Third Italy: Lessons for Developing Countries», *Americas Program*, draft, Fall, 1992.

**Pan A. Yotopoulos**
Stanford University

1. - The issue of convergence is currently trendy. Although the formal literature started with Baumol 1986, its origins go back to a question Kenneth Arrow, 1974, raised in his Nobel Prize Lecture. Arrow observed that inequality in economic development among countries is not readily amenable to the neoclassical explanation of differences in physical and human assets per capita. This explanation poses two problems: how did these differences in assets came to be in the first place? And, in any case, the differences in income seem much too vast to be explained by differences in factor endowments. Especially on the latter question, international trade, and more specifically capital mobility across borders would be expected to reduce differences in wages, thus restoring equality in rates of growth.

Arrow provides his own explanation for the persistent international income inequality. There exist differences in production possibility sets of different countries. This reduces the issue to incomplete information, since differences in production possibility sets say something about the transmission of knowledge across countries. Therefrom the origins of the endogenous growth models that incorporate various types of market incompleteness and allow for per capita output differences to persist (Romer 1986, Lucas 1988, Murphy, Shleifer and Vishny 1989). The empirical evidence, however, on the initial question posed by Arrow is still incomplete. The most credible result at present is that convergence may well occur locally, defined as in economies with the same initial conditions; it does obtain globally, since economies with different initial conditions, such as literacy rates or educational endowments, fail to converge (Durlauf and Johnson 1992).

The most obvious extension of this volume topic is to apply the insights from the convergence literature to supra-national/sub-national groups. Does convergence occur within economic groups? The experience of Europe's Common Market would be most valuable. Does it happen within/between socio-economic classes in a country? Future research might profitably examine the issues related to "trickl-ing-down" and to appropriate "locomotives of growth".

2. - Some seemingly counter-intuitive results that cropped out may have a plausible explanation as "place holders" for more tradi-tional factors that enter economic growth. Physical capital does not seem to account for much of the measured growth. A flow-concept subset of it, e.g. investment in mechanical/electrical equipment, seems to do better. On reflection, that should not be surprising. Capital stock concepts are composed of notoriously non-homogenous components with different durability (life expectancy), vintage, and physical depreciation characteristics. What matters in production analysis, however, is not capital stocks but annual streams of services. The proportionality relationship between the two is more likely to be constant, the more homogeneous (e.g., same durability) is the capital concept used. This may well explain the better performance of capital equipment as compared to a more aggregate capital stock concept (Yotopoulos 1967).

Similarly, telephones came up as a good explanatory variable of rates of growth. Telephones have been also found to correlate quite well with sundry other developmental variables, including the birth rate and the death rate (negatively) and thus the demographic transition (positively). But is the causation from phone conversations to prevention of births? It is more likely that telephones are a place-holder for increases in income at the left tail of the distribu-tion, where income matters a lot. As such, telephones may be better than traditional income concepts that are open-ended variables. It is conceivable that doubling per capita income might still leave unal-tered incomes of the poorer households. But doubling telephones, or radios cannot be easily done without bringing in new consumers into market, the phoneless poor whose incomes might have in-creased (Yotopoulos 1977, Ch. 2). I predict that as long as we lack any more reliable indexes of income distribution, telephones will continue to be a good predictor of a fair amount of good things in development.

3. - Continuing on the unbundling of the aggregate capital stock, education was singled out as a good "soft" factor that accounts for endogenous growth — especially the *level* of education, as opposed to its rate of change. But here also we have to be cautious. The Philippines is credited with having a good level of higher education — which has produced a good flow of Philippine nurses and doctors to the rest of the world but little development for the Philippines. Closer at home, Greece has the highest number of economists per capita in the world. I would like in fact to propose the *Y*-1 Theorem which states that economic development is inversely related to the number of economists in a country (properly measured and normalized).

4. - The specter of overvalued domestic currencies has often been raised in this volume and elsewhere as extremely damning for the prospects of development. No-one would knowingly advocate overvaluation, but the same caution should be exercised on under-valuation. Moreover, humility should prevail in our acknowledging that we do not really know what is the "right" nominal exchange rate and in case of doubt I would rather err on the side of overvaluation, especially for developing countries. It is true that overvalued domestic currencies tend to flood the country with imports and to stave off exports — unless there are controls. But it is also true that undervalu-ation turns nontradables into tradables, and can thus account for excessive import substitution (Little, Scitovsky and Scott 1970), and for expensive (in terms of domestic resources) over-exporting — not only of traditional commodities but also of natural resources and teak forests, of the choicest real estate (through foreign purchase), of the best scientists (braindrain), and ultimately of a country's treasure and national heritage. The *Big Mac PPP Index* (the price of McDonald's hamburger in various countries) finds the Russian rouble the most undervalued currency in the world (*Economist*, April 18, 1992). While undervaluation may solve some of Russia's problems in the long-run, in the short-run Russian rocket scientists work for Silicon Valley companies (from Russia) for $80 a month *(Wall Street Journal)* and Russian art treasures are rapidly becoming a huge export success. This is hardly conducive to economic development.

5. - In closing I would like to propose the *Y-2 Theorem*: a competent and honest Government never hurts the cause of development.

I will leave the statement elliptical, as it was left in this year's meetings. Perhaps it can be elucidated in the future.

# Index

499